Boycotts, Buses, and Passes

BOYCOTTS, BUSES, AND PASSES

*Black Women's Resistance
in the U.S. South and South Africa*

PAMELA E. BROOKS

University of Massachusetts Press

AMHERST

LC 2008031443

ISBN 978-1-55849-678-1 (paper); 676-7 (library cloth)

Designed by Dean Bornstein
Set in Adobe Caslon Pro and Myriad Pro by dix!
Printed and bound by Sheridan Books, Inc.

Library of Congress Cataloging-in-Publication Data

Brooks, Pamela E., 1952–
Boycotts, buses, and passes : Black women's resistance in the U.S. South and South
Africa / Pamela E. Brooks.
p. cm.
Includes bibliographical references and index.
ISBN 978-1-55849-678-1 (paper : alk. paper)—ISBN 978-1-55849-676-7 (library cloth :
alk. paper)
1. African American women—Southern States—Political activity—History—
20th century. 2. African Americans—Civil rights—Southern States—History—
20th century. 3. Government, Resistance to—Southern States—History—
20th century. 4. Civil rights movements—Southern States—History—
20th century. 5. Southern States—Race relations—History—20th century.
6. Black women—South Africa—Political activity—History—20th century.
7. Blacks—Civil rights—South Africa—History—20th century.
8. Government, Resistance to—South Africa—History—20th century.
9. Civil rights movements—South Africa—History—20th century.
10. South Africa—Race relation—History—20th century. I. Title.
E185.86.B696 2008
305.48'896073-dc22
2008031443

British Library Cataloguing in Publication data are available.

To my parents, who taught me how to fight and who are fighting still in their elder years—I am grateful.
And to Ronni.

Contents

Acknowledgments

I always loved sitting at their dining room table just listening to their loud and funny stories about when they were "young gals" growing up in Washington, D.C., in the 1930s and '40s. My great-aunts Mary B. Smith and Arnette B. Jones were special women, partly because of the unguarded versions of family history they shared with us, but also because their generosity and resilience directly benefited our transplanted family. Big Mary and Aunt Arnette were the second and third daughters of Mrs. Hallie Magruder Armstead, a domestic worker in private families, a splendid cook, and a pastry chef in a few of the downtown Washington hotels. My aunts followed their mother into domestic work when they were still very young, but they did not in any way enjoy the work, and once they had reached their mid-teens each decided to leave it behind as soon as other opportunities presented themselves. Wartime Washington was still a tightly segregated city, but the newly expanded job market provided an occupational outlet for them. They became factory workers and hotel elevator operators, and eventually they were the first Black women hired as clerks at the Washington Gas Light Company in the city's downtown. The stories my aunts told about their work experiences led me to think about some of the political choices other Black working-class women made in order to better themselves, their families, and their communities. Their wisdom, revealed with such wit and sharp insight, inspired me to pursue my research in Alabama and South Africa and to do justice to the stories of Black women activists in their names.

The stories of all but a few of the women activists encountered in these pages could not have come to light without the energy, insight, and material assistance offered by many people. The practice of writing has largely been a solitary endeavor for me, but I have found that the task of bringing this book into being has required the efforts of more than just one. In addition to honoring my aunts' initial inspiration, I am happy to name here those who have contributed their own gifts to this project.

I am greatly indebted to Pat Manning, scholar of world history and historian of French West Africa. At its inception, when I was unsure about the project's execution, Pat immediately saw the feasibility of the study, found money to help with my initial research trips, and put me in touch with colleagues in Johannesburg. Pat read draft after draft of the manuscript—his insightful comments and good will proved invaluable, and it gives me great pleasure to have found in him such a good friend and colleague. Likewise, from the very beginning Bob Hall, consummate historian of the African American experience, believed in this project, and helped me better understand how this work might fit within a diasporic paradigm. Both Pat Manning's and Bob Hall's unswerving faith in me and in the importance of the work was of enormous value to me as a single parent with a great deal riding on her shoulders. I also found encouragement in the early stages from Ron Bailey, who was the first to interest me in going back to school; Robin Chandler provided advice and support for my first trip to South Africa, and Leslye Smith, always positive and helpful, reminded me at critical moments that I could do what was before me.

Members of the history department at Northeastern University were also encouraging during the project's early stages. I want to thank Felix Matos-Rodriguez, Jeffrey Burds, and Bill Fowler for their very useful early criticism. Thank you also to Christina Gilmartin, Laura Frader, Gerry Herman, Adam Mc Keown, and Clay McShane, and to Ms. Nancy Borromey for her tireless efforts on my behalf. I am especially grateful for the company and conversations of several other colleagues, including Sarah Swedberg, Yinghong Chen, Eric Martin, Jeff Sommers, David Kalivas, Whitney Howarth, and Deb Johnston. Judith Rollins deserves special thanks for the near-miraculous rescue she performed—this is a much better book because of her early critique and her conviction that I should keep going until the manuscript saw publication.

Belinda Bozzoli and Philip Bonner at the University of the Witwatersrand in Johannesburg shared valuable resources and helped sharpen my thinking over the course of several discussions. A number of other scholars aided this book immeasurably by critiquing early versions, asking key questions, and ultimately providing encouragement: Iris Berger, John Bracey, Lisa Brock, Margaret Burnham, Vicki Crawford, Robert Edgar, Françoise Hamlin, M. Bahati Kuumba, Shula Marks, Elliott Skinner, Michael Thelwell, Jeanne Toungara, and Rhonda Williams.

Eugene Cedras of Alexandra, an activist during the 1980s, introduced me to that amazing community and drove with me from Johannesburg to Durban. Staff at the Alexsan Kopan Community Center in Alexandra, including those in the African National Congress office and the branch library housed there, were both welcoming and helpful, as were the knowledgeable and enthusiastic staff members of the Alexandra Heritage Office, especially Ntebogeng Timba and Boitumelo Khunou, who helped me locate and speak with a few key veteran women activists from the bus boycott era. And I owe special thanks to my mother's colleague in the anti-apartheid movement in Boston, Themba Vilakazi, for providing much needed help and understanding during my first extended stay in South Africa. Vivian and Willard Johnson provided excellent advice and pointed me in the right direction on that same first trip. Aggrey Mbere, who died too young, helped me brainstorm people to talk with and always welcomed me whenever I was in Johannesburg. During more recent trips to that throbbing city, which I have come to love with all its contradictions, I am very grateful for the perfect kindness and support shown to me by the Shayi and Pandeka families: Frank and Maria Shayi, their children Blessing and Siphiwe Pandeka, and their grandsons Rhulani and Junior. In Pretoria, I thank Precious, Stanley, and Piwe Kumalo for taking time out of their busy schedules to invite me and my dad to their home, and for helping me get to the fortieth anniversary celebration of the 1956 women's march to Pretoria.

I am indebted to the expertise of the archivists at the Cullen Library at the University of the Witwatersrand and the National Archives in Pretoria, and to the sublime competence of the folks in the Interlibrary Loan departments of Oberlin College and Northeastern University. The archivists at Tulane University's Amistad Research Collection, Esther Van Driel and Andre Mahommed at the Mayibuye Collection at the University of the Western Cape, the archivists at the Mugar Library's Special Collections at Boston University, Dr. Cynthia P. Lewis, archivist at the Martin Luther King, Jr. Institute for Nonviolent Social Change, the archivists at the Special Collections of the Levi Watkins Library at Alabama State University, the archivists at the Special Collections at Central State University in Ohio, Ms. Jacqueline Brown at the Wilberforce University archives, and Dr. Gwen Patton, archivist at the H. Councill Trenholm State Technical College in Montgomery, all provided access to important materials, and I thank them for their help.

I am grateful to the members of the Research and Development Committee at Oberlin College, who, along with Pam Snyder, director of the Office of Sponsored Programs, awarded me two H. H. Powers travel grants that enabled me to get to South Africa. Dean Jeff Witmer has also been very generous with essential funding. Fellow members of the African American

Studies department deserve thanks for their collegial interest in the progress of this book, in particular my longtime friend Caroline Jackson-Smith, as well as Meredith Gadsby, Johnny Coleman, Yakubu Saaka, and Booker Peek, who read an early version of the manuscript and offered useful criticism. Other patient colleagues at Oberlin and beyond responded willingly to requests for guidance and comments, too, including A. G. Miller, Jan Cooper, Pat Mathews, Harlan Wilson, Pablo Mitchell, Gina Perez, Gillian Johns, Frances Hasso, Wendy Kozol, Ben Schiff, Sarah Schuster, and Charles Peterson.

Most especially I want to thank the women who took time from their own lives to sit with me and tell me their stories. I knew none of them before our interviews began, yet they graciously shared with me some of the most intimate, painful, and personal moments in their lives. Many of these tough, vibrant women are the contemporaries of my great-aunts, and reminded me of them in ways that made it hard to leave them. Some, like Mrs. Maggie Resha and Mrs. Idessa Williams Redden, have passed on, so I can only hope that they would have enjoyed seeing themselves and their colleagues portrayed here. But others, including Mrs. Emma Mashinini, Mrs. Beautie Mae Johnson, Ms. Joyce Piliso Seroke, Mrs. Bertha Mashaba Gxowa, and Ms. Gwendolyn M. Patton, are still actively committed to working for justice. I owe all of them a great deal for their critical support and their assistance in pointing me to other women who, on their recommendation, agreed to speak with me. I am forever in their debt.

This book could not have seen publication without the expertise of the good people at the University of Massachusetts Press. I am grateful to the editorial talents of Joan Vidal, Carol Betsch, Mary Bellino, Bruce Wilcox, and especially Clark Dougan, who picked me up, by phone, off the floor on more than one occasion. Thank you to Kate Blackmer for her wonderful set of maps.

Lastly, I want to thank the friends and family members who urged me forward and helped me stay halfway sane. Polly Attwood and Wendy Sanford nourished me and my daughter through this long haul in countless ways, as writers, scholars, and friends. Likewise, other women friends and colleagues embody in their own lives and work a unique understanding of how to encourage one another's creativity, and I thank Ellen E. Pinderhughes-Green, Ann Holmes Redding, Marian Mollin, Jean Sherlock, Christine Sloane, Diane Wiltshire, Pamela King, Marilyn D. Parker-Brooks, and Brenda Grier-Miller for that. My loving aunts, Evonne B.

Furey, Elaine B. Sutherland, Eloise B. Allen, and Mil Brooks, have each witnessed every stage of this project and enthusiastically urged me forward. My sisters, Dianne L. Brooks, Angela Y. Brooks-Adams, and Gail Brooks, and my brother, Frederick Brooks, also lent their encouragement. My parents continue to astonish, instruct, and inspire me. My father, Owen H. Brooks, shared an informed understanding of the South and of the Black freedom movement in which he participated. Still a young man when he went to Mississippi in 1965, he is today a marvelous living resource, battle-scarred and weary, perhaps, but always penetrating in his analysis of the nature of white domination and of the best forms of resistance. My mother, Erma B. Brooks, a fine intellect, a stalwart campaigner since her Progressive Party days, and an endless source of support and wise counsel, has carried me through every step of this process. She was my most valued critic and eager listener. And most of all, there's Ronni, who has spent the majority of her life on this long journey with me, first as a child and now as a member of the next generation of fine scholars. She kept me aware of what matters most in this process: laughter, patience, stubbornness, and love, all of which she has supplied in great abundance. To her and to my parents, this work—whose shortcomings I alone fully claim—is proudly and lovingly dedicated.

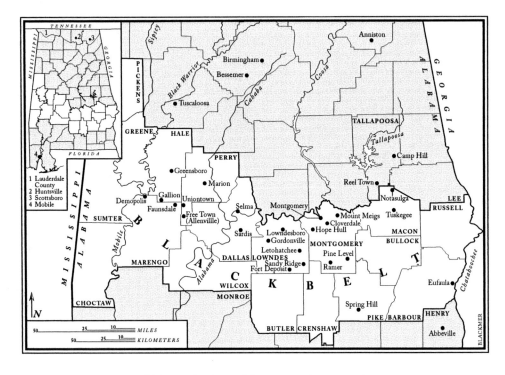

Alabama (with neighboring southern states).

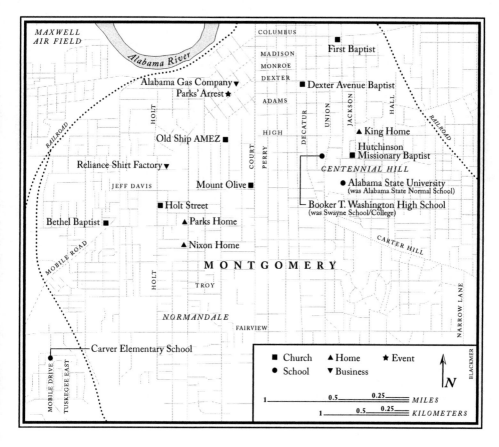

Montgomery, Alabama.

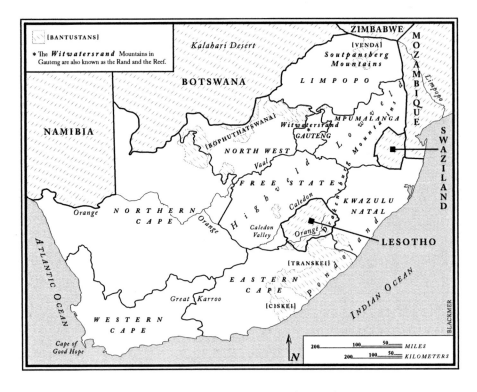

South Africa (with provincial divisions).

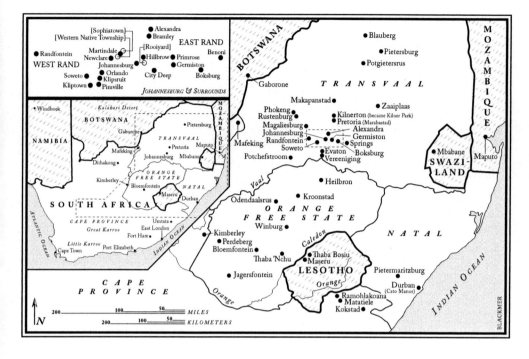

Greater Johannesburg (with Alexandra and Soweto).

Boycotts, Buses, and Passes

INTRODUCTION

I'm going to stay right here and help these things straighten out.
—*Mrs. Idessa Redden, Montgomery, Alabama*

All those campaigns kept us working and saying, "Freedom in our lifetime."
—*Mrs. Bertha M. Gxowa, Johannesburg, South Africa*

In the heart of Montgomery, Alabama, Mrs. Idessa Redden, a slender eighty-four-year-old, sat comfortably in her well-appointed living room. A lifelong activist in the Black freedom struggle, Mrs. Redden recounted stories of how she joined the National Association for the Advancement of Colored People (NAACP) in her mid-twenties, made repeated attempts to register to vote during the 1940s, and finally succeeded in registering in 1949. By the 1950s she was working with Rufus Lewis, a respected local activist, helping to register voters. In early December 1955, Mrs. Redden's cousin informed her that the Black riders of Montgomery had decided to boycott the city buses and that a meeting would be held at the Holt Street Baptist Church on Monday night, December 5. Mrs. Redden recalled the promise she felt at this first, hugely successful mass meeting of the 1955–1956 Montgomery bus boycott:

> When I heard Dr. King speak that night, I was amazed. I never screamed louder in a church before in my life. But that night I screamed to the top of my voice, "Lord, you have sent us a leader." It was just something about him that was different from all other men. And I was willing to follow him. Because I had walked the streets of Montgomery and wondered to myself, "Why do Black people have to live in places like this? Why do Black people have to throw their dishwater out the back door?" I didn't know all about the sewage system then, 'cause mostly where Black folks lived there were no sewers.[1]

An ocean away in Johannesburg, South Africa, Mrs. Bertha Mashaba Gxowa, a member of Parliament from the district of Gauteng, recalled a time when a seat in the legislature was unattainable for any African, let alone for an African woman. This exclusion from political life and the apartheid regime's liberal use of force against the Black population spurred her activism. By 1952 she had become a top-flight organizer among a host of outstanding women activists. During the mid-1950s, twenty-year-old Bertha Mashaba combined her work as an employee of the African Clothing Workers' Union with her work as a member of the African National Congress (ANC) Youth and Women's Leagues, volunteering her time to participate in the 1955 Congress of the People, among other campaigns. From that two-day meeting came the eloquently articulated vision of a truly democratic South Africa, the Freedom Charter. Mrs. Gxowa recalled the struggle:

> Of course, one of our slogans was "Freedom in our lifetime." All the campaigns that were important, the writing of the Freedom Charter . . . all those campaigns kept us working and saying, "Freedom in our lifetime" and saying, "This is what we want the country to be governed under. This is what we want for the people. This is how we want the people to live. There shall be houses for all; the door to learning and education shall be open; all shall be equal before the law; there shall be security." I mean, all of the parts of the charter we kept in the campaign for the internal government to [use to] draw a constitution for everybody—a constitution that protects every man, woman, and child in the country. These are the rights of the people.[2]

Although Mrs. Redden and Mrs. Gxowa lived in different countries, were subjected to different systems of racial oppression, worked on different issues, and engaged in different campaigns, the resonances of their activism and the broader struggles that they represent inspire a compelling comparison. The histories of oppression, the role of historical memory in their politicization, and their demands for human and economic rights connect the struggles within the African diaspora—struggles that emerged separately, but coterminously, in a world in which the racial and colonial balance was under siege. During the 1970s and 1980s, these and other similarities helped establish useful common ground that united U.S. and South African exiles and activists in the demand for U.S. sanctions against apartheid. During the 1950s, however, before African Americans and Black South Africans had more vigorously begun their collaborative assaults against the apartheid state, Black women in both countries had initiated a round of mass actions that aimed to eliminate white supremacy.

For Black working- and middle-class people in Jim Crow Alabama, who lived under their own version of apartheid, the beginning of the Montgomery bus boycott in December 1955 helped launch a renewed effort to achieve full freedom in the South and across the United States. The activism of women in Montgomery—symbolized, in part, by the resistance of Mrs. Rosa Parks—is akin to the activism of women in South Africa during both the Alexandra bus boycott and the anti-pass resistance. In Montgomery, thousands of Black women—primarily domestic and factory workers, but also teachers and clerks, some young and some elderly and many without regular means of transportation—steadfastly refused to ride the city buses for more than a year. They walked in protest of the many indignities and dangers they faced on a daily basis. By 1954, Black men in Montgomery had already begun to forgo riding the buses in an effort to avoid arrest, fines, jail time, or all three, which were meted out by hostile bus drivers who wielded police powers in the face of such minor infractions as sitting in the wrong place, moving too slowly, talking back, or attempting to resist abuse in any other way. With few Black men riding the buses, Black women, children, and elderly riders were even more vulnerable, and were left to find their own ways of protecting themselves.[3]

For Black women in South Africa, the fare hikes and poor service that made travel to and from the white neighborhoods of Johannesburg costly and dangerous prompted their involvement in the Alexandra bus boycott of 1957. For three months, sixty thousand Black residents of Alexandra and many more from other townships on the Rand chose to walk the nine miles into Johannesburg rather than pay the exhorbitant bus fare that threatened to destabilize already precarious family budgets.[4] Against the backdrop of deepening mass resistance of the 1950s, the favorable outcome that resulted for the Alexandra boycotters raised the possibility of other actions of dissent against the intransigent Afrikaner Nationalist government. Vigorous women's anti-pass and anti–Bantu education demonstrations from the mid- to late 1950s—protesting passes that restricted women's movements and Afrikaner control of African education, respectively—extended the range of the movement to address additional critical concerns of the Black community. Despite arrests, bannings, and the breakup of their leadership, Black South African women persisted in demonstrating their opposition to the apartheid state.

Montgomery and Johannesburg, two sites of reverberating protest within Africa and her diaspora in the 1950s, are firmly linked by liberation ideology, by time frame, and by the pivotal component of women's activism. Although at first glance these events may appear to be isolated and unrelated, when the stories of these "ordinary" women are set side by side,

the similarities in their local and regional challenges to white supremacist systems become apparent. By building Black schools, churches, and
labor unions or by migrating to cities and establishing new urban communities, African Americans in the U.S. South and Black South Africans
both succeeded in subverting oppressive systems. When the histories are
viewed separately, similarities, especially those that reflect the experiences
of women, are often overlooked. When they are taken together, however, the struggles of the women in both movements encourage a global
vision that suggests the imminence of colonial and neocolonial power in
retreat.

Although Mrs. Redden and Mrs. Gxowa were unacquainted with each
other's work in their respective freedom movements, each was a prominent
participant in a significant worldwide struggle for the liberation of African
peoples. Yet few scholars, activists, and students on opposite shores of the
Atlantic are aware that the struggles of these women activists ultimately
helped to define their era. For younger progressive activists, particularly
women, an important aspect of their heritage—including an understanding
of the necessary persistence and dedication to both Black liberationist and
Black feminist goals—has therefore escaped notice. For many, their training
has been deprived of the wisdom derived from Black women's vision. In-
corporating individual experiences of oppression (such as enduring rape or
doing white people's dirty work) can translate them into acts of resistance.[5]
In short, as time passes, memories fade, bodies weaken, and new power brokers begin to write their own versions of history, the necessity to search out
and leave behind guiding, principled testimony for Black descendants and
other invested peoples urgently beckons. In focusing on women's knowledge, experiences, and leadership in a global context, I aim to challenge
common assumptions about what history is, who writes it, and for whom it
is written. The inaccurate assumptions may be that disenfranchised Black
women do not make history, that they do not have the attributes required
to write it, and that those who count themselves among the intellectual
elite have no interest in learning from it.

This book, however, does more than address previous historical gaps and
even disinterest in recognizing the political agency of Black women. Comparative analysis compels the reader to reconsider how global transformations occur and why. Considering the perspectives of seemingly powerless
Black women sheds light on how disenfranchised constituents within
transnational communities ultimately helped to topple white supremacist

regimes. This is neither a story that unfolded overnight nor a tale that has had an ending. Nevertheless, for more than a century, women have acted in small, discreet, individual, collective, overt, and rebellious ways that, when taken together, have resulted in new patterns of political resistance and change.[6]

That long history of struggle corresponds to the long history of white domination that stemmed from the colonial period. Despite the fact that the history of African peoples at home and in the Americas is replete with examples of devastation and loss, I aim to show how such traumas motivate and strengthen black peoples who are intent on being free. The lessons learned from enslavement and emancipation in the United States, for instance, which were passed from one generation to the next as an important cultural product, provided some with greater resolve. In the face of British imperial power, artillery, and Boer land thefts, Black South Africans learned the names of such ancestors as the BaSotho king Moshoeshoe, as true reminders of an independent past. In a wider context, the history of the African diaspora has shown a clear intellectual, religious, and political engagement. At least since the nineteenth century, African American, Black South African, and other African-descended missionaries, students, educators, emigrationists, and Pan-Africanists have shared a practice and discourse of liberation. At every juncture, the participation and leadership of women have been integral.

Although racism lay at the very core of the existence and struggles of these women, this book is not a simple recounting of antiracist agitation by Black women. As contemporary theorists such as Patricia Hill Collins, Audre Lorde, Evelyn Brooks Higginbotham, Deborah King, and E. Frances White have shown, Black women's lives are lived at the nexus of multiple identities and oppressions, which include but are not limited to race, gender, class, sexuality, and ethnicity. This multiplicity of experience, in turn, has had everything to do with how Black women fashioned a politics of resistance—one that is based substantially in women's interests and that is understood within a broader scope of liberationist ideals.[7] Women such as Queen Nanny, the rebel Maroon leader in colonial Jamaica; Claudia Jones, the Cold War–era, Trinidad-born radical activist of Harlem and London; Adelaide Casely Hayford, a Pan-Africanist and the founder of a girls' school in Sierra Leone; and Amy Jacques Garvey, the leader of women activists in the Garvey movement, expressed what I see as an early protofeminism while they advocated Black liberation.[8] At critical historical moments, these women and their ideological descendants expressed a "woman-centered consciousness"—an important re-visioning of a more nationalist project. In contrast to the approach of Black men, Black women who have raised the level of discussion about what constitutes freedom have demanded an incorporation of their own differences and those of others and have even dared to criticize the shortcomings of the male leadership. Refusing to allow their issues and opinions to remain outside the more masculinist discourse of nationalist politics, the women activists of the 1950s pushed their movements toward a more militant stance.[9]

The experiences of these women, which appear in all their complexity in this book, engage the question "What was it like to be a daughter, mother, wife, worker, organizer, teacher, leader from a rural area who migrated to the city and joined a political movement to eradicate white supremacy?" A series of forty oral interviews conducted between 1995 and 2006 was designed to elicit the whole life histories of some thirty-five women, who generously answered this question and others and gave further insight into their motivations, organizational frameworks, and political views. Through these and other oral and written narratives, the women activists reveal a wealth of knowledge, wisdom, humor, and pain, exposing a long and ongoing history of struggle for freedom, justice, and human dignity.

In addition, in this book I highlight the development of the political consciousness of these activist women and their invaluable demonstrations of leadership at critical historical moments. External political forces, such as the 1940s decolonization movements among African and Asian peoples and the accompanying language of self-determination helped to develop their consciousness. Another critical force, World War II, invigorated a global political economy that in many cases spurred the migration of hundreds of women from their rural homes to cities, in search of jobs and freedom. Neither Idessa Redden nor Bertha Gxowa migrated from a rural home, but others in these pages did so, and both groups of women—rural and urban—took advantage of expanded employment opportunities that eventually served to radicalize their politics. New conditions in new urban and work environments catapulted some into labor unions and labor organizing, in many cases spurring a different kind of working-class consciousness and preparing them for participation in the freedom movements. Both Mrs. Redden and Mrs. Gxowa share examples of how their labor organizing experiences increased their political awareness. In addition to seeking a healthier existence and the material resources necessary for urban living, migrant women sought opportunities to educate their children and to join or create religious, social, or political organizations with other women.

An important aspect of this consciousness-in-the-making is revealed in their later activism: The rabble-rousers of the Women's Political Council (WPC) and the Federation of South African Women (FSAW) took on a rebellious yet respectable demeanor and articulated a strongly woman-centered ideology. Although they emerged before the onset of the official second-wave feminist movement and did not identify themselves as feminists, the women of these two organizations understood that they were acting against institutions, systems, and laws that discriminated against them *as women*. Rather than remain bound to a constricting set of white "normative" definitions of womanhood, these protofeminist Black women walked the bus routes in hats and high heels, were imprisoned with their babies on their backs, or defied their "madams" by refusing to meekly do as they were bid. In so doing, they constructed a bold and respectable brand of political resistance.

For the present generation of young men and women activists (as well as old-time agitators, veteran campaigners, and other interested parties) who face a host of global challenges, women such as Idessa Redden and Bertha Gxowa offer a number of lessons: First, groups of "ordinary," disenfranchised, and seemingly powerless women can successfully confront powerful states and, in the process, transform their societies. The key word here is *ordinary*, which in so many ways they were not. For the most part, they were not well schooled, they did not belong to the social elite, and they often possessed few economic resources. Yet these women had plenty to say about the source and meaning of the many injustices under which they lived. They communicated their acute dissatisfaction to similarly situated women and men in their communities, persuading them, by example, to put everything on the line for freedom. Mrs. Gxowa and Mrs. Redden and their many women compatriots are the very embodiment of what Marxian theorist Antonio Gramsci termed "organic intellectuals." In fact, the presence of these forceful organic intellectuals significantly alters the definition of leadership within the two freedom movements. Many of the 1950s women activists formed a critical middle tier of local leaders, "bridging" their grassroots communities with the more formal organizations and the more remote male leadership.[10] Contemporary women activists stand on the shoulders of earlier activists such as Mrs. Redden, Mrs. Gxowa, and the many others who speak in these pages.

·{ 7 }·

A Note on the Organization and Methodology of the Book

This book presents a mid-twentieth-century Black women's political consciousness and activism that stem directly from the history and experiences of the nineteenth and early twentieth centuries. Rather than provide a formal comparison of separate case studies or a global examination of the trans-Atlantic world, I have sought to acknowledge how regional developments and local communities of women and men figured significantly in effecting change throughout the African diaspora. In the excavation of the landscape of the 1950s activists and their movements, it became apparent that a much larger story was unfolding. As a result, the topography of the women's early lives and their heritages are uncovered in the chapters that lead up to the mass demonstrations of the 1950s, and the main events of the boycotts and pass resistance are revealed in the final chapters. Nineteenth- and early twentieth-century communities, organizations, and institutions figure prominently in the early struggles and collective campaigns fought against colonial rule or segregationist systems. The book proceeds from the mid-nineteenth century, where a practice of women's resistance and activism was formed within multigenerational communities and families that were undergoing rapid, fundamental change. In the beginning and middle chapters, which include the early lives of the women as they advance to the mid-twentieth century, the early development and values of the communities that harbored resistance in many forms—churches, schools, unions, women's social and economic clubs, occupations, and, most of all, habits of survival—also emerge as critical to the formation of Black women's liberationist and protofeminist consciousness.

In the United States the memory of enslavement held different meanings for men and women, and the experiences of Black women in captivity and after emancipation helped determine the types of resistance to white supremacy that they enacted. Similarly, a legacy of free and independent African peoples deriving sustenance from landed societies with a tradition of close communal ties and patriarchal power formed the precolonial and colonial background against which the South African women measured some of their contemporary losses. I treat both subjects in chapter 1. In chapter 2 I address working- and lower-middle-class women in the so-called New South and the Orange Free State who participated in building Black independent institutions and protest while they sought better lives within the urban context. In chapters 1 and 2 I highlight the persistence of habit and tradition within the two trans-Atlantic communities. In chapters 3 through 6 I cover the women's youth in rural and urban settings, migrations to the cities, work, union organizing, radical political legacies, social networks, early formations of political organizations, and the first 1950s mass demonstrations. Particularly in chapter 3, the rural backgrounds of some of the women activists reveal not only rich and proud heritages but also the models of competence and integrity that contributed to their sense of well-being. In chapter 4 I consider the process of urban migration more closely and show the women's leisure activities—such as those spent in home missionary groups—as experiences that laid the groundwork for later, more overtly political organizing. By chapters 5 and 6, the women activists have witnessed the more radical politics of the 1930s and 1940s. The Communist Party in both locations—majority Black in Alabama, with the same potential in South Africa—acting on its international imperative of Black self-determination, seeks ways to fuse political interests among the Black (and some white) working and middle classes in order to offer aggressive resistance against a virulently hostile white supremacist political economy. In chapter 6, women's activism is the springboard to the formation of overtly political organizations during the increasingly militant decade of the 1940s and World War II. Finally, in chapters 7 and 8, the women are engaged in full political resistance against the state as they demand a new accounting of women's issues from both their movements and their relationships with men. The discussions in chapters 7 and 8, especially, engage the question of where a protofeminist practice emerges and becomes useful in the understanding of Black women's political activism and leadership in the later twentieth century.

To tell this story in full scale, Black women stand center stage in the narrative. The voices of the women activists as girls, young women, and ardent disrupters of the status quo direct the reader's thinking about the entire transnational landscape of Black resistance. Fittingly, and as an overture to the history and analysis that follow, I open each chapter with the thoughts and perceptions of women activists of the 1950s. These overtures (usually set in the 1990s) are designed to move the larger story forward and back to the women's recollections of their political consciousness-in-the-making. Similar themes run through both the overture and the chapter that it introduces, helping to provide a more complete picture of the story of each chapter.

The oral histories of such dynamic women activists as Bertha Gxowa and Idessa Redden enliven the narrative with a vivid portrayal of the risks they took in confronting their white employers, their husbands, the male leaders, and the white power structure. In their descriptions of their early experiences and in their physical bearing, it was clear that they did not accept the monikers "poor" and "marginal" as accurate representations. Many of the women "historians"—or "keepers of information"—remembered the fullness of their prepolitical pasts, when parents and extended family members found ways to provide them with the necessities of life and modeled how to stand up to naked injustice with pride and dignity.[11] Their sometimes long, digressive narrations are rich in wisdom, logic, common sense, personal experience, noteworthy worldviews, and community knowledge.[12] Viewing the women's own truths as they themselves see them helps locate the wellspring of events and emotions that tie them so profoundly to their communities. If Montgomery and Alexandra, Lowndes County, and Western Native Township are any test, then such communities serve as important laboratories for social justice movements—movements that clearly have been led, sustained, and safeguarded by a host of women such as Idessa Redden and Bertha Gxowa. These remarkable women provide inspiration and faith in the possible at uniquely challenging moments in the twenty-first century.

~~~~~~~~~~

IN THE BEGINNING

Early Resistance among Enslaved and Free Women, 1721–1870

ONE Easter season, well before the 1955–1956 Montgomery bus boycott had become a daily reality in the lives of the Black residents of Montgomery, Ms. Ora Lee Bell, a domestic worker in the affluent Cloverdale section of the city, took all five of her young children downtown to purchase their new Easter outfits. Ms. Bell was particularly interested in finding white baby-doll shoes for her girls that season. She wanted good shoes for her children this time, not the cheap, stiff ones on sale at Weber's Department Store. Perhaps she would find better-quality, more comfortably fitting shoes at the Belko and Hudson Department Store, she thought, although she knew that her shopping was likely to be restricted to its Negro section and that, if she wanted to shop at Belko's at all, she would have to enter the store from the rear.

Gwen Bell, Ora Lee Bell's middle daughter, remembered the indignity of that particular shopping trip: "We couldn't go in on the Dexter Avenue side.... We had to go on over on [to] the Washington Street side ... [even though] the front of the store was over on the Dexter Avenue side." When it came time to try on the shoes, the salesman would not allow it. Yet Ms. Ora Bell insisted; she did not want her children to suffer the pain of ill-fitting shoes as they had in the past. "And he told my mother, he said," Gwen recalled, "'Well, you can take them pickaninnies and get out of my store.'... And there were several people telling her to be quiet, you know; [they] said, 'Don't argue with him; just go on.'" Still, Gwen's mother was not deterred; she continued to softly, but firmly, protest. As the salesman became more irritated, he pushed her, ordering her out of the store. The children rallied to their mother's defense, encircling the salesman and waiting for his next move. It was a tense moment, one that could have easily escalated into a dangerous, even deadly, situation for the Bells. 'You know," explained Gwen, "because all five of us [felt], 'Don't you touch my mama!' we were ready to attack him, and she said, 'He's not worth it; let's keep on. He didn't hurt me.... [W]hen you hurt them is when you don't spend your money in their store.'" [1]

Before the onset of the 1955–1956 Montgomery bus boycott, the Black residents of Montgomery had, for decades, experienced similar indignities in a wide variety of settings, including department stores, restaurants, hotels, parks, municipal buses, work spaces, and city neighborhoods. Black people generally—especially when they acted as independent agents rather than as, for example, nannies or chauffeurs—enjoyed only limited access to the public spaces in the city. They were reminded daily, by the law and by public postings, where they could and could not go and how they were to interact with white people. The Bell family, therefore, did not need to be persuaded to join the Montgomery bus boycott movement. A potent but rarely highlighted aspect of the Montgomery bus boycott was the economic boycott of the downtown stores. As the bus boycott extended its reach, lasting significantly longer than anticipated, the lost Black patronage of the stores helped to sway the white business community in the face of the often fractious negotiations at City Hall.

Half a world away, Black South Africans also found their daily lives severely constricted by white oppression. Most emphatically from World War II onward, they too engaged in antiracist resistance in protest of the severe political and economic conditions, when miners' strikes, pass resistances, and bus boycotts erupted along the Witwatersrand in the Transvaal. Between January and March 1957, more than fifteen thousand people boycotted the Alexandra Township Public Utility Transport Company buses and walked the nine miles to central Johannesburg in protest of bus fare hikes. Even a "one-pence" increase in bus fare meant that Black families on the Rand would face such difficult choices as whether to pay their rent or buy their children shoes. If for a Black family in Montgomery the unrestrained ability to try on the shoes they sought to purchase symbolized a critical marker in their existence as a free people, for many Black children in Johannesburg, South Africa (as in Montgomery as well), even the ownership of a pair of shoes symbolized that freedom.

To a small child in Johannesburg, South Africa, a pair of socks and shoes held a more practical than symbolic meaning. Although Emma Mashinini felt fortunate in some ways, she remembered clearly the hardships associated with being Black and disempowered. Like Ms. Ora Lee Bell and many other Black women in the U.S. South and South Africa, Emma Mashinini's mother was a domestic worker. Her father worked and was required to live at a dairy many miles away and was able to visit his family only once a week. Their combined wages provided for the upkeep of their family, which included eight children.[2] In 1936, when she was seven years old, Mrs. Mashinini was forcefully removed from their home in City Deep to make way for white people. After City Deep, her family moved to Sophiatown, the vibrant, crowded, often dangerous multiracial freehold community where petty traders, political leaders, and working- and middle-class women and men lived until its obliteration in the mid-1950s. "From Sophiatown I was now sent to a Salvation Army school in the municipal Western Native Township nearby, where I discovered how few of my classmates had started school at the correct age. My family was fortunate in other ways, too. I don't remember any of us running around without shoes, and I had a raincoat, unlike many of the children, although since I was sickly in those days I knew that whenever it rained I'd get tonsillitis anyway, and be unable to go to school. . . . We always wore socks and shoes. Amongst poor people this was a particular pride," she recalled.[3]

This sense of pride or worth as measured by a pair of shoes may be difficult to imagine from a modern-day U.S. standpoint. These recollections from the 1930s and 1940s reveal, however, the lack of recourse for Black people in the face of the myriad economic, social, and political injustices of the segregated South and pre-apartheid South Africa. For Black women in particular, in the first third of the twentieth century, these injustices still called to mind an earlier disregard of their physical persons—their bodies, unlike those of men, were exploited for the future workers they could produce and for the work they could perform in service to their own and others' households. For those who were considered mere "beasts of burden," shoes were an unnecessary luxury that would not enhance the hard labor of multiple childbirths or a lifetime in the fields or kitchens of their fathers, husbands, chiefs, and bosses. At the dawn of the twentieth century, and by the look and substance of the lives of the majority of Black women, slavery in Montgomery had died hard, and subordination in Johannesburg was becoming even further entrenched. For instance, Black women in both locations were grossly undereducated and worked in the least remunerative job categories. They could not vote (whereas some Black men could), and they were often subject to the wishes of men or to strong familial obligations. Still forced to fend off frequent physical attacks by white and Black men, Black women seemed to form a unique class of the most powerless. Yet, despite their enslaved or even quasi-free status, many Black women found important ways to subvert the restrictive expectations that their superiors held for them. This early history of Black women's perseverance under enslavement in the United States and during the precolonial and colonial periods in South Africa holds significant meaning in the chronicle of women's resistance, Black liberation, and the 1950s political uprisings.

In this chapter I explore, within a historical framework, the contours of Black women's social and economic lives—from enslavement to Reconstruction in the United States and from the precolonial to the colonial periods in South Africa. I explain how a mature social and political consciousness among Black women emerged more forcefully, by the 1940s and 1950s, as sustained political action. To be sure, I argue for the long-term view of Black resistance—a resistance cultivated among families and communities of enslaved and nominally free peoples that ultimately resulted in powerful and effective movements for liberation. I hold that the earliest political experiences of the women activists, although sporadic and short-lived, were fostered by their own grandparents or by the conditions that prevailed during their grandparents' generations and before. For it is among enslaved women in the United States that—by, for example, refusing to engage in sexual relations without choice or perfecting work routines in their own interests—Black women first developed a practice of challenging white demands. Similarly, among South African women during the precolonial and colonial eras, exercising choice in what to cultivate or raise for the economic benefit of the collective household or finding ways to exert their (limited) influence through their sons or husbands contributed significantly to women's agency and to the formation of their future political voice.

Clearly, Black women's political consciousness and activism began long before the boycotts and pass resistance of the 1950s. From enslavement to emancipation and through colonialism, Black women fomented small but significant political resistances and victories on the road to Black liberation. Their actions can be cited as important forerunners; indeed, they provide the historical context in which future resistances could be launched. Thanks to early examples set by capable male and female ancestors, Black women could look more confidently to the promise of future victories. In a local context, during and after enslavement, the labor and agency of Black women were necessary ingredients in their people's survival and continued resistance to oppression. At the same time, Black women helped two economic regions to expand their considerable fortunes within a burgeoning worldwide market economy. As larger political and economic forces loomed about them, enslaved and nominally free Black women continued to find ways to challenge forces over which they had little recognized control and to use whatever leverage they had to take their families and their communities beyond survival to a better way of life.

Women's Enslavement and Resistance in Alabama

For three of the Montgomery bus boycott activists—Mrs. Beautie Mae Johnson, Mrs. Amy Collins Harris, and Mrs. Rosa McCauley Parks—slavery was something they heard about almost daily from the grandparents they lived with in their early childhood. Stories of survival in the Alabama Black Belt, often bitter, punctuated their personal histories and provided them with a reference for the experience and its cost. During slavery, Black people cultivated an array of resourceful behaviors to use to their advantage. The work of enslaved women and their resistance to the exploitation inherent in that system is part of the long history of Black struggle in Alabama.

The story of a once-free Choctaw people who gave the word *Alabama* its meaning—"clearers of the wood or thicket," or "those who clear the land"—bears some resemblance to the histories passed down among several generations of AmaZulu, AmaXhosa, Khoisan, or Southern BaSotho.[4] African and Native American history and folklore are replete with tales of war and exile—in each case, the native peoples became dispossessed of their lands and then subjugated to white authority. In nineteenth-century Alabama, Native American and African histories converged. Once they arrived at the trans-Mississippi region, the original home to the Choctaw, Chickasaw, Cherokee, and Creek nations, African captives found their reversed fortunes tied to those of the new master landowners.

Extending the cotton frontier to the Mississippi River and beyond, white Alabamians were poised to make money in a new market economy. As Black Belt cotton and land prices boomed (but not without the predictable economic busts) from the late 1810s to the 1830s, in came the surveyors, banks, land speculators, politicians, planters, small farmers, and enslaved Black workers in ever increasing numbers. With Alabama admitted to the Union in 1819, the population of the new state stood at nearly 128,000 by

1820. Approximately one third of the population was made up of persons of African descent, all but 571 of these people were enslaved, and nearly half of the almost 42,000 enslaved men and women in Alabama were female.[5]

Slavery in Alabama had actually begun with the development of the colony of French Louisiana. As early as 1701, the governor of the colony had advocated the importation of Africans in order to meet growing labor requirements. In 1721 the first few ships carrying seven hundred African captives arrived in Mobile directly from the Guinea coast and Angola.[6] Thereafter, the Western, or Indian, Company pledged to import "three-thousand blacks" within the next twenty-five years. The cost of an enslaved worker—payable in rice or tobacco—rose from $176 in 1721 to a high of $373 in 1734.[7] By the 1830s the price had jumped to more than $750, peaking in 1860 at $1,600 for a competent field hand, and twice as much for a skilled hand.[8] Until the Civil War, the insatiable demand for unpaid labor among the Alabama "laborlords"[9] continued unabated.

Although between 1820 and 1850 the number of enslaved persons increased more than eightfold, the proportion of women to men remained fairly even.[10] Women's dexterity in picking cotton, skill as plow hands, and established capacity for hard physical labor all accounted for their equal number among plantation workers.[11] Based on cotton production, the first fifty years of the political economy of Alabama depended greatly on the unpaid labor of its Black men and women.

Of course, demand and skill were not the only factors that influenced the cost or value of a bondsman or bondswoman. A healthy woman of child-bearing age was valued for her ability to produce additional enslaved workers. In 1834 the Alabama State Supreme Court ruled that "a jury would place a higher value on a female slave promising issue than on one of contrary description."[12] In 1852 an Alabama planter who sought redress from the courts after having purchased three enslaved women who could not bear children was awarded the return of his investment.[13] Indeed, enslaved women who had given birth to numerous children were often advertised for sale as "good breeders" whose reproductive abilities would help increase their owners' wealth for generations. If, as Kenneth Stampp states, slave owners did not routinely force the breeding of enslaved women for immediate profit, they reared them "with an eye to their marketability."[14]

The testimony of Rose Williams demonstrates how owners manipulated the reproductive lives of enslaved women. When she was sixteen years old, Williams's owner selected an enslaved man named Rufus as her mate and ordered them to "bring forth portly children." At first, Williams refused, but—under the threat of punishment by whipping and by the retaliatory sale of family members—she ultimately relented: "There it am. What am I to do? So I decides to do as the massa wish, and so I yields. I never marries, 'cause one experience is enough for this nigger. After what I does for the massa, I never wants no truck with any man. The Lord forgive this colored woman, but he have to excuse me and look for some other for to 'plenish the earth."[15] Williams's decision not to marry reclaimed from her owner her reproductive power and challenged the myth of complicit and oversexualized Black women who invited the sexual attentions (read: assaults) of their white, male owners. Like Celia (Newsom), Harriet Jacobs, Sojourner Truth, and many whose stories have not been told, Rose Williams is counted among women who—determined to take control of their minds, bodies, and (re)productive labor—personify the first strains of a Black feminist consciousness and practice.[16] For African American women of the post–World War II generation in Alabama—only two generations removed from enslavement and making claims to respectability on public byways—an understanding of this awareness of choice about the treatment of their physical persons from their collective past was essential.

Along with Black women's reproductive potential, their seemingly inexhaustible capacity for labor was valued highly. Over the many generations from enslavement through freedom, this capacity for and efficiency in work helped sustain legions of Black families and communities. The owners of enslaved women reaped double rewards from the labors of their bondswomen as cooks and field hands, performed in service to both white and Black families.[17] In the 1930s, at age 101, Charity Anderson recalled how hard she had worked as an enslaved woman in Monroe County, Alabama: "I sure could wash, iron, knit and weave, bless you, [and] I could finish my days' work around the house, and then weave six or seven yards of cloth. I've washed, ironed and waited on the fourth generation of this family. I learned the children how to wash, iron, weave, and knit. I just wish I could tell these young children how to do."[18] As clearly as Anderson expressed pride in her value to the white family for whom she toiled nearly all her life, she revealed her importance to the persistence of Black communities. Organized, purposeful, and capable of moving effortlessly from one task to the next, Anderson turned domestic work into a high and enduring art that proved indispensable in freedom. Freedwomen who were in a position to capitalize on such skills collected the proceeds from their paid domestic labors, which could provide shoes or an education or even ultimate liberation for family members even among succeeding generations.

During enslavement and emancipation and through at least the first decades of the twentieth century, the work responsibilities of enslaved and nominally free women began in childhood and changed little from one generation to the next. According to several of the Works Progress Administration (WPA) narratives of former slaves edited separately by George Rawick and Benjamin A. Botkin, Black children—who were considered half-hands—were nevertheless expected to pull their weight. Often Black children began by caring for other children or by performing small jobs around the house, grounds, or fields. Jenny Proctor, a field hand in Alabama, recalled, "I 'tended to the children when I was a little gal and tried to clean the house just like Ole Miss tells me to. Then soon as I was ten years old, Ole Master, he say, 'Git this here nigger to that cotton patch.'"[19] From the time she was a very young girl, Carrie Davis remembered, she "was used for [a] housegirl and to help keep the yards and bring in water. Us wore mostly slips woven in homemade looms and it was orsanberg and homespun, Sunday and Monday the same, [and] our shoes was made out of tan yard and they was brogans and hard as rocks."[20]

Even wearing the coarse, heavy cotton used as grain sacks and heavy, "hard-as-rocks" ankle-high work shoes, many enslaved children felt fortunate only to keep warm, dry, and protected from the natural elements. They had more pressing worries to preoccupy them. Jenny Proctor remembered eating what she thought was a discarded biscuit and paying for the infraction with a severe beating.[21] Mary Ella Grandberry recounted, "Plenty times us had to go without breakfast. . . . [U]s worked 'til dinner time just the same before we got anything to eat."[22] Oliver Bell recalled the emotional toll of watching his mother being whipped: "Ole Marsa made her pull her dress down 'roun' her waist and made her lay down cross the door and he taken a leather strap and whipped her, and I remembers crying."[23] Mary Ella Grandberry concluded, "I don't remember much about when I was a child. I disremembers ever playing like children do today. Ever since I can remember I had a water bucket on my arm totin' water to the hands. If I wasn't doing that, I was chopping cotton."[24]

In addition to the specific skills they acquired as uncompensated workers, children learned a particular awareness of their role and position as members of a subordinate people. Working alongside parents, relatives, or older fellow bondspeople encouraged an important group consciousness needed for individual and collective protection, if not for a sense of well-being. Young Mingo White helped his mother avoid suffering fifty lashes to her back by assisting at night in the spinning and carding of her daily quota of thread once her other work was completed.[25] The common form of gang labor, which included young children as partial hands, served as a training ground for group cooperation, as young workers watched full hands help one another to meet work quotas or encourage one another to keep pace by the rhythm of their singing. By joining the "trash gangs"—which generally comprised women with small babies, pregnant women, and women past childbearing age—pubescent girls learned from other women about cooperative work, female socialization, and men and sex.[26]

Some adult women field hands fulfilled their work obligations at the plow. In a gendered division of plantation labor not always rigidly applied, plowing was generally reserved for men and hoeing for women. Subject to a woman's skill and strength and the needs of her owner, she might also be required to plow. Oliver Bell remembered his mother working as a plow hand. In one of the narratives compiled by Rawick, in testimony evocative of the story of Sojourner Truth, a woman known as Aunt Clussey insisted, "I could plow as well as any fiel' han' Massa had and put the harness on besides."[27] In Lee County, Alabama, however, Sara Colquitt's combined labors as field hand and household worker suggest a more typically varied female work experience:

> Miss Mary was good to us but us had to work hard and late, from 'fore day light. I worked in the field every day and would take my littlest baby and tie it up to a tree limb while I hoed and worked, to keep ants and bugs from getting on it. . . . I was one of the spinners too and was given six cuts to do on a reel at a time, and do it at nights lots of times too. I'd help cook at the house when the real cook was sick or had [to cook for] a heap of company. Us cooked on a great big fireplace with arms hanging over the coals, to hang pots on to boil and us had three legged skillets to fry in, that set over coals, [and] then us cooked sho'nuff bread, ash-cakes, the best things you ever ate, nothing like it these days.[28]

Colquitt was sold a second time "for $1,000 to Mr. Sam Rainey of Camp Hill, Alabama." Rainey paid top dollar for Colquitt's valuable productive skills and proven fertility. She remembered the overseer on Sam Rainey's place as especially brutal—someone who would "whup you in a minute, put you in the buck and tie your feet, whup you a [far] sight."[29]

The versatility, skill, and endurance of enslaved women workers helped determine the fluidity with which owners and overseers who were looking to extract the most from their female workforce transgressed gender divisions. The fact that, as a woman, Colquitt was expected to perform reproductive labor no doubt enhanced her sale. This did not, however, exempt her from working "hard and late" in the fields, where she had to work out the logistics of providing for her smallest child's safety and care. Immersed in a labor system propelled by coercion and sex as much as by capital, Colquitt was hardly immune to the common practice for both men and women of being beaten "in the buck"—bent over, hands bound to shins, locked in a crouching position by a stick that ran behind the knees and in front of the elbows.[30] Oliver Bell's testimony confirms the particularly gendered, if not sexualized, practice of whipping enslaved women who have been stripped to the waist, breasts exposed, and forced to lie prostrate as if in preparation for "Ole Marsa's" pleasure. Ultimately, it is not difficult to see how Angela Davis made the link to power and punishment being visited on the bodies of enslaved women in the form of rape. According to Davis, such sexualized violence was designed to ensure white men's dominance and root out any notions of resistance among enslaved women and men.[31]

That such competent women workers confronted and resisted their total degradation as women and as human beings within an economic and social system designed to deny both should, however, be no surprise. This nineteenth-century collective history would come to establish a basis and in some cases the methods from which Black women drew their future resistance to political, economic, social, and sexual injustice. Enslaved women often practiced forms of resistance aimed at ensuring the care and safety of their children, if not their communities. Fannie Moore remembered her mother's repeated struggles to protect her children from the overseer: "I never see how my mama stand such hard work. She stand up for her children though. The old overseer he hate my mama, 'cause she fight him for beating her children. Why, she git more whuppings for that than anything else."[32] In considering flight, women were hard-pressed to leave their children behind or expose them to the dangers of life on the run. Enslaved women more often chose periodic truancy or absenteeism as their mode of escape.[33] In his poignant narrative, for instance, Frederick Douglass remembered sharing only a few brief visits with his mother when she stole away from her home plantation at night in order to spend time with him.[34]

Because food rations for enslaved workers were usually insufficient, cooks and other household workers often took food from their owners' kitchens. Colquitt admitted, "All us niggers was fed from the big kitchen and sometimes we would steal more food than we was given but we wasn't hungry none."[35] In another of the narratives compiled by Rawick, a woman known as Aunt Rachel who professed to have been "the finest of cooks," admitted being "a little careless when it come to the ownership of victuals." Her interviewer explained, "She will 'borrow' meal, flour, meat, and sugar, and then when chance presents itself, she will 'borrow' from the same pantry to 'pay it back.' She often says 'When you find a nigger what won't steal victuals when he's hungry, you'll find hair growing in the palm of that nigger's hand.'"[36] According to Aunt Rachel, "stealing" food was a common practice among hungry bondspeople, and in a manner that suggests twentieth-century domestic workers' "pan toting" of leftover or staple foodstuffs as a kind of compensatory wage, she was not above using dissemblance to claim her due.

Enslaved women also used other tactics of resistance—such as feigning illness, reducing their work pace, refusing to perform certain tasks, breaking implements, poisoning food, or behaving in a disruptive manner—in order to modify the terms of their labor. Rather than quit, mid-twentieth-century domestic workers in Montgomery and Johannesburg—including political activists such as Amelia Scott Green and Naomi Setshedi—also expressed dissatisfaction with their employers by refusing to perform certain tasks, by staying home, or by talking back to the mistresses of the households in which they were employed. It would seem that, since the days of enslavement, those with the least power had learned and practiced similar methods within the long tradition of Black women's resistance to white domination.

Away from the master's gaze and the overseer's whip, however, enslaved women and men resisted complete control of their minds and bodies by finding opportunities to create family, community, and leisure activities. Enjoyment of leisure time during enslavement established a set of practices that were continued in freedom. Coming together for communal festivities or for worship helped Black people develop a collective consciousness that could act as a buffer against the worst aspects of enslavement or life under the heel of Jim Crow.

Corn shuckings, holiday celebrations, dances, and marriage ceremonies were occasions for fun, laughter, and release. Camp meetings, church gatherings, and funerals not only provided additional opportunities for socializing; they also helped connect enslaved women and men in a powerful community of faith. At age 100, Martha Bradley recalled, "When we didn't go to church, we'd get together in the quarters and have preachin' and singin' amongst ourselves."[37] Preaching and singing *away from the white folks* perhaps recalled an African expression of the most sacred kind performed in community—an expression that helped foster among African Americans an independent consciousness and identity apart from the assumptions of white people.[38] The sense of spirituality and religious expression of the slave community acted as refuge, resistance, and promise of freedom all rolled into one. In the brush arbors, at separate church services, or even under the watchful eye of the masters, the meetings, songs, and fervent prayers of enslaved Black people—indicative of their strong religious conviction and the belief in their ultimate liberation—persisted. Embedded in the lyrics of a well-known song is the idea of freedom as imminent and not just a consequence of death:

> Steal away, steal away, steal away to Jesus
> Steal away, steal away home,
> I ain't got long to stay here.
>
> My Lord, He calls me,
> He calls me by the thunder,
> The trumpet sounds within-a my soul,
> I ain't got long to stay here.[39]

Whether in the here and now, in the lifetime of an enslaved person, or in the spiritual hereafter, faith in God was often equated with faith in eventual freedom. Freedom might be found in a song about stealing home to Jesus or in the Union's liberating soldiers; either way, for Black people, faith and freedom were intermixed in the experience of bondage. After emancipation, the new freedom and faith were called on to sustain Black women and men through times of great violence and despair. In later periods of political disenfranchisement and economic failure and throughout the modern freedom movement, Black people drew heavily on a wellspring of faith often expressed in song. Invoked as a form of communal prayer during marches or in hot, crowded jail cells, many movement freedom songs emerged directly from such spirituals as "Steal Away" and "Oh, Freedom!"

Structural Changes and New Challenges

The great paroxysm of the Civil War released Black people into a chaotic South characterized by physical devastation, economic disaster, bitterness, violence, confusion, and displacement. Newly freed Black women and men in Alabama confronted this chaos as they struggled to secure and provide the most basic necessities, search for lost loved ones, and fulfill an elusive freedom. In 1860 Black people in Alabama numbered 437,770, of whom 435,080 were enslaved. By 1870 the total Black population stood at 475,510, which represented nearly half the aggregate population of Alabama,[40] and the majority of the Black population of Alabama still lived in the fertile Black Belt, with Montgomery and Dallas Counties (and their respective cities of Montgomery and Selma) accounting for the highest numbers.[41] The population of Black Belt voters was key to the leveraging of political power by the Republican Party in Alabama during Reconstruction. Similarly, in the post–World War II era, Black residents of Montgomery and Dallas Counties were among the leading activists invigorating some of the most difficult campaigns in the modern freedom movement. Political disenfranchisement and intimidation, two hallmark characteristics of the post–Civil War era, again proved formidable to those in the Black Belt who were looking to change the status quo during the 1950s and 1960s. The Black Belt population of the Reconstruction period, roughly half of which (not unlike its twentieth-century counterpart) was made up of women, represented a collection of families and communities that needed all available hands to forge their political and economic survival in the midst of Ku Klux Klan violence.

Memories of Klan presence in Alabama just after the Civil War remained fresh for many, including Mary Ella Grandberry. As a "big gal," Grandberry experienced the terror of Klan night riders in the early days of freedom:

> Right after the war the Ku Klux got after the colored folks. They would come to our houses and scare us most to death. They would take some of the niggers out an' whup them and those that they didn't whup they tied up by their fingers and toes. Those Ku Klux would come to our windows at night and say: "Your time ain't long acomin'." The Ku Klux got so bad that they would even get us in the daytime. They took some of the niggers and throwed them in the

river to drown. They kept this up 'til some folks from the North come down and put a stop to it.[42]

Spreading quickly from Tennessee into Alabama and across the South after 1866, the Klan used its terror tactics against Black communities that were becoming mobilized as groups of newly constituted citizens who sought equal rights. Black men and women took their demands for suffrage and equality—the twin markers of true emancipation—into the streets and into public spaces, holding demonstrations, mass meetings, parades, and conventions.[43] Where Grandberry's vivid account implied her understanding of the reasons behind such violence, Ellen Parton's testimony before a joint committee of Congress in 1871 clearly exposed white men's continued use of rape as a political weapon:

> They came on Monday, Tuesday and Wednesday. . . . [O]n Wednesday night they came and broke open the wardrobe and trunks, and committed rape upon me; there were eight of them in the house; I do not know how many there were outside; they were white men. . . . I called upon Mr. Mike Slamon, who was one of the crowd, for protection. . . . [H]e then took me in the dining room, and told me I had to do just what he said. . . . [A]fter he got through with me he came through the house and said he was after the Union Leagues.[44]

Mike Slamon's unapologetic use of sexualized violence against Parton suggests that the practice was the contemporary norm. Black women paid dearly for the democratic freedoms that only (some) Black men could fully exercise.

Denying Black women the right to vote did not keep them out of the electoral process, however. Freedwomen were fully involved in making political decisions that they believed would benefit their families and communities. As one scholar of early Alabama history found, "The women were converted to Radicalism long before the men, and almost invariably used their influence strongly for the League."[45] More recently, Elsa Barkley Brown interpreted women's "influence" to mean that Black men and women viewed the voting process, or the ballot, "as collectively owned" and that the emphasis placed on family and community in the post–Civil War period meant that everyone was included in the political process.[46] Together, between 1871 and 1877, Black voters elected to Congress Benjamin S. Turner, a Selma freedman and successful merchant; James T. Rapier, a freeborn man from Lauderdale who was educated in Canada; and Jeremiah Haralson, a self-educated freedman and former field hand.[47] At the same time, Black people continued to agitate for a greater participatory role in and a greater share of the bounty within the Republican Party.

Seeking a new economic self-determination, the former bondspeople took seriously the Radical Republican promise that they would be granted "forty acres and a mule."[48] When the proposal was rejected, those who wished to make a living from the soil (as the majority did) had little choice but to enter the debt-laden sharecropping system, which lasted well into the first half of the twentieth century. Any approximation of fair competition with white people in a free (and corrupt) market system proved virtually impossible. Black families were ultimately forced to live at the barest levels of subsistence as old and new planters desperately sought to resume their prewar levels of production. Turning now from their former position as labor lords to politically powerful landlords, the white bosses used every conceivable political and economic ruse—rigged labor contracts and disenfranchisement; taxation; excessive charges for tools, seed, and animals; and harsh vagrancy and restrictive apprenticeship laws—in an effective assault on Black independence and mobility.[49] These economic conditions for the post–Civil War generation applied similarly to the generations still eking out a living as sharecroppers and hired hands after World War II. For many rural daughters and future activists in the Montgomery boycott (even those born in the city) who knew firsthand the hardships of such conditions, the determination to bring about a new order of social justice and economic independence for Black people grew from their experiences.

Chickens for Shoes

During the 1860s and 1870s, Black women chose to stay out of the fields as much as possible, and Black families placed an unprecedented emphasis on the education of their children in the quest to assert their independence and equip themselves for a future in freedom. Although freedwomen took advantage of opportunities to earn extra money by selling whatever surplus they could cook or cultivate, Black women also sought ways to replace outside work responsibilities with work for their own families. Family decisions about where, when, and by whom Black women would be employed were aimed at keeping them safe from white male scrutiny and sexual assault.[50] The practice of taking in laundry neatly fulfilled the need to earn money for the household while it created its own form of labor autonomy. Women who successfully avoided the precious few wage labor options open to them were most often "the wives and daughters of able-bodied men."[51] Accused by hard-pressed prospective employers of attempting to emulate the white middle-class values of a "domestic" white womanhood and confronted with considerable attempts to subordinate them and demean their role as women, Black women chose to assert their own variety of respectability. These consistent demands for their own respectability, which constitute a strong stance in defense of their interests, help locate aspects of the subsequent political activism of Black women as distinctly protofeminist. In spite of the economic and political structures that kept so many Black women in Alabama poor and disenfranchised, their claims to respectability—most apparent at such historical moments as the post–Civil War period, the 1896 formation of the National Association of Colored Women's Clubs, and the era of the Montgomery bus boycott—helped ignite their sustained resistance against all forms of Black inequality.

In addition to the pursuit of economic independence, the effort to attain literacy played an essential role in Black women's historic struggle to win a true and just freedom. The freedwomen and men of Alabama, as elsewhere, understood the importance of being able to read labor contracts and the power of a letter of confirmation presented to a prospective employer. These and other incentives made them eager to take advantage of the limited opportunities for schooling on the plantations and in the cities following emancipation. On a plantation near Selma, for instance, a group of field hands built a schoolhouse not far from where they worked. The contract they drew up with their employer stated that they would build the school and pay the teacher's salary and the employer would furnish the materials.[52] Since no system was yet in place to support public education and thus no public funds were available for *any* Alabama resident, freedmen and freedwomen had no choice but to pay for their education out of their own meager resources, a practice that continued well after Radical Reconstruction. In fact, Black women were known all over the South for selling "chickens for shoes": They used the proceeds from the sale of their chickens and eggs to buy shoes for their children so that they could walk to school in the winter.[53] Congregational, African Methodist Episcopal, Baptist, and other national religious groups sent missionaries to the rural and urban South to educate the children and win the hearts and minds of thousands of new converts.[54] They had their work cut out for them, however: In 1870 a mere 15,815 Black people attended school in the state, and two decades later 69.1

percent of the Black population ten years of age and older—over half of them women—remained illiterate.[55]

African Women and Precolonial African Societies

South Africa is a country of many proud lineage and ethnic groups who, jointly and independently, fought against British and Boer imperialism in a centuries-long struggle for Black liberation. The BaSotho-BaTswana peoples, indigenous to the areas that later became known as the provinces of the Transvaal and Orange Free State, were among the many groups of African peoples who found their social, political, and economic institutions disrupted by the European tradition of land appropriation and capital accumulation. As African peoples offered continuous resistance to European demands for land and labor, their institutions became strained and their ways of life drastically changed. It is these institutions and lifeways, established among free and independent peoples, that offer contexts for understanding not only the integrity of a people before subjugation but also the source of their resistance and its ability to empower future generations.

The stories of several of the 1950s activist women who testified about their involvement in the South African freedom struggle begin with an acknowledgment of the importance of the long history and traditions of their people. This is the case for the BaSotho-BaTswana activists Mrs. Maggie Resha, Mrs. Florence Siwedi, and Mrs. Ellen Kuzwayo. Although their ancestors were not enslaved peoples, the hated passbook that, at some point after 1956, each was required to carry may well have made them feel that they were "slaves in [their] own country."[56] These were women who came from proud lineages whose women fulfilled roles as providers for their families and their communities and exerted their own brand of influence on their men. The precolonial roles of women set certain limits on their subjugation and provide important sites of resistance.

Speakers of SeSotho and SeTswana in north-central South Africa, who—at the time of the Dutch arrival—were already living in what would become the western Transvaal, believed that the first people, their most ancient ancestors, came with their cattle from the Northeast. For this reason, when the BaHurutshe bury their dead, "they place the face of the deceased person in that direction."[57] The BaHurutshe, one of the major lineages and polities of the BaSotho-BaTswana peoples, also claim that there was a hole in their country, out of which the first men came with their cattle, and that their footmarks can still be seen today.[58] Although the two explanations of origin may seem slightly at odds with each other, they share the important intersection of men, cattle, and place.

Early in the nineteenth century, the SeSotho- and SeTswana-speaking peoples lived primarily between the Limpopo and Orange Rivers, north and west of the Drakensburg Mountains in the present-day North West and Orange Free State provinces. Centuries before, the earliest BaSotho peoples settled primarily in the Magaliesberg region—a well-watered and well-wooded area named after the BaKwena founding ancestor, Mogale— and then divided and dispersed from that region.[59] The northernmost people among the BaSotho were the BaTswana of modern Botswana and the lands lying southward, among whom the earliest offshoots were the BaKgalagadi and the BaFokeng. The Southern BaSotho—formed into a single organized group by their paramount leader, Moshoeshoe, during the mid-nineteenth century—were located roughly in the area of present-day Lesotho. Moshoeshoe's people are linked genealogically with the Ba-Hurutshe, a much larger group, chiefly lineages with such offshoots as the BaKwena, BaKgatla, BaPedi, and BaTlokwa. A third large group of Ba-Sotho lineages includes the BaRolong and their offshoot, the BaTlaping. Last, linked by language and custom but not necessarily through any of the major lineages, the Lovedu and Phalaborwa of the Lowveld and the Birwa of the northern Transvaal round out the remaining BaSotho groups.[60]

Different in language, history, and custom from the Nguni speakers of the southeast and coastal regions, the SeSotho- and SeTswana-speaking peoples built their hut foundations of stone. They herded cattle, goats, and a few sheep and cultivated sorghum, beans, pumpkins, melons, and gourds. They also hunted game for meat. The valuable long-horned BaSotho cattle and pack oxen provided milk and transport and were used as items of trade. Surplus grain was also a valuable trade commodity; by the 1830s the BaSotho had begun to cultivate maize, which they used to establish trade relations with the Europeans.[61] The BaSotho built their large, sprawling settlements on hilltops of the Highveld and tilled their fields in the areas below. Several European travelers and early missionaries reported estimates of sixteen thousand (BaHurutshe) to twenty thousand (BaTaung) people living together under a single independent chief during the first quarter of the nineteenth century.[62]

In a largely bifurcated system of labor, BaSotho men performed the traditional tasks of hunting and herding They were also well known for their skill as metalworkers, producing valuable copper, iron, and tin trade and domestic goods. Among the BaRolong, in fact, oral tradition teaches that the founding lineage developed the art of forging, from which their name is derived. Their ancestral totem (the iron and hammer—*tsepe* and *noto*) has been celebrated in ritual dance performed as history and pageant.[63] Ba-Sotho men were also skilled in leather work, wood and ivory carving, and fashioning fur pelts and ostrich feathers for ceremonial use. In addition, men cut and hauled wood for building purposes, cleared new fields, and sometimes assisted in fieldwork.[64]

For their part, BaSotho-BaTswana women performed the primary economic activities linked to the maintenance of the household.[65] Indeed, the household constituted an efficient economic unit of production: a husband, a wife, and their children residing in one household, for which the woman was largely responsible. (In this polygynous society, a man could head several smaller households of women and children.)[66] In addition to carrying on the family lineage, women were the primary producers of agricultural goods for consumption and exchange. In groups that resembled the Alabama trash gangs, married women and their unmarried daughters worked their families' grain fields. Women hoed, planted, weeded, shooed away birds, harvested, and threshed. Periodically, sometimes in mixed-group work gangs, men and children assisted in planting (men cleared new fields), weeding, harvesting, and (in later decades) even threshing.[67] In addition to serving as cultivators, women collected the grasses that they used to thatch their roofs and built and repaired the mud walls of their homes and the walls and floors of their granaries and courtyards. Women also gathered and prepared wild vegetables and other foods, brewed beer, collected wood and dung for fuel, and hauled potable water for their families. Women and men wove baskets, and women potters made earthen jars large enough to hold ten to twelve bushels of grain.[68] Women sometimes tended the sheep, goats, and donkeys; they also cared for the pigs (known in Lesotho as "the cattle of women") and the chickens.[69]

Although early nineteenth-century BaTswana women performed essential social and economic work roles, they also experienced—sometimes severe—gender subordination. They were, however, far from their characterization by some as mere "beasts of burden."[70] Not all women shared the same degree of subordination and lack of power. "Within [southern African] kin-based systems, the status of women and girls was situational, determined by their lineage position, not by inherent gender categories."[71]

Sisters and daughters of male heads of households within various patri-lineal societies generally commanded greater respect from wives outside that category. Problematizing the notion of complete female subordination to an all-male rulership was the fact that as a married woman grew older, her status (and thus the respect she commanded within the society) gener-ally increased.[72] Among the AmaMpondo (an Nguni-speaking group lo-cated south of the BaSotho at the Eastern Cape), whose division of labor greatly resembled that of the BaSotho-BaTswana, a wife—as the principal grain producer—was afforded significant "bargaining power" and was "wel-comed as an economic asset by any group with which she elected to live."[73] AmaMpondo women were not the, "beasts of burden" Margaret Kinsman understood; rather, they were "economically self-supporting, and their sta-tus was in no way servile."[74]

Nineteenth-century BaSotho women of Lesotho were the "primary agents of accumulation and growth" in the Lesotho economy because this growth was in not only the men's interests but their own. Women labored to increase the prosperity of their households and thus of their society. Al-though their labor came under the indirect control of their chief, women householders had the ability to make certain economic decisions. When the care of pigs was introduced in BaSotho society, women gladly took up their supervision to enhance the household food stores. Displaying fore-thought and initiative, in the severe famine of the 1820s, BaSotho women worked effectively to increase surplus food and grain for their own and their children's consumption and cooperated with other women in the harvest of their grain in order to increase their own food supplies. They also produced surplus craft goods to trade for food and other household items.[75] Actively participating in reducing their economic dependence, BaSotho women made conscious beneficial choices. They developed a strong sense of their own capabilities as women as they purposefully deployed the female collec-tive. In the process of working collectively—like the enslaved women in the U.S. Black Belt in the 1820s—the elder women inculcated their daughters with an understanding of women's autonomy, which was to benefit them and their people.

A wonderful example of the autonomy of southern African women that strongly contradicts the "beasts of burden" analogy comes from anthro-pologist Monica Hunter, who performed her research living among the AmaMpondo in the 1930s. The story takes place one hundred years after the era of Kinsman's findings and among a different group of people, but it is nevertheless instructive of the important influence of some wives over their husbands. While living at Ntibane, Hunter knew of a man who had wrongly accused and then beaten his wife for her alleged infidelity:

A husband came home drunk one night, stormed at his wife for having left the beer-drink without him, accused her of having gone home with another man, and finally tied her up to the hut-pole and thrashed her. She ran away to her own people the next morning. Neighbors knew that the accusation was unjustified, and that she had come straight from the beer-drink alone to prepare food for her children. The only other woman on the *umzi* [kinship group and its dwellings] was an old crone beyond work. The husband found himself in difficulties for water, firewood, and food, and begged assistance from neighbors. The women refused. "And now," they said to me with satisfaction, "he is living alone, just like a wild animal, cooking for himself." [76]

Not only did the wronged wife abandon her abusive husband and seek recourse from her own family; the women of the husband's community also refused to participate in any further persecution of the wife. Clearly, the subordinate position of women in this society had its limits; in the face of such injustice, the women exerted their own power of choice. Apparently, a sense of the female collective, or female solidarity, took precedence over the well-being of the man, who was humiliated, mocked, and made to fend for himself, "just like a wild animal."

With respect to the alleged unmediated subordination of BaSotho-BaTswana women, it is important to bear in mind—within a context of political and economic power, especially during the period before white rule—the complete subordination of all the members of the society to the overarching (though not unquestioned) authority of the chief. In BaSotho-BaTswana societies, the *kgosi* (chief) is the hereditary head of the government until his death, and he is succeeded by the eldest son of his great (first or most important) wife. During much of the nineteenth century, his duties extended over a wide range of activities within the polity or larger society, where—aided by his advisers—the chief held final responsibility for matters of public policy and law, social and economic activity, and appropriate responses to natural and human-made disasters. The person and position of chief was highly respected by the people and by those from whom tribute was paid in labor and goods. The chief's virtues and most important deeds were widely extolled in praise-poems, and he was addressed ceremonially at all times. [77]

An exception to the designation of the eldest male of the royal house as chief or king is found among the Lovedu of the northeastern Transvaal Lowveld, who at least since the mid-nineteenth century have recognized the rulership of "women in their own right." According to the anthropologist Eileen Krige, the hereditary Lovedu queen Modjadji has enjoyed renown as a rainmaker and is sometimes consulted by other chiefs when royal succession is in dispute. The queen may take for her own household any number of "wives just as though they were men,"[78] and may be assisted and advised by other women who serve as district heads. Notable also is the position of the *rakhadi*, or paternal aunt, who is among the advisers to the ruling king or queen and who can serve as regent for her nephew until he comes of age or is ousted (sometimes by her own son). Like her male counterparts, Modjadji is expected to conclude her reign after the passage of four circumcision schools (roughly forty years) by committing ritual suicide. Although in most other indigenous South African societies women may have remained literally and symbolically outside the chief's *kgotla* (court, court of law, or council chamber), among the Lovedu a woman has held the ultimate power.

European Incursions in a Time of Troubles

With the nineteenth century came a rapid increase in white impingement on African political and economic independence. As European missionaries sought to control African minds and souls, other white settlers moved east from the Western Cape to claim control over African lands from the Atlantic to the Indian Oceans. Although written documentation of women power brokers during this age of continuous African resistance to white conquest is scarce, the examples that follow illustrate that African women did not stand by in silence.

Early in 1813 the Missionary Society of London sent the Reverend John Campbell to inspect the physical and spiritual condition of its recently organized missions in South Africa.[79] Campbell's observations, recorded in his diary, provide a firsthand account of life among the BaSotho-BaTswana peoples, including an understanding of their early relationships with other European and African groups. He traveled by wagon into BaTswana territories with his party of missionaries and interpreters—among them Adam Kok, leader of the Griqua (a people of mixed European and Khoisan ancestry from the Eastern Cape). Campbell was anxious to make new converts on behalf of the society upon reaching the BaTlhaping capital, Dithakong, but he had to wait more than a week for the BaTlhaping chief to return from a hunting trip so that he could request permission to begin his work.

Finally, summoned before Mothibi one evening, Campbell made his pitch. Mothibi had no intention of allowing the missionaries to live among and convert his people; he did, however, express an interest in having some of the children "learn the Dutch language." Seizing this opening, Campbell showed Mothibi how "things could be written in his language." Campbell noted, "We read to him the names of his predecessors and all his family. For the first time he smiled, on hearing their names read over, and seemed full of astonishment and pleasure." After Campbell assured the chief that he would not interfere in matters of government, Mothibi told Campbell, "SEND INSTRUCTORS, AND I WILL BE A FATHER TO THEM."[80]

Turning the colonial mission on its head, Mothibi shrewdly referred to himself as father. Western missionaries who engaged in just such paternalistic discourse proliferated throughout the BaSotho-BaTswana territories and all of South Africa during the next 150 years.[81] In this instance, Mothibi's authority could be negotiated to suit the purposes of the Europeans as long as their purposes also suited his own interests. Wisely assessing the political climate, Mothibi wanted some of his children to learn Dutch, the language of the first colonizers. Sisters and wives sometimes advised the chief on matters of importance, and in this case the woman Campbell calls "Mahootoo," Mothibi's younger and clearly favored "great wife," had intimated to Campbell that she would use her influence on his behalf.[82] Granting the missionaries their toehold seemed to hinge, however, on the chief's pride in both the BaTlhaping ruling lineage and his place in it. Campbell astutely convinced Mothibi that he, his children, and generations to come could read in SeTswana the names of Mothibi's earliest ruling ancestors. By allowing such instruction, Mothibi and Mahootoo had helped set into motion significant processes—Christianization, "civilization," migration, and proletarianization—that they and other African people could not foresee.

Disruption and change on the early nineteenth-century Highveld did not stem only from the many incursions made by the West in pursuit of world markets and world minions for Christ. Indeed, before the "white man's burden" could be shouldered on a larger scale, the widespread disruption caused by the formation of the AmaZulu state and the Shakan revolution spurred massive dislocation and depopulation among the Nguni-, SeSotho-, and SeTswana-speaking peoples of central-southern Africa.

Shaka's social and military revolution, characterized by his consolidation of numerous peoples into the AmaZulu kingdom, precipitated a radical transformation of African and European peoples and governing systems. As a consequence of the *Difaqane*, as the dispersion or forced migration is known in SeSotho, a new social and political order obtained on the High-veld. A new generation, including at least one woman, quickly recognized the value of leveraging its power against the outside African and European forces. By playing one against the other, they hoped to maintain and per-haps increase the lands so vital to their survival.[83]

During the 1820s and 1830s in the "time of troubles," the *Difaqane* gen-erated unprecedented competition among the SeSotho-, SeTswana- and Nguni-speaking peoples for diminishing grain, cattle, and other food sup-plies. Many old settlements disappeared, some abandoned after attack by displaced groups of AmaZulu, such as Mzilikazi's AmaNdebele, on the run from Shaka to the Transvaal Highveld.[84] Some of the older and stronger BaTswana societies, such as the BaPedi and BaVenda, managed to hold onto their lands and their people with mixed success. Others, such as the AmaHlubi (Nguni speakers), succumbed to annihilation at the hands of more powerful opponents. In response to the eradication of many peoples and the departure of the more powerful AmaNdebele, two BaSotho groups managed to consolidate their independent power and embark on a process of regeneration (one more successfully than the other).

One BaSotho polity, the BaTlokwa, was led by the queen regent 'Man-thatisi, described as "a mighty woman [sitting] at the head of an invinci-ble army, numerous as the locusts, marching onward among the interior nations."[85] In BaSotho tradition, she is acknowledged as an exceptional figure. Beginning her regency in 1813, well before the colonial period, 'Man-thatisi governed as an "honorary man." According to an early researcher of BaSotho traditions, she headed the chief's *kgotla*, "discuss[ing] politics . . . [and] the policy of the [BaTlokwa] during her regency was made by her alone."[86] Thomas Arbousset, a French missionary who visited the area be-tween the upper Caledon River and the Vaal, found 'Manthatisi to be "a woman of great intelligence" who possessed "a sweet and agreeable expres-sion" heightened by "a regular countenance and an elegant figure."[87] 'Man-thatisi's resourceful leadership enabled the BaTlokwa to survive the ravages of the *Difaqane*. The queen regent absorbed survivors of disintegrating Ba-Sotho and Nguni-speaking communities, extended her territorial range, and maintained her central stronghold atop the mountains on the north side of the Caledon.[88] Her reign lasted only until about the mid-1820s, however, at which time 'Manthatisi yielded to the decisions of Sekonyela, her son and successor, who apparently lacked his mother's insight and generosity.[89]

Easily the most gifted leader of the southern BaSotho, one who thoroughly understood the necessity of practicing a new, more pragmatic, collective brand of state politics, was Moshoeshoe. For Mrs. Maggie Resha, a direct descendant of the revered chief, Moshoeshoe represented the independence for which all Black South Africans had to fight in the 1950s. His successful reign provided Mrs. Resha with a strong sense of her heritage, her birthright, and her people's long history of struggle.[90]

The son of a minor headman of the Monaheng branch of the Ba-Kwena, Moshoeshoe pulled his people together during the waning days of Shaka's reign and managed to increase his fortunes over those of Sekonyela. Moshoeshoe took other Nguni and SeSotho speakers under his protection and located his capital atop the seemingly impregnable Thaba Bosiu in the Little Caledon Valley. He made alliances with other more distant BaSotho and BaTswana chiefs and by the early 1830s had consolidated this collection of diverse peoples and language groups into a single state that would become known as Lesotho. Transcending ethnic barriers and forging unity in the face of European divisiveness—well before the African National Congress (ANC) policy of nontribalism—Moshoeshoe formed a unified political state. As Moshoeshoe acted out a beneficial nationalist impulse, amassing lands and cattle in pursuit of security, his people became known as the BaSotho.[91]

Moshoeshoe preferred conciliation; however, when it was necessary, he ably fought to defend his position. In the 1830s he had learned at the hands of the armed and mounted Kora and Bergenaars (an offshoot of the Griqua) that in order to maintain his sovereignty he would need guns and horses. The BaSotho benefited greatly from this insight during the wars against the Boers in the 1850s and 1860s. The British, who had replaced their earlier desire to bring Moshoeshoe under their control with a hands-off policy in the chaotic Transorangia region, posed a lesser threat.[92] Moshoeshoe managed to stave off the Boers until 1868 by cultivating a relationship with the British that he used as leverage. He steadily increased his supply of guns and horses, buying from any available source, including sympathetic missionaries.

Defeat finally came at the hands of the Boers, however, when they pursued a scorched-earth policy against Moshoeshoe. In the final hour,

Moshoeshoe's earlier appeals to the British for help were answered by their 1868 annexation of "Basutoland" as a British Crown colony. A strong argument for annexation, an act of political self-interest, lay in preventing the Boers from appeasing their appetite for land at the expense of the British Crown. The Boers' ability to drive a land wedge between the Cape and Natal would, after all, be greatly increased if Moshoeshoe were brought to his knees. Under Philip Wodehouse, the new high commissioner, therefore, the British transferred the BaSotho to their own jurisdiction.[93]

Moshoeshoe died in March 1870, at the age of eighty-four, just as the British and Boer officials were haggling over the boundary between the Orange Free State and British Basutoland. Although he had lost significant land north of the Caledon, Moshoeshoe's people had gained protection from becoming dispossessed subjects in their own homes. More skillfully than any other in the central Highveld, Moshoeshoe had encountered the West in a manner that honored his past and the traditions of his ancestors as he pragmatically, intelligently, and honorably faced an uncertain future. At the height of his reign, he had created a powerful state out of chaos, put Western missionaries and technologies to his own use, and protected his people from exploitation by Boer farmers. Along the way, he had commanded enormous respect from his community and from Europeans who sought his favor or his recognition of their authority. As one French missionary observed, "The chief bent upon me a look at once majestic and benevolent[;] his eyes, a little weary it seemed, but full of intelligence and softness, made a deep impression on me. I felt at once that I had to do with a superior man, trained to think, to command others, and above all himself."[94]

"A superior man," as Moshoeshoe surely was, taught many that resistance to white settlement was not necessarily futile. By all accounts, however, Moshoeshoe was still a man of great status and power in a world dominated by men. Demonstrating the full extent of that power, he allegedly beat to death his "great wife,"'MaMohato, for being unfaithful to him with one of his close advisers.[95] Women, including those who were deemed "honorary men," who outrightly rejected the traditions or rules governing their lives were to be discredited and severely punished. Although some African women found important ways to exert their own agency— 'Manthatisi's compassionate governing, Mahootoo's use of her discretion, BaSotho women's economic decisions—those actions were taken in ways that did not detract from the prerogatives of men. There is no question that in the precolonial and colonial eras African women were invaluable to their families and societies and that at the same time they faced subjugation.

By 1868 Moshoeshoe's people—like the Black Republicans and Union Leaguers of Alabama toward the end of Reconstruction—came to understand that overt forms of political resistance, although valiant, did not always yield clear victories. Effectively disenfranchised by 1877, Black citizens of Alabama had to find their own means of mounting a campaign of resistance against white supremacy; they pursued education, built institutions, and stubbornly worked to pay off their sharecropping debts. Ultimately, in the hope of retaining their territorial integrity, Moshoeshoe's people had to supplant the struggle to eliminate the disruptive presence of the Boers with the risk of an uneven alliance with the British. As the political economies of these regions continued to develop, however, making increasingly harsh demands on Black men and women for their labor and tribute, African Americans and Black South Africans made important adjustments to their political circumstances. In both locations, during the time of industrialization and racial segregation, the resourcefulness of Black women was often the key to these adjustments and to the persistence of their communities in the pursuit of a better life.

Chapter Two

NO WASH OR PASS

Institution Building, Migration, and Protest, 1867–1918

Mrs. Thelma Glass, a tall and striking woman in her mid-eighties, retired many years ago from her position as a professor of political and cultural geography at the historically Black Alabama State University in Montgomery. "I think world events made [teaching] so interesting," she observed. "Things that were going on all over the world . . . and why people from certain areas had ideas [interested me]. One of the most exciting things was [that] Africa came into prominence in my last three or four years. . . . Ghana was the first [in 1957] and then Nigeria [in 1960]." During the mid-1950s, Mrs. Glass experienced the rumblings of a different sort of Black independence, when Mrs. Rosa Parks refused to relinquish her bus seat to a white person and the rest of Black Montgomery followed suit. Continuing to teach her geography classes full time and to serve as a member of the Women's Political Council, Mrs. Glass was also eager to participate in the 1955–1956 bus boycott movement. She attended meetings regularly, testified on behalf of Martin Luther King, Jr., at his boycott conspiracy trial in March 1956, and refused to be intimidated when the King home and several Black churches that actively sponsored the boycott were bombed. "I wasn't afraid to do anything!" Mrs. Glass reported. "The bombings . . . just made me more determined to keep working."[1]

Across the Atlantic, in the last region of the African continent to realize Black independence, Joyce Piliso Seroke contemplated the meaning of the new South African democracy: "I was one of those who said [freedom] won't happen in my lifetime—that's how stringent the repressive laws were."[2] Like Mrs. Glass, who earned her teaching degree from the all-Black Alabama State College, when Mrs. Seroke graduated from the South African Native College at Fort Hare in 1956, she was prepared to teach. As one of only a handful of women students at Fort Hare, however, she had attained more than pedagogical training. At the predominantly male school, she had come into political consciousness—a hard-fought process that required that she learn how to speak for herself. During the 1952 Campaign for the Defiance of Unjust Laws, as an eager first-year student, Mrs. Seroke attended the contentious Fort Hare branch meetings of the African National Congress (ANC) Youth League. As new members, she and other young women had to find ways to defend their right to speak and overcome men's attempts to silence them:

> At the very serious student meetings men would shout and say freshers were supposed to be seen and not heard. And if you wanted to make your point, they would howl and say, "Sit down, woman! Sit down!" Our group would say the only time these men [will] take us seriously is if we also talk sense and they [will] see that we're not just standing there only to be seen. Our talk must be about issues and be informed. And when we raised our hands, we must be brave and not be intimidated, and then we had to develop a slogan: "Chairperson, will you protect me? I want to make my point, your protection." And the girls would chime [in], "Protection! Protection!" And finally the men would stop, and we would start talking.[3]

Mrs. Seroke followed her mother into the teaching profession, joining the faculty of the school that Charlotte Manye Maxeke and her husband, the Reverend Marshall Maxeke, helped found only a short distance from Johannesburg: Wilberforce Institute in Evaton.[4] In 1959, after three years of teaching, Mrs. Seroke made the difficult decision to leave Wilberforce. After the imposition of the 1953 Bantu Education Act, which gave the Afrikaner government full control of African education, she feared that the top-notch instruction that she and other teachers were providing for their students would become compromised. Eventually, she became a trained social worker in Soweto, and—operating under the auspices of the Young Women's Christian Association (YWCA)—she took up community organizing in Soweto, helping to provide women with material necessities while she raised their consciousness about women's political and economic disabilities. Her university days had provided the political foundation she needed to become an effective teacher and organizer who understood that her fight was about more than national liberation.

Joyce Seroke and Thelma Glass, both teachers educated at well-known

Black institutions, believed that their education and training had equipped them to share their knowledge with their communities by helping to develop the minds and widen the experiences of a new generation of Black youths. This effort, however, constituted only part of their contribution to the greater struggle for freedom, for they were not content to sit and watch as others participated. As Alabama State and Fort Hare helped nourish members of the movement leadership, Thelma Glass and Joyce Seroke counted themselves among the many women who became determined to participate in the struggle on an equal footing with men. Their brand of activism included community organizing, institution building, and direct action. Fostered and sustained by the examples of their parents, these "mothers of the[ir] nation[s]"[5] gave a new voice and a maternalist, if not a protofeminist, meaning to the generations-old liberation impulse.

The lives of these women also reveal the central role that Black institutions—particularly churches, schools, and women's networks—played in Black human rights struggles. In this chapter I examine the prolonged efforts at institution building in Black Montgomery and the early examples of collective action in South Africa and Alabama that challenged racial hierarchies and Black marginalization. Black institutions that were critical to the success of the 1955–1956 Montgomery bus boycott included Alabama State College, First Baptist Chruch, and Dexter Avenue Baptist Church. Linked thematically to the mid-twentieth-century boycott is the Montgomery boycott that took place in 1900, which was replicated during that period in many parts of the urban South. Similarly, in South Africa, Black women's pass resistances of the 1950s were preceded by a successful campaign against passes for women that took place in the city of Bloemfontein in the Orange Free State (OFS) in 1913. The 1913 campaign helped to spawn the formation of the Bantu Women's League, the forerunner to the ANC Women's League, which Joyce Seroke joined in the 1950s.

The political awakenings among Black communities in Alabama and South Africa in the late nineteenth and early twentieth centuries took place within a global context of capital accumulation and economic expansion. Black workers, whose labor could be deployed to the mines and to urban households of the rapidly industrializing U.S. South and South Africa, were key components in the successful growth of new sources of white wealth. The twin factors of worker migration and the development of the pass system emerged initially in Kimberley and Johannesburg—the primary sites of early industrialization in South Africa—just as formerly independent African peoples lost their lands and acquired exploitive colonial taxes. The increase in the African population on the Rand and the creation of Alexandra and Sophiatown as future sites of bus boycotts and pass resistances establish both location and political precedence.

Similarly, the permanence of Black Montgomery rested on the ability of its inhabitants to find employment and establish local churches and schools. Schools for Black children and adults were initially housed in churches; in fact, the first classes of the Alabama State Normal School were held in a place of worship that participated in the 1955–1956 bus boycott: Beulah Baptist Church. Recreational activities, economic ventures, missionary societies, and Bible study classes made use of church facilities. Occupying the political, economic, social, and ideological center of many a Black community—and certainly that of Montgomery—the church added meaning to every facet of Black life. It is no accident that in the South, where conventional political life was so constrained for Black people, the Black church acted as the independent, institutional arm of the 1950s freedom movement.[6] As migration to the state capital offered new possibilities for Black Alabamians who sought a clear break from an often bleak past, the establishment of permanent church "homes" proliferated throughout the greater Black community, focusing collective efforts on group solidarity and material well-being. The story of the successful formation of Alabama State, although fraught with politics and compromise, is one in which the Black community of Montgomery exercised its collective will.

In 1881 and 1913, respectively, the Atlanta washerwomen and the Bloemfontein middle- and working-class women protested their nominal positions within the political economy. As in Atlanta, the political practice of the OFS women offers an early lesson in organizing that both women and men called on repeatedly. For Black women, such protests grew out of their respective histories, but the protests must have surprised those who believed that the only recourse for any women—not just lower-class or working-class women—was to trust their fortune to the largesse of others much more favorably positioned.

Black Montgomery in the Making

Emancipation signaled the beginnings of significant Black migration to urban areas in the South. In Black Belt Alabama between 1870 and 1880, the Black populations of Selma and Montgomery saw substantial increases.

Montgomery grew particularly rapidly during this period, nearly doubling its 1870 population a decade later, with a Black population of almost ten thousand.[7] More opportunities to attend school and worship, a greater sense of security from white violence, opportunities for better-paying work, and a wider variety of social outlets drew Black people to the cities.[8] While the potential of independent land ownership in rural areas remained important, the urban centers offered Black southerners a better market for trade and enterprise, attracting artisans, entrepreneurs, women domestic workers, laundresses, and traders.

The growth of Black Montgomery during and immediately following Reconstruction centered on the development of separate Black churches and schools, the diversification of paid work opportunities, and access to political participation. Montgomery is situated on the Alabama River approximately in the middle of the Black Belt, two geographical features that originally dominated its interests and encouraged its growth. When it became the state capital in the mid-1840s, the state business and political leaders and the men and women who served them began to meet to talk politics and business in the capitol and in the parlors, taverns, and brothels of the bustling riverfront town. Part of the welcoming allure of Montgomery to its Black inhabitants may have been that the headquarters of the Alabama Freedmen's Bureau was located there during Reconstruction. Certainly, the expansion of the city limits to include the outlying Black wards and precincts encouraged increased Black political participation in city and state government.[9] During Reconstruction, for instance, the Black citizens of Montgomery formed Union Leagues, which helped to politicize the Black community further. As a result of their collective efforts, in 1868 twelve Black policemen (half of the city force) were elected by a city council that included two Black men.[10]

In 1867 the seven-hundred-member Black congregation later known as the First Baptist Church separated from its white parent body and became the first independent Black Baptist church in Montgomery. After purchasing land on Columbus Street and erecting its wood-frame building, the church grew to be one of the largest in the South before the northward migration of Black southerners.[11] Thirty-one women's names were among the forty-five listed as prominent and hard-working members who "enter[ed] into covenant as one body in Christ."[12] In 1880 the well-respected church played host to the organizational forerunner of the national group of Black independent Baptists: the National Baptist Convention, USA.[13] When the women organized their national Woman's Convention Auxiliary to the National Baptist Convention in 1900, Susie C. Foster of Montgomery was elected the treasurer of the executive board alongside the corresponding secretary, Nannie Helen Burroughs.[14] Susie Foster was the daughter of the Reverend James A. Foster, the second pastor of First Baptist Church. An active member of her church, she taught Sunday school classes and organized "cantatas and suppers" in order to raise money for the church and the normal school.[15] Miss Foster also taught at the Alabama State Normal School and, like many Black women, typically combined several community and church activities in an effort to solidify two important Black institutions.[16]

In 1877, ten years after the establishment of the First Baptist Church, a disgruntled group of First Baptist members, perhaps at odds over issues of class, split from the main body to found their own church. They constructed their permanent house of worship on the corner of Decatur Street and Dexter Avenue.[17] In the shadow of the Confederate flag atop the capitol building, the Dexter Avenue Baptist Church became a small but prosperous "deacon's church." There the lay officers insisted on a high standard of training for their ministers and a healthy degree of sovereignty for themselves and for the membership.[18] Eventually, First Baptist and Dexter Avenue Baptist overcame their differences and worked together on spiritual and political matters that affected the greater Black community of Montgomery. Indeed, their future cooperation in the leadership of the 1955–1956 Montgomery bus boycott helped solidify the community and ensure the success of the boycott.

If, during the brief window of racial justice represented by Reconstruction, Black residents of Montgomery were seized with the spiritual fervor of church building, they were no less enthusiastic about the establishment of a school that offered education beyond the tenth grade. In the heart of the Alabama Black Belt in 1873, the state legislature chartered the Alabama State Normal School and University at Marion, a "school for colored students and teachers."[19] Earlier, in 1866 and 1867, the Freedmen's Bureau and the American Missionary Association had assisted the Black citizens of Marion in their quest to build an independent school for their young people. The Black residents of Marion had organized a nine-member board of trustees and had raised five hundred dollars for the land and the school building in return for the staffing of the school by the two organizations.[20] In 1871 the state joined the project, providing a small amount of funding and appointing a new majority-white board of commissioners and a new principal, who oversaw instruction in normal education. William Burns Paterson, a native of Tullibody, Scotland, who became president in 1878, led the school through its most difficult transition and relocation to Montgomery in 1887. In a letter to Principal Booker T. Washington of Tuskegee Institute, Paterson explained why his school had to leave Marion: The white cadets of Howard College, who resented having the Black students in their midst, had been assaulting Black students who did not step off the sidewalks in order to allow the cadets to pass. Thereafter, the Howard College trustees had made clear their intention to have the Marion school removed.[21]

As in Marion, influential white citizens in Montgomery opposed the relocation of the school to their city. Moreover, reluctant to see another Black normal school located "so near his doors," Booker T. Washington quietly used his influence to have the school move to Birmingham.[22] Vigorously advocating relocation to their city, however, the leading Black men of Montgomery helped galvanize support among all Montgomery citizens. Jesse Duke, the editor of the Montgomery *Herald* and an outspoken Black leader, used his influential platform to write in support of the school. Henry A. Loveless and his brother Anderson, successful Black businessmen, helped raise money for the school. Local established clergy—including the Reverend A. M. McEwen of Dexter, the pastors of Old Ship African Methodist Episcopal Zion Church and Beulah Baptist Church, and James A. Foster of First Baptist Church—also lent their support to the relocation. Foreshadowing the mass meetings of the 1950s bus boycott, the Black citizens of Montgomery met en masse in their churches, beginning at Old Ship, as a way to generate enthusiasm and raise money for the new school.

By the middle of August 1887, the Black citizens of Montgomery had made good on their pledge to raise the funds to purchase land and to lease and erect more buildings. The Alabama State Normal School was to be located in a growing Black neighborhood called Centennial Hill, near the Congregational Church and the Swayne School for Black elementary students.[23] On October 3, 1887, the Alabama State Normal School opened in facilities that were on loan from Beulah Baptist Church: two former storefronts and a few private homes in the neighborhood. Many of the white citizens of Montgomery engaged in a last-ditch effort to prevent the operation of the school. They secured an injunction against the institution on the ground that the legislature had misappropriated public funds by providing assistance to a Black school that was not overseen by the state superintendent of education. Their plan backfired. On February 23, 1889, the Alabama legislature placed the State Normal School at Montgomery under the supervision of the board of commissioners and authorized the school to offer only elementary, secondary, and normal education courses.[24] Forty years later, Alabama State Normal was trading graduates with Tuskegee Institute to fill faculty positions and had earned notoriety as the "largest school for Negro teachers" in the United States.[25]

The state had at last appropriated enough money to keep the school doors open, but it had deprived Black people of the opportunity to benefit from a full college curriculum. By the 1880s the prevailing political winds had changed. Gone were the heady days of Radical Reconstruction, when the Black vote could ensure city police appointments and representation in Congress. As Booker T. Washington later urged, Black people in the South had to accommodate themselves to the tenor of the New South ideology, seeking less political participation among the Republicans and more of the economic stability that the Redeemer Democrats could support. To build this stability, Black people were urged to remain in the South as laborers and farmers "tilling field[s]" and supporting an old agricultural regime—dependent once again on the availability of their cheap labor—disguised as new.[26] In addition, Black people were to seek a particular kind of vocational or industrial education, much like the curriculum that Washington offered at Tuskegee Institute.[27] In a bow to white supremacy and a Jim Crow system that predominated across the country, and most notably in the South, educational choices for Black people had become narrowly defined by the 1890s. If the Black citizens of Montgomery expected their new state college to provide a liberal education on par with that of the state university for white students near Tuscaloosa, they would be greatly disappointed. A state-supported liberal arts college or university curriculum for Black students in Montgomery would have to await a new day.[28] In the face of the limitations imposed during the racially oppressive eras of Redemption and Jim Crow, the Black people of Montgomery had succeeded in building three important institutions—First Baptist Church, Dexter Avenue Baptist Church, and Alabama State Normal School—all of which would come to figure prominently in the 1955 boycott.

The economy of the New South, which was built on industry and agriculture combined, offered new opportunities for Black citizens of Montgomery who were in a position to take advantage of them to develop a middle-class community. Still, the majority of African Americans in Montgomery were situated precariously between survival and subsistence. Many Black men found work as unskilled day laborers: digging wells, constructing sewers, and working on streets, in railroad yards, and on the docks.[29] Of course, these jobs often involved unhealthful, unsafe, unsteady, low-paying work. For the better-paying jobs in such skilled or semi-skilled employment as machine operation, plumbing, carpentry, and printing, Black men faced stiff competition from white workers. Most white workers refused to train Black men, choosing to relegate them to traditional "Negro jobs" in manual labor and personal or domestic service.[30] Some enterprising Black women and men found other means of making ends meet. They hawked almost anything they could raise, find, or collect, from rags to flowers to sweet "watermillions."[31] But these supplementary forms of income did not provide a living wage. In comparable southern cities such as Atlanta—the capital of Georgia and the gateway to the New South—Black wage earners seldom earned as much as thirty dollars per month. In fact, in 1877 an Atlanta newspaper reported, "Smart colored washerwomen make $15 a month in this city."[32]

In the days before automatic washing machines, electric irons, and spray starch—in Atlanta, Montgomery, or in any other location—a washerwoman's work was long, arduous, multiply tasked, and exhausting. Those who had the means gladly hired others to pick up the dirty, heavy bundles on Mondays; wash, dry, iron, and fold; and return the items in clean, fresh, neat piles on Sundays. During the summer of 1881, however, Atlanta's "washing Amazons" united to declare that they would not do the washing without fair compensation.[33]

As Atlanta readied itself for the first-ever Cotton Exposition scheduled to take place in early October 1881, twenty Black women and a few men organized in early July the Washing Society, a trade union for independent laundry workers fashioned on the model of a secret society. On July 19, the Society called the washerwomen to strike for higher wages after publicizing their new organization through the city's churches and recruiting members door-to-door. Dubbed the "washing Amazons" by their critics, the women set their goal at the reasonable rate of $1 per dozen pounds of wash. The women's canvassing and publicity efforts were successful; in three weeks their numbers had grown from the initial 20-odd members to a reported 3,000, a great many of whom were middle-aged married women with children and households to help support. But confrontations between women supporters and those as yet unaffiliated with the union gave the city and the police an excuse to direct state power against the strikers. It was hoped that what arrests and fines could not quell, a new City Council license fee or tax on each of the Society members would accomplish.

Meeting at the Wheat Street Church, the washerwomen hammered out their response to the proposed licensing fee in a letter to Mayor Jim English. Turning around the threat of extinction via taxation, the women made it clear that they would pay the licensing fee, whether it was twenty-five or fifty dollars, in order to *"control the washing for this city."*[34] Moreover, the women kept as a priority the protection and extension of their community interests, astutely correlating the situation between them and the city with the situation between their draymen husbands and the city. The women insisted that they could "afford to pay these licenses" and added, "[We] will do it before we will be defeated . . . and then we will have full control of the city's washing at our own prices, as the city has control of our husbands' work at their prices. . . . Don't forget this. . . . *We mean business this week or no washing."*[35]

The washerwomen were keenly aware that although their labor might come cheap to the white women householders and boardinghouse owners of Atlanta, they could seize this important political moment to declare that labor under their own exclusive control. Refusing to be cowed by the machinations of the city fathers, the women of the Washing Society sought nothing less than a monopoly of their industry. Quietly, on August 15, the City Council rejected the proposed licensing fee. Meanwhile, during the period of the washerwomen's strike, hotel waiters demanded and received higher wages, and in September, just prior to the opening of the exposition, cooks, maids, and nannies in the city also demanded fair pay.[36] So close to the doors of Montgomery, a political consciousness had emerged with force among the Black working-class women of Atlanta, a consciousness that could not have been alien to their sisters in the growing capital of Alabama.

The washerwomen's strike in Atlanta is an important example of (ostensibly powerless) working-class Black women who defended their interests and maneuvered their way through a system created to keep them completely subservient. Black Atlanta women served as successful models of good organization and timing for others as well. Taking advantage of the indispensability of their own cheap labor to urban life, they used the power of their collective voice to gain both political and (especially) economic leverage. In other cities across the industrializing South—such as Jackson,

Mississippi, in 1866, and Galveston, Texas, in 1877—washerwomen were similarly moved to take action on their own behalf.[37] Black working-class women in the South thus established important precedents in building a collective political consciousness.

A Boycott of the Streetcars

At the very beginning of the twentieth century in Montgomery, during the entrenchment of the New South's Jim Crow policies, an important portent of the future modern civil rights era took place. The signal event—the boycott of Montgomery's streetcars—began during the summer of 1900 and lasted for as long as two years.[38] Black residents of Montgomery, Atlanta, New Orleans, Mobile, Jacksonville, Houston, Little Rock, Richmond, Memphis, and many other Southern cities during the century's first decade, took issue with a host of new ordinances that required segregated seating and a more rigorous enforcement. Neither in Montgomery nor in the other cities did Black riders expect the white trolley conductors to treat them with respect while enforcing the new local laws. And to Black women the issue of respect and equal treatment on the public byways was of great concern in the late nineteenth and early twentieth centuries just as it was in 1955–56. In fact, Southern Black women with their national regional counterparts discussed the issue of segregated seating on public conveyances at several of the biannual conventions of the National Association of Colored Women's Clubs (NACW). Several local Alabama clubs sent delegates to these meetings representing a sizeable contingent of women—three Montgomery clubs (the Sojourner Truth Club, the Woman's League, and the Ten Times One Club),[39] Margaret Murray Washington's Tuskegee Woman's Club, Selma's Woman's Mutual Improvement Club, and clubs from Eufaula, Notasulga, Mt. Meigs, and Greensboro were among them. In successive meetings beginning in 1896 and continuing at least through 1904, the issue of the "Separate Car Law" following on the heels of the Supreme Court's *Plessey* decision in 1896 prompted not only discussion but recommendations for action.[40] At their 1896 inaugural convention in Washington, D.C., NACW delegates all but called for a national boycott of segregated railroads:

> We hereby condemn unreservedly the excursions and picnics of our race which patronize the railroads in the states where the separate car law is in operation,

and pledge ourselves to do everything in our power through the press and pulpit to educate race public sentiment on this point. The recent decision of the U.S. Supreme Court convinces us that we must depend upon ourselves in this matter. *So long as we continue to spend thousands of dollars every year on needless excursions, we enrich the railroads at our own expense.* Cut off this source of revenue because of the "Jim Crow Cars" into which the *wives, mothers, sisters and daughters* of the race are forced to ride and the railroads will fight the separate car law through self-interest.[41]

At its 1904 meeting in St. Louis, the NACW shifted its concern over segregated conveyances to include city streetcars: "Whereas, Some of the Southern cities have introduced separate street cars, Be it Resolved, That this body condemn such action, and that in all such states and towns the clubwomen unite in trying to *induce our people to refrain from patronizing street cars* and running excursions from town to town, thus encouraging the railroads to continue their unjust discrimination."[42]

The Alabama and NACW women knew that Black people had little recourse beyond taking matters into their own hands and boycotting the "Jim Crow Cars." Although the clubwomen laid the blame squarely on the unconstitutional Supreme Court ruling and the national penchant for perpetuating racial prejudice, they were not above chastising Black people who participated in "needless excursions [that] enrich[ed] the railroads" and undermined their rights as free citizens. Effectively deploying a politics of respectability based on their status as "wives, mothers, sisters and daughters," the Black clubwomen of Montgomery, along with their sisters in other metropolitan organizations, enthusiastically supported the boycott movement in the South.

In September 1900 the Atlanta *Constitution* took note of the "surprising persistency" of the Montgomery boycott, reporting that transportation company receipts had "fallen off fully 25%." The article continued, "All efforts heretofore made in Alabama to organize strikes among the negro miners ... have proved unsuccessful and it has been believed that no considerable number of negroes could be organized for any length of time ... [yet] they have almost entirely refrained from riding."[43]

The Montgomery boycott was so effective that by 1902 the trolley company had suspended enforcement of the Jim Crow law and the City Council had amended the ordinance to require that an empty seat be available elsewhere in the car before a Black person could be compelled to vacate his or her seat.[44] The initial success of the boycott proved that Black people in Alabama could be successfully mobilized to support sustained action against white domination. Unfortunately, however, the Jim Crow laws ultimately won out on the Montgomery streetcars and elsewhere.

Until the bus boycott of 1955–1956, Montgomery quietly resumed its segregated seating arrangements. What the city ordinance attempted to accomplish in 1900, common practice succeeded in accomplishing after 1902. Just the same, African Americans in Montgomery had made an important economic point. Instead of using any political voice they commanded at the time, Black streetcar riders had used their feet as economic leverage against the trolley company. Indeed, Alabama Democrats had succeeded in winning a state constitutional convention, which in 1901 effectively removed the franchise from Black and low-income white citizens alike. Raising the slogan "White Supremacy! Honest Elections! and the New Constitution! One and Inseparable," the Democrats made no apologies for their theft of the Black vote. Members of the Black Alabama leadership—including Booker T. Washington and William Hooper Councill, a rival educator—presented several mild protest petitions to the convention, all but begging for "some little share" of political power. In the final analysis, however, no meaningful share was forthcoming.[45] If Black travelers who visited Montgomery had to endure segregated facilities, they could look forward, perhaps, to clean railroad waiting rooms for Black patrons maintained by the women of the NACW as part of their own brand of pragmatic accommodation to Jim Crow.[46] Not until the onset of the 1950s and 1960s Black freedom movement did the leveraging of both political and economic power in Montgomery earn white supremacy its first permanent defeats.

Industrialization and Women's Protests in the Transvaal and the Orange Free State

As Moshoeshoe and Philip Wodehouse engaged in negotiations designed to protect the BaSotho people, a series of discoveries that had global implications forever changed the face of the southern African continent. The discoveries took place where the Cape Colony, the Transvaal, and the OFS meet, a region that came to be known as Griqualand West. Near the confluence of the Vaal and Orange Rivers, numerous small diamonds were found between 1867 and 1868, but it was not until March 1869 that the discovery of an 83.5-carat stone indicated the profitability of future finds in the area.[47]

As thousands of eager prospectors arrived from various parts of southern Africa to work the river and dry diggings, disputes arose among the Griqua, the Transvaal and Free State Boers, and the British over who would control the diamond fields. By late 1871, fifty thousand diggers, including many from England, Europe, Australia, and the United States, were hard at work on individual claims. They washed, sorted, and carted away the unearthed rock. At the same time, individual claim holders dealt with a stream of middlemen connected to the various diamond houses of Europe or made their own sales at Cape Town or Durban. Unplanned and of concern to the British at the Cape, the mining camp known as Kimberley rapidly grew at the edge of Griqualand West outside any administrative control. Ostensibly in the interest of maintaining law and order, the disputed land claims were cleared to the Griqua, who then appealed to the British for protection. Predictably, in October 1871, before the Boers of the OFS could claim Kimberley, the British responded by annexing Griqualand West as part of the Cape Colony. As the diamond claims proliferated, the demand for cheap labor, particularly the muscle power of Black men, increased. By 1872 at least twenty thousand Black men were working the diamond fields in twenty-man crews.[48]

The mineral revolution in southern Africa was not complete, however, until the spectacular gold-bearing reefs along the east-west "Ridge of White Waters," or Witwatersrand, were discovered in the mid-1880s. Although individual prospectors had been panning for gold since the 1850s, deep gold mining did not begin in earnest until the rich reef finds of 1885 and 1886. The gold found on the Rand was inferior in quality to the gold found in Australia and Canada and it had to be extracted from deep and difficult rock formations that required the considerable capital and labor of large-scale operations; nevertheless, there was a lot of it.[49] Backed primarily by British capital, the city of Johannesburg sprouted virtually overnight, as the skilled *uitlanders*, or foreigners, from Europe, North America, and Australia rushed to the gold fields in search of wealth. By 1888 forty-four mines were operating, and by 1890 the workforce had topped one hundred thousand.[50] Seeking to minimize production expenses in the face of unexpected increases in the cost of transportation, fuel, equipment, and other supplies, mine owners restricted the number and variety of jobs performed by skilled white workers and began to rely more heavily on the lower-paid African workforce. Between 1890 and 1912, the number of African workers increased from 15,000 to 189,253.[51]

At both Kimberley and on the Reef, management regularly bemoaned the difficulty of finding African laborers who would work increasing numbers of hours for low wages. European employment of African migratory workers was not a new concept by the time of the diamond and gold discoveries, but African men found new demands on their time and personal independence increasingly encumbering. Since the 1840s, throughout much of southern Africa, BaPedi, BaTswana, and BaSotho men had been engaged as laborers in the small but growing market economy with European traders. Especially after devastating cattle losses through war, disease, and drought, African societies sent their young men to work as temporary laborers for the British or the Boers. This work pattern enabled the BaSotho to replenish their stock, meet their bride-wealth obligations, and buy guns and blankets with the sterling they had become accustomed to earning.[52] Recruited by agents in league with their chiefs or arriving at the mines on their own, African men who earned thirty shillings per week quickly discovered that their labor was worth more at Kimberley. In the mid-1870s, for instance, African men who worked elsewhere as day laborers earned two shillings per day; those who worked as domestic servants earned one pound, six shillings per month; those who worked as farmhands earned one pound, one shilling per month.[53] To keep workers on the mines longer, the British began charging the BaSotho a ten-shilling hut tax in 1870 and began to tax gun purchases as well. Joining this trend, the Boers instituted an exit tax from Kimberley; those who could not pay were forced to work on Boer farms. During the 1870s, when African societies were still self-sufficient enough and the official apparatuses were still weak enough to afford a measure of African autonomy, such schemes (with the exception of the hut tax) met with limited success.[54]

With this autonomy African men could choose to work for as few as two weeks or as long as six months, depending on their proximity to the mines and the need for agricultural production at home. In addition, African men exhibited a propensity for exchanging employers while working in the mines or for quitting when working conditions proved too dangerous. Outside promises of higher wages, poor health conditions, ill treatment by employers, and local wars were also frequent causes for leaving. During much of the 1870s, African workers had successfully resisted full proletarianization by the diamond industry, but this situation would not last.[55] During the late 1870s and early 1880s, in successive waves, as the AmaXhosa,

Griqua, BaPedi, AmaZulu, southern BaTswana, and BaSotho suffered defeat by the British and the Boers, more African men were forced to turn to the mines for their livelihood. Worsening political and economic conditions necessitated increasing resourcefulness from African societies in the rural areas of the Transvaal and OFS.

A key component in the migration process that both spurred men to seek income and enabled them to leave home was the value of women. During cattle shortages young men could earn enough money at the mines to purchase the cattle necessary to make a bride-wealth payment (ten to thirty head of cattle was the generally accepted range). Bride wealth secured a young man his wife and thus his fields, his household, and the continuation of his lineage. Lands could be retained only as long as they were in use—that is, as long as a man's wife (and his children) worked them. A man's lands, his wife or wives, and his children provided an important safety net in the context of an increasingly harsh process of industrialization. Until women became migrants themselves, men depended on them to remain at home and contribute to the production of goods and the reproduction of their societies.[56]

In addition to the loss of political independence among African peoples, other constraints against African migrants wed them more securely to the mines at Kimberley. Conditions at Kimberley were replicated at the Johannesburg mines and ultimately provided the model for policies aimed at African men and women who migrated to urban areas. New and old mechanisms designed to develop stricter worker discipline, control labor costs, and increase profits were established during the 1870s and 1880s. Critical to the extension of these control mechanisms was the joining of state and capital in the application of new laws at Kimberley enacted by the Cape Parliament after 1881. With the assistance of the British colonial state, mining companies erected a complex web of laws that criminalized the behaviors of African workers who were still reluctant to surrender their mobility completely. Such laws brought about mandatory worker registration at the labor office, dictated the issuing of passes to all legitimate workers, and established worker locations and the concept of the closed compound. Vigorous prosecution led to increased use of the courts and jails in dealing with these "criminals."[57]

The notorious masters' and servants' laws, which attempted to disguise the race-specific intent of the laws that extended only to African workers, were reminiscent of the Alabama slave codes and the postwar U.S. Black codes of the nineteenth century. The laws in Kimberley set curfews, established police patrols to enforce the pass requirements, and disallowed sales of liquor to workers without the written permission of their "masters." African miners could be randomly searched, a "Kaffir or other colored person" without the support of fifty white claim holders was prohibited from owning a digger's permit, and written contracts of no less than three months were mandatory between employers and their "servants."[58] Provoked by their anxiety over allegedly rampant theft of diamonds by Black workers, employers were empowered to beat, fine, and imprison suspects. Again, like the corrupt convict labor practices in the coal mining industry of Birmingham, Alabama, that targeted African American men, convict labor was introduced to the Kimberley mines in 1886 as a means of increasing the workforce and extending the terms of labor by a year or two.[59]

By 1883 the Kimberley mining industry had instituted strip searches for all miners, but they were imposed primarily on Black workers. In a bid to control and regiment the labor of African men and, at the same time, join the interests of the white workers to their own, mine owners segmented the workforce by race, keeping the bulk of Black workers unskilled and in positions subordinate to those of the white skilled workers. By 1885 Black migrant workers were living in closed, all-male compounds or in one of at least seven worker locations on the outskirts of town, separate from the white population of Kimberley. The compounds, which were fenced and guarded to facilitate searches and surveillance and to prevent the free movement of workers, were particularly oppressive. As a way of instilling worker discipline and routine, overseers sometimes marched Black workers who lived in the compounds to and from the mines in gangs.[60] Despite the restrictions, Black men continued to desert the mines, management found it difficult to conduct body searches twice daily, and in 1884 Black men joined with white workers in a strike against the Kimberley mine in protest of the searches.[61] The strike was brief, however, and the workers were severely punished for their efforts. To the frustration of the owners, the specter of cross-racial worker solidarity loomed large, with the full and uncontested proletarianization of Black workers remaining in question through the early part of the twentieth century.

Left to fend for themselves at home, in some cases, African women retained as little as 10 percent of their original land holdings, as they helped to bear the responsibility for payment of the ubiquitous hut tax. As their husbands, fathers, and brothers left home for longer stretches of employment in the mines, the daily lives of African women—faced with starvation and disease—became more onerous. Women's increased responsibility for food production became immediately apparent as the amount of arable land decreased and subsistence agriculture had to be intensified with the decrease in available hands. Women adapted to the changing conditions of rural production by altering what they produced. They sponsored and organized the cultivation of less labor-intensive and higher-yielding crops such as maize, which replaced sorghum as a staple.[62] In addition, in the 1870s the BaSotho adopted the cultivation of winter wheat during the colder months, when more male labor was available. Women also reallocated their time, by performing fewer household tasks, such as weaving and pottery making, in order to spend more time cultivating. By the late nineteenth century, however, the labor of BaSotho women had become less intense as family land-holdings were subdivided and agricultural production depended on failing and deteriorating soil.[63]

As economic conditions worsened, loosening traditional patterns of social organization, African women began to experience a greater sense of their own autonomy. In the face of the colonial defeats, chiefs no longer had the power to direct their people's fortunes; as a result, women and men sought their fortunes elsewhere. Women first migrated to white-owned farms, mission stations, and the newly emerging towns and cities late in the nineteenth century. Women who were single, whose husbands had deserted them, who were vulnerable to land pressures, or who were impoverished or had few resources (such as widows) were among the first to leave their rural homes.[64] African women exercised courageous personal choice in their decisions to leave, contravening the authority of their chief or other males at home. By 1911 the South African census had placed the number of African women living in South African towns at just under one hundred thousand, or 19 percent of the total African urban population.[65]

BaSotho women were among the early groups of women who migrated to the Cape and OFS farms and towns and to the Rand. In 1898, for instance, the son of Mashopa and grandson of Moshoeshoe complained that his "runaway" wife had absconded to the OFS. Fetching her back, he provoked the Mashopa rebellion between the BaSotho and the British.[66] During the Anglo-Boer War of 1899–1902, Bloemfontein proved to be a fruitful destination for many BaSotho women, since it offered them employment as washerwomen to the military garrison. Except on the Rand, where African men dominated the domestic service job market, household work offered women important employment opportunities. Laundry work and other occupations in the more informal sectors of the economy, such as beer brewing, hawking goods, and prostitution, offered women the meager monetary resources with which to sustain themselves and their families in the growing town locations.[67] Small numbers of BaSotho, Mfengu, AmaXhosa, AmaZulu, Shangaan, and Thembu women migrated to the Rand in 1896, and another wave of AmaZulu women arrived there between 1906 and 1908 and created their own work hawking goods or brewing beer.[68]

Forced out of Natal and Zululand by Bambata's rebellion to the one-pound poll tax, by drought, and by cattle disease, a "batch of Zulu Servant Girls"[69] was among the first of the women to make their way into the domestic service sector on the Rand. This event was especially noteworthy in light of several factors that impinged on women's entrance into this field of work. Even white women employers' fears of the "black peril" or of being sexually assaulted by Black men (a common theme throughout the U.S. South during this period) could not dislodge the Zulu "houseboy" from his favored position in their homes.[70] Ironically, reflecting similar concerns, African American families often chose not to send their daughters or wives into service among white men for fear that they would be sexually abused by their employers. In any case, African women did not predominate in this critical area of employment (considered traditionally female in the United States); in colonial and postcolonial Africa, at least until the 1920s or 1930s, household positions were held predominantly by African men.[71]

Because, unlike men, they were not yet required to carry passes, African women migrated more freely into Johannesburg and settled more permanently in the growing conglomeration of mining camps and segregated worker locations. In fact, the presence of African women may have inadvertently contributed to the mine owners' insatiable demands for readily available and inexpensive sources of labor. A number of impromptu settlements on the Rand that had sprung up among Black workers who sought housing had gained reputations as unseemly, unsanitary, and unsafe. As the Chamber of Mines and the state received increasing pressure to address the problem of "natives . . . travelling unhindered from one end of the Witwatersrand to the other," the Cape government considered several approaches, which, in practice, acknowledged the permanent existence of African women on the Rand. The more formal mine locations were established as part of the array of government agency policies aimed at enhancing the availability of Black labor while restricting the free movement of Black people. In 1902 J. M. Pritchard, the chief inspector of the Native Affairs Department, justified the move to the more amenable mine locations this way: "The principal reason advanced in favour of mine locations is that certain natives, who have worked for long periods on the mines and whose services are particularly valuable, have become married or 'attached' to women and if they were not permitted to live with these females in some such place as these locations they would leave the mine. Many of such natives, having worked for years on the mines have practically made their homes here and have become skilled labourers."[72]

Mining locations, which housed the families of Black workers, helped form the nucleus of the growing collection of Black townships in Johannesburg before and just after the formation of the Union of South Africa in 1910. The municipal township of Klipsruit, twelve miles to the southwest of central Johannesburg and on a site slated as a sewerage farm, was founded in 1906. The townships of Boksburg (1909), Germiston (1912), and Randfontein (1914) were also developed in successive distances from the center of Johannesburg. In the freehold townships of Sophiatown, Martindale, and Newclare (located near the center of the city) and Alexandra (nine miles to the northeast), which opened to Black residents officially in 1912, private developers permitted Black people to purchase and own their own stands.[73]

Transportation for the workers to and from their jobs in Johannesburg (except in Sophiatown, Martindale, and Newclare) proved problematic. In the early formation of the city (as in the 1940s and again in 1957), some employers refused to compensate their workers for the costs of long-distance transportation. Two possible remedies presented themselves: (1) By 1912 the Johannesburg City Council had issued several thousand permits to employers, allowing them to house their workers within the city limits, and (2) in 1908, mine married quarters—where married men were permitted to live with their wives—were more strongly proposed as alternative sources of housing.[74] In each case, African women helped establish permanent communities of Black urban inhabitants on the Rand that included a more fully formed and stable workforce. Significantly, they lent their labor to the more informal sectors, where their beer brewing, laundering, street hawking, and even prostitution could contribute to the income of the family. In fact (like the labor of Black women in the cities of the New South during the same period), their labor formed the underpinnings of capital accumulation among the industrial elite.

"We have done with pleading!" 1913 Women's Anti-pass Protests

By 1913 African women, their economic status, and their early politicization had formed an important nexus of people and conditions in several OFS municipalities, including the state capital and largest city, Bloemfontein. The 1913 women's pass resistance presaged a complex of issues that emerged in fuller force on the Rand more than four decades later.[75] In fact, linking intergenerational ideology and practice, some of the 1913 Bloemfontein women activists encouraged the women of the 1950s to persist in resisting the new pass laws of that era.[76] Since the inception of the pass laws in the 1880s, the only South African province that had actively enforced women's compliance was the OFS. Even so, African and Colored[77] women had never fully acquiesced to the purchase of the residential or employment permits, and they petitioned the government at the Cape for repeal. Both middle-class and working-class Black women—wives and daughters of the tiny Black leadership, teachers, and independent washerwomen—expressed anger over the sexualized violence meted out by the OFS authorities.[78] Both groups of women were angered as well by attempts by white employers to limit their economic opportunities and force them into domestic service.[79]

Before 1913 the Black political male leadership had led a more modest, and largely ineffective, protest of petitions and small delegations to the Cape. In 1912—proceeding without the men who led the South African Natives National Congress (SANNC)[80] and the African Political Organization (APO)[81]—OFS women formed their own political group, the Orange Free State Native and Colored Women's Association, to lead their own resistance against passes for women. They gathered five thousand petition signatures in protest of the passes and traveled to Cape Town to speak to the minister of native affairs. In the very early stages of organizing, Charlotte Manye Maxeke, a teacher from the Eastern Cape and SANNC activist who had been educated in the United States, served as an inspiration for the women. By the end of May 1913, with positive action apparently not forthcoming from the Cape government and in protest of continued police harassment and arrests, the women had decided to flout the laws and risk arrest for noncompliance by moving the protests to a new level of civil disobedience. Alongside their middle-class and working-class leaders—among them Catharina Simmons, Katie Louw, Georgina Taaibosch, Maria Modisapude, and Aploon Vorster (described in one Bloemfontein newspaper as a "jet-black Mozambique lady")[82]—women of various ages, determined and often unruly, marched in unprecedented numbers. Many wore the blue ribbons of the British suffragists, publicly destroyed their passes, and served hard jail time for their efforts.[83] On June 6, 1913, six hundred women, some carrying sticks (and some using them on the heads of the police), marched to the magistrate's office in angry protest of the passes, insisting, "We have done with pleading[;] we now demand!" Similar protests spread to other OFS towns, including Kroonstad, Winburg, and Jagersfontein.[84]

The women raised funds for their sustained efforts throughout the rest of the year and into the next, widely publicizing the issue of the pass laws through their organizational network. Although the onset of World War I drew attention away from their cause, members of the OFS Native and Colored Women's Association continued their letter-writing campaign to solicit support anywhere they could—including from sympathetic white South Africans. In a letter addressed to "all friends of our people," Katie Louw, as secretary of the association, asked for the support of a proposed parliamentary bill "repealing the Municipal Pass Law to native and colored women." She stated, "We hold that any law which compels women to carry passes can have no justification on the ground of utility, expediency, or any other grounds whatsoever, as it is degrading, harsh, arbitrary, vexatious, and leads to the committal of vice and is no protection to respectable and law-abiding women. . . . We may add that this is the only Province where women have to carry passes, and it would be a fitting climax and a gracious act on the part of the Union Government to have this law repealed."[85] By 1920, although the municipal women's pass laws had not been repealed in the OFS, they had been relaxed in several regions. In 1923 the revised set of national pass laws formed under the Urban Areas Act exempted women altogether.[86] The periodic eruptions into pass resistance by women after 1913, in combination with a national government in conflict with the farming interests of the OFS over the issue, exerted enough pressure on local officials to hinder enforcement of the laws. Ultimately, the interests of the mining-dominated Cape government—the protection of a reliable stream of workers to the mines—won out over those of the OFS farmers. By the mid-1950s, as women increasingly sought jobs in the cities and towns, control of the labor of Black women and men had surfaced once again on a national level. Intended especially to stem the migration of women from the bleeding farms, a more forcefully implemented round of laws that aimed at effective "influx control" and job protection for white workers rested most fundamentally on requiring passes for women nationwide.[87]

An important aspect of the 1913 demonstrations, however, was women's skillful use of their political leverage. Taking matters into their own hands, they pushed past the deliberate pace of the men, combining diplomacy with more threatening disruptions in the streets. Their collective and determined activism had brought the volatile issue of women's passes to a head and had severely undermined the effectiveness of Boer policy. Moreover, building on the momentum gained in the widespread anti-pass campaign and placing new emphasis on action on behalf of their own interests, Black women formed a new women's organization in 1918.

Founded by Charlotte Manye Maxeke, the Bantu Women's League came into existence as an arm of the ANC. Maxeke was every bit as able an organizer, strategist, and leader as her male colleagues in the SANNC; her talents and accomplishments were equally noteworthy. Her only disqualification for full membership in that organization was her sex. Although she was thoroughly displeased with the unequal status of women in the parent body, Maxeke continued to work for African freedom through the ANC and, in the 1930s, the National Council of African Women.[88] As an educator, the first Black probation officer of the Johannesburg municipal courts, a religious leader, a wife, and a mother, Maxeke had lived the daily struggle that Black women waged in an effort to safeguard their families and communities. She was an ardent champion of Black women, who consistently demanded that every governmental agency and political institution respect their roles as mothers and householders who were entitled to make their own economic decisions. By the mid-1930s, Maxeke had earned wide admiration among Black South Africans, who called her the Mother of African Freedom.[89] Maxeke and the veterans of the first women's anti-pass campaign had articulated a protofeminist politics that "opened the road" to future activism by women.[90]

The boycotts and demonstrations of the 1880s and 1910s were political antecedents to women's activism in the 1950s U.S. South and South Africa. Black women clearly were not afraid to lodge strong opposition to the state and to the industrializing economies of the two regions. As the nascent Black communities of Montgomery, Johannesburg, Atlanta, and

Bloemfontein tested the limits of new segregationist practices, however, forms of resistance that were less amenable to mass action subsumed their protests. Working-class women in Bloemfontein and Atlanta shared similar economic concerns that hinged on their ability to exercise choice, but Black women in the U.S. South did not have to confront a system that required official sanction of their presence in the city. With the dismantling of slavery and the Black Codes, the "modernized" Jim Crow practices were less about Black people's movements into and out of the city than about their separation from white people in schools, in neighborhoods, and on public conveyances. Different, too, was Charlotte Manye Maxeke's explicitly political leadership. Margaret Murray Washington of Tuskegee Institute led the state and national organizations of Black clubwomen at various times between 1895 and 1918, but her stance (unlike that of Maxeke) was similar to that of her husband, and (also unlike Maxeke) she refrained from engaging in overt political action.[91] The political behavior of Black women—contingent on serious threats to the interests of women and at times especially militant—ran its course throughout the twentieth century. In the 1950s, women activists from rural backgrounds, whose resistance stemmed from the struggles they faced on a daily basis, revealed the earliest aspects of political consciousness.

Chapter Three

WHEN WE WERE JUST GIRLS

Rural Life Challenges in Black Belt Alabama and
Pre-apartheid South Africa, 1920s–1940s

Eighty-three-year-old Amy Collins Harris remembered spending her childhood and adolescence in the Black Belt Alabama village of Free Town, which was officially known as Allenville at the time. She recalled a place where her large family, which included numerous extended members, fashioned a comfortable self-sufficiency undergirded by a cooperative spirit of interdependence. Founded in Hale County in the 1860s, Free Town was established on land that John Collins IV, a white man, bequeathed to his three mixed-race sons who regarded themselves as Black. Richard Collins, Mrs. Harris's great-grandfather, was one of the three brothers, who each received a thirty-five-acre plot on which to farm and settle. According to Mrs. Harris, because several other white landowners had divided their property among Black farmers who eventually came to own their own land, Free Town was known to African American families as a site of independent land ownership.[1]

In addition to owning their own farms, the Black men and women of Allenville were skilled in a variety of occupations. Amy Harris's father, Richard Gaylord Collins, was a bricklayer, plasterer, and cement finisher who worked jobs away from home in order to bring in extra money. She recalled that the Carringtons were carpenters ("that was a family that married one of the Collins ladies"),[2] as were the Ashes; Buck Lewis was a bricklayer, as was one of the Burks; and Son Burks was a blacksmith who had a shop about five miles away in Faunsdale. Mrs. Harris's mother, Fannie Collins, was a talented seamstress and nurse who cared for both Black and white people. Some of Mrs. Harris's best memories involved learning how to sew as she sat on her mother's lap, her small feet on top of her mother's as she operated the treadle, intently focused on the stitching as her mother guided her hands along the material. This was the way older family members and other artisans in the community passed down skills to subsequent generations: "The older [ones] in that community, look like it must have been in the system that one person picked up from the other. 'Cause we had several carpenters in the area, bricklayers, cement finishers and all, and I don't know no training school any of them went to."[3]

The town and farms of Allenville also supported several mills and at least one dry goods store that were owned by members of Mrs. Harris's extended family. Peter Collins, her father's first cousin, owned a molasses mill, and another Collins family member owned grist and sugar mills as well as the dry goods store, which extended credit to anyone who needed it: "He would do that for everybody in the community; they brought their corn. And he didn't charge them [money]; he just get a toll. He get, if it was two, measured by pints, you get two and he get one. That's how he got his pay for grinding it for you."[4] Even more generous with her time and expertise was Mrs. Harris's mother, who rarely accepted money for her nursing services: "Oh, she didn't accept no pay. All them was kin folk."[5]

From this family came a Montgomery bus boycott participant who was proud to claim her Free Town heritage. Mrs. Harris believed that her community had helped her develop her independent spirit and resourcefulness as she witnessed autonomous Black people all around her making their own way in the world and helping others to do the same. In the heart of the Jim Crow South and in the middle of the culturally rich and once fertile Black Belt of Alabama, Amy Collins Harris formed a consciousness of place, defined, in part, by Black resistance: "See, I was born free. I never had . . . we didn't have to beg nobody for nothin'. We had everything we ever needed. Might not have had everything we wanted, but we had enough to live comfortable. . . . I never knew no hard times. . . . We always had plenty to eat, plenty to wear, 'cause Mama could take anything and make us clothes out of it, and I made my first dress at [age] nine."[6] Participating fully in the active life of her community, Amy Collins learned what it meant to feel free. Nostalgically using the term *community* to describe the attitudes, feelings, and practices of the people she associated with home, she recalled, "It was a community of family folks, and everybody got along, and everybody lived together, and it was just lovely."[7]

· · ·

In the rural district of Matatiele in the Eastern Cape Province of South Africa, Matabello Magdeline Tsiu was born a child of the BaSotho.

Maggie Resha—as she was later known to her ANC Women's League co-members—was the second child of Tsekiso Tsiu, the son of an Anglican missionary, and Moselantja Mokhele, the daughter of a prosperous farmer. Early on she was aware that her paternal lineage was intertwined with that of the royal house of Lesotho. Through the art of combining history with memory and storytelling, Maggie Tsiu learned from stories passed down by her BaFokeng ancestors who formed a direct link to Moshoeshoe through her great-great-grandfather RaTsiu and his father Ntsukunyane. As Maggie Tsiu learned from family history, "RaTsiu had succeeded his father Ntsukunyane as king. . . . His nephew Moshoeshoe had already proved himself, according to the rituals of those days, as a brave young man, and he clearly had all the qualities required for leadership. So, RaTsiu over-stepped his own son, Tsiu, and handed his authority over to Moshoeshoe as a necessity to save the BaSotho nation. RaTsiu, however, remained the young chief's counsellor, or prime minister, if it was today."[8]

Thus, the rulership of the BaSotho passed to the heirs of Moshoeshoe rather than to the Tsius' direct line. In the meantime, Rantsiuoa, Mrs. Resha's great-grandfather, had only one child—a daughter, Ntsiuoa, whose two sons became his direct heirs.[9] One of the sons, Malitse, Maggie Resha's grandfather, was the first family member to convert to Christianity. He had made his conversion at Kimberley, where both brothers had become mine workers. According to Mrs. Resha's understanding of the family history, Malitse's older brother, Mosoeu, believed this Western faith to be a "madness, and something not fit for people with royal blood."[10] Eventually, however, Mosoeu converted, and he and his brother became Anglican missionaries to the villages of the district of Matatiele. Malitse was asked to open the church mission of St. James at Hankasele, some thirty miles from the family's home at Ramohlakoana. By the time Malitse and his BaHlubi wife arrived at St. James, three of their children—including their eldest son, Tsekiso Tsiu, Maggie Tsiu's father—were already born.

The white Anglicans offered to send Tsekiso Tsiu to college (presumably to train for the ministry), but he declined. Instead, Mrs. Resha's father migrated to Johannesburg to work for the railroad. There he became familiar with the work of Clements Kadalie and joined the Industrial and Commercial Workers Union (ICU).[11] His marriage to Mrs. Resha's mother, Moselantja Mokhele, a Christian and member of the St. James community, had been prearranged by his father. It was delayed, at her father's insistence, until she finished her industrial course at Mariazell College. The marriage was consummated when the *lobola-bohali* of "eleven head of cattle and a horse" was made to the Mokheles. According to Mrs. Resha, her grandfather Mokhele was furious at the extravagant *lobola* made on his daughter's behalf: "He told them that he was not selling his daughter, that he had lots of better-looking animals, and that five or six head of cattle would have been sufficient to seal the bond of friendship and relationship between the two families.... Indeed, the day my mother went to her in-laws after the marriage, she was sent with two fat cows for milk and ten sheep for meat as a present from her father."[12]

Matabello Magdeline—Maggie's full given name, Matabello, means "hope" in SeSotho—was born in 1923, the second of nine children. At the age of one year, she was given to her mother's unmarried sister, Maylia, to raise on their father's farm at La Grange, about seven miles from St. James. For much of her early life, Maggie Tsiu knew no mother other than Maylia, a domestic worker. Shortly after moving the entire family to the farming community of Klein Jonas (when Maggie Tsiu was still quite young), her grandfather died. Her memories of her grandmother, Motseoane-Mmatau, however, were vivid and loving. From her grandmother she learned her prayers. She also learned from her, "[The Europeans] have taken our country and they have money."[13]

Maggie Tsiu remembered how hard the people of Klein Jonas, especially the women, worked to produce good harvests and to raise their children with minimal resources. She recalled that most children went without shoes; she counted herself among the lucky ones because she had a pair of white tennis shoes that she was allowed to wear only to church. She also remembered, however, that "many people ..., in those days, had good crops ... [and that] the soil was still fertile." Her grandmother had two huge storehouses for maize and sorghum. She recalled that the work was often performed communally during the seasons of weeding and harvesting and that young people whose families were without cattle or goats often helped on their neighbors' farms in exchange for milk. She recollected the "spirit of community" that infused the families of the villages with a sense of connection and well-being:

What made life bearable was the spirit of community that was always very high in the villages.... There was also no shame in asking for such items as tea leaves, sugar, salt, etc. from a neighbor. This community spirit of sharing is very deep-seated in Africans. It descends from the first mouldings of our human relations, and is part of our culture and traditions, and I imagine it is this that has kept the African people as a nation proud of its culture despite the hardships and humiliations that have been our lot since the arrival of the colonisers.[14]

. . .

It is this sense of community that transcends the differences in and ties the backgrounds of Amy Collins Harris and Maggie Tsiu Resha. Both enjoyed relatively prosperous childhoods, and for both that prosperity was accomplished with the help and cooperation of relatives, neighbors, and friends. Both experienced important examples of sharing and assistance, tempering the notion of individual success as an absolute model of achievement. For both young girls, an understanding of mutual obligation and reciprocity that had everything to do with how families and communities survived and thrived provided them with a lasting image of accomplishment.

For the women who later migrated to the urban centers of their respective countries, the lives they had led in the rural U.S. South or on the more loosely regulated reserves or mission stations in South Africa during the 1920s and 1930s held important meaning. First and foremost, a strong connection with home, family, and the native land of their ancestors was bound up in the rural beginnings and identities of Mrs. Harris, Mrs. Resha, and other women activists like them. Amy Collins Harris is quick to link her heritage to her paternal great-grandfather and his two brothers, who staked their claim to a portion of the land in Hale County and who became prosperous and independent farmers. Maggie Tsiu Resha proudly claims blood relationship to a revered king of the BaSotho and expresses equal pride in the maternal grandfather who turned a piece of land into the foundation for the autonomy of his family. These ancestors, men and women who made the most of modest opportunities, left for their granddaughters much more than fond memories of happy childhoods. They left them a pride of place and of principle: that if Black people have good land to work, resources to draw from, and a community of people who pull together, they need not suffer.

For Mrs. Harris and Mrs. Resha, and for countless other women of their generation who grew up in rural settings in the 1920s and 1930s, chores and work, schooling and church, siblings and extended family fit integrally within the fabric of their daily lives. In these large families, even children's hands were useful; chores were divided among children and adults—among women and men and among girls and boys. The work was often hot and tedious; children went to the fields at a young age and learned by example from the adults. Attendance at school and church brought temporary relief from the work routines, bringing families and extended kin together—sometimes over long distances—for those important moments of shared community. Intruding in the lives of rural Black people who were often caught on the edge of the political economy of white-dominated societies, however, were the evils of living under a system of white supremacy.

In this chapter I examine the contours of the lives of Amy Harris and Maggie Resha as they grew up in the midst of the important influences of family, church, and school in the rural environment. Their conscious-ness of place and the intergenerational links that were established helped define their consciousness of self. In addition, their spiritual rootedness and religious practice, begun among family and friends in their small, close-knit communities, contributed to their cultivated belief in the possible. Although rural schooling was, perhaps, not as effective a conveyor of the socialization process during this period, with children beginning school at a later age and leaving at an earlier age, parents knew that education was an important escape route from the cycle of poverty and illiteracy. Young children acquired many skills under the equally important tutelage of their men and women kinfolk. Amy Harris's mother and others who, more often than not, stood at the center of their families' and their communities' sur-vival provided their daughters with important instruction in a variety of skills and attitudes, from caring for people in need to quilting, cooking, and farming—tasks that were frequently performed communally or in the company of other women. By direct observation of the social and economic strategies of the women in their communities, the future activists of the 1950s generation were empowered to take responsibility for leading their own political struggles. The young girls learned, by example, the values, be-haviors, and worldviews that contributed to a growing awareness of the in-justices they faced and the means with which to overcome them.

Raising Daughters in Black Belt Alabama

At the turn of the nineteenth century, Alabama was an overwhelmingly rural state. Although out migration had begun by 1910, forty years after slavery the bulk of the Black population was still firmly planted on Black Belt soil. Despite the loss of just under 1 percent of the total Black rural population between 1910 and 1920,[15] in the 1920s and 1930s, the overall rural character of Alabama had remained unchanged. In 1920, 78 percent of the 900,652 Black people in the state (nearly two-fifths of the total population) were still living in rural areas.[16] More than half (54 percent) of the rural Black population was twenty years of age and under, and slightly more than half (51 percent) of the Black people ten years of age and older who lived in the country were female.[17] Between 1920 and 1930 the total Black population of the state increased 5 percent, but the rural Black population decreased 4 percent. In fact, since 1910 the rural Black population had experienced a steady decline, whereas the Black urban population had increased (with the most significant increase—36 percent—occurring between 1920 and 1930).[18] Still, in 1930 the number of Black urban dwellers (268,450) was well under half (39 percent) of the Black rural population of Alabama.[19]

During this period Black children in rural Alabama did not regularly attend school beyond the elementary grades. Not surprisingly, the state record of illiteracy among Black children and adults, both rural and urban, compared dismally with that of the rest of the nation. Consistently, from 1890 to 1910, the Black population of Alabama aged ten years and older posted the second highest rate of illiteracy—40 percent in 1910—behind Louisiana (with nearly 50 percent).[20] For the same age group between 1910 and 1920, the illiteracy rate for the rural population declined from 43.5 percent to 34 percent; by 1930 the illiteracy rate for the rural Black population had decreased only to 30 percent. During this period the rate differed little between the sexes; Black women, rural or urban, fared little better than Black men in gaining access to literacy instruction.[21]

With the state refusing to fund schools for Black children or protect them from illegal labor (the legal age for leaving school was fourteen) and with few Black teachers in the workforce, it is little wonder that the illiteracy rates were so high. In 1918, for instance, only three four-year high schools were available to young Black people in the entire state, and 50 percent of elementary-aged Black children in the state attended school for under five months.[22] In 1920 fewer than 2,500 Black teachers were available to teach the 160,579 (out of 250,641) Black children between the ages of seven and seventeen who attended school.[23] In the rural communities, only 128,922, or 62 percent of the Black children who were eligible, attended school. By 1930, as the Depression deepened, 70 percent of Black children in rural Alabama aged seven to seventeen attended school; however, that number declined to only 44 percent for sixteen- and seventeen-year-olds.[24]

Growing up in Montgomery County during the 1930s, in the "shadow of the plantation" (as a comparable area in neighboring Macon County has been described),[25] Ethel Mae Smith Alexander and her younger siblings lived the array of rural experiences that these statistics affirm. Born in 1925 on her father's tenant farm, some sixteen miles from the city of Montgomery, Ethel Mae was the first of Loveless and Ella Ann Smith's four children. "I was on the farm all my life," Mrs. Alexander recalled.[26] The vast majority of families in Montgomery County in 1930 were engaged in some form of agricultural work. Whether they were landowners, cash or share tenants, or farmhands, they inherited an economic system much like that of the old antebellum plantations.[27] In the face of such twentieth-century plagues as boll weevils, drought, debt, an increased dependence on fertilizers, and unscrupulous treatment by landowners, Loveless Smith and other Black farmers persisted. Some tenaciously held on to the land that they had earned through hard times and hard work. Others continued to farm because, as renters or sharecroppers, they lacked the resources to risk changing occupations. For the Black farmer, whether owner or tenant, cash was scarce, and general store or commissary advances in food, clothing, and other supplies were the rule. In a system in which the majority of farmers earned less than a hundred dollars annually, their Herculean attempts at breaking the cycle of debt and dependence seemed destined for failure.[28] A case in point was one Macon County farmer who discovered that there was no limit to his landlord's dishonesty. After he had turned over to the landlord all that he owned or had raised, Mr. Adams was told that he was still $53 in debt. When the farmer requested a "bill that said how [much] for each thing," he was assessed an additional $255.98. "When you working on a white man's place," Adams explained, "you have to do what he says, or treat, trade, or travel. He jest closed out and got all we had."[29]

Fortunately for the Smith family, life on the Arrington farm in Montgomery County was not quite as harsh as it was for the Adams family one county away. As a child, Ethel Mae Smith worked hard, learning at her mother's side the many tasks required of subsistence farmers in Black Belt Alabama. Chief among these tasks, of course, was picking cotton: "My brother and I and two other children worked alongside with my mother. She could just grab that cotton." They learned to pick enough cotton to earn fifty cents for a day of labor: "This man had a farm called Harvest Farm. We'd work out there—hired out by the day to try to make it. I made fifty cents a day. Fifty cents a hundred pounds of cotton. You had to pick a hundred pounds of cotton and you made fifty cents.... We had a long croker sack. . . . [W]hen we packed that, my brother and I, we knew we had the hundred. She would let us rest up in the shade. We no good when we're tired."[30]

At the time, exhaustion from picking cotton all day in the oppressive heat of the Black Belt South was no doubt the universal complaint of farming children. Sara Brooks, a freeholder's daughter in west-central Alabama who was born a generation before Ethel Mae Smith, was not afraid to put it bluntly: "Pickin cotton was the tiredest thing! You had to stoop down all the time and pick it and put it in the sack hangin on your side. And then when you move, you gotta pull the sack. Then when it get full, you have to go way over and put it in the basket and then come back. That stoopin with the sack hung on your back, draggin up and down the row! Oh, that was the most tiresome thing I ever seen!"[31] Neither the method of gathering the cotton crop nor the weight of the croker sack itself had changed since the antebellum era, when the strong backs and nimble fingers of enslaved women had helped to enrich the planter aristocracy of the deep South. Unlike her cousin Rhoda, who was a fast picker, Sara Brooks said she sought to rid herself of the croker sack—some seventy years after the official demise of slavery—by cheating her way through the finger-numbing chore:

> Rhoda picked a hundred pounds by noon and she probably picked two hundred in a day, but I couldn't pick hardly a hundred in a day. I couldn't pick cotton. I hated that cotton pickin business so bad! I'm so glad now that I learnt not to cheat [at home], but I would cheat when I'd go off to pick some cotton at other people's place. I'd pull off the green bolls and wrap them in the cotton. And cockleburs—them sticky balls that grow on a bush—I'd pull them off, even, and wrap them up in the cotton so it'd make it weigh. . . . Those little stickers on the boll always got into my fingers . . . and my fingers would be *so* sore . . . and look like because I cheated, I still never had up to what the other peoples had cause maybe I was spendin up too much time wrappin up the bolls.[32]

Even the incentive of earning a pre–Depression era seventy-five cents per hundred pounds of cotton was not enough to spur Sara to quicker (and cleaner) efficiency. Admitting that her shortcut probably hurt her more than it helped her, she recalled, "Oh, tryin' to make a dollar . . . [o]h, you're gettin' good money if you got seventy-five cents for a hundred pounds. But out of all the cockleburs and all the cotton bolls, I couldn't make a hundred in a day."[33]

Like Sara Brooks and other farming daughters, Ethel Mae Smith learned how to do more than chop and pick cotton, cultivate a garden, and raise livestock. As the oldest girl, she helped her mother around the house. "[T]hen it helped me when I got in my own house," she observed. Her mother taught her "how to can, how to cook, how to wash," she explained. "Like I say," she continued, "I was the oldest, and I was responsible for the rest of the children, see. They put me in charge. So we worked in the fields and when it come time to cook, my mother put the meat on and . . . [a] little later [we'd] put the vegetables on and get the bread ready and everything. So I learned that. That was in the country."[34] Learning these domestic skills prepared a daughter not only for heading her own household but also for working under a white "mistress." The feisty Sara Brooks would rather go fishing on a rainy day than sew work dresses under her mother's watchful eye. Sara paid for her impatience:

> [Momma] would cut it out for us, and we would make em ourselves. But I could never sew—I never did have patience enough to sew. I would hurry up and I would be the first one to get finished because I'd make long stitches. Then I'd say, "I'm through, you all. Lookee here!" And my mother would look at it, she'd say, "Take it loose." She'd make me take it out and do it again. . . . Momma, she would tell us if we didn't learn how to sew and cook and wash and clean, when we'd grow up and get married and have our own children, we wasn't gonna know anything and nobody was gonna put up with us.[35]

Rose Zell Lawrence, the daughter of tenant farmers Reese and Pearlie Lawrence of Lowndes County, also remembered that her mother kept track of how well her children performed their chores. The first of eight children, she too felt the weight of learning to complete her tasks correctly: "Mother taught us at an early age how to do different things in keeping house, and we were washing, back in those days, on a rub board. They had no washing machines. Oh, she looked at you! And if you were washing something on the rub board and you weren't washin' it so clean, and you took it out the wash, you had to wash it over until it was clean, 'cause you couldn't hang it on the line if it wasn't clean."[36]

Lillie Means Lewis, also of Lowndes County, remembered a similar fate when her mother found dirt on the clothes and sheets that her daughter washed. Mrs. Lewis learned by constant repetition the tedious process of laundering and the care that had to be taken to ensure that "nary a speck of dirt" made its way to the line:

We had no pumps. . . . [We] let the buckets down in the water, and then draw
the water from the well and tote the water; put it in the pots, put the pots
out, and boil the clothes outside. Boil them clothes, and then take them out
and wash them again. Then rinse them through three or four [basins of]
water. The last water we rinsed them through had to be blueing water. Then
my mother would hang them . . . [and] then she would come down the line
and inspect them, and if they wasn't clean, she was going to take them down.
She didn't take them off and hand them to us. She would just take them off
and drop them, and take them off and drop them down, and take them off and
drop them down. And [she] stepped on them as she went.

Now we got to take them up and get all of that dirt off of them. Then go
and wash them all over again, and you better make sure that nary a speck o'dirt
she could find this time. . . . Lord, I thought she was the meanest mother in
the world, but afterward I have to look back and I say, "Thank you, Momma!
Thank you for the way that you trained me."[37]

The family laundry was a perfect vehicle for mothers to instill in their
daughters the importance of following instructions precisely. Painstaking
neatness and cleanliness were crucial attributes for those who would successfully ply their skills in the domestic service trade. This generation of
mothers had learned these skills from their mothers before them, and if
they were fortunate enough to be able to avoid the kitchens and parlors
of the surrounding white communities, the fate of their daughters was not
so ensured. As the worsening economic conditions of the 1930s continued
to plague Black farming families, rural daughters were forced to leave the
farms for more lucrative employment in the cities. Especially during the
war period, Black women such as Amy Collins Harris (who managed to
find a factory job in Montgomery in just one day) had little difficulty finding industrial, domestic, and other low-paying work. Once employed, their
level of expertise would, in great measure, determine whether they remained
employed.

Times may have been lean for Ethel Mae Smith and her family, as they
were for most Black people during the 1930s, but communities of farm
families tended to live within helping distance of one another. The members of Amy Collins Harris's extended family of blood relatives and in-laws
all lived in close proximity, sharing both goods and services in Free Town
in Hale County. Sara Brooks's father generously took in and cared for a
number of relatives, including his mother; his disabled brother, Jim; and
his sister's two children, Rhoda and Molly (whose mother, Georgia, lived

within walking distance). Ethel Mae Smith's paternal family members lived and worked together on the Arrington farm in Montgomery County for many years. Her father's parents were still living there when Ethel Mae and her siblings were children. In addition to cultivating cotton, her uncles and aunts worked the dairy farm there. She recalled how they cut the hay to feed the cows, and she described the surroundings: "[There were] nothing but two houses on this place where I was living. People lived 'round in the quarter—that's what they called it—but it was a long way from us, from our relatives. You would have to go around the woods—same thing to go to school." In the same part of the county Mrs. Alexander's maternal kinfolk, the Irving family, lived on the Grier place. "We could walk over there. We did walk there to see my grandparents," she said. Being connected to so many aunts, uncles, and cousins made her feel "real good" as a child. When there arose the need, for example, one of her aunts made her a dress for school:

> They didn't take us to church like we do our children now because we didn't have anything. . . . But when I got up bigger and started off to school . . . the clothes that I had—I remember so well . . . probably two or three dresses. My daddy's aunt made this dress for me, and then . . . I picked cotton—I remember they always worked—[and they] picked cotton and bought me this pretty green dress, kinda like a little wrap-around, [that] I remember quite well. I got me some black slippers and wore them with yellow socks. I took care of them real, real good. I didn't wear them [at home], and my dresses, I'd wash them at night for school, let them dry, get up, and press them. I remember one time where I washed my clothes, I had a flour—a twenty-four-pound—sack. That was a big sack! I ripped that sack open and then washed it, and then tied it around me, and then washed my clothes for the next week to go to school with.[38]

For the most part, rural children looked forward to going to school and church as opportunities to get away from the fields and—as Sara Brooks described it—to keep "things [from] gettin dull."[39] Parents in Black Belt Alabama and all over the rural and urban South, however, knew that for their children education could spell freedom from ignorance and exploitation. For its part, collective worship at church served to knit together the soul of a hard-pressed community. For rural Black folk, however, considerable creativity was necessary to access both. During the 1920s and 1930s, many of those who had been fortunate enough to attend elementary school had to forgo the possibility of a high school education. The few who had the opportunity to enter one of the county training schools for Black students received an education that was in no way comparable to that of the high schools open to white students. Supported initially by a combination of private and state funds, the training schools were designed to produce rural elementary school teachers who would follow a curriculum that ran along "agricultural and vocational lines." Black students found that the "faulty standards and equipment" of these schools contributed to the insufficient preparation for college entrance that they provided.[40] Education for Black people in Alabama, especially those who paid shares or rent for the privilege of working the old plantations, was intended to keep them minimally equipped to continue in a dying occupation, unprepared to do anything other than the lowest-paying, lowest-skill labor.[41] Not surprisingly, some of the women activists who became domestic or factory workers in Montgomery had not gone beyond the sixth, seventh, or eighth grades.

Rose Zell Lawrence, one of the fortunate few (and one of only fourteen in her class), completed the twelfth grade, graduating at age twenty from Lowndes County Training School in 1948. She attended elementary school through the ninth grade in her hometown of Gordonville, completed her education at the training school, and went on to teach elementary school in Lowndesboro and Sardis for three years. When there was no more money to pay for her certification courses at Alabama State in Montgomery, Ms. Lawrence quit teaching to work as a cook in a Selma hospital. She later left her cooking job to help her father on the farm, and in 1954 she left the farm for Montgomery, where she became a domestic worker in the Wool family home on Narrow Lane Road. Although she remained in domestic service thereafter, she always regretted not having had the money to continue her teaching career: "Oh I loved it, loved it, loved it! Yes, and I loved all of the people that I met. In Sardis were family people. Everybody I met [said], 'Oh, I'm kin to you, Miss Lawrence. . . .' And the children were so nice, and after the children being so nice, all their parents and things were so nice. They didn't ever want us to even leave, and we didn't want to leave them, but . . ."[42]

When Ms. Lawrence first began teaching at the one-room Hopewell School in Lowndesboro, she was responsible for the entire curriculum for twenty-four children in the first through sixth grades. In her next placement, in Sardis, she taught approximately forty students in the first and second grades, alongside two other teachers, who taught the third-fourth, and fifth-sixth grades. At the other extreme of the rural school experience, Amy Collins and her siblings walked two miles each way, to and from their one-room school in Allenville, where they were taught by their cousin Annie Collins. They shared classroom space with some fifty children of all ages, from grades one through six. Amy and her older sister, Mary, then attended the Lincoln Normal School in Marion, a private institution for Black students in Perry County, one county east. Because it was too far to walk to Marion, the sisters boarded with three other girls from nearby Black Belt counties: "Yeah, we went up there and we stayed in a home that the school owned, [with] a lady and her husband, Mr. and Mrs. Rogers. We washed for ourselves, but they did the cooking. . . . I stayed there one year because Mary met her husband. He finished that year, and they got married, and then I didn't go back."[43]

After Amy Collins finished the seventh grade at Marion, she did not attend school for a while. Later she resumed her education at the Perry County Training School, only ten miles from her home. She remained at the training school until 1937, through eleventh grade, when she left to marry her childhood sweetheart, Henry Brown. She was already twenty-one, and she was eager to be on her own and start her own family. Looking back, however, she wished that she had finished high school and gone on to college and that her oldest brother, Richard, had completed his education at Tuskegee Institute: "I told him that was a bad example for the rest of us, 'cause if he had finished, all of us would have went on. But . . . [only] one out of the eight graduated from high school, and that was Minnie [the youngest]. . . . Will left his graduation year and went to New York. I left the year before I graduated and married and went to New York. And so he set a bad example. Papa and them should have whipped his butt . . . [to] send him on, [or they should have] carried him on back there!"[44]

Ethel Mae Smith Alexander and Lillie Means Lewis were not as fortunate as Amy Collins Harris or Rose Zell Lawrence. Their educations were aborted much earlier—Ethel Mae Smith's after the sixth grade and Lillie Means's after the eighth grade. Ethel Mae Smith left school at age fifteen to marry and to help support her family because her parents had separated. Lillie Means left to help her parents farm in Sandy Ridge until she married shortly thereafter at age twenty-one and moved to Montgomery. Both women scrambled for outside work as they raised their families and struggled with their difficult first husbands. Lillie Means Lewis's work at two furniture-manufacturing companies totaled more than thirty years;

Ethel Mae Alexander held several low-paying restaurant jobs, did domestic service day labor, and was employed as a community service worker before she finally retired. Not until Mrs. Alexander's children were well grown and she was working at the local Community Action Program did she attempt to complete her education. "I did get some certificate," she explained, "[but] my load got heavy, and I dropped out again. I couldn't take it all."[45]

Outside of school, attending church with family and friends helped adhere young daughters to a community of strong, faithful members, many of whom served as models for the younger generations. Church, for many, was obligatory. For Amy Collins Harris, however, observance of the Sabbath and church attendance were important and welcome family rituals. Sunday apparel had to be washed, ironed, and set out each Saturday, because "wasn't no irons going up in the house on Sunday."[46] Since their inception, rural churches commonly depended on an "absentee pastorate"—originally associated with the early evangelical itinerant preachers—to lead their congregations. Especially during the period of World War II and the significant migrations to urban centers, there were not enough clergymen to service the numerous small country churches.[47] Pastors therefore often tended more than one church to enable communities to meet and worship together on a regular basis. The pastor for young Amy Collins's church, who lived in Mississippi, traveled every Sunday to Allenville, where he and his wife stayed overnight with relatives. The congregation at Sara Brooks's church met only once a month, but on the intervening Sundays she and her family regularly attended three other churches. Lillie Means and her family attended two churches each month—Beautiful Diamond Methodist Church on the first and third Sundays and the Baptist Church on the second and fourth Sundays.[48]

Schooled in the Black Baptist tradition, Amy Collins and her older sister, Mary, "joined church" when Amy was seven years old. Mrs. Harris recalled complete participation in her church community: "Oooo, yeah! We came up in Sunday school at Bethlehem Baptist, down there right in the community. [We had church] every Sunday: Sunday school, church, BTU—that's Baptist Training Union, [an] evening program for children, mostly." Certainly the church was considered the lifeblood of the community, supporting members through every stage of their lives. People were baptized, thus becoming members of their churches, at an early age; attended Sunday services regularly, including services at churches affiliated with outside denominations when their home churches could not meet; held offices of responsibility on, for example, the Usher Board, or Missionary Board; and were honored by having their good works celebrated upon their deaths. As a young person, Amy Collins rarely missed a church activity: "I attended Sunday school. I sang in the choir and whenever we had programs—you know, we had programs for Easter and Christmas—and I participated in everything."[49] Amy Collins Harris shared her talents and came to understand how integral her presence was to her community through her participation in the activities at Bethlehem Baptist Church.

For the women who later became political activists, stories of slavery recounted by their grandparents, who were small children at the time of emancipation, held important lessons. In the rural communities in every corner of the state, former bondswomen and bondsmen provided the bridge between a difficult past and a more promising future. Through those who had experienced or heard firsthand tales of the injustices of slavery, the young girls came to appreciate the value of struggle and perseverance. As one former domestic worker observed about the experiences of her family members during slavery, "Those times? No, they didn't forget; they didn't let you either."[50] Embedded in the collective act of remembering this profoundly painful past is the act of affirming the experiences of family elders by continuing to pass their stories from generation to generation.

Belco Herst, who was born during slavery, was one such elder who imparted to the members of his family valuable lessons from his past. Herst's granddaughter, Mrs. Beautie Mae Osborn Johnson, who had been employed as a factory worker and a beautician in Montgomery, remembered her grandfather as an important figure in her life. Born in 1915 in Hope Hull, Montgomery County, Beautie Mae Osborn was raised among her mother's people on her grandfather's farm. Their large extended family, which was headed by her grandparents, Belco and Annie Herst, included her five aunts and uncles and their children. Beautie Mae Osborn enjoyed a close early relationship with "Papa Belco," as she called her grandfather. "That's the daddy that I mostly knew," she recalled. Her own father, Jim Osborn, had left his family to work in the mines and mills of Birmingham and Detroit. Julia Herst Osborn, Beautie Mae's mother, had remained with her five children to help run her father's farm, until she moved her family to Montgomery in 1930. It was on the farm that young Beautie Mae Osborn, later a staunch supporter of her union and of the Montgomery movement, heard her grandfather tell the stories that would become indelibly imprinted on her own consciousness.[51]

Proudly, Mrs. Johnson recounted some of Papa Belco's life: "He was a well-to-do farmer, because he had a wagon; he had a double-horse buggy [and] a single-horse buggy. He had things, you know. Now, he wasn't highly educated like my father's side, but he had a lot of common sense." Still, Mrs. Johnson wished to set the record straight with respect to her grandfather's ability to read and write, since a family history had noted that he "could not read or write after the Civil War ended." Citing this information as inaccurate, Mrs. Johnson insisted, "I know he could read; that's wrong. . . . I know he could read, because he taught me how to read." Continuing to recount his life story, she recalled, "And he told me all about his boyhood, you know. And when they took him and brought him over here, they put him in a cage, and his mother and father were screaming and hollering that that isn't fair . . . and begged [them] to buy them too, but the Hersts wouldn't buy them. . . . [The slave traders] brought him on a boat . . . to America, and the Hersts bought him. [They had a plantation] over in Letohatchee in Lowndes County. That was during the slavery time."[52]

One of Papa Belco's stories was well known in the Herst family. He recalled overhearing a meeting in which white people insisted, "The Negro is behind and . . . will always be behind."[53] Black people, they were saying, are nothing, have nothing, and should never aspire to be anything. To his granddaughter and the rest of his family, however, Papa Belco proved these white people wrong. He owned his own land and remained an independent farmer most of his life, enabling his children and grandchildren to move beyond his own limited success. Papa Belco's stories of slavery and his later experiences in the battle against white supremacy greatly influenced his family. For young Beautie Mae Osborn, they provided the inspiration to think differently about her own options, to consider how she might avoid serving white folks. Neither she nor her mother accepted the foregone conclusion that they should labor in the homes of white people. "I never did no housework, and my mother never did no housework, either. She worked for the WPA [Works Progress Administration]. . . . She did some sewing. That's the only job I know she ever did besides farming," Mrs. Johnson declared.[54] Beautie Mae Johnson never cleaned white people's houses, and after the age of fifteen she no longer farmed. Implicit in her job choices was the notion that she would not be left behind.

In the case of Rosa McCauley Parks, both maternal grandparents had experienced slavery. Her grandmother Rose Edwards (for whom Rosa was named) was five years old when the Civil War ended, old enough to remember how the plantation owner's valuables were buried in the ground to hide them from the Union soldiers. After the war, Rose's parents (Rosa Parks's great-grandparents) managed to purchase a twelve-acre farm on the Wright plantation in Pine Level, Montgomery County, where they had been enslaved. Just as she would have done if slavery had continued, six-year-old Rose trotted off to live in the "big house" to attend to the demands of the Wrights' small child. The family of Sylvester Edwards, Rosa Parks's grandfather, had fared far worse than that of his wife, Rose. Sylvester Edwards was the fair-skinned child of the plantation owner and one of the enslaved women who worked in his house, both of whom died when he was very young. As an orphan and perhaps as a physical reminder of his relationship to the former owner, he was severely abused, suffering regular beatings by the former overseer, who now owned the plantation. He was denied shoes and food, surviving on scraps secretly provided by other Black people. Rosa Parks noted, without apology or remorse, that her grandfather developed a deep hatred for white people. As Mrs. Parks recalled, "My grandfather was the one who instilled in my mother and her sisters, and in their children, that you don't put up with bad treatment from anybody. It was passed down almost in our genes."[55]

Sylvester Edwards used every opportunity to mock the supposed superiority of white folks. Taking advantage of his fair skin, he would introduce himself by his last name, shake hands with unsuspecting white men, and call them by their first names (forgoing the obligatory "Mister"). Freely, he transgressed the code of racial etiquette between African Americans and white people. Those who performed such acts of resistance to the assumed subordination of Black people, who "forgot their place" in a world no longer bound by the legal sanctions of the slave system risked severe repercussions. The gradual formulation of a complex of customary and de jure practices represented by the term *Jim Crow* was designed to elicit from the former bondspeople and their descendants a special deferential countenance and bearing. Although the Jim Crow system proved an effective method of social control, instilling in Black people a sense of inferiority, it did not eliminate excessive displays of white violence.[56]

As the lynchings and race riots of the early twentieth century confirmed, the threat of white violence was pervasive in the lives of southern Black people. It was this fear of racial violence that Rosa Parks remembered feeling in 1919, when she was six years old, as she and her grandfather Sylvester Edwards watched groups of night riders pass by their door. In a show of force that she believes was aimed at an emboldened and impatient group of returning Black war veterans, the Ku Klux Klan embarked on a frenzied period of terror-inducing night rides near the Edwards home in Montgomery County. Ready to defend his home and his family, Mrs. Parks's grandfather "kept his double-barreled shotgun close by at all times," preparing to take a few Klansmen with him if necessary. "I can remember my grandfather saying, 'I don't know how long I would last if they came breaking in here, but I'm getting the first one who comes through the door,'" recalled Mrs. Parks.[57]

As a national organization, the Klan had been revitalized in 1915 atop Stone Mountain in Georgia, stimulated by the debut of D. W. Griffith's *The Birth of a Nation*, the overlong cinematic paean to the birth of the Klan. From Stone Mountain, recruiters were deployed throughout Alabama, where by 1916 at least three klaverns had been organized, in Birmingham, Bessemer, and Montgomery. The "new" Klan, which purportedly represented the tenets of "100 percent Americanism," also advocated white supremacy, anti-Catholicism, anti-Semitism, xenophobia, and a Protestant "morality" that helped promote the klansmen's vigilance against vice and support of Prohibition. No strangers to the rural landscape, the Klan of this period traversed the countryside in Ford motorcars; they also enjoyed wide popularity in the cities, where jobs and economic security were believed to be the special preserve of white men.[58] Images of the Klan and of her grandfather rocking by the fire at night, with "his gun right by just in case,"[59] as she sat nearby fully dressed and ready to run, stayed with Mrs. Parks throughout her life.

White domination in the countryside was not enforced exclusively by the Klan, however, and despite what the white landowners may have wished, not all farming families gave in to intimidation. In a re-creation of some of the more insidious conditions of the slave system, as Lillie Means Lewis recalled, the white owner of the plantation on which her family sharecropped would ride among the workers to assess their performance. Mrs. Lewis remembered that on one occasion she, her siblings, and her father had all had quite enough of the allegations by the man on horseback that the Means children were poor workers:

See, my father knew better that we were doing what *he* was saying. But that man would come out across the field and then he would tell us that he wanted us to do just the way [he said]—but we would do like our father [said]. . . . We got at him one time. We ran him from across the field with our hoe, and we got at him. He come out there bothering us ... and we ran behind him to catch him. We didn't catch him, because if we had ...

And my daddy was out across the field out there, and he saw him, and he stopped his mule because he was flying ... and he met him and told him, "Don't ever," he said, "don't ever bother my children." He said, "They're doing what I said [to] do, so don't ever bother them, because if you do, [I would] be sorry for you if they had caught you. I would have been sorry for you. So don't ever go 'cross and bother them anymore. Anything you want done you tell me. Don't tell my children. Don't bother my children."[60]

In an assertion of his own independence and of his right to direct his own labor and that of his children—rights that had been denied the enslaved men who worked on the Black Belt plantations—Mrs. Lewis's father issued a warning that could easily have put him and his family in harm's way. Instead, however, it served as an example of resistance to white power that remained embedded in the consciousness of the members of his family. It was not only the father who was determined to stand up for his family; the children were prepared to stand up for themselves as well.

Could such acts of resistance be retrieved, re-formed, or reenacted by the women activists of the 1950s, modified, in part, by their experiences in the city? Indeed, as their early childhood experiences reveal, the women were infused with a social context that nurtured a sense of well-being and encouraged them to defend and to demand their rights.

Daughters of the Reserves

In June 1913, at a time when rural Black people of the U.S. South were moving to the northern urban and industrial centers, the South African Parliament passed the Natives' Land Act, an exclusionary and far-reaching law that served to divest African peoples of their lands. The passage of the act helped spawn a movement of its own, the widespread displacement and subsequent migration of Black people into the towns and cities of the former British colonies and independent republics of the Union of South Africa. A significant objective of the law, however, was to create rural "reserves" of African labor for the farms and mines of the growing dominion. There was no mistaking the separatist intent of the act, whose demarcation of "scheduled native areas" that represented the only regions in which Africans were allowed to live as independent farmers helped lay the groundwork for future apartheid laws. The writer-journalist Sol Plaatje, one of the early leaders of the South African Natives National Congress (SANNC), described the effect that the act had on every Black South African: "Awaking on Friday morning, June 20, 1913, the South African native found himself, not actually a slave, but a pariah in the land of his birth."[61]

The purpose of the Land Act was to ease the strain on and ensure a brighter economic future for the unrepentant Boers (the ostensible losers in the war with the British) in two key areas: labor and land.[62] Most troubling to the rural Boers who witnessed the rapid growth of the British-controlled mining industry was the drain on what they viewed as their supply of African labor and a rapid increase in landownership by Africans. According to many Orange Free State (OFS) farmers, there was a need for legislation that favored tenantless Boer farmers who feared competition with an increasing number of successful African "squatters," tenant farmers, and sharecroppers. In addition, growing communities of African farmers provided African farm laborers with alternative sites of employment and competitive wages; by employing African farm laborers, African farmers could further alienate their labor from and possibly even drive up the costs of white farmers. Accordingly, the Natives' Land Act prohibited Africans in the four provinces from sharecropping and farm tenancy and from purchasing or renting land outside the prescribed reserves. Before a subsequent amendment increased the amount of land reserved for African people, although Africans totaled nearly 68 percent of the population, they were allowed to own only 7 percent of the land.[63]

Like Mr. Adams and other Black Belt Alabama farmers who had to decide whether to "treat, trade, or travel," many African families preferred to move on than to see their life savings disappear into the hands of the Boers. Like their U.S. counterparts, from the 1880s on, many African sharecroppers and tenants refused to accept unsatisfactory terms of remuneration. They chose, instead, to search out more favorable agreements with white farmers in the OFS or Transvaal. During the winter of 1913, however, African farming families, the dispossessed former clients and competitors of the Boers, found themselves more at the mercy of the Boer landowners than they had ever been before. With little to no notice, African farmers were forced by law to put all of their labor, equipment, and animal resources at the disposal of their former Boer associates. Unaquainted with the full scope of the law, African families—convinced that they might find more favorable terms elsewhere—searched in vain for a better proposition. Plaatje

recorded the plight of African migrant farmers who refused to accept without protest the assumption of their defeat:

> Proceeding on our journey we next came upon a native trek and heard the
> same old story of prosperity on a Dutch farm: they had raised an average eight
> hundred bags of grain each season, which, with the increased stock and sale of
> wool, gave a steady income of about £150 per year after the farmer had taken
> his share. There were gossipy rumours about somebody having met someone
> who said that someone else had overheard a conversation between the Baas
> [boss] and somebody else, to the effect that the Kaffirs were getting too rich
> on his property. This much involved tale incidentally conveys the idea that
> the Baas was himself getting too rich on his farm. For the native provides his
> own seed, his own cattle, his own labour for the ploughing, the weeding and
> the reaping, and after bagging his grain he calls in the landlord to receive his
> share, which is fifty per cent of the entire crop.
>
> All had gone well till the previous week when the Baas came to the native
> tenants with the story that a new law had been passed under which "all my
> oxen and cows must belong to him, and my family to work for £2 a month,
> failing which he gave me four days to leave the farm."[64]

Despite, in some cases, the "determined opposition of their wives,"[65]
Boer farmers were successful in transforming an independent African
peasantry into a growing class of impoverished farm laborers. The lag time
in the practical establishment of "scheduled" or "released" areas where Africans might purchase land, however, slowed the dissolution of the African peasantry. Until a more vigorous prosecution of the post–World War II
apartheid laws could be put into effect, some resourceful African farmers in
the OFS and the Transvaal managed to find ways to circumvent the worst
aspects of the act. The experiences of one family provide an excellent example of the post-1913 perseverance of African sharecroppers.[66]

Nkgono Emelia Mahlodi Pooe, who was of BaKwena and BaSotho ancestry, was born in 1882 to a family of labor tenants who worked in the
area of Heilbron in the OFS. Late in the 1890s the family made the difficult decision to become sharecroppers. According to Mrs. Pooe, her father,
Rankwane Molefe, who was an experienced farmer, decided to try his hand
at sharecropping "even though there [were] not enough oxen to pull the
plough."[67] Over his older brother's objections to sharing any part of the
hard-earned harvest with a Boer, Rankwane Molefe plowed another field
with the use of his neighbors' oxen and eventually began sharecropping

with another family member at Zaaiplaas. When drought and locusts prevented Mr. Molefe from making any harvest, Emelia Mahlodi and her mother helped to compensate for the loss by going to work on the distant farm of an aunt, in exchange for ten bags of sorghum.

Although Rankwane Molefe eventually managed to purchase a span of his own oxen, the South African War left the family interned in a British military camp, bereft of their livestock, *trekgoed*,[68] and other resources. Taking advantage of the situation, the owner at Zaaiplaas agreed to furnish the supplies that Mr. Molefe needed, but on new sharecropping terms. Instead of the usual fifty-fifty split, Mr. Molefe would have to turn over two-thirds to three-quarters of the crop. Mrs. Pooe recalled, "We watched tens and tens of bags of maize and grain-sorghum going to the side of the Boer."[69]

In 1906 Emelia Mahlodi married a young sharecropper, Naphtali Pooe. Especially after 1913, she and Naphtali worked a series of farms as sharecroppers, and Naphtali combined farming with teaching school. The Pooes worked their land and raised their children amid communities of kinfolk. Families of the more prosperous 'croppers and the somewhat less fortunate labor-tenants worked cooperatively, sharing resources and joining work parties, much like the Black Belt farmers of Alabama. During the first year of the Natives' Land Act, when the Pooes' landlord informed them that they would have to sell some of their cattle, they were forced to move away from their tight-knit community. Refusing to sell any of his small herd, Naphtali Pooe set out by bicycle or by horse for "many long days in search of a new place where they could do sharecropping."[70] Mrs. Emelia Mahlodi Pooe recalled her husband's persistence in finding a place for them to live and work:

> [It was] as if Boers had all formed a conspiracy whereby they had vowed never to take any black men on sharecropping terms.... They would come back to report that one Boer had promised them a farm on which he wanted to settle sharecroppers. They would then go there to see what kind of soil there was and to assess the prospects of settling there. The name of the farm was Ceres. When they arrived there they discovered to their disappointment that it was an area of very poor soil with a sour grass cover—a clear indication of poor soil—which would make it very difficult to practise sharecropping profitably.[71]

Naphtali Pooe ultimately found suitable land and a willing landlord at Oorbietjiesfontein on the northern bank of the Vaal, just inside the Transvaal, where there was plenty of good grazing land and an excellent supply of water. He and his wife moved their three children to Oorbietjiesfontein, where their three youngest children were later born. Ranging far from their farm in search of a good return on their produce, the Pooes found that Potchesfstroom, a two-day journey by ox wagon, fetched the best prices for sorghum and maize.

Acknowledging the fierce competition between her family and the hapless *bywoners*,[72] who farmed "almost on the same basis as sharecroppers," Mrs. Emelia Mahlodi Pooe hinged her family's success on the effective use of women's labor:

> With us blacks, I would go out into the fields with my husband and perhaps with my children if they were already old enough. With the Boers as *bywoners* it was different. Normally their wives couldn't go out into the fields to hoe. The husband would have to do the hoeing alone. Or sometimes he would take out money to pay for whomever he could hire. With us we would hoe together with Naphtali or organise a work-party. In fact our competition with the *bywoner* was appreciated by Theuns [the landowner] himself. Theuns would remark that he had at last got the real "*Vrystaatse mense*"—people who are used to work and did . . . proper farming wherever they came from. He would say that before anyone could wake up Napthali's span would be in the fields with most part of a day's work behind him.[73]

Of course, the full use of women's labor among both BaSotho-BaTswana peoples and the Nguni speakers was a common and critical aspect of agricultural production in precolonial southern Africa and through at least the first third of the twentieth century. Although they were not generally responsible for plowing (after the introduction of the ox-drawn plow in the late 1830s),[74] women participated in all aspects of crop production, from hoeing to threshing (see chapter 1). Even raising and caring for large herds of cattle did not preclude the vigorous production of sorghum, maize, and winter wheat that—especially when herds were low and grazing was difficult—sustained African societies. As the principal growers of such crops, African women played a vital role in the fields, providing sustenance for their communities. Mrs. Emelia Mahlodi Pooe understood the significance of the role that African women played in their own agricultural production, which stood in stark contrast with the European custom of keeping their women out of the fields. She observed, too, that the Boer farmers' self-interest in fostering competition between African farmers and *bywoners* also served to stimulate success among African sharecroppers.

Fieldwork was not the only area, of course, where the labor of African women was treated as a valuable commodity. The domestic labor of women was considered part of the sharecropper's and landowner's post-harvest *akkoorde*.[75] These agreements were made during the winter, when tenants and sharecroppers (like their Alabama counterparts) trekked to the farms of other landlords in search of better terms. Looking back on her days as a young unmarried woman, Mrs. Emelia Mahlodi Pooe was aware of the value of her own and her mother's potential for domestic labor in their landlord's household, and she was proud that her father had refused to include it in the yearly *akkoord*:

> Even when he happened to have trekked from somewhere and was looking for a new place to stay on a new farm and perhaps the new Boer [landlord] wants him [my father] to give his wife to wash for the Boer's wife or that I as his daughter [go] to work in the kitchen, my father never accepted such terms in the agreement—terms according to which his wife would have to do washing for the white farmer's wife and the daughter to work in the kitchen. . . . He argued very strongly. He said to the white man: "I and I only work for you."[76]

Similarly, during the 1920–1921 season, Naphtali Pooe refused to allow the landlord to beat his eleven-year-old son, Ranchawe. Mr. Pooe chose, instead, to move his family to another farm. He barred the labor of his wife and daughters from inclusion in the *akkoorde* until the family finally left sharecropping in 1940. By the 1950s the elder Pooes had joined their sons in Soweto.

Many of the women who migrated to the towns and cities of a rapidly industrializing South Africa were among those who protested their economic and political disempowerment in the OFS in 1913 (and future political resistance by women in Johannesburg in the 1940s and 1950s was also actively supported by a contingent of rural women who had made the city their home). Just as the Bloemfontein women withheld their labor from white households and burned their passes in 1913, there were rural Black women who held firm in their insistence that they "did not work for whites."[77]

Mrs. Ernestina Mekgwe, whose mother was counted among the women who did not work for the Boers during her rural days, was born in the rural district of Rustenburg in 1906 and migrated to Johannesburg in the mid-1920s. As a longtime domestic worker in the city, she became a staunch supporter of the bus boycotts and pass resistance of the 1950s. She grew up in the western Transvaal town of Phokeng, where the BaFokeng—known as prosperous and independent peasant farmers—have successfully mixed their agriculturally based economy with platinum mining since the 1940s.[78] Mrs. Mekgwe recalled this early prosperity: "Our main occupation during those years was farming and it was really profitable. No woman ever thought of going to work for a white man.... Women got rich only through farming."[79] Mrs. Mekgwe does not describe her family as rich, although her father held three fields and owned thirty head of cattle and twelve donkeys. Her mother worked the fields, sewed for the family, and decorated the house. They grew enough produce to satisfy their needs: "At home while growing up we made about fifteen bags [of sorghum] every season and these saw us through to the next season.... When we wanted sugar we sold some, when we needed paraffin we also sold some or exchanged it for paraffin or other various needs.... We never went short of anything, [because] we ploughed and our needs were met through selling our produce, not (like) today when our lives are controlled by a small coin."[80]

Integral to the well-being of BaFokeng families and communities, as in all African societies, were the skills and labor of children. The labor of boys and girls followed the pattern for the labor of men and women—that is, the division of labor by sex (barring such special circumstances as the absence of male children) remained in place. Certainly, a girl was expected to work with her mother, helping her labor in the fields, clean and prepare the house and courtyard, cook, fetch water, thresh grain, collect firewood, run errands, and care for younger children. Phokeng girls handled the plow or even herded the cattle if the need arose. Nthana Emily Mokale—domestic worker, factory operative, and 1950s defier of the Sophiatown removals—who had no brothers, had herded her family's cattle. She had also handled all the household chores, including the cooking and washing.[81] By fulfilling the work expectations of their respective communities, both rural South African and Black Belt Alabama youth contributed to the persistence of and achieved adult status in their communities.

Many of the women activists who grew up in the rural districts of South Africa shared the experience of participating in communal work parties, or work camps (*matsema*, in SeTswana).[82] The work camps accommodated the seasonal flow of tasks—such as plowing, reaping, or threshing—too large for a single family to accomplish. This practice helped to instill in the women an understanding of the crucial nature of not only mutual assistance within the larger community but also the role of women. It was the responsibility of the person who convened the work party to arrange for the participants to assemble and to act as host to the group by supplying sufficient refreshments. The women of the host family prepared the food but often received additional provisions from other women in the community. The men and women brought their own tools and equipment, and the children ran errands and kept the workers supplied with water.

Ellen Kuzwayo, an ardent supporter of Black liberation and women's issues in her adopted home of Soweto and nationally, was born in the district of Thaba 'Nchu in the OFS in 1914. In her autobiography, *Call Me Woman*, she remembered looking forward to the convening of the work camps when she spent time on her grandfather's farm. No one shirked the responsibility of helping a neighbor with whatever was required: "Every family, including my grandfather's, the landlord's, made an effort to be represented, even if this meant seconding someone. Joining in the camp was both hard work and a celebration." A large undertaking that required a great deal of work and cooperation, the *matsema* was a special time for the community. "I anticipated the work-camps with great joy and expectation, even when I was away at college—these were the events I genuinely looked forward to on my arrival home."[83]

Once the food had been prepared and the communal meal had ended, everyone enjoyed lively singing and dance performances. The work, food, singing, and dancing were all part of what brought the community together, as Mrs. Kuzwayo recalled:

The main meal, including plenty of beer, was kept as the last event of the day. Everybody participated in this meal—men, women and children, but it was accepted in those days that *bojaloa* [homemade beer] was for the adults only. . . . The climax of the day was highlighted by dancing and singing after the day's hard work. This was a well-earned relaxation and entertainment. Womenfolk excelled in the dance "Mokhibo." "Mohobelo" and "Mokorotlo" are two corresponding dances for BaSotho men. . . . The music is sombre and the mood of the men is subdued. In some instances one man will lead as a soloist and the others respond in harmony.

On the other hand, "Mokhibo" can be performed by individual women or in pairs. The participants kneel upright facing each other. The movement is concentrated on the breasts and shoulders, extending to the arms, with an occasional neck movement. If it is done by those with experience, it becomes a real joy to watch.

"Moqoqopelo," by contrast, is a free-for-all. Those who provide music and clapping of hands stand in a circle round the main dancers. Generally, the dance is by partners, male and female. . . . It was a great joy to participate in "Moqoqopelo" as a young girl. In this fashion, every work-camp was brought to a close with great joy and excitement which lingered in one's mind for weeks or months after the event.[84]

Mrs. Kuzwayo credits the women of her rural district with the overall success of the work camps and, by implication, with the strong cooperative nature of their community. In addition to their crucial labor in the fields, the women were responsible for preparing the food for the workers and their families and producing *bojaloa*, the home-brewed beer traditionally served at important village gatherings and family events. Their brewing skills were widely known and appreciated, cultivated within each family and passed on from mother to daughter. Naboth Mokgatle, a famous son of the BaFokeng, has affirmed the importance of a woman's skill at brewing: "A woman found good at brewing beer is regarded as a copy of her mother, and the unfortunate one who cannot is also taken for granted as a copy of her upbringing. The reason given is that a woman must be in a position to entertain her husband and his guests. When men complain of hunger, they are understood to mean that they have had no beer for a long time. My mother was one of the fortunate ones who was always praised for being an expert in the art of brewing."[85]

Through a series of complicated steps, a good brewer could develop her traditional skill by trial and error. She would turn sprouted and dried corn or sorghum into *momela* and then grind and ferment it over a period of many days. Then she would boil, harden, and liquefy the substance, ferment it once again, and finally strain it and allow it to mature.[86] A woman in a rural area could earn a much coveted reputation as a skilled brewer; a woman in the city, after perfecting a shortened process that generally yielded a stronger product, could use her skill to provide enough income to support her family. In effect, for women in the city, beer brewing represented an important link between their past lives of rural independence and their struggle to live independently in pre-apartheid and apartheid-era urban areas. Such important survival skills, learned in the rural context, allowed a single woman or a community of women in the city to exhibit their independence in economic and political terms.[87]

In rural communities, mature and married women were entrusted with the training and education of their daughters as responsible and capable wives and mothers. Informal instruction took place on a daily basis, as an integral part of the everyday chores necessary for families and communities to thrive. Instruction could take the form of direct intervention in the performance of a task or indirect modeling of important behaviors and attitudes. Respect for men and for elders was strongly reinforced as was deference to white people, through the use of such appellations as "Baas," "Baassie," and "Mistress." There were, of course, exceptions, and African women may have had more leeway in expressing their displeasure over the more insidious forms of white control than did African men. Ellen Kuzwayo recalled, for instance, that her grandmother, Magdeline Segogoane Makgothi, was known for her fierce attitude in dealing with the Boers:

> Unlike my grandfather, who was a gentle person, my grandmother was outspoken and direct in her speech and dealings, to the point of being blunt....I can never forget how on one of our many trips in the family Cape carriage (a covered four-wheeler) to Thaba 'Nchu, she monitored and commented on Grandfather's driving for the whole of the journey. The bone of contention was that she felt Grandfather was giving too much space to any white farmer's cart, car or carriage travelling in the opposite direction. She repeatedly told him: "Jeremiah, you must not go more out of the way for the other traffic than is necessary. You are entitled to your portion of the road as much as they are." In a gentle way, Grandpa would reply, "It is all right, Segogoane[;] do not worry!" He was unruffled by her remarks throughout the 30-mile journey. To use the modern expression, he kept his cool, and always with a slightly remote smile.
>
> The climax of the journey came when we reached town and stopped while my grandparents did some shopping. As the couple were discussing their plans, and deciding what to do, a white lady, close to Grandma's age, approached the carriage and addressed herself to Grandma in Afrikaans, saying something like "Ek soek 'n meid wat in my kombuis kan werk" ["I am looking for a maid to work in my kitchen"]. My grandma gave her one look and without a moment's hesitation, replied: "I am also looking for that type of person—can you help?"... The white lady turned her back and left without a word. Grandpa was more embarrassed than hurt. He spoke firmly but softly to Grandma as if objecting to her reply. That incident shows just how straightforward Grandma was in her talk. It left a lasting impression on my mind.[88]

Mrs. Makgothi's attitude toward white people revealed a strong desire not to leave direct confrontation with them solely to the men. She responded to a woman and a system that routinely branded her as so much expendable labor. Kuzwayo was left with a vivid impression of her grand-mother's keen insight and quick tongue, much like Maggie Resha's memory of her own straightforward grandmother. Growing up in rural Matatiele in the Eastern Cape, south of Thaba 'Nchu, the young Maggie tried to com-prehend her grandmother's explanation for why she could not have a Eu-ropean doll: "'You cannot cry for European dolls,' she said, 'because these people have taken our country and they have money.'"[89] The importance of these attitudes toward their imposed subordination was not lost on the two young girls, who later recalled the wisdom of their grandmothers' teach-ings and became strong, independent women capable of taking the lead and speaking their minds.

Traditionally, before the more widespread acceptance of mission educa-tion for children and adolescents, young girls were expected to undergo an initiation process to achieve inclusion in the society of adults. By the 1920s and 1930s, however, this practice had become quite controversial. Many Christian-educated Africans, striving to adopt a new set of Western moral attitudes and expectations embedded in a rapidly industrializing South Africa, decried the old practices. During the 1940s, initiation ceremonies (called *bojale* or *bogadi* for young women) were still taking place in a few so-cieties, but for the majority of BaTswana, "owing to the influence of Chris-tianity [the initiation ceremonies] ha[d] long been abandoned."[90]

The initiation rituals were part of a larger regimental tradition that had not been wholly abandoned by the BaTswana. The initiates as a group were called into existence by their chief every four to seven years and named by him in a way that identified them and reflected their collective experience ("those who go with rain," for instance). These new adults were honored in celebration and respected by each member of their community. Before its demise, the *bojale* ceremony took place in the village, presumably within the view of the Western missionaries who made their way there. The complex set of rituals included explicit instruction about sex, marriage, and relation-ships with men; physical hardships and punishments; and an operation or physical procedure, such as branding on the inner thigh. The young women also received instruction in the agricultural and domestic life of the com-munity and participated in singing, dancing, and masquerading. Once the ceremonies were completed, the initiates were considered marriageable.[91]

Ellen Kuzwayo recalled that in her BaSotho village in the 1920s, when she was growing up, girls' *lebollo* (initiation, or *Lebello*, as Mrs. Kuzwayo refers to the process) was still being practiced within a context of extremely divided opinion. Because her parents were practicing Christians, they refused to allow her to undergo the traditional rite of passage supervised by some of the mothers of the community. What Mrs. Kuzwayo knew of the process she had gleaned from accounts by others and from her own observations. Unlike the boys, who were reputed to be, at best, antagonistic toward those who tried to intrude on their session,

> the girls ... were peaceful and harmless. On their return [from initiation school] they assumed an air of superiority, and openly looked down on those who had not been through this process. In addition to this, they refused to share their experience of the *Lebollo* or give any information related to it with anyone of their age group who had not been there. ... All the same I got to know that for the two or three months that the girls were there they had female tutors who were themselves graduates of that school; further, that sex education was one of the areas that was given attention.[92]

Mrs. Kuzwayo observed that the rarity of pregnancy before marriage was a direct consequence of the moral shaping combined with the explicit instruction on human sexuality provided at the initiation schools. The *basue* (women instructors in *lebollo*), she commented, "played a very important role in building up the moral standards and personal stability of young girls of that time; a very important role, regardless of the low opinion educated Christian people had about *Lebollo*."[93]

In *lebollo* lay a significant difference between the experiences of South African and Alabama women that had important ramifications with respect to the tone, shape, and content of their future political activism. South African women who underwent *lebollo*, who—together—were named, required to endure hardships, and instructed in the intricacies of sexual relations with their future husbands, were provided with a strong sense of themselves as women, separate from men. The initiation process offered a way to understand, accept, and prepare collectively for their particular set of circumstances, both good and bad, which stemmed from or impacted their condition as women. *Lebollo* was an acknowledged way to celebrate, as a group, women's exceptionality, talents, and crucial role in their communities. Such training was not formalized in the same way among African American women; in fact, few Black women in the United States during or before the 1950s could boast that by the age of sixteen their female elders had fully informed them about sexual matters.[94] In contrast, by fomenting a particular women's consciousness, African women's full immersion in a sector of their society created by and for them could later be translated into women's activism in resistance to political and economic forces. Women's passes, the exclusion of nightly bus service, the erection of municipal beer halls displacing women's beer brewing—all threatened a large cohort of married women, mothers, and grandmothers *as women*. Any definition of feminist practice in the lives of South African women should include a reinterpretation of *lebollo* viewed in this light.

In spite of the Christian community's view of the practice of initiation as heathen, the formal recognition of the collective entry of young people into adulthood was reimagined in the practice of confirmation. Ernestina Mekgwe recalled the importance of the confirmation schools as a substitution for *lebollo*. In a syncretic blending of Christian and BaTswana belief, young women and men between the ages of sixteen and eighteen were organized by the missionaries, separately by sex, after which they petitioned their chief for a name, attended several months of Christian education classes, and were celebrated at their confirmation ceremony. Once confirmed, young BaTswana men and women were expected to discontinue their education at the mission schools and assume greater responsibilities, such as finding employment or getting married. Mrs. Mekgwe remembered, "We had to attend confirmation school for three or four months. After that period we were expected to know the rules of the church well. . . . During the Confirmation Day we were then dressed up beautifully in German-style clothes. . . . My first pair of shoes I wore in 1924 for the confirmation ceremony at Penzhorn's church. . . . [My parents bought me] shoes, dresses, and this would be the first time in your life that you wore new clothes."[95]

In addition to offering instruction in the church catechism, European missionaries, often in competition with their U.S. and West Indian counterparts, taught standard school subjects, including the written forms of English and several African languages. Assisted by African student linguists, who routinely spoke a host of languages unfamiliar to the missionaries, some Christian evangelicals helped translate the Bible into SeSotho or SeTswana. Ellen Kuzwayo reported that in about 1883, her maternal grandfather, Jeremiah Makoloi Makgothi, played a significant role in the translation of the New Testament into SeRolong. Makgothi, a graduate of Lovedale Institution, was a teacher and (with Plaatje) a leader of the SANNC.[96] Ernest Penzhorn, the German Lutheran missionary at Phokeng, translated the Bible into SeSotho in the 1880s. Penzhorn's translations proved to be no guarantee that the African faithful would remain committed to his program, however. When A. A. Morrison, a West Indian ordained by the African Methodist Episcopal bishop Henry M. Turner in 1898, arrived in Phokeng offering to teach the rudiments of English, many BaFokeng Lutherans sent their children to his school.[97] Increasingly, SeSotho- and SeTswana-speaking parents, no doubt surmising the future utility to African men and women, chose the schools that taught English. Arriving in South Africa in 1913, the Reverend Kenneth Spooner, a Barbadian Pentecostal missionary, enjoyed a great deal of popularity among Transvaal BaSotho-BaTswana families. In spite of Spooner's disapproval of polygamous marriages and the use of medications in treating illnesses, parents wanted their children to benefit from his instruction in reading, writing, and speaking English.[98]

Crisscrossing the vast southern African landscape were a host of Anglican, African Methodist Episcopal, Methodist, Lutheran, Presbyterian, and other European and U.S. missionary societies concerned with more than saving souls. As the Reverend Dr. James Stewart—principal and guiding light of the Lovedale Missionary Institution—believed, Christianization would produce in African men and women the desirable effect of civilization: "If possible, we avoid doing things twice. When a man is Christianized, that is when the great change has really taken place in him[;] he is generally civilised as well."[99] Stewart and other missionaries designed their school curricula to instill in students the values and assumptions of the "morally fit" and "mentally superior" teachers and evangelists who trained them. By the mid-nineteenth century—at the instigation of the governor at the Cape, Sir George Grey, who had previously worked among the Maori of New Zealand—"industrial education" had been incorporated into mission education in order that "Bantu lads could be instructed in the civilised crafts to be carpenters, blacksmiths, and so forth."[100] Following a philosophy similar to that of Booker T. Washington of Tuskegee Institute, the Lovedale Free Church Missionary Institution and other African schools—including Ohlange Institute, established by John Langalibalele Dube, the Booker T. Washington of South Africa—aimed their instruction at the "heart, head, and hand."[101]

Among the most successful of the mission establishments was the Lovedale Free Church Missionary Institution, founded at the Eastern Cape by the Glasgow Missionary Society in 1841. Lovedale accepted students and staff from various parts of eastern and southern Africa on an interdenominational and interracial basis. At its seminary the school also trained "young men of intellectual and spiritual qualification" for the ministry, and in 1868 Lovedale added a girls' boarding school.[102] In 1898 a hospital—one of the few that served the needs of African patients—was added to the Lovedale campus, and in 1903 Lovedale began training African women as nurses.[103] The press at Lovedale, among the first to publish works by African authors, helped to provide texts for other African mission schools and also trained African students as skilled printers. Several of Ellen Kuzwayo's relatives studied at Lovedale. Her grandfather, Jeremiah Makgothi, studied printing and earned his teaching certificate there in 1878.[104] Her father, Phillip Merafe, learned printing at Lovedale and went on to practice his trade in Maseru and Johannesburg. Kuzwayo herself spent all of 1936 at Lovedale, as she recalled, "cramming a three-year syllabus into one year" in preparation for her Junior Certificate and matriculation exams.[105] She was disappointed at acquiring only the second-class pass, not enough to qualify for the matriculation class that would have entitled her to go on to the college at Fort Hare (the only school of higher education for African students at the time). Although she was happy at Lovedale, Kuzwayo decided to leave at the beginning of January 1937 to take a teaching post at the Inanda Seminary (American Board of Missions) for young women in Natal.[106]

Like their African American counterparts in Alabama, African school students had to cope with insufficient government resources and with a curriculum based on the prevailing governmental view that African youth should be trained to occupy positions of subservience. During the first two decades of the twentieth century, government grants to the mission schools on behalf of African students were piddling. Students and teachers had to make do with overcrowding, acute teacher shortages, and inadequate church facilities used as schools. In 1915, for instance, schools for European children in the "liberal" Cape Province employed 5,290 teachers for 105,742 students, whereas schools for African children employed 4,003 teachers for 137,238 students. In other words, the European school pupil-teacher ratio stood at about 20:1, whereas the African school pupil-teacher ratio stood at about 34:1. For the same year, instructors in European schools earned an average of £109, whereas instructors in African schools earned an average of £24. Similarly, in 1915 Cape expenditures for new buildings for European schools amounted to £114,664, whereas no expenditures were made for buildings for African schools.[107] In the Transvaal and in the OFS, where African families were, of course, not exempt from paying annual taxes, African students fared even worse. For the nearly 16,000 African students in the Transvaal, the government granted £15,000 toward their education; for the 10,000 or more students in the OFS, government expenditure amounted to little to none.[108]

In the 1930s and 1940s, government expenditures were still fixed within a well-defined segregated context. Ostensibly, the Union of South Africa government was responsible for funding Black education, and the provincial governments were responsible for overseeing Black education. This general arrangement persisted through much of the 1940s. The considerable taxes that African people paid supplemented the fixed central government expenditure and were subject to increase. In contrast, between 1930 and 1945, per capita government expenditures for white students increased from just over twenty-two pounds, twelve shillings to thirty-eight pounds. Per capita government expenditures for Black students increased from little more than two pounds to almost four pounds in the same period. Although the number of Black students who attended school nearly doubled, in 1945 most Black students were concentrated in the lower grades; only 3.4 percent were in grades beyond primary school.[109] As a result, of course, the same poor educational conditions that had existed in 1915 obtained overall during this period: Teacher shortages persisted; many instructors were inadequately trained; books, furniture, and other school supplies were insufficient; and school buildings were inadequate.

In 1930, at age seven, Maggie Tsiu began her schooling in Matatiele in the Eastern Cape, just outside the former Transkei. By law, Mrs. Resha recalled, Black children were not to begin school before age seven. Parents who adhered to traditional customs, who had not recorded the birth dates of their children, had to instruct their children in counting to seven on their fingers or by using small stones, to ensure that they were prepared to answer any questions about their age. Mrs. Resha recalled that she walked to the schoolhouse, some three miles from her home, without shoes and that she endured the school day without food. The school building housed several groups of children—Sub-A, Sub-B, and Standards 1–3—in two rooms. Only the Standard 3 class, which was taught by the principal, merited a room of its own; all other classes were crowded together in a single room. Mrs. Resha described the conditions:

To ease some of the disturbance [of a crowded classroom], classes were held outside when the weather was good. Inside, we used to sit on benches to listen to the teacher. But, when it came to writing, we used to kneel on the floor and use the benches as desks. In Sub-A we wrote with a slate pencil on black slates, while from Sub-B we used exercise books and pencils. Among the lessons we took were reading, writing, arithmetic, poetry, and music; we also learnt sewing, weaving mats and baskets, dictation, and mental arithmetic.[110]

By the time Maggie Tsiu was ten or eleven years old, she was able to transfer to a school in Ramohlakoana (seventy miles from her grandmother's home), which included instruction through Standard 6. Students came from all over the region, including Lesotho, to receive instruction in the higher grades. Maggie Tsiu's aunt, a domestic worker and seamstress who earned fourteen shillings per month, took responsibility for paying her school fees, which amounted to fourteen pounds to twenty-eight pounds per year.[111] The students' coursework at Ramohlakoana included English, SeSotho, arithmetic, history, geography, physiology and hygiene, nature study, music, sewing, and cooking. Students also took part in sports activities. At age sixteen, over the objections of her paternal grandmother—who perceived education for girls as no more than extraneous knowledge—Maggie was able to continue her schooling. Many considered the three-year preparation for the Junior Certificate and the teaching profession to be education for boys. According to prevailing notions, since girls were to marry and raise families, they had no need for education that did not further that purpose. Indeed, Maggie's sister was attending St. Margaret's, an industrial school that offered courses in cooking, knitting, and weaving. Maggie's mother, however, was a woman of independent thought who insisted—despite the economic hardship that it would entail—that Maggie be allowed to break from custom and become the first girl from their area to "take boys' education."[112]

In 1939 Maggie Tsiu began her studies for her Junior Certificate—which included English, Xhosa, Latin, and biology—at the Welsh High School in East London. In January 1942 she successfully completed her Junior Certificate course of study, passing the Form III examination that entitled her to train as a nurse. Mrs. Resha recalled that while she was studying at the Welsh High School, she was "taken on visits to museums, aquariums and many other places connected with [the] lessons." She also recalled that she and her fellow students were allowed to take their classes in biology and in physiology and hygiene at the better-equipped white high school for boys nearby. In line with the segregated social practices of the time, noted Mrs. Resha, "[we] had to wait until after they had finished their lessons before we could go there for our lessons."[113]

On a visit to her hometown of Matatiele during the six-month hiatus between the end of her exams and the beginning of her nurses' training in July 1942, Maggie Tsiu noticed how much the landscape and the people had changed since she had left three years before. Viewing her community from a privileged, Westernized perspective, Maggie had to come to grips with the rapidly deteriorating conditions in which her people were living. Maggie's maternal grandmother attributed the increasing impoverishment of her people to their exploitation by the white folks who had taken over their country. Gone, Maggie observed, were the large flocks of sheep and cattle that could no longer be sustained on exhausted soil. Gone, too—having migrated to the cities in search of work—were the many young men and women with whom she had spent her childhood. Only a few had had the privilege of being schooled beyond the primary grades; fewer still had had the opportunity to pursue the Junior Certificate. Maggie Resha recalled that she came to the shocking realization "that for an African child to get [an] education, was like a camel passing through a needle's hole."[114]

Still, the daughters and sons of the rural South Africans, like those from Alabama, found ways to educate themselves, worship together, and eke out a living on the lands that they were fortunate enough to own or stubborn enough to 'crop. The young men and women were among the last generations to experience a direct line of traditions and practices that stemmed from the independent African peoples or the formerly enslaved African Americans. Those traditions had proved vital to the collective survival of people who contended with forces that were bent, it would seem, on their very destruction. Instead of bearing witness to their parents' or grandparents' demise, Ellen Kuzwayo, Maggie Resha, Amy Collins Harris, Rosa Parks, and others of their caliber learned from their elders practical skills and courageous attitudes that translated into the competence and conviction that they exhibited throughout their lives and especially during the eruptions of the 1950s.

Ms. Charlotte Manye (Maxeke), most likely at the time of her graduation from Wilberforce University in 1901. (Wilberforce University Archives.)

Alexandra boycotters walking at dawn, 1957. Photo by Eli Weinberg (UWC-Robben Island Mayibuye Archives).

Policeman checking belongings during Alexandra bus boycott, 1957. Photo by Eli Weinberg (UWC-Robben Island Mayibuye Archives).

Domestic worker and policeman, Johannesburg, 1950s. Photo by Eli Weinberg (UWC-Robben Island Mayibuye Archives).

Women's march to Pretoria, August 9, 1956. *From left:* Ms. Rahima Moosa, Mrs. Lilian Ngoyi, Mrs. Helen Joseph, and Ms. Sophie Williams. Photo by Bob Gosani (BAHA).

Woman walking in the African tradition during the 1955–1956 Montgomery bus boycott. Photo by Don Cravens (Getty Images).

Walkers during the 1955–1956 Montgomery bus boycott. Photo by Don Cravens (Getty Images).

African National Congress supporters during the Treason Trial, Johannesburg, 1956. Photo by Eli Weinberg (UWC-Robben Island Mayibuye Archives).

Nurses' demonstration, Soweto, 1958.
Photo by Bob Gosani (BAHA).

Mrs. Bertha Mashaba Gxowa at the African National Congress Women's League office, Johannesburg, 2006.

Michael Motshele and Mrs. Rachel Maredi Motshele, Alexandra, August 1997.

Mrs. Florence Nomathamsangqa Siwedi, Soweto, July 1997.

Reliance Manufacturing Company workers, n.d. (Photo courtesy of Mrs. Beautie Mae Johnson.)

Union organizers at their open-air social, n.d.: Frank Gregory (*top row, third from left*), Mrs. Beautie Mae Johnson (*bottom row, third from left*), and Edgar Daniel (E. D.) Nixon (*middle row, third from right*). (Photo courtesy of Mrs. Beautie Mae Johnson.)

Mrs. Beautie Mae Johnson, Montgomery, April 1997.

Mrs. Irene Williams (*left*) and Mrs. Cora McHaney (*right*), Montgomery, April 1997.

Mrs. Ethel Mae Smith Alexander and Ezekiel Alexander, Montgomery, April 1997.

Mrs. Amelia Scott Green, Montgomery, April 1997.

Mrs. Maggie Tsiu Resha,
Ramohlakoana, Eastern Cape,
July 2001.

Mrs. Kate Mxakatho, Soweto,
July 1997.

Chapter Four

"LOOKING FOR BETTER"

Montgomery, Johannesburg, and the
Urban Context, 1920s–1940s

I N 1924, when Rosa McCauley left rural Pine Level without her mother for the first time, it was to continue her education in Montgomery. She would attend the Montgomery Industrial School for Girls, a private school for Black girls—known informally as Miss White's—that was run and staffed by white women from the North.[1] Rosa and her younger brother, Sylvester, had been attending a school in Spring Hill—some eight miles from their home—where their mother, Leona Edwards McCauley, taught. Despite frequent bouts of tonsillitis, young Rosa usually walked the distance with her brother. She knew, however, that if she wanted to continue beyond the sixth grade, she would have to venture to Montgomery and pay tuition for the privilege. Rosa had spent time with her mother in Montgomery during the summers when Mrs. McCauley attended Alabama State Normal to update her teacher certification. The decision to send Rosa to school in Montgomery was eased by the fact that the McCauleys had relatives there. While she was a student at Miss White's, Rosa lived with her mother's sister, Fannie Williamson, and her four children. In order to help defray the cost of tuition, Rosa worked at the school cleaning classrooms. She also assisted her aunt Fannie, who had a job cleaning at the Jewish Country Club.[2] No stranger to work, Rosa had helped in the fields, milked cows, cooked, washed, quilted, and performed general housekeeping chores on the Pine Level farm from a young age.[3] Rosa's acceptance at Miss White's at the age of eleven had been contingent upon her repeating the fifth grade there, but by midyear, she had already been promoted to the sixth.

At Miss White's Rosa enjoyed the "usual classroom subjects, like English and science and geography."[4] She also enjoyed the domestic science courses, including cooking, sewing, and caring for the ill. As it turned out, she would soon put these skills to use, nursing her mother and grandmother back home at Pine Level and running the household, until she married at the age of nineteen. Traditionally, however, this kind of training was provided to young girls by the women in their communities. Certainly, this fact contributed to the opposition of many Black people to the Hampton-Tuskegee model of education, which they believed prepared their young people for no more than subservience.[5] In contrast, what Rosa liked best about her time at Miss White's was the way her teachers emphasized self-respect: "What I learned best at Miss White's school," Mrs. Parks recalled, "was that I was a person with dignity and self-respect, and I should not set my sights lower than anybody else just because I was black. We were taught to be ambitious and to believe that we could do what we wanted in life. This was not something I learned just at Miss White's school. I had learned it from my grandparents and my mother too. But what I had learned at home was reinforced by the teachers I had at Miss White's school."[6] During the period of the boycott, the sense of dignity and self-respect that Rosa McCauley Parks carried throughout her lifetime was apparent to many. Early in life, she had demonstrated an inner strength and sense of fair play. As a young girl, she had assertively defended herself and her younger brother against bullying by neighborhood white boys in Montgomery. "The habit of protecting my little brother helped me learn to protect myself," she recalled. "I had a very strong sense of what was fair."[7]

Rosa McCauley finished the eighth grade at Miss White's before it closed in 1928. She attended ninth grade at the Booker T. Washington Junior High School and then completed the tenth grade and part of the eleventh at the Alabama State Normal laboratory school before leaving to take care of her ailing grandmother. During the early 1930s, when Rosa was studying at the laboratory school, a public high school education was not available to Black students in Montgomery. As the educator and writer Horace Mann Bond put it, in 1930, "the Capital City, with a Negro population in excess of 30,000, maintained no public senior high school for Negroes."[8] After Rosa Parks returned to Montgomery as a married woman in 1932, she finally had the opportunity to complete her high school education.[9]

. . .

Born in 1913, the same year as Rosa Parks, Kate Mxakatho—a stalwart African National Congress (ANC) Women's League campaigner during the 1950s—began school in her rural hometown of Makapanstad, to the north of Pretoria in the former South African Transvaal. Kate Mxakatho's Ba-

Sotho parents were both educated Christians who wanted their eldest daughter, Kate, and her seven siblings to have an education. "It is said that I didn't want to play with the other children who were not at school. I went to school at the age of eight. Then the schooling was from [age] ten." Kate Mxakatho thus began her education early and went on to take teacher training courses at Kilnerton Institution, a Methodist boarding school about eighteen miles east of Pretoria. When she completed her training, she was sent back to her home district to teach the early primary grades at a small mission school. "I loved school," Mrs. Mxakatho recalled. "Even now if I could go back to school, I would be there in a minute. I loved reading." She also had a passion for the teaching that she began in 1936 and for her hometown community of people, who taught her so much:

> I loved it, and I knew the happy thoughts of children. If one says . . . "May I please go out?" the next one will follow [and] then the third. What I used to do to them is that when one comes [and then] the second one, [I would say,] "Oh, just let's break." When they come back, I say, "You've all gone to the loo. . . . Now we are going to study. No nonsense, eh?" What I didn't like to do was to use the rod. . . . Where I was was at home. I was at home with children. And old people were my best friends! I learned a lot from them. About oppression I got [a lot] from them.[10]

The stories the elders told about their forced conscription by the Boers during the 1899–1902 Anglo-Boer War made a deep impression on young Kate. In 1944, after eight years of teaching, she left because she "saw the country becoming corrupt." The school authorities, she explained, "would tell us that this subject must be done in the vernacular. Now, when it became the thing [to do] . . . most of the teachers of our type had already resigned. . . . Well, I came to Johannesburg and became a domestic servant. That is why I say it is only whites who can enter by the front door."[11]

Kate Mxakatho's political analysis came as a result of a lifetime of experiences and influences. A cousin on her mother's side, Philip Matseke, was an ANC activist and ardent believer in equal rights for African people. She felt she had grown up "knowing that we are not living in a country that is normal."[12] In Johannesburg Kate Mxakatho's views were reinforced. She listened to the street corner speeches of radical Black activists and became active in the ANC Women's League. Migration to the city, where family members had preceded her, offered Mrs. Mxakatho "backdoor" employment, which brought with it unequal social relationships with white people.

Like Mrs. Parks, whose family had nurtured in her a respect for education and a nascent politics of resistance, however, Kate Mxakatho possessed a developing consciousness that she would find the means to express in the city.

During the Depression of the 1930s and before, economic necessity had pushed young Black women off the farms and plantations, and by the 1940s such economic stimulants as World War II pulled them to the city. Whether the young women from Pine Level or Makapanstad had managed to complete their elementary or high school educations before migrating to Montgomery or Johannesburg seemed to make little difference in the job opportunities that were available to them. Often the young women came in search of higher education or a better future, as their older brothers, uncles, or fathers had done before them. Others were persuaded to join their relatives or friends in order to share in opportunities that they had found. Whatever the circumstances, the women arrived in the more prosperous cities looking for something better than what they had known in the country. *Egoli* (the city of gold), as Johannesburg was known, for the truly enterprising, might actually be the city of golden prospects.

For most Black women, the choices for paid employment in the city were few. Some form of domestic work, in private homes or in commercial establishments, was the most likely opportunity. Life, however, did not consist of work alone. Newly arrived in the city, Black women sought out familiar institutions that could help ease their adjustment to a new environment. Churches and social organizations where extended family had already established a presence were often the means through which the women, as new urban migrants, began to feel as though they were at home.

"I left there and came to Montgomery"

At the age of fifteen, Ethel Mae Smith left her family to help lighten their load and raise a family of her own in Montgomery County, Alabama. Three years later in 1943, as a young married woman, she made her permanent home in the city of Montgomery. With her eleven-month-old son in tow, she was, in her own words, "looking for better." Taking advantage of the more robust economy and stronger job market that existed during World War II, she was among the millions who participated in the nationwide process known as chain migration. Through this process, rural Black people who sought employment in the industrial cities of the South, North, and West linked themselves to a network of relatives and friends who already lived in the city.[13] Her paternal aunt, Ethel Lee Smith, who worked as a maid at the Dexter Hotel, helped her get a job at the hotel and welcomed Ethel Mae (now Belser) and her family into her home while they saved to get a place of their own. As she left the last plantation, Ethel Mae was unsure whether her husband, Will Henry Belser, would follow her, but she knew that, in any event, she had to get away from the country. There had to be something better for her than the hard life she had lived as the young wife of a laborer or 'cropper:

> I tell you what I did. In the country, he said that he was going to move farther back down the hill, and I didn't want to go. I left. He followed later. . . . If you had seen it [where we were to live], you wouldn't want to go back down there neither . . . because it was way back down the hill. . . . I couldn't have seen my mother when I got ready—or any other part of the family. I went down there [to see the place]. It's all a white man's place, but I didn't like that place, and I left there and came to Montgomery. I've been here ever since.[14]

The homes of many Black Belt tenants, sharecroppers, and laborers were rough wood cabins with few amenities other than, perhaps, a wood stove and a few pieces of furniture. Typically, they were not equipped with indoor plumbing, had no nearby source of clean water, and were far from the nearest neighbors.[15] Finding his wife gone, Will Henry grabbed his belongings and followed her that very same day.

Quickly discovering that the hotel job paid too little to survive on, Ethel Mae Belser sought work elsewhere in the city. Determined to stay in Montgomery, she found a job waiting tables at the Douglas Cafe on Monroe Street. Mrs. Alexander recalled that her inexperience may have been obvious: "I did like that work, but at that time, being young and just from the country I wasn't smiling a lot, so I didn't make a lot of tips like some of the people. I would hear the soldiers—there were a lot of soldiers down there. There was a USO [United Service Organizations center] right next door to there. They would say, 'You're not smiling; you're not going to get a tip.' You know, I'm just a young person from the country, but I like it [anyway]."[16] Still, she proved resourceful in moving on to the next job if one failed to suit her. She received help from her network of family members in caring for her baby son and found jobs at a commercial laundry, at another High Street cafe, and as a day worker for various military families at Maxwell Air Field. She and Belser had two more children before their marriage broke up in the mid-1940s. She stayed at home with her children when they were infants and resumed work once they were old enough to be left in the care of others. She attended church once a month in the nearby town of Ramer and became a member of Bethel Baptist Church in Montgomery in 1950. At the bus stop one day, on her way to work, she met the man who became her second husband, Ezekiel Alexander. He purchased a car during their courtship, and they were married soon thereafter, in 1947.[17]

Through the same migratory process, Amy Collins left for Montgomery in 1942 to join cousins who were already in the city. She felt that it was past time for her to be on her own, away from her parents' protection, taking care of herself and her son. William Washington, Amy Collins's cousin, had arrived in Montgomery to attend Alabama State Normal. His sister, Fannie Washington, who followed him, found work at the Reliance shirt factory. She met and married Frank Matthews, a plasterer, and together the couple bought a house, where William, Fannie, and Frank lived. As William Washington prepared to enter the army, Frank Matthews died suddenly. At his funeral, Fannie Matthews asked her cousin Amy Collins if she would like to join her in Montgomery:

> After the funeral was over, we went to Fan's house, and she told me, she said, "Amy . . . William fittin' to go in the service, and you back home. . . . Why don't you come up here and stay with me?" I said, "You have to write Mama." I said, "You know when you go back home, it's just like 'fore you ever left there." She said, "I write Aunt Fannie."
>
> She wrote Mama. My daddy didn't want me to come 'cause he said he could take care of me anytime. I told him, "No." I said, "I'm grown now; I need to take care of myself." So, Mama and I together, we talked to him, and I came. I got up there that Saturday on the bus, and she took me to the factory that Monday and I got hired.[18]

Amy Collins had already left home once. Just after her unexpected wedding to Henry Brown in 1937, the young couple had left Allenville for New York, where her two oldest brothers and older sister had migrated earlier that decade. Richard and John Collins frequently visited their parents and other family members in Alabama, and when they returned to New York from one of those visits, they took their sister Leola with them. Once Leola had settled in a job and a living situation, her husband joined her in Mt. Vernon, New York. Because she and her husband lived in the home of the white family they worked for, they had to make different living arrangements for their three children. "She left the children. The oldest child was four, the middle one was two, and the baby was eleven months. She left them with us, with Mama, and I was there. So we did for them. And when the oldest one was fourteen, Leola came and she carried them with her."[19]

Like her older brothers, Leola visited her family often and, after one of those visits, she returned to New York with her younger sister Amy. Before she became pregnant with her first child, Amy Collins (Brown) found a job as a live-in domestic worker, but that lasted for only about three months. Unhappy in her marriage and in New York, she returned to her family in Allenville in 1939. Then in 1942 she left her small son in the care of her parents and joined her cousin in Montgomery. In Montgomery she soon found a church home at Bethel Baptist, where Fannie Matthews was a member, and joined both the choir and the Usher Board. Happy in Montgomery, she determined that this was where she would begin again. "I liked the people that I met and I liked the church. . . . I just liked it," Mrs. Harris explained.[20] She also liked George Harris, whom she had met through Fan's young man, who was stationed with him at Tuskegee in the 378th division, 4th battalion of the U.S. Army Airborne. Amy and George Harris were married in 1944 before he had to ship out for Okinawa. In 1946, when her husband was discharged from the army and they had a place on Troy Street, Mrs. Harris brought her eight-year-old son, Henry, to Montgomery to complete the family circle.[21]

The positions most often available to Black women in Montgomery were low-paying domestic, factory, hotel, and restaurant jobs. Still, they offered Black women an economic independence that they had not known in the country. The World War II–era economy brought with it the freedom to change jobs and employers. The opportunity to reap the benefits of future prospects in an urban context was as enticing to Black women as it was to Black men. Even in the face of low-paying jobs, the dangers inherent in traveling alone, and pressing concerns about the care of their children, Black women chose to risk their futures on the possibility of a new and better life.[22]

According to the U.S. census for 1940, the three areas that employed the highest numbers of "nonwhite" women in Montgomery were, in descending order, domestic service, nondomestic service, and manufacturing. Of the 6,793 "nonwhite" female workers in Montgomery fourteen years of age and older, nearly 5,000 were employed as domestic workers, more than 700 were employed in service jobs outside of private homes, and almost 500 were employed in factories. Only 92 Black women held clerical positions, but 409 held unspecified professional positions—most likely, for the most part, in the teaching and nursing professions, since in all of Alabama that year only one Black woman practiced law and only five Black women practiced medicine.[23]

The salaries for Black teachers were notoriously low in comparison with those of their white counterparts. In 1930 Bond reported that, in the Black Belt region, the per capita expenditure for the salaries of Black teachers of Black children were $2.73, whereas the per capita expenditure for the salaries of white teachers of white children were $31.99.[24] According to Mrs. Irene Williams, a retired teacher from Montgomery, in the 1930s and 1940s Black schoolteachers in Montgomery County earned $27 to $28 per month and typically boarded with individual families, who provided them with both food and housing.[25] On the other end of the wage scale, a woman who lived in as a domestic worker in Montgomery during the early 1940s could hope to earn only between $4 and $5 per week.[26] According to Mrs. Amelia Scott Green, a retired domestic worker from Montgomery, day labor paid even less—sometimes half the wage for a live-in domestic worker, or $2.50 per week.[27] Piecework at the shirt factory paid very little, especially at the outset. In the early days at Reliance Manufacturing Company, women shirttail hemmers earned 25¢ per hundred completed shirttails. Mrs. Idessa Redden recalled that in her early days at the factory during the late 1920s, she earned $9 every two weeks. By the end of her tenure there, during World War II, she was earning about $45 every two weeks.[28] Thus (especially during the war period, when factory double shifts became commonplace), Black women teachers applied for jobs at Reliance during the summer months, when school was not in session—a practice that sheds some light on the tenuousness of their middle-class status.[29]

Although the Black women workers of Montgomery may have owed the majority of their days (and frequently their nights as well) to white families or to factories, hotels, laundries, schools, and restaurants, some portion of their evenings and weekends belonged to them. Some spent their leisure time in the county juke joints or private social clubs, fraternal organizations, or the Black movie house on the east side. On Sundays, however, the overwhelming majority of the African American population could be found in any one of the many Black churches in the city. Serving by far the highest percentage of the Black population were the Baptist churches, among them First Baptist, Dexter Avenue, Beulah Baptist, Bethel Baptist,

Hutchinson Missionary, and Holt Street. Founded by the early twentieth century, these were several of the churches that were active in the 1955–1956 bus boycott. Women played a critical role in carrying out the mission of the Black Baptist church, which was not only to nurture the spiritual development of the congregation but also to help provide the material needs of the wider community. They usually supported several other domestic and overseas missionary projects as well. In a church that stood solidly at the center of community life, providing a space for the social interaction and empowerment of Black people, women figured prominently in its local, regional, and national organizational structure.[30]

Ms. Gwen Bell, a member of Holt Street Baptist Church throughout her life, recalled her mother's full-time involvement in the missionary society of their church. The General Missionary Society at Holt Street began during the pastorate of the Reverend A. W. Wilson, who had come to Holt Street with his wife, Mrs. Annie Mae Wilson, from a small church in Macon County in 1939. A vigorous organizer, Mrs. Wilson capitalized on the energies of the churchwomen, inaugurating five mission circle groups: the Matrons, the Youth Group, a kindergarten for small children, regular Bible study, and continued care for the needy. After Gwen Bell joined the church at age eight, she regularly attended Sunday services with her mother and her siblings and accompanied her mother to the Circle #3 missionary meetings during the week:

> I started when I was with my mother 'cause I used to go to Missionary Society with her. I learned to sing hymns from attending Missionary Society. When you went to Missionary Society, you could just feel something, because the people would just sing the hymns, what we call the Old One-Hundred. They would start off singing, [and] then talk awhile and sing awhile with it. . . . "Father I pray . . ."—you know, like that. I learned to do that. I also learned the meaning of prayer [by] listening to the people pray.
>
> Gussie Nesbit could sing a hymn, and she was serious about anything pertaining to religion. And whenever the circle meetings [met] from house to house, she would have that meeting—she would sing and pray for thirty, thirty-five minutes. And then they would have the Bible lessons, teach the Bible lessons, and they would serve refreshments. The meetings would last about an hour and a half to two hours. And she would always have what you would call a fun time at the end of every meeting, and she could make you laugh.[31]

Gwen Bell saw the missionary circles as part of the collective work of the women members of Holt Street, culminating in the annual presentation of the Women's Day Program, which was usually held the third Sunday in November. The meetings were both enjoyable and productive—the women were expert fund-raisers. While they contributed to the overall mission of the church, they also pooled part of their proceeds to support the attendance of local women delegates at the National Convention held in September:

> What it is is for the women to get together, meet[ing] at certain times, according to your schedule, and to study the Bible. And [the purpose is also] to do mission work, [to] go out and visit the sick or something if somebody needs help and come back to the General Mission, which is held the Monday after the first Sunday. All groups come together, and they will make a general report of what they have done for a whole month for the community. Each circle will make their report.... They would raise money for the purpose of going to the convention.... That was ... the large financial goal. The other was to give to the sick, to those who needed the utilities paid. Or, you know, sometimes there were families where the children didn't have clothes or whatever, [or the mission might be to] buy medicine, different purposes.... We had to pay anywhere from fifteen to twenty dollars a month, this was your [circle] quota.... See, Holt Street was known for helping people. It didn't make any difference [who you were]. It was known for helping.[32]

The hundreds of women church members who ministered to the needs of their urban neighbors were vital to the growth and development of the churches of Montgomery and to the many important programs they sponsored. Missionary church work was quite involved, but it was also an opportunity for women, many of whom were former migrants, to create their own spaces for relaxation, enjoyment, and sisterhood during their off-hours. Montgomery churchwomen were known not only as expert fund-raisers but also as capable administrators in the distribution of those funds. In the process of strengthening their churches and their communities spiritually and materially, women gained valuable experience in public leadership, which they put to use especially at the convention level, where they became full participants in the ongoing discussion of Black empowerment.

Many of the young rural women who made their way to Montgomery arrived with little to recommend them as prosperous urban dwellers. Their early lives in the country had familiarized them with the realities of hard work, little income, inadequate education, and the constant struggle against white supremacy. Those who were able to gain a more stable economic footing in the city in their later lives could credit their preparation through the baptism of fire in the lessons of survival that they had learned from their elders as young girls in the country. Their rural upbringings in Hale, Lowndes, and Montgomery Counties taught them various forms of resistance to injustice, buffered by strong ties to their communities of friends and family. These ties also assisted the women in their successful transition from rural daughter to resourceful wife, mother, and employee. In rural South Africa similar transitions took place.

"Going to Johannesburg . . . was like a means to an end"

When Black women without qualification beyond the Junior Certificate who had been teaching in rural South African primary schools chose or were forced by circumstance to migrate to the cities, they found few jobs outside of domestic or factory work. Teaching primary school children was itself a rewarding experience for many, but it was difficult to parlay into other kinds of work in a market in which so few jobs were open to Black women.

In a situation similar to that of Kate Mxakatho, Mrs. Rachel Maredi Motshele—an ANC Women's League activist during the 1950s—tried nurses' training after teaching primary school for several years and finally had to abandon teaching altogether for employment in Johannesburg. Rachel Maredi was born in 1923 on a farm near Pietersburg in the northern Transvaal, the youngest of nine children. She was educated with her twin brother at mission boarding schools and completed her Junior Certificate at age seventeen. She went on to spend two years in teacher training at Kilnerton and was posted at a primary school at Blauburg in the Transvaal for four years. She described the location as "rural, rural, rural," adding, "There was nothing!"[33] Rachel Maredi taught for another four years at a rural school at Carlsrhue before she tried her hand at nurses' training in response to the urgent need for nurses during World War II. After only two weeks in training at Pietersburg Hospital, Rachel Maredi realized that she did not have a strong enough stomach for the job. When she returned to teaching at Potgietersrus, the Nationalists had come to power and were beginning to weed out teachers who would not or could not instruct their children in Afrikaans:

> They introduced Bantu education. And when I said I don't know about Bantu education, I was expelled from teaching . . . because I would not teach Bantu education, something I myself did not know what it was. I didn't know what it was. They musn't be taught history; they mustn't be taught geography; they mustn't be taught English; they mustn't be taught what and what. It must only be in their own language—only in Afrikaans. I was not taught Afrikaans at school then. . . . So we were asked at this time by [Hendrik Frensch] Verwoerd [the prime minister] to go and teach Afrikaans in our own language.[34]

Faced with the problem of what kind of work to pursue and where to find it, Rachel Maredi decided to join her eldest sister, a domestic worker in Johannesburg, who lived with her family in Alexandra, on the outskirts of Johannesburg. Arriving in Alexandra for the first time in 1949, Rachel Maredi had never seen so many people in one place before: "No, no. It took time; it took time. My God! I really just didn't know. . . . What were these people doing? Where do they come from? Where are they going to? And then to find [that] twelve of them come from one yard! And I don't see houses; I only see a big bunk like this. And I say, 'What's happening?' It really surprised me." Rachel Maredi found work near the sprawling, bustling city of Johannesburg when she responded to a newspaper advertisement placed by a "very nice Jewish couple"[35] who lived in Bramley. She also found her future husband. On a Sunday afternoon just after church, while she was having tea with a friend at an outdoor cafe near Park Station, she met Michael Motshele, a handsome young man in an army uniform. She thought he was quite rude at the time, but he would not be dissuaded from wooing her, and in 1953 they were married.

Frances Goitsemeng Baard did not teach for as many years as Rachel Motshele or Kate Mxakatho. Born in 1908 to educated BaTswana parents in Kimberley, Frances Goitsemeng completed through Standard Six at mission schools in Bechuanaland (Botswana) and Greenpoint Township, just outside Kimberley. During her second year at the Perseverance Training School for Black teachers, when Frances Goitsemeng was sixteen or seventeen years old, her father's sudden death forced her to leave school to find a way to support herself. Her brother-in-law found her a teaching job at Perdeberg in the Orange Free State, where she taught for more than a year: "It was almost like a farm school. Some of the children were small, but some of them were nearly as big as me! I was teaching general subjects to all of the children, ABC, and the 1, 2, 3, and so forth. I taught those children reading and writing for about a year, and things were going quite well for me. Then they told me I must leave the school because they wanted a qualified teacher and I was not qualified."[36] Forced out of the primary school teaching profession, she had to scramble to find a job as a live-in domestic worker in Bloemfontein and Port Elizabeth.[37]

Like the majority of Black women in South Africa, Frances Goitsemeng had received training that prepared her only for unskilled labor in a society that reserved the skilled and well-paying jobs for white people. She was unhappy with her job in Bloemfontein. She disliked domestic work—the wages were too low; the employers were "rude"; and, as a live-in worker, she had to leave her two small children with her brother in Kimberley. In Port Elizabeth, Frances Goitsemeng stayed with a former school friend while she took advantage of the enhanced job market at the onset of World War II and found work with more amiable employers who paid better wages. In 1947, after she had married Lucas Baard, a former classmate from Kimberley, and had her fourth child, Mrs. Baard finally left domestic work behind. She found a job in a canning factory that enabled her to go home to her family at night.[38] Becoming more politicized through her factory work, and ultimately joining the ANC Women's League, Mrs. Baard went on to become a magnificent voice for national liberation and trade union organization and an outstanding leader among the women who were active in political resistance.

Juggling the demands of family and work in the fast-paced, over-crowded, segregated, often dangerous urban areas, where such amenities as indoor plumbing were available only to white people, these women from rural backgrounds managed to create spaces where they could express their ingenuity, flexibility, and creativity. Most ingenious of all was their ability to turn month after month of inadequate pay into enough to sustain their families in the costly industrial cities of South Africa. Rent was high, and food was expensive. Children's school fees had to be paid, and in several Black areas of Johannesburg residents were charged for access to water and sewerage. In 1935 no Black male worker on the Reef who earned an average twenty shillings per week could come close to supporting his family without the incomes of his wife, children, and boarders.[39] A woman supporting her family on her own faced a particularly difficult struggle. Yet Black women not only found ways to earn money to buy furniture; pay their church fees;

and keep their children clothed, fed, and in school; they also found time to participate in the vibrant life of their communities.

Young women who migrated to the city, often after completing their confirmations, usually went directly into domestic service jobs to support themselves or to contribute to their families' upkeep. For some women, however, as the ardent 1950s activist Mrs. Naomi Setshedi testified, there were other reasons for migrating to the city:

> Going to Johannesburg or any of these towns was like a means to an end[;] it also had some adventure in it. Even if I had stayed at home I would not have starved. There was a sense of freedom about staying on your own in Johannesburg, and things like furniture [that] we had seen others bring as fruits of their work in the towns urged us to follow suit. We had all seen our older sisters returning from such towns with beautiful dresses, shoes. . . . Men always took notice of such girls and our sisters always had many boyfriends around them.[40]

Direct kin and extended networks of kin, people from home who had already made the transition to the city, helped to establish the young women in their jobs. At age eighteen, with the aid of her older brother, who worked at a dairy in a Johannesburg suburb, Mrs. Setshedi recalled, she found a place to stay with a female relative. "I found that woman very helpful, because she also kept her ear to the ground, trying to find out whether there was a job for me. She ultimately got me a job."[41] Women domestic workers earned an average of three pounds per month in the 1920s, a sum that remained unchanged into the mid-1930s.[42] For these wages, Black women who worked in white households were expected to perform duties that included caring for the children and cooking, cleaning, and washing for the family. Domestic workers typically occupied small, cold backyard rooms on the premises, where occasionally they were permitted to entertain friends. On their traditional Thursdays or partial Sundays off, they might get together with friends at church or at Zoo Lake. Young women often met young men through their friends or relatives.[43] By the time young women were married and raising their own families, however, full-time, live-in domestic service had to give way to a form of domestic work that could more easily accommodate their needs.

Thus, many adult working-class women turned to part-time domestic work (usually taking in laundry) or to beer brewing, street hawking, or even prostitution in order to make ends meet. Women's labor was just as integral a part of the city economy as of the rural indigenous and capitalist economies. In the mid-1930s a woman could earn anywhere from two shillings, six cents for one day of washing to forty-five shillings (two pounds, five shillings) per month washing for two European families every week.[44] Women could also rent their sewing machines to their neighbors or charge a small fee for making them dresses, skirts, aprons, or blouses. Some sold snuff from the tobacco leaves they ground; others sold fruits or vegetables on the streets. The income from these sales was often nominal, however. Beer brewing, an extremely labor-intensive task, was by far the most lucrative enterprise. In the mid 1930s good beer brewers in Rooiyard, a Black community in central Johannesburg that has since been demolished, could take in between three pounds, ten shillings and four pounds, ten shillings per month from weekend sales.[45] Thus, considering that in 1927, according to the Joint Council of Europeans and Africans, the minimum monthly expenditures for a Black family of five for rent, food, and other essentials (excluding clothes and furniture) should amount to roughly six pounds, ten shillings, women's beer earnings were an essential supplement to the income of men.[46]

Beer brewers ran the perpetual risk of police raids, fines, and imprisonment for their illegal activity. For a woman with small children, living on the edge of subsistence, these risks were high. Women took to creating alcoholic beverages that brewed faster or without boiling. The popular Barberton, made from bread, yeast, brown sugar, and water, often garnered a heavier fine for its brewers; *skokiaan* and the infamous "kill-me-quick" were two other potent and popular brews that could be made in time for weekend sales if police found and destroyed the buried stash begun earlier in the week.[47] The municipal beer halls designed to raise revenues from Black people also posed a threat to independent women beer brewers. In 1939, the women responded by effectively boycotting the municipal beer hall in the Western Native Township.[48] Clearly, despite the threats, Black women in Johannesburg were making a statement about the importance of this work to their economic independence. Ida Molefe, an anti-pass activist in Randfontein who was originally from Phokeng, admitted that she "managed to buy and sell liquor ... [buying it at] a bottle store in town." She explained, "The bottle store owner was in favour of me, [so] that was why he did not report me to the police. . . . I was once arrested because of selling homemade beer known as *mgomboti* in our language and fined eight rand.... I made more money [than by working as a domestic] and I was able to buy furniture for my house."[49] For Ida Molefe the gains outweighed the risks.

Also balancing out the risks and hard work was the lively and colorful urban culture that grew up around the beer-brewing trade, which opened avenues for expression in a multifaceted African social life.[50] As the proprietors of the ubiquitous *shebeens*—the rooms where music, dance, and beer all came together—women played a major part in the birth of the musical forms that have characterized the distinctive sound of South African jazz for several generations. On Saturday nights, when miners, houseboys, cooks, and washerwomen came to the townships looking for entertainment and for release from the boss's scrutinizing gaze, the *shebeen* "queens" had cleared out their rooms of extraneous furniture in preparation for the infusion of restless workers. Typically, the hosts would hire a pennywhistle band or a lone *marabi* musician, prepare "fatcakes" and other food, and preside over the proceedings well into the early hours of the following morning, all in exchange for a small fee. Larger dances and concerts where big-band performers perfected U.S. and South African musical styles were also venues for liquor and home brew and attracted both working-class and middle-class patrons. During World War II, the Jazz Maniacs of Sophiatown and other big bands were hired to play for Black servicemen in the Allied forces.[51] To the delight of their audiences, outstanding women vocalists, such as Dolly Rathebe, Susan Gabashane, Thoko Thomo, and Miriam Makeba, fronted both big bands and small during the 1940s and 1950s.[52] Implicit in the songs, music, dance, and illegal liquor was a politics of cultural resistance that would not be stilled by the frequent appearance of the policemen's *khwela khwela*.[53]

For Black women in the cities, leisure time included more than the culture of beer brewing and beer consumption. Women were members of organized groups through their churches, through the Young Women's Christian Association (YWCA), and through their schools. Perhaps the most visible of the women's groups were the *manyano* prayer union associations of the Methodist church and other denominations. Proud exemplars of spiritual zeal, members dressed in uniforms with colorful collars, blouses, jackets, hats, and sashes. The *manyano* groups formed throughout rural South Africa in the late nineteenth century and in Johannesburg in the early twentieth century.[54] These organizations, which emphasized women's prayer and devotion to their faith, were reminiscent of the women's missionary circles of the Baptist churches. The *manyanos* ultimately claimed an independent identity that did not fall under the supervision of white missionary women. By 1937 the first African woman president had been elected to a three-year term as head of the Methodist prayer unions.[55]

The *manyano* groups, which were formed within an efficient administrative structure highlighted by the annual meeting, were generally led by ministers' wives. Many domestic workers and washerwomen were counted among the organizations' regular membership. Women met on Thursdays to pray for the spiritual well-being of their families and their communities. During Sunday services, members assisted their ministers in prayer and song. They took care of the ill, supervised young women, and raised money for missionary or other purposes. Women members who did not heed the call of the organization to stop brewing beer in order to promote sober and morally healthy homes were not awarded the prized silver brooches for distinguished service. Despite this tension, by 1940 Reef membership totaled approximately five thousand women. In these groups African women gained valuable experience in organizing other women and in handling and disbursing their own funds. Although collectively the groups were a valuable arm of the church, their individual activities did not tend to center on activist Christian notions of social justice. Lilian Ngoyi, future leader of the Federation of South African Women, noted that *manyano* members enthusiastically wailed for Jesus Christ at Easter time as though their tears were enough to alleviate his (or their) suffering.[56] Nevertheless, even without becoming a self-identified political entity, *manyano* women sporting their colorful uniforms loudly enacted a politics of resistance at the 1956 women's anti-pass demonstration in Pretoria.

Also providing mutual support and practical organizing experience were the women's savings organizations known as the *stokvel*. Somewhat akin to domestic workers' penny-savers' clubs in the United States,[57] *stokvel* participants met in round-robin fashion at each other's houses and donated to the hostess a sum of money intended to augment her household or other expenses. In times of urgent need, the *stokvel* provided its members with the same sort of economic cushion offered by any other mutual benefit society crucial to Black community survival. Ellen Hellmann recorded *stokvel* activities in Rooiyard during the mid-1930s, and the practice continues throughout the city today.[58] Because the *stokvel* was also begun as a way to dispose of the beer left over from the sales of the previous week, some, like Nthana Mokale, regarded *stokvel* activities as immoral. Nevertheless, many have been willing to join the groups and risk the criticism. Naomi Setshedi, for instance, took part in the *stokvel* "against her conscience," because, in her words, "I found them very helpful."[59] In addition to operating in many instances as investment groups, the *stokvels* have served as social clubs in which women can find sympathetic ears for their troubles, joyful expression in their music, enjoyment of the food they prepare, and edification in the speeches made. Thus, the *stokvel* has remained a strong manifestation of women's imaginative self-sufficiency.

. . .

In the new urban context, familial links often provided the necessary first steps to jobs, housing, and new social interactions. Propelling women out of their rural family environment was a determination to find something better than the declining economic conditions the country could offer. As older brothers, uncles, and fathers left their families for Birmingham, Kimberley, Montgomery, Cleveland, or Johannesburg, rural daughters followed to create their own new beginnings in the city. Leaving the country did not mean leaving behind their roots, however. The important people, markers, and feelings came along. The rural U.S. South and rural southern Africa were fertile ground for lessons of social injustice for Black people. Important examples of the resistance of their elders provided future women activists with living witness of how to speak out boldly to those in power and survive to speak out boldly again.

The women often found employment in the city that mirrored their work experiences on the farms. Daughters of sharecroppers skilled in the art of beer brewing turned this art to their profit. Limited in their choices of employment, young women from the country often took jobs that extended their domestic roles into the paid workforce. Few women could get by without performing some sort of domestic labor in the city—cleaning, cooking, and laundering in private homes, in hotels, in cafeterias, in cafes, and in commercial laundries or sewing or canning food in factories. Domestic work—even if only a part-time supplement to income from other sources in the informal sector—seemed unavoidable. For U.S and South African women, entrance into the manufacturing sector came slowly, with the rigid color bar that was in place for the relatively few women employed. Factory wages for Black women, although extremely low, were still higher than any income that they had ever had in the country. Women's wages were used overwhelmingly to benefit both family and community.

During their leisure time, women found ways to meet and support other women in their communities. Segregated spaces—townships, churches, women's organizations—proved fertile ground for their individual and collective energies and provided valuable outlets for their many skills and talents. As they came together in women's groups, they nurtured the attributes of self-sufficiency and collective female action taught in childhood. In pooling their critical material and moral support through networks and organizations, Black women honed the skills that they would put to use in the 1950s uprisings.

Ultimately, the early lives of these rural daughters prepared them for the many changes they would experience in the city. Their rural upbringing, which instilled in them a sense of their history, a pride in their self-sufficiency, and a willingness to persevere in the face of difficult odds, contributed greatly to their marked transformations. As urban women, they became attuned to the people and processes that would control them and sought ways to resist this control as they cared for their families and communities. In the process, they gained valuable preparation for the wide-scale political resistance of the 1950s that was soon to come.

Chapter Five

"MY POLITICS WERE INFLUENCED FROM THE TRADE UNION"

Raising Political Consciousness, 1930s–1940s

IN 1928 the New York–based Reliance Manufacturing Company opened a plant in the capital city of Montgomery, in the middle of the Alabama cotton belt, where there was easy transportation and a healthy supply of cheap Black labor. The factory, which produced men's shirts and (later) blue jeans and navy uniforms, employed some 254 workers at its peak, most of them Black women.[1] During the 1930s several attempts to organize the plant failed; however, in 1945, at the suggestion of (and with the labor connections of) Edgar Daniel (E. D.) Nixon, a leader of the 1955–1956 Montgomery bus boycott, the plant affiliated as Local 490 of the Amalgamated Clothing Workers of America (ACWA), a member of the Congress of Industrial Organizations (CIO). One of the sewing machine operators who was active in the drive for union representation was Beautie Mae Osborn Johnson.[2]

After completing the ninth grade and migrating to Montgomery from her grandfather's farm in Hope Hull in 1930, Beautie Mae Osborn went to work at Reliance Manufacturing Company. By the end of her tenure, she had spent nearly thirty years as a "swing" worker, moving from job to job in the factory according to where she was needed. She fitted the forms of shirts on a special machine, faced and blocked sleeves, sewed center button strips on the fronts of the shirts, and trained and supervised other women in the use of the industrial sewing machines. In her early days at the factory she was paid according to how many pieces she could complete. "But if you didn't make nothin', then you didn't get anything," she explained. Before minimum wage was enforced in her shop, she could make between $1.25 and $1.50 a day. In 1940 minimum wage at Reliance was only 25¢ per hour.

By 1959, her last year at the factory, Mrs. Johnson was making $25 to $30 per week.[3]

In 1934, at age nineteen, Beautie Mae Osborn met and married a cutter, Charlie Johnson. The cutter jobs, skilled and higher-paying positions at Reliance, were reserved for the men. Very few women made it to the cutting room. No Black woman was ever hired for any clerical position at the plant. The administrative staff was all white, and (apparently in an effort to keep it that way) the plant manager, Clarence Giesing, was hired out of Kalamazoo, Michigan. When ACWA was finally successful in launching a local at the plant in 1945, Mrs. Johnson was among the enthusiastic workers who had voted it in. Thereafter, she became a shop steward, traveling to out-of-state meetings for her local. Already a registered voter in the state of Alabama when the plant became unionized, Mrs. Johnson nevertheless credits her union activity with helping to politicize her thinking: "See, I was a member of the AFL-CIO [American Federation of Labor–Congress of Industrial Organizations], and they believed in [integration], [and] they were trying to get some people ready so that they could integrate and [they were] trying to get them registered . . . and then I did quite a lot of traveling going different places for my union. . . . And they would always talk about that we needed to integrate and [that] we had to quit taking a little talk on integration, because, see, that's what [the governor,] Big Jim [Folsom,] did was talk."[4]

When other Black and white union organizers questioned her about conditions in Alabama, Mrs. Johnson admitted, her answers were at first quite uncritical. During the period of stepped-up migration out of the South, however, Mrs. Johnson had to face what she would do—stay or go:

> Now really and truly I did a lot of traveling going different places, and many times . . . I'd meet upon girls in the train station, and when they'd find out I came from the South, they started asking me questions about Alabama and about how we were being treated. But I didn't think nothing about it at that time. . . . And so . . . I said, "Oh well, I know my place, and since I know my place, I don't have any problem." And [later I realized] my place is supposed to be anywhere where I put my money, but you know, I didn't think too much about it. And then finally I started thinking about that you go and put your money in the bus, and then you had to go to the back to come in the back door. I started thinking about it. Well, when I started thinking about it, then I did something about it. I went and bought me a car! But when all my

friends . . . started leaving, I didn't want to go—even when my husband left. That's why we went on and separated . . . because I didn't want to go. I told them somebody had to stay here and make this a better place to live.[5]

. . .

In the 1940s, on the other side of the Atlantic Ocean, the mobilization of Black workers into labor unions in South Africa resembled the difficult fight that Black men and women had endured in the U.S. South. Many South African workers, like their U.S. counterparts, found their way to the movement for national liberation through their earlier union experiences. One such worker was the daughter of a garment worker in Johannesburg who was a former employee of her father's all-Black union: the "tall, bespectacled, [and] lively" Bertha Mashaba Gxowa. Bertha Mashaba, as she was then known, left a lasting impression on the late and legendary Helen Joseph, her organizing partner during many of the African National Congress (ANC) and Women's Federation campaigns of the 1950s.[6] Helen Joseph's memoirs[7] depict a young and energetic Mashaba, who threw herself wholeheartedly into the often frenzied pace of organizing within a growing movement for national liberation. "I had to join!" Bertha Mashaba Gxowa insisted, "for who else would do it? Who else would go to their homes and where they were? . . . There would be no one. . . . We had to mobilize the women and tell them about the evils of the pass laws . . . to conscientize them and bring them out of their homes."[8]

Bertha Mashaba, the first of eight siblings, was born and schooled in Germiston Location, an urban area on the East Rand, roughly fifteen miles from Johannesburg. Her mother, Maud Mashaba, had to travel long distances by foot or by bus to and from her job as a domestic worker in Primrose, a suburb of Germiston. Often she did not see her family for weeks: "In fact, we were actually raised by my grandmother . . . because [my mother] was a live-in domestic worker. She used to live in and come when she stayed off . . . once a month, twice a month, depending on the people she worked for."[9]

After completing her Junior Certificate, seventeen-year-old Bertha Mashaba went to work for the African Clothing Workers' Union, which was organized by and for African men who were employed in the garment industry. Among the first Africans hired to work in that industry in the Johannesburg area, Bertha Mashaba's father, John Mashaba had been among the founding organizers of the union.[10] Most of the African workers were unskilled and were paid a miserable "7 and 6," or 75¢ per week (about 1.50

rands in the early 1950s). Mashaba, however, was a skilled worker, a cutter like Charlie Johnson, but his weekly earnings of £14 (or about 28 rands) were hardly enough to support a family of eight children in the 1950s. Also a member of the rejuvenated ANC, Mashaba fused trade union politics with a growing politics of national liberation. He thus exposed his daughter to a movement and ideology that borrowed heavily from the demands and tactics of trade union politics:

> In fact, my politics were influenced from the trade union. That's why I joined politics. I went up to my JC, it's standard 9, and then I worked for the union. They sent me to commercial school to learn shorthand and bookkeeping. I was working there as a general worker in the office, attending Wage Board and shop steward meetings as a typist and I became interested. We were organizing workers to collect [membership] subscriptions of workers. We waited for them outside of the buildings—we couldn't go in. We wanted to conscientize them about workers' rights. That's where I developed politically.[11]

In 1952, at the age of eighteen, Bertha Mashaba joined the ANC Youth League "among the first batch from the Germiston area."[12] Simultaneously, she joined the Women's League and in that same year became one of the youngest members to participate in the Defiance Campaign against Unjust Laws. She was among the founding members of the Federation of South African Women and helped to organize women's participation in the framing of both the Freedom and Women's Charters. By October 27, 1955, twenty-one-year-old Bertha Mashaba was already the Transvaal secretary of the Women's League and a veteran organizer who contributed her own energy and know-how to the success of the first women's demonstration at Pretoria. She was the national organizing secretary for the massive women's demonstration in 1956. Bertha Mashaba, as her ANC Women's League compatriots sometimes still call her, continues her work today as a member of Parliament from the district of Gauteng. The struggle is not over, she has asserted, and the work continues just as painstakingly as it did when she was an organizer for the African Clothing Workers' Union. That work prepared her for the long struggle ahead and equipped her with the tools of person-to-person organizing that she so ably employed during the many women's campaigns of the 1950s.

· · ·

For both Mrs. Johnson and Mrs. Gxowa, their early factory and trade union experiences had an important influence on their lives and on their activism in the freedom movements of the 1950s. Their political awakening in the 1930s and 1940s began with their exposure to the trade union activities implemented on behalf of Black working people. First, as both Mrs. Gxowa and Mrs. Johnson admit, their understanding of the plight of Black workers and Black people in general had to be "conscientized." They had to begin to question and seek answers to why Black people continued so long under white domination. Mrs. Johnson pondered her own place in segregated Montgomery, and Mrs. Gxowa recognized the injustice in the employment circumstances of her parents. This consciousness-raising led them to union work in their efforts to resist the racist controls that bound them. Union organizing then took on a broader application, with Mrs. Johnson becoming active in voter registration and Mrs. Gxowa becoming active in the ANC Youth and Women's League. Aldon Morris has highlighted the care with which they carried out the daily, often tedious, face-to-face organizing necessary to mobilize people for important campaigns. Linking the members of their communities with the organizations they represented and winning the respect and trust of adherents, Gxowa and Johnson came to inhabit the invaluable political space of what Belinda Robnett calls "bridge leaders."[13]

Montgomery's and Johannesburg's activist women were clearly influenced by the political currents of the 1930s and 1940s that held important sway during their political coming of age. At least some of the women who participated in the boycotts and pass resistance movements of the 1950s were longtime radicals from the labor movement, the Communist Party, and other vanguard associations that called for fundamental and ultimately far-reaching social change. Events of the 1940s—World War II, the crumbling of Western imperialism, and the struggle of Black people within Africa and the diaspora to end their subordinate positions to those for whom they had fought against fascism—constituted an important context within which a new political activism could take root. After their own and their menfolk's participation in World War II, Black women had to confront the contradiction between the democratic rhetoric of the era and the reality of their racially segregated lives on the homefront. The story of Florence Siwedi (later in this chapter) represents one set of dilemmas originating from World War II experiences that set her firmly on the path of resistance.

In this chapter I look at women's political activism in Montgomery and Johannesburg during the 1930s and 1940s. On the Alabama side, several important themes emerge as key to women's later activism. The powerful example of 1930s southern injustice in the Scottsboro case affected the political development of Rosa Parks and linked her to an important model of activism. Black Alabamians played a principal role in organizing the mines, mills, farms, railroads, and garment industry, and in Montgomery the figure of E. D. Nixon, for whom Mrs. Parks had worked, loomed large among union and political activists. Established in the early 1930s, Highlander Folk School in Tennessee prepared many organizers to wage local struggles, including the 1955 uprisings in Montgomery. In South Africa, garment and other secondary industry workers produced a host of Black and African labor leaders who later called for complete national liberation. Emma Mashinini was one leader whose factory experience and friendship networks helped engender her later political activism. She was not unlike other African women who had to "push [their] arse[s]"[14] beyond reasonable limits to comply with the demands of their white bosses. Yet in the 1940s, Black workers on the Rand were willing to set their own limits and insist on their own set of demands in order to succeed in their Alexandra bus boycotts. In both the U.S. South and South Africa, despite the differences in scope and circumstance, important precursors to grassroots organizing not only signaled the possibility of fair economic conditions but also helped to bring about a significant change in future power relationships.

Organizing in Alabama

When nine Black youths from Tennessee (the youngest twelve or thirteen and the oldest nineteen or twenty years of age) were hauled off a freight train heading west through Alabama on March 25, 1931, they could not have imagined the long, complicated, painful ordeal to come. Arrested and jailed in Scottsboro, the boys were indicted five days later for the alleged rape of two young white women—Victoria Price and Ruby Bates—who had hitched a ride on the same train. In early April, in a series of trials that lasted only three days, the Scottsboro Boys, as they came to be known, were convicted by an all-white male jury and sentenced to die in the electric chair in July. Timely interventions by such players as the International Labor Defense (ILD) of the Communist Party, the National Association for the Advancement of Colored People (NAACP),[15] the Scottsboro Defense Committee, and the Supreme Court kept the pressure on the corrupt Alabama court system and its eager henchmen, preventing the defendants' executions and allowing them to appeal. For nearly two decades—throughout the many trials, demonstrations, petitions, and hearings; two landmark Supreme Court decisions that expanded the scope of the Fourteenth Amendment; and Ruby Bates's retraction of her rape allegation and admission that she and Victoria Price had fabricated the story to avoid vagrancy charges—the defendants did not find justice. In 1937 charges against four of the nine were dropped, but not until 1950 were the last two of the remaining five men either paroled or set free by the state of Alabama. In 1950, when Haywood Patterson—a defendant who had managed to escape to the North—was arrested by the Federal Bureau of Investigation (FBI), the governor of Michigan would not allow him to be extradited to Alabama.[16]

By the beginning of the Cold War period, although the long ordeal for the men had finally ended, the lasting effects of the case remained for Black southerners in particular and oppressed Black people in general. In a poignant and prophetic statement that evoked the experiences of freedom movement participants in the U.S. South and South Africa, Haywood Patterson proclaimed in his memoir, "I have had a great struggle. But I want the world to know I am unbeaten."[17]

Many Black Alabamians who came to the defense of the Scottsboro Boys had their own horror stories of white violence to tell. Indeed, the 1930s witnessed a number of cases in which advocates for poor Black defendants applied public pressure in order to protect their clients from a fate of certain death as a result of either the legal system or mob lynchings. With the initial reluctance of the Alabama NAACP to become involved, in case one or more of the youths turned out to be guilty, the ILD took on the job of galvanizing support for both the Scottsboro Boys and other Black defendants accused or rape or murder, offering free legal services as they publicized the horrifying details of their cases. The NAACP quickly recognized and came to resent the success of the ILD, whose Birmingham membership had grown to three thousand people by 1934.[18] Fear of association with communism precluded a lasting and effective partnership between the NAACP and the ILD. More moderate, reformist, and middle class and less mass based at the time, the NAACP failed to find common cause with the more militant, antiracist, anticlassist ILD. As a result, the membership of the ILD was overwhelmingly Black and from the low-income and working classes. In part because of the very competent and public defense of the Scottsboro Boys, Angelo Herndon,[19] and others, low-income and working-class Black men and women in Alabama became empowered with a political voice and a collective memory of resistance against white supremacy—attributes that would have great importance for subsequent generations of activists in Alabama and throughout the South.

Two of the Montgomery residents who got caught up in the feeding frenzy that took place at the Scottsboro courthouse were Raymond and Rosa Parks. Married in December 1932, the couple had been introduced by a mutual acquaintance and had become friends during the spring of 1931, when the case originally came to trial. Raymond Parks, a barber in Montgomery who was ten years older than his wife, was, in her words, "the first man of our race, aside from my grandfather, with whom I actually discussed anything about the racial conditions. And he was the first, aside from my grandfather and [our neighbor] Mr. Gus Vaughn, who was never actually afraid of white people." A member of the NAACP, Raymond Parks was also the first activist she had ever met. Clandestinely involved in raising money for the Scottsboro defense, he freely talked with his young sweetheart about the importance of the case. After the couple was married, Parks continued his activism for the case and for other efforts by Black radicals and activists in and around Montgomery.[20]

Mrs. Parks remembered one of the activists with whom her husband worked was a woman from Montgomery County named "Captola": Capitola Tasker and her husband, Charles, were sharecroppers who had organized for the Communist Party affiliate the Share Croppers' Union (SCU) during the 1930s. Staunch Communist Party members, they worked tirelessly to organize low-income workers—sharecroppers, tenants, and farm workers—into a mass organization that advocated higher wages, maximum working hours, and nondiscriminatory practices. The Taskers quietly produced leaflets in their home, which were distributed (to those who came in for a "trim") from the Montgomery barbershop of a Black Communist Party organizer named Al Jackson.[21] Raymond Parks may have met the Taskers through Jackson, as a fellow Black barber, or through their mutual work for the Communist party. Mrs. Parks recalled the danger and risk of her husband's underground political activities:

I was proud of [Raymond] Parks for working on behalf of the Scottsboro Boys. I also admired his courage. He could have been beaten or killed for what he was doing. . . .

I remember a meeting we had when we were living on Huffman Street in what they called a shotgun house. . . . It was the first meeting we'd ever had at our house and it was in the front room. This was the first time I'd seen so few men with so many guns. The table was covered with guns. I didn't think to offer them anything—no one was thinking of food anyway. . . .

I can remember sitting on the back porch with my feet on the top step and putting my head down on my knees, and I didn't move throughout the whole meeting. I just sat there. I guess there were about half a dozen men. I can't even remember who they were, although I probably knew them. After the meeting was over, I remember, my husband took me by the shoulders and kind of lifted me from the porch floor. I was very, very depressed about the fact that black men could not hold a meeting without fear of bodily injury or death. Also I was reminded of the time I was a child and I sat next to my grandfather waiting for the Ku Klux Klan to ride down on us.[22]

The Montgomery police, like the Ku Klux Klan, rode at night in an effort to intimidate—in this case targeting those who participated in the cause to free the Scottsboro defendants. Mrs. Parks recalled that when the couple moved from Huffman Street to South Union, the police continued their harassment of her husband and anyone else who was suspected of radical activity. In fact, she recalled that two nights before the police appeared on South Union, riding up and down on motorcycles, they "had killed two men who were connected with the group Parks was with, people Parks knew well." Raymond Parks managed to elude the police by entering the house from the back door, but his wife continued to fear for his safety. Mrs. Parks recalled another incident with a policeman shortly thereafter. At the Montgomery train station a policeman spoke to her in a threatening manner, forcefully shoved her aside, and, because she had not yet had the opportunity to purchase a ticket, refused to allow her to board the train. Feeling disrespected and racially targeted, she noticed that another Black woman had teasingly caught the policeman's attention and was laughing as he "sort of swung his club in her direction."[23]

Although Mrs. Parks linked these incidents in her mind, at the time she was unable to pinpoint the meaning of their relationship or respond to the confrontation with conviction. With the Scottsboro case clearly at the nexus of sex, race, and class relationships in Alabama and throughout the South, the electrically charged atmosphere kept white people belligerent and Black people on their guard. In a society dominated by white men accustomed to having the power to exploit Black women sexually, the highly publicized alleged rape of two white women by nine Black youths left Rosa Parks and all Black women particularly vulnerable to attack. Feeling abused and humiliated by the policeman, Rosa Parks did not miss the sexual innuendo of his interaction with the other Black woman at the train station, who—in the face of white male power—seemed to choose to meet the stereotype of Black women as Jezebels or prostitutes head on. Mrs. Parks, like many Black women under similar circumstances, had no intention of risking her good name or her family's precarious safety by challenging the policeman or even by sharing the incident with her husband. By December 1955, however, Rosa Parks was no longer willing to keep silent.

As the Scottsboro case and others like it demonstrated, in the 1930s Alabama was not a place conducive to the efforts of the more radical leftist political organizers. While the Depression tightened its noose around the neck of an already weakened farm and industrial economy in the state, putting men and women out of work and throwing farmers off the land, Communist Party and other labor organizers faced stiff opposition from an intransigent group of industrial leaders. Landowners and state authorities joined the list of those who were willing to brand anyone who worked for a change in the status quo as a Communist. Invariably, the explosive issue of race figured prominently as the divisive wedge used by those who sought to avoid, at all costs, an encroaching labor movement that actively organized both Black and white workers.[24] At the same time, low-income Black people—industrial workers, the unemployed, sharecroppers, and farm workers—sought to improve their dire economic circumstances in a way that recognized their particular struggles against racial discrimination, by turning to organizations that were not afraid to confront the institutions of white supremacy. Viewing the Communist Party as the only group prepared to uphold the interests of low-income Black men and women in Alabama in the 1930s, many joined its overwhelmingly African American membership. A majority Black membership in Alabama meant that a politically savvy Black working class could work to align its own economic and political interests with the active effort of the Communist Party to pursue "Negro self-determination in the Black Belt." The Communist International (Comintern)–inspired platform in the U.S. South encompassed jobs, labor organization, relief, an effective Scottsboro defense, and civil rights.[25] This increased political activity meant, however, that both Black and white radicals and labor organizers had to prepare for efforts at political repression by the state and the local power structure that would dog their every move.

The shoot-outs at Camp Hill and Reeltown in Tallapoosa County in the early 1930s, for instance, are indicative of Black Alabamians' willingness to use militancy to defend their right to organize and to demand fair treatment. When officers tried to break up a Communist-organized sharecroppers' union meeting, one of the attendees fired on them. Soon thereafter a group of white gunmen gathered around Camp Hill and proceeded to Reeltown, severely beating Black sharecroppers in the region and riddling their homes and cars with bullets. Ned Cobb's graphic testimony of his 1932 ordeal at Reeltown attests to Black farmers' use of armed self-defense against white men when reasoning failed. Pushed to take a stand that could have cost him his life, Cobb—who was severely wounded in the shoot-out—recalled, "I didn't have no voice. . . . But when I wouldn't stand under their whip they arrested me for *bad* crimes . . . fightin a crowd of sheriffs over what was mine and what was my friend's."[26] Cobb and other Black men and women suffered a heavy loss in terms of lives, property, and means of livelihood: White violence under the protective guise of the officials who participated reached an alarming pitch in the aftermath of such defiance. In angry but muted response to the rampaging, Communist-phobic county and city authorities, the ILD and SCU led a mass funeral procession numbering more than three-thousand people through the streets of Birmingham for the martyred men at Reeltown. Their march boldly displayed the "deep red hammer and sickle" on banners draped across the dead men's caskets. By 1934 and through the ever-worsening conditions of the Depression, in the Black Belt counties of Lowndes, Macon, Montgomery, and Dallas, SCU membership among the Black farmers hardest hit by evictions and falling farm prices had increased by leaps and bounds.[27]

Similarly, in the Alabama coal, steel, textile, and commercial laundry industries, labor organizing among Black and white workers was slow, difficult, and bloody, especially for union organizers and members who were also affiliated with the Communist Party. In May 1934 the local Birmingham leadership of the International Union of Mine, Mill and Smelter Workers (Mine Mill) were encouraged by their predominantly Black membership to call a strike for higher wages, shorter hours, and recognition of the union. The affected iron and steel companies did not hesitate to call in the police, fire and evict workers, and refuse to negotiate. In the confusion and violence that followed, two strikebreakers were killed and many workers were wounded. Although state troopers were called in, they proved ineffective against the fire bombings and gunfire between the two sides. At the end of the strike, in late June, Mine Mill was hard pressed to find any benefit—they had failed to win recognition and had gained only a negligible increase in wages. In the spring of 1935, between twelve hundred and fifteen hundred Black women laundry workers in Birmingham walked out in a strike supported by Communist Party miners, only to face vicious intimidation by laundry and dry cleaning proprietors wielding billy clubs and throwing fire bombs. With only the support of the radical labor elements, the laundry workers were forced to abandon their fight for union recognition and concede defeat.[28]

Black and white Communist Party members of Mine Mill and other labor unions bore the brunt of antilabor violence perpetrated by the civil authorities, an invigorated Klan, company thugs, and common vigilantes. The severe repression of the Depression-era strikes in Alabama put the Communist Party and labor organizers on notice that they would have to find ways to work together on behalf of workers, Black people, and the lower-income classes. If the Scottsboro case was any example of the fragile state of affairs for building political coalitions in the deep South, the most radical elements of the labor movement would have to soft-pedal their Communist Party allegiances in favor of a more inclusive liberal stance. At the same time, the integrationist-minded NAACP leadership faced criticism from inside and outside their own organizational ranks for failing to become more actively involved in the plight of the Black working class. The NAACP was admittedly impressed by the success of the Communist Party–sponsored Unemployed Councils, the determined and effective ILD, the Southern Tenant Farmers' Union, and the newly formed CIO (with help from the Communist Party) in winning the hearts and minds of Black working men and women. In 1935 the NAACP hierarchy considered a shift from its more traditional civil rights and legalistic approach to a more proactive "concern with the economic needs of the black masses."[29]

Facilitating the gradual turn of the NAACP was the 1935 decision by the Congress of the Comintern to launch the popular front (and its 1937 decision to launch the democratic front) with leftists and liberals to combat antilabor repression and promote civil rights. At the same time, it should be noted, South African Communists faced similar ideological turns wherein, first and foremost, self-determination for Black South Africans could (at least theoretically) lead to the "dictatorship" of an overwhelmingly Black proletariat. In South Africa, however, Communist Party members ultimately received a more welcoming reception from their Congress allies within the popular and democratic fronts than did their comrades in the United States. Precluding the consummation of any Communist Party–NAACP accord was the opposition of the leadership and board of the NAACP, among them Walter White and Roy Wilkins, who stood staunchly against Communist Party ideology and practice. They saw the Communist Party as thoroughly unreliable, if not dangerous to Black people, capable of conveniently turning its attention away from the priority of achieving Black equality in favor of pursuing its own political interests whenever Moscow called. However, the willingness on both sides of the Communist Party–NAACP divide to entertain broader notions of political activism than were typical of each helped to lay the groundwork for a growing Black militancy and a coalition of leftists and liberals that would prove crucial to the success of the freedom movement to come.[30]

E. D. Nixon of Montgomery, Alabama, was one of the important links between the radical labor movement and the Black southerners who increasingly insisted on economic and political justice in addition to civil equality. Nixon was an amazingly energetic and politically astute leader of the Black citizens of Montgomery, who ably combined his several interests and allegiances into a single fluid body of lifetime work: justice for Black people. In 1928 Nixon, who worked as a porter for the Pullman Company, joined the Brotherhood of Sleeping Car Porters (BSCP) after hearing the founding president of the union, A. Philip Randolph, speak at a meeting in St. Louis. Nixon recalled:

When I heard Randolph speak, it was like a light. Most eloquent man I ever heard. He done more to bring me in the fight for civil rights than anybody. Before that time I figure that a Negro would be kicked around and accept whatever the white man did. I never knew the Negro had a right to enjoy freedom like everyone else. When Randolph stood there and talked that day, it made a different man out of me. From that day on, I was determined that I was gonna fight for freedom until I was able to get some of it myself.[31]

During the 1930s Nixon remained a staunch union man while the struggle for company recognition and AFL affiliation was being waged by Randolph and his lieutenants. Integral to the effort to keep union hopes alive during the fight to gain recognition and a contract were the efforts of the Ladies Auxiliary of the BSCP. "We had a women's auxiliary. They would have fish fries and raise some money," Nixon explained. Local auxiliaries composed of the female relatives of the BSCP members were organized in 1925, at the same time that Randolph organized the brotherhood. Their purpose was to provide moral support and funds in strike situations and to add legitimacy to, if not a unified familial front on behalf of, the prodigious efforts of Black working people to gain entry into a labor movement controlled by white men. Their program in the 1930s and 1940s was to offer African American women an education in labor history and consumer consciousness. The Ladies Auxiliary also offered a real alternative to Black women's organized political participation in such organizations as the National Council of Negro Women, which (like the NAACP) emphasized watchdogging the promises that the federal administration made to Black professionals.[32] In the process, at least some of the working women of Montgomery gained important political experience in and exposure to a race ideology that took a new working-class and militant form.

As the BSCP won affiliation with the AFL, its long-pursued contract with the Pullman Company, and the right to a closed shop after 1938, Nixon handled grievances against the southern representatives of the company out of his Montgomery office. "The southern white man," he said, "couldn't see why he had to abide by a contract that was agreed upon by the Company." One of the early grievances that he appealed to the National Labor Relations Board through the BSCP was his own. Again, in a peculiarly southern sexual double standard, Nixon was written up for talking to "some woman." When he pointed out that the woman in question was his wife and demanded the same respect for her that his white supervisor would have demanded for his own wife, he was punished for his impudence by being put on mandatory leave without pay. In his hearing before the National Labor Relations Board, Nixon was exonerated. "The Pullman Company had to pay me for all the time lost," he noted. "And [the company was instructed] that my record be clear[ed] of all charges."[33] A big man with a commanding voice and a strong union background, Nixon seemed to have little difficulty responding forcefully to people who were in positions of authority.

The Reliance Manufacturing Company workers who tried repeatedly to organize sought Nixon's help. He encouraged them to continue to seek union representation, and he put them in touch with Lucille and Ed Whitt, CIO organizers in the South. Ultimately—through a series of clandestine organizing meetings in the Whitts' and others' homes in Cleveland Court and at the Elks' Club—Local 490 of the ACWA was formed in April 1945. Frank Gregory (a cutter and friend of Nixon's), Beautie Mae Johnson, and Amy Harris were three of the first six officers elected to head their local.[34]

Amy Harris reported earning perhaps 30 dollars every two weeks when she began as a third trimmer at Reliance in 1942. A trimmer, Mrs. Harris explained, used very small, sharp scissors to cut away the stray threads of a garment. Being third trimmer "meant I was the third one to get the shirt!" An employee had to work three weeks before being paid for two weeks' work, "leav[ing] a week in the hole," she recalled. Amy Harris never hesitated to join the group that organized on behalf of the ACWA. Her reasons for joining the push for affiliation were quite clear:

> I guess I was just with the gang that wanted it, 'cause a lot of people didn't want it, and I was always for advancing. . . . I just wanted to do better. If there was any such thing as doing better and progressing, I was for it! I realized that [it was kind of dangerous], but I went on anyway. I say I [can] try anything one time. . . . We were trying to improve the salary, [as] one of the main things, trying to get a raise, and then we wanted some improvements around the plant, like longer time for lunch period, things like that.[35]

In addition to longer lunch breaks and increased pay, according to Mrs. Harris, a more intangible reason, no less important than pay, prompted her to become a member of her union local: "Well, you could feel like you wouldn't be pushed around from one job to the other for no good reason. You know, they hire somebody else and demote you. You felt like you had somebody to speak for you and [to make sure that you would] not be pushed around."[36] Listening to the union representatives discuss the pursuit of equal pay for equal work, Mrs. Harris came to understand the value of the organization and the validity of the notion that Black women were entitled to a standard of fair play, equal treatment, and justice: "'Cause they would tell us in the meeting that you weren't supposed to be treated different, that if you were doing the same work, you was supposed to be getting the same pay. You wasn't supposed to be pushed back if you felt like you were doing a good job, [and they should not be able to] demote you, give your job to somebody else."[37]

In 1948 Mrs. Harris joined her colleagues from various southern locals of the ACWA at a conference at the Highlander Folk School in Monteagle, Tennessee. The school—which had been founded in 1932 by Myles Horton, the son of poor, white sharecroppers—had become a "halfway house" that figured prominently in several mid-twentieth-century U.S. movements for social change.[38] Many of the innovative features of the philosophy and practice of the school were quite radical for the time. Foremost in its approach was a strong belief in the efficacy of worker education for use in the advancement of democracy. Highlander provided early and lasting support of unionism in the South and a capable staff committed to the valuation of the wisdom and experiences of low-income, oppressed southerners. The school promoted a strong belief in the ability of ordinary people to create solutions to their own complex problems. Moreover, in 1940, in recognition of the need for the school to eradicate its own set of Jim Crow practices, Horton informed all unions with which he was affiliated that his school would associate only with organizations that did not discriminate against Black workers.

Because of the lasting relationships between the school and its more radical CIO affiliates, Highlander early acquired a reputation as a Communist organization. As a result, it suffered serious recriminations by law enforcement and the state of Tennessee and experienced numerous bomb threats. In 1949 the CIO chose to discontinue its relationship with Highlander, citing Horton's refusal to sever ties with unions that had ignored the anti-Communist provision of the Taft-Hartley Act (which outlined federal government requirements for unions). In 1961 the state of Tennessee used the technicality of the sale of beer without a license to close the doors of the Highlander Folk School. Shortly thereafter, the school relocated to Knoxville, and in 1971 it moved to rural New Market, Tennessee.

In the early 1950s, however, Septima Clark,[39] Bernice Robinson, and Esau Jenkins were instrumental in establishing the renowned citizenship education programs at Highlander, which became the model for the voter registration program of the Southern Christian Leadership Conference (SCLC). Under Clark's skillful and progressive leadership, the citizenship education programs served thousands of people dedicated to understanding and demonstrating the process of participatory democracy. Included in that number was Rosa Parks, whose experience with Clark and others at Highlander helped to fuel her NAACP activism.[40]

Pictures that Amy Collins Harris kept to document her experience at the Highlander Folk School show her enjoying her time with the Highlander staff and the thirty other Black and white delegates from fifteen southern locals. Union delegates from Mississippi, Alabama, Tennessee, northern Georgia, and West Virginia convened in Monteagle from August 14 to 15, 1948, to participate in the first ACWA education conference held for the southern delegates. There Mrs. Harris and her fellow conferees learned many "practical union-strengthening techniques" via "discussions, dramatizations, [and] demonstrations."[41] As a shop steward, Mrs. Harris had been elected as a delegate to the Monteagle conference. Her mission was to return with ideas from the training she would receive there to incorporate into the fall and winter programs scheduled at her local. She listened to suggestions from the staff and other delegates in both formal and informal groups. She learned enjoyable techniques that had been found to be useful in the development of group cohesion, and she learned to put to use music and songs adapted from southern folk and church styles for labor movement purposes.[42] At Highlander, Mrs. Harris found a reservoir of resources to buoy her political activity. By 1948 Amy Collins Harris's union and voter registration work had stood her in good stead for the boycott to come.

Organizing on the Rand

During the World War II era, Johannesburg was a vital, rapidly expanding, politically charged city full of multiethnic diversity and labor intensity. As in the United States, rapid and sizable urban population growth resulted as much from the enormous pull of industrialization that began in the mid-1930s and increased during the war years as from the push of severe rural impoverishment. Malnutrition, disease, overpopulation, droughts, and soil depletion all played a real part in driving African men and then women off the land. In 1936, for instance, the Industrial Legislation Commission of Enquiry reported that among 45 percent of the African population on the reserves the average per capita income totaled two pounds, sixteen shillings, seven cents.[43] Out of this income came the various head, hut, and poll taxes, which might amount to an estimated one pound, ten shillings per family.[44] If the reserves were becoming less hospitable to the African population, however, so too were the cities. African migrants felt the constraints of the Urban Areas Act of 1923, which allowed municipalities stricter control over the movements of African peoples through new pass laws, segregated housing, and increased police patrols. Yet in spite of the risks, many African men and women had little choice but to leave their increasingly barren homelands in search of jobs in the cities. In fact, in a sweeping two-pronged assault on already dispossessed peoples, the Native Trust and Land Act and the Native Representation Act promulgated by Prime Minister J. B. M. Hertzog, both of which were passed in 1936, eliminated the possibility for

Africans to purchase land and disenfranchised Cape Africans. Any opportunity to seek legal remedy was now removed.

Certainly Johannesburg was one of the fastest-growing cities on the African continent, with a population of just under a million in 1951. In 1946 the African population in the city had reached 387,175, 36 percent of whom (or 139,900) were women.[45] White women, many of them the daughters of cash-strapped rural Afrikaner farming families, were first off the Orange Free State (OFS) and Transvaal farms in search of factory or clerical jobs on the Rand.[46] African women, for their part, were slower to leave the rural areas, since—with their men already at work in the mines—their labor was needed on the reserves, and they were slower to enter the manufacturing industries once they arrived in Johannesburg. Moreover, African women had fewer employment options than did white women who migrated—they were left with the lowest-paying domestic service jobs. As in the United States during World War II, white men who left manufacturing jobs for the armed services or for other higher-paying jobs were often replaced by white women. As many white women found their way into clerical positions, Black women took low-skill, low-wage jobs in the factories. Hired after Colored and Indian women, African women were the last to be considered for employment. In the Transvaal clothing industry, for instance, between 1937 and 1947, the number of African women workers increased from 8 to 873, while the number of Colored women increased from 250 to 3,078. In the same manner, African women received the lowest pay, with the greatest margin of difference occurring between the wages of African women and white men.[47]

Protected by government tariffs and further stimulated by internal demand, the secondary industries—clothing, food processing, textiles, chemicals, construction, metal products, machinery, transportation equipment—expanded rapidly from the mid-1930s through the war period. In the early World War II years, as real wages began to rise and as wartime labor shortages provided jobs for more Black workers, manufacturing surpassed mining in employment and in the value of goods produced.[48] In the meantime, under Hertzog's Pact government (a coalition of Afrikaner Nationalists and the conservative Labour Party), African men—with their contracts of service regulated by the increasingly intricate pass laws—had been prohibited from qualifying as employees (as opposed to servants) since 1924. The Industrial Conciliation Act, as it was called, which established a

Wage Board that could consider minimum wages, also legalized the practice of collective bargaining and recognized the existence of trade unions for white workers. Quite openly, the act protected skilled jobs for white men and prohibited African and Indian men from belonging to registered trade unions.[49]

Nevertheless, African men continued to find jobs in urban industrial centers and—often assisted by Communist Party members—continued to form their own worker organizations. Clements Kadalie's Industrial and Commercial Workers Union (ICU), headquartered in Johannesburg after 1925, was one such organization (if not liberation movement) that sought to organize all Black workers—rural and urban, men and women, clerk and miner—into "one big union." According to the scholar and contemporary activist Edward Roux, "The first constitution of the I. C. U. was written for Kadalie by a Cape Marxist and modelled on the constitution of the Industrial Workers of the World."[50] This was true too for the African unions formed in the late 1920s and early 1930s, including the African Laundry Workers' Union; the African Clothing Workers' Union led by Gana Makabeni (formerly of the ICU); and unions of African workers in the baking, dairy, printing, chemical, and other industries that received material and ideological support from members of the Communist Party of South Africa (CPSA).[51] When the Council of Non-European Trade Unions was formed in 1942 under Makabeni's leadership for the express purpose of winning full legal recognition for African unions, twenty-nine affiliates from the Johannesburg area were represented. By 1945 the organization had extended its reach to include several industrial areas outside Johannesburg (Pretoria, Bloemfontein, Kimberley, East London, Port Elizabeth, and Cape Town), representing 119 unions and 158,000 members—some 40 percent of the nearly 400,000 African workers in manufacturing and commerce.[52]

According to Emil "Solly" Sachs, secretary of the Garment Workers' Union (GWU) and CPSA member, African women began to enter the garment industry on the Rand in 1940, as employers sought to stem labor shortages during the period of rapid wartime expansion. Sachs reported that by 1944 more than one thousand African women had taken jobs in the garment industry in the Transvaal. In his investigation of the conditions of the term *employee* under the Industrial Conciliation Act, Sachs found that contrary to prevailing opinion and to previous practice of the Industrial Council for the Clothing Industry, African women were covered under the terms of the act and were entitled to its wage and union member benefits.

Employers were slow to honor the findings of the GWU, but in December 1944 the Supreme Court ruled that Christina Okolo (who had brought the test case) and "all other African women" were, indeed, "employees." As a result of the court ruling, employers were forced to bring the wages of African women into line with union agreements and extend to African women additional benefits. Some women saw their weekly wages increase from one pound to two pounds and also qualified for quarterly increases that could bring their wages up to four pounds, twelve shillings per forty-four-hour work week after two and a half years. In addition, the women were entitled to four weeks' paid leave and also qualified for unemployment benefits.[53]

The Supreme Court decision could not reverse the establishment of a separate union division for Black workers, however. Predictably, the majority of white women co-workers in the GWU had become dissatisfied with the growing presence of Black women. Sachs blamed the formation of racially separate union branches on "the majority of the members [who] had not yet reached a sufficiently high standard of education and tolerance." Once the Colored workers' Number 2 branch was established in 1940, it was only a matter of time before segregated entrances, elevators, offices, and shop floor partitions were created to maintain the women's separation. Anna Scheepers, a prominent white GWU member, represented many when she declared, "We do not object to their working in the factories but we do not want to mix with the coloured workers."[54] On at least one occasion, Sachs had to quell an uprising by white GWU women. During one such instance, they had refused to work and were prepared to lynch a Creole woman who had just been hired by their employer in order to meet the wartime production demand. Ultimately, Sachs was able to shame the good "Christian" women into getting back to work and into accepting their new co-worker. Class consciousness had yet to trump racial animosity. The belligerent attitudes of white women toward their Black "sister" workers and fellow union members should have come as no surprise to white organizers in South Africa. In a country that was racially divided and hostile to Black success, racially inflected shop floor antagonism merely mirrored the World War II–era conditions in which they occurred.[55]

Emma Mashinini—staunch union activist and future leader of the GWU and later the Commercial, Catering, and Allied Workers' Union of South Africa (CCAWUSA)—recalled the harsh conditions of the clothing factory and the tensions between white and Black workers and management. Her first factory job was making military uniforms at Henochsberg's in the mid-1950s. Three days after the company opened a branch factory on Charles Street in Johannesburg, Mashinini was hired as a trainee machinist. Her work experience was similar to that of many Black women who were hired during the boom time of the war period:

> I remember my first day very clearly. It was November, and when I walked into that building it seemed to me that there were hundreds of people rushing this way and that, and a terrible volume of noise, with a lot of shouting—"Come on, do your job!"—that kind of thing. It was completely bewildering. Immediately [when] I got there, on my first day as a worker, I was started on the machines, working very close to people who had already worked as machinists at other factories, so I was a struggler from the start.
>
> I remember most of all how they cursed us when we couldn't keep up. I was in a department headed first by an Afrikaner called Mrs. Smit and then by a German-speaking man, Mr. Becker. He used to shout and scream at us, sometimes for no reason at all, and it wasn't unusual for ten people to be dismissed a day. They were always saying you had to push. They would say, "*Roer jou gat*," which means, "Push your arse"—"Come on, push your arse and be productive". You would be on the machine sweating, but they would tell you, "*Roer jou, roer jou*"—"Push, push, push", and you would push and push. No one would ever say, "Okay, that's enough. Good." You were working for a target. You'd know there was a target you had to meet, and at the back of your mind you were concerned about the welfare of your children. You would be torn in two, because you were at work and in your mind you were at home. This is the problem of the working mother: you are divided. You are only working because you have to.[56]

Added to Emma Mashinini's concern about being away from her children was her concern about whether she could do her job well enough to keep it. A perfectionist by nature, she soon found that "it was not possible to chase perfection along with production. They made the choice for you, and they wanted production." Laboring under the constant fear of dismissal, she suppressed her anger at having to work for, as she put it, "a tiny wage, which we needed in order to survive." She started her day at five o'clock in the morning (well before her three children were up) by making sure that a friend, family member, or neighbor was available to wake the children for school. Leaving her children a simple breakfast and clean clothes to wear, she headed from Orlando to her job in Johannesburg, arriving by seven in order to be ready to begin work at half past seven. Lunch and tea breaks during the work day were taken on the fly, and not until seven o'clock in the evening did she return home to prepare dinner for her family. Her husband at that time shared neither his time nor his earnings with his family. Laundry and other household duties fell entirely to Mrs. Mashinini, who shouldered alone the considerable demands of both work and family. These were hard times, when money was scarce and Emma Mashinini had little energy for outside activities.[57]

Still, as Mrs. Mashinini recalled, after she prepared her children for church on Sundays, she found simple joy in the quiet and relaxation of walking with them to the Sunday service:

> There was no time to sit and laugh and talk. No time and no energy. Even going to church, trying to cope with catching them, getting them to wash, finding their socks, always shouting. Only on the way there, walking out of that house and holding their hands—I think that was the only loving time I had with my children. Just holding their hands and walking with them to church.
>
> That was the happiest time. They would be sitting there, and going off to Sunday School or whatever, and you could sit down and relax, and listen to someone. Even today I love to go to church, only now my company is my grandchildren instead of my children.[58]

Mrs. Mashinini also looked forward to gathering with other township women at one another's homes for *stokvel* meetings. This was a time for letting down their defenses, forgetting their immediate personal concerns, and enjoying the warm company of friends over tea or other beverages served by the hostess. The *stokvel* provided the women with not only an opportunity to socialize but also an economic boost—this was a way to improve their financial situation and engender a sense of community and sisterhood:

> So we set up the *stokvels*, where we could pool our resources. The members decide what is the greatest need. It could be a ceiling, a refrigerator, ... pots, or anything that you could not pay for yourself. The members collect money in proportion to their wages, and put it into a pool for one person in the group to purchase what has been decided. After that they pass on to the next person, and the group identifies another pressing need, and so it goes until you find that each person in the group has managed to buy some household gadgets without getting into a hire-purchase contract, which has been disastrous to many a housewife.[59]

Mrs. Mashinini acknowledged an additional function of the *stokvel*—it provided a forum in which women could discuss any topic, including current affairs and politics. She explained, "After the money has been collected the women start conversing about current affairs, sharing their problems, which leads them to politics. And that is why African women are often much more politically aware than their Coloured and Indian counterparts, who do not have the opportunity of meeting in such a way." Common concerns among African women—such as their inadequate wages despite union participation, overcrowded living spaces and forced removals from their homes, the inferior education available for their children, poor health care, and chronic poverty—were all conversational fair game. Invariably, these conversations led to a common understanding of the evils of white domination and the government policies that were designed to keep Black people separate and multiply disadvantaged. The social-savings groups acted as important sites of resistance for African women.[60]

The period during and immediately after World War II added a host of stresses to those that already burdened the Black community. For most Black people in Johannesburg, massive housing shortages combined with the struggle to keep up with the rising cost of living overshadowed Prime Minister Jan Christiaan Smuts's fear of the eventual demise of segregation and his temporary relaxation of the pass laws in 1942.[61] Nevertheless, he maintained the practice of segregating the South African armed services, kept weapons out of the hands of African men, relegated African men in the military to service jobs, and discharged African men with many fewer benefits than their white and Colored comrades in arms.[62]

Early in the war, some members of the CPSA took the opportunity to campaign against military recruitment of Black men and women. Dr. Yusuf M. Dadoo, a well-respected leader of several non-European coalitions, was arrested for issuing a strident address in pamphlet form, directed to all non-Europeans who were considering enlistment. Dadoo pointed to the great disparity in pay between white and Black volunteers and challenged his readers to consider the hypocrisy: "You are being asked to support the war for freedom, justice and democracy. Do you enjoy the fruits of freedom, justice and democracy? What you do enjoy is pass and poll-tax laws, segregation, white labour policy, low wages, high rents, poverty, unemployment, and vicious colour-bar laws."[63]

Nevertheless, of the more than 300,000 men recruited into the South African armed services, 114,000 were Black, and they would have little to show for their efforts at the end of their service. Michael Motshele, an Alexandra storekeeper, minister, and ANC activist during the bus boycotts, remembered his tour of duty as a laborer in the South African army under General Den Piener in North Africa. His war experiences parallel those of many African American veterans of World War II who still carry the scars of having inferior status in their own ranks as they fought the Nazi forces. Motshele was paid ten rands[64] per month for performing "general labor needs" in depots and training camps. When the war "was heating up" in the desert and the Germans took Tobruk, Libya, without much opposition, Motshele was among the troops who surrendered, and he served eighteen months as a prisoner of war in Germany. After the war, he knocked around Johannesburg and the Rand seeking any kind of general labor, sold used clothes to miners where he had once worked, and became politically active and joined the ANC. He recalled Alexandra as a seedbed of political activity during the 1940s, and he wanted to take part in it. "I'd seen other Africans governing themselves," he says, and so "I joined the ANC to fight for freedom."[65]

Similarly, Florence Nomathamsangqa Siwedi, an ardent ANC activist and veteran of the South African Red Cross, who served in North and East Africa during World War II, credited her war experiences with raising her political consciousness. Mrs. Siwedi, whose mother was a domestic worker in Johannesburg who had to leave her daughter in the care of relatives while she worked, completed her education through her Junior Certificate in a string of Anglican boarding schools between the Cape, Natal, and the northern Transvaal. In 1942, at the age of sixteen, she arrived in Johannesburg ready to pursue nursing training at the General Hospital. Only four months into her class's training, the South African Red Cross Society "took them to go and serve in the Second World War." It is unclear whether her service was voluntary or coerced (although it is clear that her nurse's training was interrupted and that her service was obtained without the consent of her parents), but her three-year stint in the war effort changed her outlook in many ways. She resented the "£5 pocket money" that she and her comrades received for their work; however, her experiences proved useful if not always positive. She cared for the wounded and the sick, Allies and Germans, helped identify them at the field hospitals and camps, learned how to make clothing for the South African soldiers, and learned to work in mixed groups of people toward a vital common goal. Upon her return, she pondered the meaning of it all:

So we [the] South African Red Cross Society, the World Red Cross Society, we were allowed to go and serve them . . . food wherever we could. There was no distinction. And then from there those [men] would just take their numbers, they had bands with their numbers here, and [they] sent their numbers to their different camps, and then they know who they are, and they will send their messages to their families, wherever they belong to in the world. I was very young, and we were homesick, traumatized, all that. And I will tell you that we never got counsel. . . . [W]e never got counseled who served there. When we came back, we got nothing. Now, we don't know about the soldiers, what the soldiers got, but we, we got nothing.[66]

Florence Siwedi returned to South Africa in 1945, and the following year she joined the ANC Youth League: "That was in 1946 when we began to go into politics deeply because we felt that we served for nothing, you see. And then that's when we turned to the African National Congress. I was a youth in 1946, [and] then I joined the movement in the Youth League. The way we were living whilst we were struggling in the war, in the South African Red Cross, we were a mixture. And then when we came back to South Africa, we were separated again: White Only, Coloreds, Indians, Africans. We were separated." This separation was hurtful and humiliating in her dealings with friends with whom she had shared binding experiences in the war:

Now, as friends from there [the war], when we wanted to meet each other, say, my European friend[s,] like Edith, could not come in the location. I was able to go to her in town, because our parents used to go to town and work, but she was forbidden to come into the location as a European. . . . She was my friend . . . but it was now that separation which . . . traumatized us, and we were never recognized after that. So imagine for the service[men and -women], we were told that things will be better because King George VI is coming to tour in South Africa.[67]

The British king did little to alleviate the problems that Black South Africans faced on a daily basis. He did nothing to remedy Florence Siwedi's missed opportunity to become a nurse. He did nothing to increase the low wages that she received as a kindergarten teacher in Johannesburg or to improve the unlit, overcrowded conditions of the living spaces that Black South Africans were forced to inhabit in Alexandra.

Alexandra was often referred to as the Dark City, because electricity was not available in most of the homes or on most of the streets. During the well-known gangster period of the 1940s and beyond, most people lived in fear of the infamous gangs that roamed the streets under the cover of night—the Msomi, Americans, and Spoilers (the Americans and Spoilers were reportedly imported from Sophiatown). The gangs helped establish Alexandra as a rough and tumble urban outpost. Alexandra offered enterprising Africans the opportunity to hustle unsuspecting residents or to offer "protection" to, for instance, the many illegal beer brewers. Some of those who were less inclined to use illegal means of exploitation purchased property in order to charge rent, exempt from the strictures of the 1913 and 1936 Land and Trust Acts. Established in 1912 as an African freehold township, nine miles from the center of Johannesburg and outside the city limits, Alexandra was not subject to the same tenancy constraints and pass laws that applied to Black residents of other areas. Moreover, because the township did not come under the administrative jurisdiction of the Johannesburg City Council and neither provincial nor state authorities wished to take responsibility for its myriad problems, Alexandra was left largely to govern itself. Despite its high unemployment rate and unsanitary conditions, the fact that Alexandra was well out of reach of both effective policing and the immediate power of state authority made it attractive to Black people—the unemployed, the self-employed, domestic workers, laborers, and a tiny middle class. By 1942 estimates placed the population at well over sixty thousand.[68]

Between 1940 and 1945, the residents of Alexandra responded to several attempts by the Alexandra bus companies to raise the fare between the township and downtown Johannesburg; with only a modicum of organized leadership, they successfully boycotted the buses until the original fares were reinstated. The most prominent and longest-lasting of the boycotts occurred in August 1943 and November 1944. Fare increases of one cent per ride could amount to nearly one shilling per week, which could amount to as much as 9.5 percent of a family's income (well beyond what most African families could afford).[69] Before the war, housing and transportation costs for Black workers were comparatively low in Alexandra, but wartime inflation changed all that. Meanwhile, the Alexandra bus companies, having wrested exclusive control of the township transportation market from a handful of Black entrepreneurs, aggressively sought to protect their right to maximize their profits on the backs of their Black ridership. For the privilege of riding the bus to the city, residents of Alexandra had to endure chronic overcrowding, long delays, and higher weekend rates in a system that did not provide a reduced fare for workers who were employed in locations between the city and Alexandra. Under this same "no-stages" system, moreover, if a domestic worker who was employed within the city limits but well beyond the downtown sector wanted to be sure that she had a seat on the bus home from her job, she would have to take one bus to the center of the city and then another bus to Alexandra.[70]

On August 3, 1943, with the fare increased from four to five cents, Alexandra residents boycotted the buses. Shortly thereafter, the Emergency Transport Committee, which was composed largely of white liberals, established a ferry service to help residents get to and from work. J. B. Marks, committed Communist, trade unionist, and ANC activist, addressed crowds at the downtown bus terminus at Noord Street, urging continued participation in the boycott. The Johannesburg press, which proved sympathetic to the boycott, published information geared toward helping boycotters obtain rides and appealed to employers not to chastise employees who walked to work. Police presence was nominal and unobtrusive. Still, by August 8 no progress had been made in lowering the fare. Alexandra residents rejected several proposals suggested by the bus companies, the Johannesburg City Council, and other interested parties. On August 9, after a mass meeting in the township, more than ten thousand people marched to Noord Street in protest. On August 11 the central government announced resumption of the four-cent fare, pending the findings of a commission established to investigate the issue of transportation for Africans on the Rand.[71]

The commission report favored the bus companies, and seven months later the fare on the Alexandra buses was again raised to five cents, this time subsidized by employers. On November 15, 1944, the day the one-cent increase was to take effect, Alexandra again launched a widespread boycott of the buses. Many of Alexandra's residents—schoolchildren, day laborers, washerwomen, the unemployed—had little or no opportunity to claim the employer subsidy. The police no longer exhibited a permissive attitude; the first day of the boycott they arrested marchers and intimidated drivers who provided rides for the boycotters. This time the goals of the boycott seemed to cover a broader set of issues than the one-cent increase. According to a statement made early on by Dr. Alfred Xuma—president of the ANC, part-time medical officer of the Alexandra Health Committee, and a representative delegated to speak to the bus companies on behalf of the boycotters—the 1944 boycott would "bring to public notice the deplorable conditions under which the Natives live."[72]

Through several severe rainstorms and hailstorms, Alexandra residents continued to walk back and forth to work each day in long columns that consisted of hundreds of people. Hilda Watts (Bernstein), CPSA member elected to the Johannesburg City Council from the district of Hillbrow the year before, recalled the sight of miles of creative boycotters in 1944: "After a month of the boycott, the character of the daily procession had changed. At night the road to Alex[andra] was packed with bicycles, a tremendous procession of them. While thousands still had to get lifts or walk, more and more bicycles were being borrowed from friends in other townships, or supplied by employers."[73] Again, white supporters on the City Council, from the Labour Party, and as employers offered rides and tried to reason with the Transportation Board and the bus companies.

December came, and the boycott remained unresolved. A City Council subcommittee recommended that the council subsidize the increase through the use of coupons, at a sum that would cover three months. When the Smuts government rejected the plan, Alexandra residents, through the Workers' Transport Action Committee, resolved to continue their boycott. In a mass meeting held on December 20, Alexandra residents decided to hold a sit-down strike, which was later put off until January. According to Hilda Watts, however, people in the township protested the curtailment and prosecution of independent lorry operators by throwing "a cordon across the road" to prevent the empty buses from entering Alexandra.[74] As pressure built, the City Council offered to ask the bus company owners to resume the four-cent fare "until the coupons could be printed." By January 4, after a mass meeting resulted in acceptance of the terms of the settlement, the buses were again rolling. The weekday fare remained at four cents; the Saturday afternoon fare increased to six cents. On Sundays and holidays, riders paid seven cents. The bus companies were subsequently bought out by a new group of private owners who formed a "public utility corporation," which ultimately dispensed with the use of the coupons and reinstated the four-cent fare.[75]

Those who participated in or witnessed the boycotts learned some valuable lessons. The boycott proved to be an effective weapon against outside controls; other communities adopted its use, and Alexandra repeated its initial success in 1957. Under the leadership of the Workers' Transport Action Committee, represented in part by the Communist Party and ANC activist Gaur Radebe, Alexandra residents and their spokespersons were empowered to make their own decisions and entrust their representation to their own delegates. Through the mechanism of the mass meeting, ordinary women and men became politicized and adept at communicating their demands to those in power. Moreover, the formidable unity and determination that Alexandra residents displayed proved the power of mass action and served as an example for future action. The possibility of successful mass action opened the doors to a much wider set of demands: liberation and the elimination of apartheid.

Between 1944 and 1947 African women and men launched a series of squatter movements on the Rand to protest the acute housing shortages created in part by municipalities that refused to acknowledge them and precipitated by the labor demands of World War II. Thousands of squatters set up communities in areas adjacent to Orlando, Pimville, and Alexandra. Women figured prominently in these movements, organizing their own associations in Pimville and Alexandra, resisting police, and participating in a 1947 march through Johannesburg.[76] In 1945 women in the Springs location, many of them beer brewers, boycotted the municipal beer halls and landed in jail. Between 1943 and 1944 women organized cooperatives to purchase food at reasonable costs. In 1947 in Kliptown, on the other side of Johannesburg, women sent a deputation that included the CPSA activist Josie Mpama to the Johannesburg City Council to protest high prices and inadequate food distribution.[77]

In 1944, a year before the ANC introduced the pass laws issue to the Manchester Pan-Africanist Congress in Britain,[78] Alfred Xuma joined with a host of notable Communists—including Yusuf Dadoo, Josie Mpama, Edwin Mofutsanyana (Josie Mpama's husband), J. B. Marks, and Moses Kotane—to form the National Anti-Pass Council. Their mission was open protest against the pass system.[79] Xuma was ready to forgo the well-worn strategy of appealing to the state for relief in favor of a stronger protest, and he urged the ANC branches to form anti-pass committees that could work together. Xuma was not averse to linking the interests of his organization with those of the Communist Party in order to achieve results.

In fact, Johannesburg and the Rand were a hotbed of African resistance during the 1940s. Black resistance in Johannesburg was not unlike resistance by African-descended and Asian peoples in other parts of the world, who took advantage of the increasingly liberal and democratizing tendencies that grew out of the Western powers' brush with fascism. The personalities, ideologies, and rhetoric of the anticolonial movements on the continent of Africa and throughout Asia were enormously effective in helping to coalesce political groups and individuals into what would become a powerful oppositional force. African Americans too were alert to the opportunities to refuel their opposition to white supremacist systems that radical movements and the war presented. As an integral part of the social movements of their communities, Black women in Africa and the United States used the organizing experience they had gained in the 1930s and 1940s to build structures that could ignite even stronger resistance.

~~~~~~~~~~~

Chapter Six

LAUNCHING NEW NETWORKS

Black Women Organizing for Change, 1940–1950

Mʀs. Cora McHaney and Mrs. Irene Williams, now retired, are counted among the dedicated Black women teachers of Montgomery, Alabama. Mrs. McHaney—prim in appearance, sporting earrings, a pin at the V-neck of her dress, and a white knit headband that frames her smooth brown face—is originally from Florida. Mrs. Williams—tall and elegant, with a warm, broad smile that lights up her attractive features—is native to Alabama. Proud of their long years of service in the Montgomery city and county school systems, both women embody the practice of teaching as a means of social elevation and racial betterment. In education and social status, Mrs. McHaney and Mrs. Williams represent the ethos and aspirations of many among the Black middle class. Their experiences as the youngest children of large, rural families that struggled to send their daughters to school during the early decades of the twentieth century, however, provide a more nuanced characterization of their status in the Black community. Moreover, as teachers in the late 1930s and 1940s, their small salaries and occasional bouts with unemployment, forced them to supplement their incomes by performing day labor for white families and by working at the Reliance Manufacturing Company. As Black teachers in a segregated public school system overseen by white administrators, both Mrs. McHaney and Mrs. Williams risked serious repercussions as active participants in the Montgomery bus boycott.

"Oh, McHaney was more active than I was," Mrs. Williams recalled. "See, because she was out sick for a while . . . she could participate more. But those of us that were still working, we couldn't, or else we could be fired." Still, Mrs. Williams was an active member of Beulah Baptist Church, one of the churches where mass meetings were held during the boycott and where volunteer drivers picked up and dropped off people who needed rides. "The teachers, we were rather leading a double life," Mrs. Williams explained. "Some were politically conscious in an Underground Railroad fashion. I gave money and participated on the q.t."[1]

Mrs. McHaney recalled, "I joined the WPC [Women's Political Council] before the boycott. I knew Mary Fair Burks [founder of the WPC] from State Normal—she taught us at summer school." Many WPC members were drawn from the elementary and secondary school teachers who, like Mrs. McHaney and Mrs. Williams, kept their certification up to date by taking classes at Alabama State. "I was also a member of the Prince Hall Masons [Order of the] Eastern Star with Mrs. A. W. West [a Montgomery bus boycott activist]. She was the Worthy Matron, and we talked about protest instead of Eastern Star business!" During the 1940s Mrs. McHaney taught at several small county and large city elementary schools. In the late 1930s she served as principal of a small county school that employed five teachers and taught six grades; she came to the city system in 1941. During World War II she taught in the county again, but she was back in Montgomery teaching at Carver Elementary School in 1951. "And I registered to vote with Rufus Lewis [a well respected local activist] in the forties, maybe '42 or '43. I was not afraid to take a stand. I was an excellent cook. I told Superintendent Dr. C. T. Dannelly, 'I can do something else; I won't starve!' . . . I stuck my neck out! I picked up people, I went to all the mass meetings, and I took a day out of school to attend the trial."[2]

Both women were clear in their conviction that they had something significant to offer. "We helped out a lot," claimed Mrs. McHaney. "We kept the boycott going. If we hadn't pitched in, the folk would have had to ride. And it made me feel good—this was a good purpose, a good cause, and I was with my folks trying to integrate. If you hadn't taken a stand, it wouldn't have been a success."[3] Mrs. Williams concurs: "We achieved a closeness, a cohesiveness that otherwise wouldn't have come into being. You don't have to make a lot of noise just to be a participant. . . . Still waters run deep. . . . [H]owever you live will show in your face."[4]

Such women activists served their colleagues and associations well. They raised money through the networks of their local and national women's organizations, they drove riders to and from their destinations, and they voiced their enthusiasm in the mass meetings. They were no strangers to struggle, and they felt a kinship with those who occupied more working-class positions. "Pitch[ing] in" where they could offer material or moral support, Mrs. Williams and Mrs. McHaney were motivated by not only a sense of injustice but also an understanding of their vested interest in the plight of their community.

Similarly motivated by a sense of justice and community, Mrs. Maggie Tsiu Resha, age seventy-eight, proudly recalled her South African heritage, her land, and the long struggle for freedom that her people have waged. "We must never forget that Africa belongs to us. That is what we were fighting for,"[5] she asserted. Like Mrs. Williams and Mrs. McHaney, Mrs. Resha grew up in a large extended rural family of independent farmers who struggled to afford her education. In the 1940s, during World War II, Maggie Tsiu was a student in eastern Pondoland at the Holy Cross Hospital run by the Anglican church. While she was far from home at the remote mission station, she read *Bantu World*, a popular, well-respected newspaper that catered to the interests of Black South Africans. There she first read about the African National Congress (ANC) and its leader, Dr. Alfred B. Xuma. Admittedly naïve about politics at the time, her discussions with other nursing students about ANC activities were limited, "as nobody really understood much about the subject."[6]

In 1948, however, when Maggie Tsiu married Robert Resha, an organizer and journalist who worked with the ANC, her political understanding deepened. The young Mrs. Resha was happy to become part of a rejuvenated movement for Black liberation in which a growing number of people were infused with an activist spirit. Mrs. Resha recalled that in the early days supporters sang freedom songs to mobilize young people to join the ANC. Ida Mtwana, elected provincial president of the ANC Women's League in 1949, was especially good at teaching people the songs that motivated them to get involved: "We had a freedom song which went: 'Vuma silibale igama lako' (Agree that we write your name!). When that song was being sung, people would flock to the stage, holding their subscription fees of two shillings and sixpence to join the ANC. People were proud to be members of Congress, since it gave one a sense of mental liberation . . . [to be] engaged in doing something about apartheid."[7]

By 1952, as the ANC launched its nonviolent direct action Defiance Campaign against the unjust apartheid laws, women became increasingly involved in the liberation movement under the auspices of the Women's League. In Sophiatown, Maggie Resha continued her activism as a member of the league:

I was elected first as secretary and later as chair [of the branch]. . . . By the early Fifties [the Women's League] was a powerful force within the ANC nationally. Women organized house parties every month to raise funds for the organization, since its only form of income was from membership subscriptions. But, chiefly, [the Women's League] began to arouse women to be involved in campaigns to fight against racist legislation which directly affected them as women, disabilities which eroded their progress as African women.[8]

Maggie Resha and her husband agreed to "write their names" on the roll of South African freedom fighters. In 1962 that full-time commitment forced them to flee South Africa with their family and, while in exile, to organize and raise both funds for and international awareness about the ongoing struggle to liberate their country. Inherent in that struggle for Mrs. Resha and other Black South African women was their understanding of the necessity to "fight against racist legislation which directly affected them *as women*."[9] After 1949, women held their own meetings within the parent body of the ANC, while the WPC women of Montgomery organized under their own auspices to voice their long-held concerns. After 1948, Black South African women felt especially targeted by the policies and programs of the new Afrikaner Nationalist government—for instance, by the emphasis on the extension of passes to women, proscriptions aimed against the education of their children, and the very destruction of their homes. Black women in Montgomery, for their part, were not as directly targeted by gender as were their South African counterparts. Wherever segregated bus seating in the South existed, however, Black women were vulnerable to the rough treatment and lack of respect meted out by bus drivers who were given the right to exercise police power. In both the U.S. South and South Africa, Black women built parallel autonomous organizations within their movements in order to exercise their political agency and protest the offenses that they suffered as a consequence of their sex.

In late 1943 the Women's League was reestablished at the ANC annual meeting at Kimberley, and in 1946 the WPC was organized in Montgomery, Alabama. Both auspicious events occurred, however, within the larger context of a more militant Black activism that surrounded World War II. In 1946, worker unrest in the gold mines of the Witwatersrand engendered a huge and unprecedented protest by Black miners. The leaders of the strike were directly linked to the Communist Party and to the fledgling Congress Youth League (CYL) of the ANC, both of which sought ways to galvanize a mass-based, growing membership into future mass actions. In Montgomery and in many locations throughout the U.S. South, the National Association for the Advancement of Colored People (NAACP) pushed for Black voter registration and continued to dismantle the Jim Crow system by bringing education and voting regulation cases to the federal courts. Other local political groups organized specifically to disrupt the racialized power dynamics in the state, especially where Black populations nearly equaled or outnumbered white populations. Rosa Parks, Mary Fair Burks, Jo Ann Gibson Robinson, Idessa Redden, Beautie Mae Johnson, and Amy Collins Harris—all activist women in Montgomery who confronted the many inequities that Black people in their city faced—looked back on the strategies they employed.

Black Politics in Montgomery

During the 1940s E. D. Nixon used his position as head of the local branch of the NAACP (and later as state president) to intervene on behalf of any Black person he could help. Following the first NAACP Supreme Court victory—the 1938 case against the segregated law school of the state of Missouri—Nixon had helped reinvigorate the few NAACP branches across the state.[10] Thus began the slow but steady NAACP march *against* legal segregation in the South and *toward* full citizenship rights. Modeling his actions after his union grievance activities, Nixon used his own personal brand of audacity, under the auspices of the NAACP, to chip away steadily at various forms of Alabama injustice. Even following the bombing of his home shortly after he became president of the Montgomery branch of the NAACP, he persisted in uncovering acts of white violence against Black people. In one instance in the late 1930s, he investigated the case of a woman who was beaten to death by a white sheriff. Nixon received a tip from a white man who wished to remain anonymous, advising him to find the woman's sons, who had witnessed their mother's death. Nixon demanded that their testimony be included in the grand jury hearings, but in order to have the young men subpoenaed, he had to approach the sheriff responsible for the beating death to insist that the young men's testimonies be entered into the official record and that they be compensated for their travel expenses from Birmingham to Montgomery. The unlettered sheriff was reportedly dumbfounded at both Nixon's nerve and his speedy calculation of the cost of the brothers' mileage. As Nixon later recalled, "Of course, he was acquitted. The woman died 'from causes unknown.' But he couldn't believe his eyes. He just couldn't believe a Negro had the courage to challenge him. I had nothing on me. If I had a pocket-knife and had been arrested, that's all they needed."[11]

When Rosa Parks joined the NAACP in 1943, Nixon was still head of the local branch. She originally joined the organization after seeing a picture in the *Alabama Tribune* that showed her old school friend Mrs. Johnnie Carr attending a meeting.[12] Johnnie Carr was the secretary of the Montgomery branch, and Mrs. Parks decided to go to a meeting in the hope that she would run into her friend. Mrs. Parks later recalled:

> In December of 1943 they were having the annual election of officers meeting, and I went to it. That day [Mrs. Carr] wasn't at the meeting, and there were just a few men, maybe a dozen or fifteen. I paid my membership dues, and then they had the election of officers. I was the only woman there and they said they needed a secretary, and I was too timid to say no. I just started to take minutes, and that was the way I was elected secretary. There was no pay, but I enjoyed the work, and [Raymond] Parks was very supportive of my involvement.[13]

By the early 1940s, Rosa Parks had come to know Nixon as fearless and direct in the face of white hostility. Indeed, in Mrs. Parks's words, he had a reputation "as a person who had enough courage and dedication and concern to approach the white people in power on issues that concerned us. We thought he had plenty of courage and nerve."[14]

Together, E. D. Nixon and Rosa Parks took on several cases in defense of Black women and men in Alabama who had been victimized by white supremacist laws and customs. Mrs. Parks listened to people's complaints, prepared depositions, wrote letters and press releases, attended and recorded the proceedings of meetings, answered phones, and fielded myriad requests. With valuable assistance from the attorney Arthur A. Madison, a native of Alabama who practiced law in New York, the Montgomery branch redoubled its efforts to increase the number of Black registered voters. Field officers from the national office of the NAACP assisted Madison, Nixon, and Mrs. Parks in launching voter registration drives. Mrs. Parks and her mother, Leona Edwards McCauley, were among those who participated in the early forays to the courthouse. After two unsuccessful (unexplained) attempts at registering to vote in 1943, Mrs. Parks managed to register successfully in 1945. She had had to pay her poll taxes retroactively from the time she turned twenty-one; the total amounted to $16.50, no small sum for a person who earned no more than $20 per week at the time.[15] No matter how hard they worked, Mrs. Parks recalled, the small victories of the few who managed to register during the 1940s did not outweigh the bitter disappointments.

Sex, violence, and the specter of southern-style "race mixing" lay at the heart of a number of cases that Nixon and Mrs. Parks investigated. With the help of Nixon and Mrs. Parks, Andy Wright, one of the young men accused in the Scottsboro case, was paroled and then hired as a truck driver in Montgomery but too few cases ended with a positive resolution. During the summer of 1945, Nixon and Mrs. Parks were among the many, both Black and white, who attempted to assist Mrs. Recy Taylor, a Black resident of Abbeville, Alabama. Six armed white men had forced Mrs. Taylor into a car and then raped her. The sheriff of Henry County intimidated at least one of Mrs. Taylor's supporters off the case, and even with the confession of one of the assailants, two grand juries refused to indict any of the men for the crime. Another case that took place during the 1940s involved eighteen-year-old Jeremiah Reeves, who naïvely entered into a romantic liaison with a white woman. When their affair was discovered, Reeves was slapped with a rape charge. Despite his mother's many appeals and persistent NAACP efforts to save him, Reeves spent the next three years on Death Row, and at age twenty-one he was executed.[16]

In 1943, the same year that she joined the NAACP, Mrs. Parks endured a humiliation that was perhaps prophetic of what was to occur in December 1955. She was put off a Montgomery bus because, in her words, she "didn't follow the rules." After boarding the bus and depositing her fare, she neglected to step back off the bus and board in the rear, as was the convention before the boycott. When the bus driver demanded that she reenter the bus at the rear, Mrs. Parks refused; having already reached the back of the crowded bus, she stood where she was and would not budge. The bus driver grabbed her by the sleeve and hauled her through the bus and out the front door. According to Mrs. Parks, he was a "mean . . . rough-looking" man who wielded a gun, was endowed with police power, and looked ready to strike her, but she responded by saying, "I know one thing. You better not hit me." The driver refrained from physically harming Mrs. Parks, but the experience left her determined never to ride his bus again. For their part, the other passengers at the rear of the bus declined to come to her aid; in fact, they grew impatient and disgruntled with her stubborn refusal to follow the rules. Their resentment, Mrs. Parks explained, was not uncommon during the 1940s, "when people took a lot without fighting back."[17]

Despite this apparent complacency and the local failures of the NAACP, by the end of the war Black people in Alabama and across the South had become more politically emboldened since the radical activities of the 1930s. Black participation in World War II, the democratic rhetoric useful in its prosecution, and the 1944 NAACP victory in *Smith v. Allwright* (which outlawed the white primary in Texas) helped spur an increased demand for the expansion of democracy. African Americans in Alabama and in many other southern states vigorously pursued the right to vote and joined the NAACP in growing numbers. In a campaign that aimed to appeal to a more mass-based membership in the South, local branches increased their official membership from fifty thousand in 1940 to nearly four hundred thousand by 1946.[18] The NAACP linked Black southerners to a national network of resources, including organizers and lawyers, that could be put to effective use in addressing other issues of local concern, such as voter registration and increased educational opportunity. Led by a committed leadership of middle- and working-class African Americans, the NAACP branch networks battled to obtain political clout for the masses of Black people in the South. In 1941, for instance, Charles Gomillion a Tuskegee professor, helped found the activist Tuskegee Civic Association in Macon County, Alabama. As a returning World War II veteran, Gomillion joined a suit against the Macon County Board of Registrars for failing to register Black voters. Rather than meet the legitimate demands of the complainants, the board suspended operations for more than a year. In 1942 the NAACP field organizer Madison Jones commented on recent political activity by Black southerners: "There is a definite interest in the intelligent and effective use of the ballot manifested everywhere I go. I do hope that movement spreads."[19]

In 1946 Ella Baker, assistant field secretary and director of branches for the NAACP, traveled through the South holding meetings and workshops among the constituencies in an effort to further stimulate activity on the local level and take the concerns of the branches to the national office. She also held leadership-training conferences, one of which E. D. Nixon and Rosa Parks attended in Jacksonville, Florida. Baker's training sessions on voter registration emphasized the critical nature of following "the legal victories that have been won against the white primary with vigorous registration and voting campaigns."[20] In the 1946 Alabama gubernatorial campaign, Black voters contributed considerably to the election of Big Jim Folsom, who had run on a progressive platform favorable to African Americans, workers, and people who depended on state aid, which supported expanded access to public education and the abolition of the poll tax.[21] Despite Folsom's promising victory, his tenure as governor remained contentious, and state politics became even more divisive in 1948, as the States' Rights, or Dixiecrat, Party set up headquarters in the Big Mule[22] city of Birmingham.

Alabama Democrats had turned once again to waving the bloody flag as the state and national (Harry S. Truman) forces advocated real electoral reform capable of enfranchising and substantially increasing the political clout of African Americans. In the ensuing fratricidal war—especially in several Black Belt counties where the Black population came close to equaling or outnumbered the white population and where many Black people and former Democrats voted Republican—this platform proved damaging to the ruling party. Facing stiff opposition, Black registered voters in Alabama increased slowly in number: from 1 percent in 1947 to 5 percent in 1952.[23] After the *Brown v. Board of Education* decision in 1954, rabid segregationists in Alabama and across the South—fearing African Americans' potential for political power and economic advancement and the racist notion of Black men's sexual aggression against white women—coalesced in a resurgent Ku Klux Klan and its more bourgeois counterpart, the White Citizens' Council. As the plain-talking father of Charles Dobbins, the liberal editor of the Montgomery *Examiner*, had remarked to his son even in the 1930s: "We don't have politics in Alabama based on issues. All our politics is race."[24]

The Formation of the Women's Political Council and Women's Activism

Undeterred by the resurgence of the Klan, Black residents of Montgomery continued to agitate for change. In fact, one of the most prominent Black Baptist churches helped foster that agitation. Since his arrival as pastor of Dexter Avenue Baptist Church in 1948, the legendary Reverend Vernon Johns had exhorted his largely middle-class parishioners to stand up for themselves politically and economically, checking their own class biases at the door. An important figure in the Black activist community of Montgomery, he provided a critical politicized space in which various key figures of the boycott movement could connect. Demonstrating a personal commitment to racial justice, Johns had refused to enter the Montgomery buses at the back and had been chased out of a white restaurant by gun-toting men when he attempted to integrate it by entering and asking to be served. After a group of police officers viciously beat a Black motorist, he advertised his sermon on the large bulletin board outside his church: "It's Safe to Murder Negroes in Montgomery."[25] Neither his renowned biblical scholarship nor his audacity in challenging racial injustice could be denied.

To the displeasure of many of his parishioners, Johns had also taken up the practice of selling fresh fish and produce from a truck in front of the church as a lesson in the dignity of ordinary labor and good business sense. In 1952, forced by those who feared his disregard for their conservative middle-class status, Johns finally resigned his post at Dexter.[26] Some, however, had been encouraged by the disquieting spirit of their pastor: Mrs. Mary Fair Burks organized her women colleagues at Alabama State College into the WPC; Rufus Lewis became involved in voter registration; E. D. Nixon continued to urge greater activism within the NAACP locals across the state as he organized the Progressive Democratic Association; and Mrs. Jo Ann Gibson Robinson and other WPC women worked to change Jim Crow practices in Montgomery. By September 1954, when the young pastor and newly minted doctoral recipient from Atlanta, the Reverend Dr. Martin Luther King, Jr., arrived in Montgomery to take over the helm at Dexter, an important sector of the Black community in Montgomery had already been politically primed.

In 1946 Mrs. Mary Fair Burks, an English professor at Alabama State College in Montgomery, organized the WPC.[27] One historian described the organization, which was vigilant in holding the city administration accountable for its unfair segregationist policies, as "the most militant and uncompromising organ of the black community" before the boycott.[28] In founding the organization, Mrs. Burks had resolved to find a useful outlet for her growing anger and frustration with the Jim Crow practices in Montgomery. Seeking "to do something more about segregation," she looked especially toward other Black middle-class women to help bring about needed changes. At the base of her determination lay her exposure to the more balanced race relationships in Ann Arbor, Michigan, where she had attended graduate school. A personal confrontation with the all-white Montgomery police department also motivated her to act: Shortly before the formation of the WPC, she had been arrested for what amounted to a minor traffic violation—her car had come too close to a white woman who was getting off a city bus. After making several polite objections to the officer who arrested her, Mrs. Burks discovered that her middle-class status offered no defense against the policeman's club. Forced to accept her own vulnerability in the face of state power, she came to realize the futility of "waging [her] own personal war." As Mrs. Burks explained, "My arrest convinced me that my defiance alone would do little or nothing to remedy such situations. Only organized effort could do that. But where to start?"[29]

As Mrs. Burks recalled, one of the Reverend Vernon Johns's warnings to his church members against their self-satisfied smugness followed closely on the heels of her arrest and proved to be the catalyst she needed.[30] She looked to her church members to provide not only a base of inspiration but also the necessary footsoldiers for the cause. The members of her congregation, however, displayed a decided "complacency" and assumed "masks of indifference or scorn." Undeterred, she pressed on, focusing her organizing efforts on her women friends and colleagues:

> I was a feminist before I really knew what the word meant and so I dismissed the hard-faced men, but I felt that I could appeal to some of the women. I played bridge with them, but more important, I knew that they must suffer from the racial abuse and the indignity accorded all blacks, even though they were somewhat insulated from it. Their outward indifference was a mask to protect both their psyche and their sanity. I believed that I could get enough such women together to address some of the glaring racial problems.[31]

Although it was not her intention to address only women's issues within the new organization, Mrs. Burks later acknowledged her protofeminist tendencies. She was aware that racial injustice knew no sexual limitations and that women's political activism did not rest on the involvement of men. Like any good organizer, she worked with the people she could most easily reach: women whose experiences in many ways mirrored her own.

On the Sunday following her arrest, Mrs. Burks formulated her idea of an organization of Black women dedicated to fighting racial injustice in Montgomery. She spoke with some fifty women—drawn from among the parishioners at Dexter and her colleagues at Alabama State—in the hope that she could interest them in participating in an initial organizational session. Some forty women, most of whom had their own humiliating tales of racial discrimination to tell, came together at that first meeting in the early fall of 1946. These early members of the organization were decidedly middle class in education and in economic status. They were, for the most part, professional women—public school teachers, college professors, principals, supervisors, social workers, and nurses—all sharing the agenda of becoming politically involved. Mrs. Burks recalled that as the women debated what they should call their group, she was very clear on this point. She strongly believed that the name should reflect their three-pronged program: political action, protest, and education in the form of voter registration; the desegregation of city buses and parks; and political education of both Black youths and adults. By a narrow margin, the women voted to name their organization the Women's Political Council. Among the principal goals of the organization, Mrs. Burks admitted, "we did not consider overthrowing *Plessy*."[32] As she explained, "Only a miracle could do that. What we could do was to seek political leverage as we protested racial abuses."[33] Even without taking on the fight that the NAACP had been waging constitutionally since the late 1930s, however, the WPC women broke new ground in Black women's political activism not only in Montgomery but also across the South.[34]

Women who figured prominently in the 1955–1956 bus boycott joined the organization at its inception or soon after, including Irene West, Bertha Williams, and Thelma Glass.[35] One of the early WPC recruits, Mrs. Thelma Glass, recalled, "I knew it was something I wanted to do.... [Y]ou didn't have to beg me to come to a meeting." By 1950 two other women who would be crucial to the organization during the bus boycott and to Dr. King's Montgomery Improvement Association had joined the WPC: Mrs. Jo Ann Gibson Robinson and Mrs. Euretta Adair. Mrs. Glass, a graduate of and for many years a faculty member in the history department at Alabama State, recalled the drive and energy of their leader, Mrs. Mary Fair Burks:

> She was an unusual person for her time—always demanding the best in quality and everything for a Black person and to some people, I guess, a dreamer. She was good enough to be a part of anything that existed.... [I had] known her since the time I was an undergraduate.... She was just as active in cultural activities. For example ... she organized [a club called] Great Books in Literature.... [N]ot only was she interested in political uplift but she was [also] interested in quality of society—all things. She was in all things, almost from the ground up.[36]

Mrs. Glass's own reasons for becoming involved in the WPC combined a unique brand of mid-twentieth-century political activism with a late-nineteenth-century conception of social elevation common among middle-class African American educators and other professionals across the South:

> You know, I kind of think that maybe this idea of me working to improve the quality of life in the Black community and to move above mediocrity . . . I guess it came with me from high school or early college. In other words, it embarrassed me that Blacks would make excuses for things. I was an individual who always felt—don't make any excuse for me because I'm Black. Hold me responsible. I can do anything anyone else can do. I guess this is one thing I tried to inspire [in] my teachers, my students, when I was teaching. Somehow, I felt that we should do the things that would improve the community. I was always interested in moving Blacks above mediocrity in every area and working with them to help them in any way. I was always interested in people, in helping people. That was just part of me—to go out and try to teach somebody the Constitution before you could vote. It made me feel good to do it.[37]

Between 1946 and 1955, the thirty to forty women of the WPC eagerly took on several projects that directly led to the decline of the status quo. One of their first tasks was to register the membership to vote. It had been difficult for even these highly educated women to satisfy the inflated literacy requirements of the county registrar. As Mrs. Burks explained, it was common knowledgethat "even Ph.D.s failed the test."[38] Nevertheless, they were wholeheartedly committed to taking and retaking the test—which required that they be able to read, write, and interpret any article of the Constitution—as often as necessary.[39] Eventually, all of the WPC women became registered voters, and in connection with their postwar voter registration campaign, they organized citywide "registration schools" that met once a week in several Black churches. They helped Black women and men learn to read and write, fill out registration forms, and understand the rudiments of the U.S. Constitution. According to Mrs. Burks, the WPC volunteers also "took them to the courthouse where they filled out the forms." She recalled, "We even accompanied them when they returned to the courthouse to check on the results of the applications." These personalized techniques, they believed, increased the success rate among the registration applicants.[40]

By the early 1950s the WPC leadership had been turned over to Mrs. Jo Ann Gibson Robinson, and the organization had expanded its program to include a public review of state and local candidates for political office.

Their review, in turn, generated a slate of candidates recommended to the voters. The WPC actively worked with the organizations of E. D. Nixon and Rufus Lewis to have the Black community vote as a bloc. The strategy of bloc voting could be effective with a comparatively small number of Black voters, especially in tight races. In these situations, according to Mrs. Burks, Black "votes often could decide the outcome." Interestingly, their white "supporters" at the Montgomery Council of Human Relations objected to the independent WPC review of potential office holders. In contrast, a few representatives of the segregated local branch of the League of Women Voters were helpful, Mrs. Burks reported, in sharing their opinions about the candidates. Clearly, despite what many white people wished to keep as their own political prerogatives, the WPC continued to work as a power broker within the Black community as it pursued its goal of changing city views of and interactions with Black people, particularly with respect to electoral issues.[41]

The efforts of the WPC, the actions of Lewis's Citizens' Steering Committee, and Nixon's work with the NAACP and other groups were not the only means through which Black people could become registered voters in Montgomery or in the state. National labor unions and their local branches throughout the South were also encouraging Black people to register during the World War II era. Since the 1930s the Congress of Industrial Organization (CIO) had been working not only to increase membership in its southern affiliates but also to organize both Black and white workers. In 1944, continuing the drive to attract workers during the war period, the CIO president, Philip Murray, declared that the union campaign to organize Black workers in the South should be seen as "a civil rights program." Moreover, he believed that the labor union program "not only encompassed the organization of workers into unions . . . but [also included] the freedom of southern workers from economic and political bondage [and was designed] . . . to exclude . . . from the South all types of racial and other forms of discrimination." Local CIO–Political Action Committees (PACs) in the South helped prospective Black voters to pay their poll taxes and hired Black organizers to help register potential voters. The Alabama PACs, which supported the successful candidacy of Jim Folsom for governor, were part of a loosely based statewide coalition of liberal (and some more radical) activists and organizations that worked on behalf of progressive change in the South.[42] In Alabama these organizations included the Southern Negro Youth Congress (SNYC), an organization of young Black women and men with ties to the Communist Party; the NAACP; the Southern Conference for Human Welfare; the CIO; and the CIO-PAC.[43]

According to Mrs. Beautie Mae Johnson, she and her colleagues at the Reliance Manufacturing Company took advantage of several opportunities—sponsored by their CIO-affiliated local, Amalgamated Clothing Workers of America (ACWA)—to discuss the importance of voting and were encouraged to register. Amy Collins Harris, one of the leaders of the ACWA local, recalled that Rufus Lewis would occasionally come to their biweekly union meetings to talk with the membership about voter registration. Mrs. Johnson remembered registering in the late 1930s or early 1940s after paying a large poll tax. Mrs. Idessa Redden first attempted to register in 1943, not long after she left Reliance. Mrs. Harris recalled having registered before she and her husband married in 1944.[44] She worked with both Nixon and Lewis, soliciting potential voters door-to-door after her factory shift:

> Oh ... this was way before the boycott. ... We were trying to get people to register to vote. We went from house to house. ... I took from Mobile Drive back to Cavalier Drive, and [a neighbor of mine] took from Mobile Drive to Tuskegee, east, and I came west. And we went from door to door teaching people about the questionnaire, the questions they would [be asked] ... [and we would] have them ... fill it out, what they would be asked when they got down there to register.[45]

For many of the women, their experiences at Reliance helped to prepare them for voter registration work, the desegregation of city public facilities, and an eventual turn to greater political and economic justice. In 1928, the same year the factory opened, fifteen-year-old Idessa Redden had already promised herself that she would never work for white women in their homes. She had had to leave high school before she graduated, in order to get a job and help out her family, but, she said, "[I] vowed to myself I was not goin' to no white folks' kitchen." Instead, she lied about her age and went to work for Reliance, where she remained for more than ten years. She learned new skills on the industrial sewing machines and was paid "in the beginning ... around nine dollars, maybe, every two weeks." This work seemed to suit her for a time, but she resented attempts by the plant manager, Clarence Giesing, to keep her under his thumb. In a manner evocative of pre–Civil War plantation methods, Giesing demanded that she provide him with information on the other employees and act as his mouthpiece. He wanted her to warn the women to stay away from social clubs after work, in the interest of maintaining factory productivity:

> And he started talkin', and he was sayin' about some of the poor work the employees was doin' and the reason why they was doin' it. So I asked him, "Why? What reason?" He said that if they wouldn't go out and stay at the BT's all night . . . —well, BT's is up here on Jeff Davis [Street]; that was the night club—they could do better work. So my answer to him was this: I said I had three reasons. First of all: "I have too much race pride to sit here and talk to you about my people." Secondly: "You not goin' to come tellin' me nothin' 'bout neither one of your employees up there in the office" (which was white). And the third one was [this]: "When these employees in this plant leave the plant property, you don't have nothin' to do with where they go at night."
>
> So then he told me I need to go up North and live! So I told him, "Naw, I don't need to go up there. I'm goin' to stay here and try to help these things straighten out." So, maybe a year later, I was bein' picked at, and so I just walked out one mornin'. . . . I had fifty cents.[46]

Mrs. Redden left the factory even though she had no money, because, as she later explained, "I just never was a person who wanted to bow to nobody in order for them to treat me right."[47] Before 1945, unfortunately, none of the workers at Reliance (much less those who were both Black and female) had any formal protection under which to appeal for fair treatment.

Black Politics on the Rand

During the 1940s three significant developments on the Rand emerged as key factors in an increasingly nationalist and multiracial struggle: (1) an outpouring of worker discontent and a shift to mass protest, (2) the creation of the ANC Youth League, and (3) the establishment of the ANC Women's League. Organizing mine workers and preparing for the African mine workers' strike of 1946, the ANC and the Communist Party of South Africa, which had begun their collaboration in 1944 with the formation of the National Anti-Pass Council, further strengthened their political ties. Meanwhile, between late 1943 and early 1944, the Congress Youth League was created under the visionary guidance of Anton Lembede, coincident with the 1943 mandate to establish the ANC Women's League.

The 1946 miners' strike grew out of a rash of worker discontent that flared on the Rand between 1942 and 1944 in the form of a series of smaller strikes that affected not only the mining industry but the growing secondary industries as well. More than sixty strikes, some without benefit of trade union initiative, shook the mining industry, the food industry, the saw milling industry, and the Johannesburg municipality. Then, in 1946, the African Mine Workers' Union led a demonstration that was unprecedented in size and overall impact. After considerable deliberation with its rank and file, the union called on its members to strike against the Rand mines for higher wages and union recognition.[48]

The African Mine Workers' strike of 1946 is known as a "watershed event" in the history of Black protest politics in South Africa. Replacing "patient constitutional protest" with mass action, the miners' strike represented an important turning point in the Black struggle and marked the beginning of a period in which state response to such actions became increasingly intransigent. The strike was an important instance of "collective moral outrage" among workers whose wages had failed to keep pace with wartime prices. The miners sought an increase from two shillings to ten shillings per day. Food scarcity and quality were real issues for the miners, who needed the wage increase, in part, to augment their meager food rations.[49] In the stratified system that the mines created, it was understood that the mine owners and managers had certain responsibilities toward their workers. The men's subordination was mediated by their expectation that the mining authorities would treat them respectfully underground, allow them certain latitude in their private lives (including the ability to engage in beer brewing free of prosecution), and listen to the legitimate complaints that had already worked their way through a system of meetings and consensus building. When the mine authorities abrogated this system of give and take, large and small work stoppages took place.[50]

At an August 1941 conference in Johannesburg attended by a wide range of ANC-organized political activists, an organizing committee was formed to establish an African miners' union. Two committed Communists were at the helm: Gaur Radebe served as president, and J. J. Majoro, a former mine clerk and member of the African Mine Clerk's Association, served as secretary. J. B. Marks ultimately assumed the presidency, inaugurating a more energetic membership drive in 1943, and by 1944 the union reported twenty-five thousand dues-paying members. In December 1943 the Lansdowne

Commission issued a report on mine and power workers' wages and working conditions. The government of Jan Christiaan Smuts and the Chamber of Mines largely rejected its recommendations of wage and cost of living increases, paid leave, and overtime pay. In August 1944 the union called a conference in which the leadership rejected the counterproposals made by the government and called for a wage board inquiry and the abolition of the compound system. The government retaliated with the enactment of War Measure 1425, which prohibited gatherings of more than twenty-five people on mining property and denied recognition of the union. Union organizers were forced to find ingenious ways to meet with the membership, often at night and under mine dumps. In the meantime, as the food quality and supply deteriorated and as starving families on the reserves pressed their wage earners for help, worker discontent continued unabated. Hunger strikes followed in 1945, and workers were fired for meeting with their union representatives in search of some relief. In 1946 workers continued to hold meetings, and in order to press their demand for the increase to ten shillings per day, random work stoppages ensued. Police reprisals were instant and brutal.[51]

By August 1946 the African Mine Workers' Union membership was ready for a call to strike. Marks had duly primed his men: "We are wrestling with a giant. . . . You have approached the mine authorities in a [disciplined] manner and put your demand to them and in every case where you asked for fish you got a serpent."[52] At the August 4 meeting, a miner named Moustache rose from the floor and moved to strike on Monday, August 12. Between Monday and Friday more than 75,000 men struck at their respective mines, resulting in 183,467 man-days lost. A force of 1,600 police, mustered to put down the strike, arrested more than 1,000 people and left more than 1,200 injured and at least 9 dead. Meanwhile, twelve mines were brought to a complete standstill, and nine others felt the effect. For its effort, unfortunately, the African Mine Workers' Union lay essentially broken, with most of its organizers jailed and facing charges of sedition, riotous assembly, or violation of the Native Labour Regulation Act. In the ensuing trials of union activists, Communists, and ANC members, however, the important alliances that had already been formed between white radicals and African nationalists became further cemented. Facing the giant with courage, the miners had helped create a new set of adversaries committed to a new trajectory of protest.[53]

The ANC Revived

Since the period from 1927 to 1928, the Communist Party of South Africa (CPSA) "had begun to break out of its isolation from the Africans."[54] Three African members—one of whom was Gana Makabeni—were elected to the Central Committee, a new emphasis was placed on training African workers, and a concerted effort was made to organize branches in the African locations and townships. By 1928 the CPSA reported that 1,600 of its 1,750 members were Africans.[55] All but simultaneously, under the left-leaning three-year leadership of Josiah Gumede, the ANC sought to restructure by soliciting individual memberships that could be grouped into branches. Gumede, who had been to Russia, looked favorably on the Communists, who "sincerely fought for the emancipation of the oppressed."[56] How to combat such oppression, however, was not always clear to the CPSA. Confusion existed over the interpretation and execution of the anti-imperialist Communist International directive to bring about a South African "Native republic," a program that paralleled the effort by the U.S. Communist Party to bring about "self-determination for the Black Belt."[57] Nevertheless, in the midst of a great deal of argument, the new Communist Party leadership of the 1930s attempted to make good on the sea change. The thesis found a powerfully persuasive advocate in the Communist Party activist James La Guma. A Black radical trade unionist from the Cape, La Guma saw in its premise a way for Africans to abandon their subservience to white people and for white people to relinquish their racial arrogance in the effort to establish a socialist state.[58]

In the meantime, the ANC, whose House of Chiefs resolved to have nothing to do with the Communist Party, was lulled back into a conservative complacency. Even so, Communists and leftists were not individually swayed from joining local ANC branches, becoming increasingly entrenched in the myriad problems that African people faced. Africans in the Communist Party were also making progress, as workers and teachers—including such capable men as J. B. Marks, Edwin Mofutsanyana, and Moses Kotane—continued to join. By 1939 Kotane—a self-taught former domestic servant, ardent trade unionist, and astute Marxist theorist from the Rustenburg district—had become the general secretary of the party. He made no mistake about his two primary allegiances: "I am first an African and then a Communist," he stated in December 1938. "I came to the Communist Party because I saw in it the way out and the salvation for the African people."[59]

Although not all factions within the ANC agreed, by 1940 the ANC—now under the leadership of Dr. Alfred B. Xuma—had become more amenable to the idea of an informal working relationship with the Communist Party.[60] In fact, during the postwar 1940s and early 1950s, as Cold War propaganda was heating up worldwide, Xuma was more successful in stemming attempts to purge the Communists from ANC ranks than U.S. labor and civil rights groups had been in their own organizations.[61] An obstreperous Congress Youth League (CYL) leader by the name of Nelson Rolihlahla Mandela—described by Anthony Sampson, who became his close associate, as "heckler and disrupter-in-chief"—seemed to relish breaking up Communist meetings during the preparation for the 1950 May Day strike. The success of that strike and the police brutality that followed it, however, helped change Mandela's view of who constituted the real enemy and who shared areas of common interest.[62]

The Congress Youth League had originated among young, middle-class men of Johannesburg whose families or educational and social experiences had previously exposed them to political affairs. The Bantu Men's Social Centre in Johannesburg, for instance, was one popular gathering place for politically minded young men and women. The Transvaal African Students' Association, some of whose members subsequently joined the CYL, frequently met there, as did many students from Fort Hare, the alma mater of several founding Youth Leaguers.[63] Unquestionably, the most outstanding thinker and personality among the cadre of professional young men determined to bring about a more active mass movement for national liberation was Anton Lembede. In 1943 Lembede—a brilliant intellectual from rural Natal who had been trained as a teacher, philosopher, and lawyer—came to work in the Johannesburg law office of Pixley ka Isaka Seme, a founder and former president of the ANC. With a small number of ANC activists—including Jordan Ngubane, a journalist; A. P. Mda, a teacher; Walter Sisulu, an estate agent; and Peter Raboroko, a Fort Hare graduate and teacher—Lembede and his group began to hash out the ideas that would be expressed in their Manifesto and Constitution.[64]

Late in 1943 and throughout 1944, the small circle of Africanists (as they later came to be known) held meetings with Dr. Xuma to gain support for their group. In the process of revitalizing and reorganizing the ANC, Xuma had abolished the House of Chiefs and called for the establishment of a new constitution. According to Mda, at the annual conference in December 1943, where the new constitution was adopted, the delegates resolved "that Congress Youth Leagues and Womens' Leagues be formed." By the following March and April, with Xuma's knowledge and apparent blessing, the CYL had issued its manifesto, had written its constitution, and had held its inaugural meeting at the Bantu Men's Social Centre.[65] Later that year the CYL summoned "all youth from the Reef, the Transvaal, and the neighbouring regions, to a mass YOUTH CONFERENCE," whose speakers would include Dr. Alfred Xuma, Oliver Tambo, and a Miss Ncakeni, addressing "The part of Women in our struggle."[66]

Women's roles in the movement were, indeed, being articulated, but their presence in the political arena remained obscure. Ellen Kuzwayo, who recalled having joined the CYL in the 1940s, was at a loss to explain why "there seemed to be no outstanding women in the ranks of the ANC movement at that time." She remembered hearing the name of Ida Mtwana but regretted that she never had the opportunity to work with her.[67] Florence Siwedi spoke about some of the responsibilities of the women on the sidelines of the CYL:

> There were some students [in] those days, like Oliver Tambo. When they came from Fort Hare, we usually used to come and make a reception for them at the Bantu Men's Social Centre in Johannesburg. . . . And then those bands usually used to come to the Social Centre to play music for the reception of the students who were coming from Fort Hare—in fact, from all the universities [to encourage them] to come and have receptions [with] the Johannesburg townships. And then when they go back again, there is . . . a farewell.[68]

The young ANC women offered valuable service as hostesses for CYL parties at the Bantu Men's Social Centre and assistants in the freedom struggle; however, their substantial organizing and leadership skills would not be tapped until a later time.

In the meantime, the young men became the primary architects of CYL policies and programs. Although in the early years specific strategies for accomplishing their goals as a group seemed to be lacking, Lembede, Mda, and Ngubane managed to produce excellent polemics on the question of African nationalism and the overall mission of the league. As stated in the manifesto, the founders understood their purpose to be to breathe new life into the national liberation movement, to stimulate in younger African men and women "a national consciousness and unity," and to act as the new "brains trust" of the ANC:

> In response to the demands of the times African Youth is LAYING ITS SER-VICES AT THE DISPOSAL OF THE NATIONAL LIBERATION MOVEMENT, THE AFRICAN NATIONAL CONGRESS. . . . The Congress Youth League must be the brains-trust and power-station of the spirit of African nationalism; the spirit of African self-determination; the spirit that is so discernible in the think-ing of our Youth. It must be an organization where young African men and women will meet and exchange ideas in an atmosphere pervaded by a com-mon hatred of oppression.[69]

Given the shifting nature of its meaning to those who stood on either side of the racial divide, the "spirit of African nationalism" proved a difficult notion for the Youth Leaguers to profess. Established or potential allies, Black or white, might be put off by its exclusionist connotations, as some were by those embodied in Marcus Garvey's powerful idea of wresting "Af-rica for the Africans" or the equally powerful image of "hurl[ing] the White man to the sea."[70] Striking a more moderate tone than Lembede may have originally intended, the CYL National Executive Committee clarified its position on African nationalism in a new manifesto in 1948:

> We of the Youth League take account of the concrete situation in South Af-rica, and realise that the different racial groups have come to stay. But we insist that a condition for inter-racial peace and progress is the abandonment of white domination, and such a change in the basic structure of South African Society that those relations which breed exploitation and human misery will disappear. Therefore our goal is the winning of National freedom for African people, and the inauguration of a people's free society where racial oppression and persecution will be outlawed.[71]

The Africanists viewed their ideology as a crucial antidote to the psy-chological damage inflicted on those cast farthest down. They underwent a lengthy period of organizing and preparation before they prodded the ANC into various forms of civil disobedience and mass action. Suggesting a more spiritual than concrete plan for increasing their membership, the CYL called for a communion with the people: "Every Youth Leaguer must go down to the masses. Brush aside all liberals—both white and black. No compromise is our motto. We recognise only one authority—the people, and our leader can only be he who is with the people."[72] ANC membership began to climb as the organization took better note of the concerns of ordinary people. By the end of the decade, the unmistakable imprint of the Africanists was evident in the Programme of Action adopted at the 1949 ANC annual conference, which included an insistence on freedom from white domination, a campaign to boycott "all differential political institutions," a one-day national strike, and a fund-raising mechanism designed to help underwrite the Programme of Action.[73] By way of the new, more inclusive language and appeal, however, Africanists, Communists, and moderates were now joined in "a long, bitter, and unrelenting struggle for . . . national freedom."[74]

The Women Organize

An additional critical ingredient that was set in motion in the 1940s proved essential to the eruption of mass actions in the 1950s. After the ANC resolved to rebuild the women's arm of the organization in December 1943, the ANC Women's League (ANCWL) was organized, with Madie Hall Xuma (wife of the president of the ANC, Dr. A. B. Xuma) elected as the first president. The roots of the rejuvenated women's section date back to 1918, when the Bantu Women's League was formed under the leadership of Charlotte Manye Maxeke, who helped organize Bloemfontein women in the anti-pass protests of 1913. Her life and work were heavily influenced by the social uplift ideology prevalent among middle-class African Americans, with whom she had spent considerable time when she was in the United States.[75] Her remarkable career reflected her strong commitment to the development of African women and to the advancement of African people overall.

Charlotte Manye Maxeke was born in the Eastern Cape in the early 1870s and educated in mission schools. After she became a teacher in Kimberley, she developed an impressive musical talent and joined a chorus of young African singers.[76] The group toured England, Canada, and the United States, and in 1895 she and several members of the chorus were offered the opportunity to study at the African Methodist Episcopal Church–sponsored Wilberforce University in southern Ohio. Adopted by the Women's Mite Missionary Society, which underwrote her college education, Charlotte Manye graduated in 1901, the first Black South African woman to earn a college degree.[77] While she was at Wilberforce, she came in contact with Dr. W. E. B. Du Bois; Du Bois's future wife, Nina Gomer;

the Reverend Reverdy C. Ransom, a "charismatic preacher" of the African Methodist Episcopal Church and (with Du Bois) a leading figure in
the Niagara Movement; and Ransom's wife, Emma Ransom.[78] Charlotte
Manye Maxeke, who was also an active member of the Women's Mite Missionary Society, spoke at their 1900 and 1901 annual regional conferences
about the African Methodist Episcopal Church in South Africa and the
need for "civilization" and temperance.[79]

Charlotte Manye married the Reverend Marshall Maxeke shortly after
his graduation from Wilberforce in 1903 and his subsequent return to South
Africa. The couple taught at various schools for African youths between the
Transvaal and the Eastern Cape, including a school at Evaton, which later
was named Wilberforce Institute.[80] Through her church and her involvement in African affairs, Charlotte Manye Maxeke advocated on behalf of
African people, adeptly speaking "different political languages" to different
political constituencies.[81] Maxeke blasted the South African government
for its harsh treatment of Black sanitation workers in 1919 and defiantly insisted that African women would not carry passes. In 1923 she clarified her
position to a Johannesburg *Star* reporter: "The natives are my people and if
I attempt to explain the case, and plead in their favour, you are not to interpret my remarks as savouring of an anti-white policy. I am a British subject,
and I am very proud to owe allegiance to the flag."[82] Maxeke maintained
a delicate political balance as she asserted her right to speak for African
people. She called on a definition of Black political identity that, although
couched in dependent terms, could not only make the claim to nonracialism but also refute Afrikaner authority.

As an early supporter of the ANC, Maxeke resented the second-class
status accorded the women of the auxiliary organization; she believed in
the full equality of women, including their right to express themselves politically. Before the 1940s, when women were barred from full membership
in the ANC and the Bantu Women's League offered only affiliate status,
she had told a friend, "They needed us to help by making the tea."[83] She
did not allow this lack of recognition to diminish the zeal with which she
approached her work in the name of Black women, however. She ardently
supported women's education and vocally fought a system that granted few
legitimate means for Black women to earn a living. From 1913 she resisted
any state plan to issue passes to women or to demand that they undergo
medical inspection as a condition of their employment. She advocated on
behalf of women and children who had been imprisoned, and in 1923 she

established a registration agency for prospective domestic workers. Maxeke's work strongly supported an ethos of respectability, and she built her arguments for improved conditions for Black women on the assumption that they had a right to their own family lives and to their own choices of employment. Speaking at a Fort Hare conference in 1930, Maxeke warned of the "many problems pressing in upon us Bantu [that] disturb the peaceful workings of our homes." Citing the negative impact of the system of worker migration on the already narrow job opportunities for women and on their ability to care for their children, she laid the blame at the door of "the European": "Thus we see that the European is by his treatment of the Native . . . only pushing him further and further down on the social scale, forgetting his responsibilities to those who labour for him and to whom he introduced the benefits, and evils, of civilisation."[84] Recognizing the imposed limitations of the political moment, Maxeke proposed that women replace men as domestic workers in safe and hospitable environments and that "Native and European women" sponsor a conference in order "to understand each other's point of view." She proposed, "If you definitely and earnestly set out to lift women and children up in the social life of the Bantu, you will find the men will benefit, and thus the whole community, both White and Black."[85] In a manner reminiscent of the writings of the early African American feminist Anna Julia Cooper and in language mindful of her audience and typical of the era, Maxeke argued for the advancement of African people through the "uplift" of African women.[86]

Until her death in 1939, Maxeke remained a staunch advocate for the elimination of practices and principles that oppressed women and men based on race *and* gender. True to her era and crucial to national liberation, she saw her work in support of women as service to the race as a whole.[87] During the 1950s women's pass resistances, a similar brand of argument, though now thoroughly politicized, promoted the respectability of African women.

In response to the 1941 ANC resolution to build a women's arm, in 1943 Madie Hall Xuma—the well-educated African American wife of ANC president Alfred B. Xuma and a practitioner of Black self-help in the United States—was elected president of the Women's League. She built on her teacher training and social work within the Young Women's Christian Association (YWCA) in the United States to advocate for what she viewed as important work for women that would make "the programme of Congress as attractive to the women as possible."[88] Josie Mpama had criticized Mrs. Xuma for assuming a distinctly apolitical stance within the new Women's League. Mrs. Xuma explained in an interview, "I decided to stay out [of politics] because this is a foreign country to me. I didn't want to get involved in controversial matters. But I once helped raise £1,000 for Doctor [Xuma] when he took over the ANC."[89] In the same interview, however—conducted as Mrs. Xuma prepared to return to the United States after her husband's death and as the state apparatus for enforcing high apartheid policies hardened—Mrs. Xuma recalled the circumstances that compelled her to work on behalf of African women: "I found that I had to do something for women here. It had to be something to make them independent. . . . Then, I hit on Zenzele—it seems to have worked too."[90] Described by one historian as "social, self-help societies that attracted a middle-class following and focused on sewing and social or charitable activities," the Zenzele, which enjoyed wide appeal, proliferated on the Rand.[91]

Madie Hall, born in Winston-Salem, North Carolina, was one of four children born to educated parents, H. H. Hall and Ginny Cowan Hall. Her father was the first Black medical doctor in Winston-Salem, and her mother combined a talent for business and property ownership with active membership in her church and community. She trained her daughter to be financially competent and to care about people "who were sick or poor or needed help." Young Madie Hall wanted to become a doctor after she graduated from Shaw University, but when her father discouraged her from pursuing a medical career, she went into teaching. "My mother didn't oppose him. She just wanted me to get that college education," Mrs. Xuma recalled.[92] Madie Hall went on to finish her undergraduate training at Winston-Salem Teachers' College, and in 1937 she earned a master's degree from Columbia University Teachers' College. In between, she taught school in Winston-Salem and at Bethune-Cookman College in Florida and worked for the YWCA in North Carolina and in Lynchburg, Virginia. It was in New York that she met her future husband, the persistent Dr. Alfred Bitini Xuma.[93]

Madie Hall, who initially refused to marry A. B. Xuma, accepted his proposal as an opportunity to serve Black people. She arrived in South Africa in May 1940 and quickly became acclimated to the new routines of wife, stepmother, and leader of the ANC Women's League. In mid-1943, Madie Hall Xuma organized a successful fund-raiser, writing, directing, and performing in the "American Negro Revue." The musical, which chronicled the history of African Americans, earned £216 for the parent body.[94] Mrs.

Xuma's organization of the YWCA-affiliated Zenzele clubs and her ANC Women's League presidency represented her most lasting and important work in South Africa.

In the Xhosa language, *Zenzele* means "help yourself" or "do it yourself." It was the motto of the African Women's Improvement Association founded by Florence Jabavu at the Eastern Cape in 1927.[95] Mrs. Jabavu was the well-educated wife of D. D. T. Jabavu, a prominent intellectual, political activist, and the first African professor at Fort Hare.[96] In 1935 Mrs. Susie Yergan—an African American woman who married Max Yergan, a YMCA missionary who worked at Fort Hare—founded a self-help organization for rural women called the Bantu Women's Home Improvement Association. The organizations and their affiliates came to be referred to as the Zenzele Clubs. Florence Jabavu's and Susie Yergan's organizations worked in ways that were reminiscent of Margaret Murray Washington's "mothers' meetings" in Tuskegee and rural Macon County, Alabama. These rural Black women's groups, in South Africa and in Alabama, focused on the acquisition of up-to-date, efficient skills in household jobs, farming, child care, health care, and hygiene.[97] Despite the fact that Mrs. Madie Hall Xuma's 1940s organization shared the same name and similar programs with the older rural associations, it appears that the organizations were not affiliated.

Mrs. Xuma's intention was to help local women in the area in and around Johannesburg. She wanted to do "something to encourage them to stand on their own feet instead of depending on other people too much."[98] Zenzele programs stressed a respectable home life and the domestic arts. After 1951, as a result of Mrs. Xuma's efforts, the clubs affiliated with the International YWCA, which opened the doors for Black women to participate in a greater variety of activities and a well-established structure of organizational and service work. In 1963 Mrs. Xuma stated, "One important job that Zenzele has been doing all along has been to train women to speak and become leaders of the community."[99] In an internal report, Zenzele women thanked Mrs. Xuma "for her inspiration and very wise guidance ... for her untinted faith in the ultimate independence of Africans and particularly the faith she has displayed in the total independence of the Womanhood of this continent."[100] In fact, some Black women of Johannesburg used their YWCA tenure to organize within the community when it was too dangerous to engage in explicitly political activity. Future leaders such as Ellen Kuzwayo and Joyce Piliso Seroke gained valuable training and experience from their YWCA work.[101]

As provincial ANC branches were established in the late 1940s, the ANCWL began to build momentum in its own right. In 1949 the ANC adopted the Programme of Action conceived largely by the more activist Youth Leaguers. With the new focus, new leaders who were more disposed to mass action replaced the Xumas as heads of their respective ANC groups. A feisty Ida Mtwana—"Youth Leaguer, moving spirit among women, orator and heckler"—became the next president of the Women's League.[102]

Mrs. Kate Mxakatho, an early activist in the ANCWL, has credited her family with instilling in her a sense of dignity and "politics"—the awareness that African people were made to withstand many forms of injustice:

> I think politics were in my family, more especially, my mother's family. My mother's cousin was then secretary of the ANC . . . Philip Matseke. He used to preach to us that whites are really trampling on our toes. As young children, when they allowed them to even organize in the schools, [he would] come and preach to us, in fact, and I grew up knowing that we are not living in a country that is normal. Then, when I came to Johannesburg, I met people like Radebe, in fact, who were in the Communist Party, and Mofutsanyana; those were the CP [Communist Party]. They used to hold meetings in street corners in Johannesburg, more especially, the [African] locations.
>
> And the ANC, we had [Elias] Moretsele; he died during the first Treason Trial. People like Robert Resha and Mandela joined when the president was Pixley ka Isaka Seme. Then we carried on 'til the Boer[s] saw that we were becoming strong[er] and strong[er].[103]

Echoing sentiments similar to those of Charlotte Maxeke, Mrs. Mxakatho expressed frustration over but would not be deterred by the subordinate role relegated to women within the parent body. Clearly, she resented the fact that women in the ANC were expected to perform domestic duties, and she relished the opportunity to organize women for more meaningful political activity: "We women were only used as scullery girls! Whenever they had conferences, we would go and cook—even though you're a card-carrying member! It was only in the 1940s that Madie Hall Xuma said to us women . . . (her husband was then president of the ANC), 'Women, the men are in Bloemfontein in the conference. What are you doing?' Then we started forming our ANC Women's League branches. [I belonged to the] Western Native Township branch."[104] Kate Mxakatho recalled her involvement in the Defiance Campaign of 1952, an excellent example of the willingness that so many women exhibited when they were called on to contribute more than their cooking skills to the movement for freedom.

During the late 1940s, Maggie Resha—the young wife of Robert Resha and later a member of the same ANCWL branch as Kate Mxakatho—began her life in politics after she was exposed to the CYL. Having accompanied her husband to a CYL meeting held at the Western Native Township Municipal Hall in 1948, she was inspired to hear the ardent members' insistence on more rapid movement toward African liberation. Aware of the limited choices open to her in a segregated society, she became commited to activism. As a newly trained nurse who held both state registration and hospital certification from Holy Cross Hospital in eastern Pondoland, she had met her husband when he was a patient at Pretoria Hospital. She loved nursing, but she hated the segregated conditions under which she had to work. A segregated hospital staff, with no Black doctors, served a segregated clientele; the Black staff was permitted to treat only the "non-European" patients. The Black nurses' accommodations were deplorable, their uniforms distinguished them by race, and they were paid one-quarter the amount paid to the white nurses, who held the same qualifications and, in Maggie Resha's words, "nursed in the same way." Disillusioned by this disparity, she coped (as many members of Mrs. Burks's congregation had done in Montgomery) by wearing "a perpetual invisible mask." [105]

Mrs. Resha's regular attendance at CYL and Women's League meetings was the perfect antidote to her disillusionment and discontent. The CYL militants, she recalled, "made fiery speeches which demanded action against the white government's oppressive laws. After that [initial] meeting, I felt so happy and relieved to hear Africans talk of fighting for their freedom; I suddenly found I had something to live for after all my depression and bitterness . . . at the Pretoria Hospital." [106] Breaking out in some of the same urgent fever that excited so many of her compatriot Youth Leaguers, she favored physical action: "Robert and I talked and talked after we came back home, because I had suggested that Africans must stop talking and fight physically to get their land back. He tried, patiently, to explain the ANC policy of non-violence." [107] Her fighting spirit was soon effectively channeled into positive action aimed at efficient removal of the structures that oppressed Black people. Like so many of her counterparts in the U.S. South, who confronted the same challenge to maintain a nonviolent stance in the face of brutality from the state and other sources, Mrs. Resha and her

ANC colleagues managed to use nonviolence as a tactic in their own brand of committed activism.

Eagerly, Maggie Resha joined the Women's League under Ida Mtwana[108] and became familiar with the purpose of the organization and with an imaginative method of recruiting women members:

> The essence of the ANCWL was to mobilise women to play a more meaning-ful role in the liberation struggle, and to watch for and resist any racist legisla-tion directed against them as women. Ida Mtwana was a very militant person and an immensely eloquent speaker. She soon called separate meetings of the ANCWL. At these meetings we decided to organise as many women as pos-sible to join the ANC. Ida had a wonderfully melodious voice, and she soon taught the women many freedom songs. . . . People were proud to be members of [the African National] Congress, since it gave one a sense of mental libera-tion, because of being engaged in doing something about apartheid.
>
> . . . In Sophiatown, when the women started to organise women into the ANC, they told all men to bring their wives to the meetings or the women would not vote for them. Men like Patrick Molaoa and others actually thanked the women for this action. Men came with their wives, and what cream of militancy would otherwise have been left idle! Many women, who . . . used to complain that their husbands had been neglecting them or were not sup-porting them because of their politics, saw the light when they started to be active in the organisation. The WL [Women's League] warnings to the men in Sophiatown [were] so effective that dozens of men bought the green ANC blouses from Lilian Ngoyi, who had designed and sewed them, as presents for their wives.[109]

In this case, the women's brand of political blackmail was successful. Husbands and wives who complained of losing each other's time to politics were encouraged to experience the benefits of ANC membership—in other words, to invest in their own political self-interests. Maggie Resha saw the Women's League become "stronger and stronger."[110] Adding to her already full life—which included two children, training in midwifery, full-time em-ployment, and partnership with an active husband—Maggie Resha became increasingly involved in the Women's League as an organizer and leader of her branch.

Meanwhile, in 1948 (the same year that Alabama and other southern white supremacists bolted from the Democrats to form their own anti-Black Dixiecrat Party), a now "purified" Nationalist Party under Daniel

François Malan came to power in South Africa. The Nationalists promised to put an end to Smuts's "lenient" policy toward Black urban migration by developing a comprehensive program of apartheid, which would dominate at least the next forty years of the South African political economy. In effect, "the age of the generals was over and that of the ideologues and technocrats had begun."[111] The grand design of racial separation did not spring fully formed from the Nationalists at that same moment, but by 1950 the Nationalists had begun to set in motion a stream of separatist legislative acts. The wide-ranging Suppression of Communism Act passed in June 1950, for example, banned individuals, organizations, newspapers, and such from actions "aimed at bringing about any political, industrial, social or economic change in the country by unlawful acts." Clearly, the objective of the Nationalists was to eliminate free speech, destroy the Black trade unions, and eradicate any other form of democratic protest or resistance. Rather than become persecuted out of existence as victims of Nationalist gestapo tactics—even with United Party opposition to the bill (which they knew would be ineffective)—the CPSA voted for its own dissolution shortly before the act was passed.[112]

The May 1, 1950, call for peaceful demonstrations and a work "stay-away" by, among others, the Transvaal ANC, the Indian Congress, the as yet unbanned Communists, and the trade unionists, in which eighteen Africans were killed and thirty were wounded, precipitated a new wave of mass actions orchestrated by the ANC and its white, Colored, and Indian allies.[113] In these demonstrations, the state found what it saw as sufficient justification for the use of extreme force. Such violence—used thereafter by a minority group that was infatuated with its own master-race ideology and self-confident enough to apply it against any and all resisters—became frighteningly commonplace. Until 1952, Communists, Black and white trade unionists who refused to accept the industrial color bar, ANC elders, Youth Leaguers, Africanists, and members of the Indian Congress, including a growing contingent of women, had to make their political way toward one another by finding reliable common ground on which to mount future actions. The decade of the 1950s, as it turned out, was dedicated to various forms of civil disobedience that were (as in the U.S. freedom movement up to the mid-1960s) distinctly nonviolent and greatly influenced by the teachings of Mahatma Gandhi. That important decade in the movement for African liberation was punctuated by a significant growth in and maturation of Black political consciousness and action by women.

Chapter Seven

~~~~~~~~~~~

"PUT MY FOOT IN THE
ROAD AND WALKED!"

Black Women Lead the Montgomery Bus Boycott, 1950–1961

At age eighty-two, Mrs. Amelia Scott Green remembered growing up in and spending much of her life within the center city Black community of segregated Montgomery, Alabama. She began school later than many of the children at the Booker T. Washington Elementary School, and in the fourth grade—like many members of her generation—she was forced to leave school to help her mother support their large family. Amelia and her mother worked for the family of Ruth Babbitt, who "was kinda on the poor side—they wasn't none of them [with] two butlers, and a cook, and a maid, and all that."[1] Amelia's mother washed for the Babbitts, and from a very young age, before she had to leave school altogether, Amelia did much of the cleaning for the Babbitt family before she headed off to school in the morning: "I'd go to work five o'clock in the morning and come back and go to school. Then on Saturdays and Sundays I'd work from 7:30 'til 3:30 for $2.50 a week. Welcome to the seven days [of work] a week! My mama washed for $1.50 a week."[2]

After she stopped going to school, Amelia held a string of day jobs cleaning house and taking care of children—"nickel and dime jobs," as she called them, where she knew that her labor was being exploited. Consequently, Amelia felt little compunction about leaving one employer for another, especially when she could be compensated in wages rather than food. "I didn't stay nowhere long," she said, "'cause I figured that I was supposed to be getting money for what I was doing, and people worked you to death, giving me something to eat [as compensation]. Then they start finding fault." She was not about to clean windows, climb up on ladders, or do any work that she felt a man was more suited to do. As she told one employer, "Miss, you don't want me to work because I ain't no mule and I ain't no fool." She credited her father with her outspoken nature: "My daddy was the kind of person, he'd tell you quick what he was and what he wasn't going to do.... I'm the same way. [I'll] come back at you, and when I come back at you, somebody is going to know that I've been there!"[3]

In 1942, during World War II, Mrs. Green's first husband, James Scott, like many of her male relatives and neighbors, enlisted in the army. At that time, Amelia Scott tried her hand at factory work, which was open to Black women and paid better than domestic work. She tried working at Capitol Laundry and then at Reliance Manufacturing Company but then returned to domestic work, cleaning for a woman who owned a boarding house that was frequented by traveling baseball teams. Earning as much as six to eight dollars a week, she managed to save enough money to buy a house. After the war, her husband migrated to Detroit, but she opted not to follow: "I told him he was welcome to go, but there wasn't nothing up there for me."[4]

By the start of the Montgomery bus boycott in 1955, Mrs. Scott had become Mrs. Green and had given birth to four children, three of whom were in school. She was cleaning house and looking after the children of a Jewish couple named Murray and Sadie Weil, who lived in an affluent neighborhood called Normandale. Mrs. Green remembered Sadie Weil as a southerner who was accustomed to exercising her power over her employee in the household and beyond, but she remembered Murray Weil as supportive and sympathetic: "The Jews caught the devil—what they call it, the Holocaust? We were doing the same thing. Murray told me that we were going to win, for what we were doing was right. She got mad with me, but he told me in front of her, and he just automatically done it. Boy, I watched her face more times than I could count. Every time she attempt to do something or say something else, he say, 'If you want it, you do it yourself.'"[5]

According to Mrs. Green, Sadie Weil fell into the familiar competition among employers of Black domestic workers for having the most compliant maid or being the most exacting mistress. Mrs. Green, however, countered Sadie Weil's claims, calling her a liar to her face when the need arose:

See, she know how being white they get together [about] their maids and things. "Well, my maid don't do that; she do this." But [when] I walked in on them one morning, she said to her sister-in-law, "Amelia ride the bus, and she's here every morning on time." I said, "You're a damn liar; I don't ride no bus. Where you get that idea from?" Then she lied to me: "I don't see where you all getting on at buying Martin Luther King a Cadillac for him." ... I say,

"I tell you one thing. If he want five damn Cadillacs, I just buy it!" I wasn't making but seventeen dollars a week. I said, "If you want somebody to ride the bus, you park your car and you go ride the bus."

There were a lot of times [before the boycott, when] we go to get on the bus, we had to go to the back door. Sometimes we could get on there, and sometimes we couldn't. They wouldn't give us a transfer. Right downtown, a many times I would walk from downtown—had paid my money at the front and went to the back. Half of the bus was for the whites up front; the other part was for the "niggers" in the back.[6]

Clearly, Mrs. Green, like countless others, had pent-up frustration and anger over the disrespect with which bus drivers treated Black riders. Routinely, before the Black passengers managed to climb aboard a bus at the rear after having deposited their fares at the front, the bus would pull off and leave them. Often, passengers who carried packages or small children would barely manage to make it on board before the driver abruptly slammed the doors shut and swung his vehicle from the curb, sending parcels and people flying in every direction. Mrs. Rosa Parks, the Women's Political Council (WPC), and the captivating voice of Dr. Martin Luther King, Jr., however, had declared an end to the humiliation that Black people endured on the buses and to the overall subordinate status that they were accorded. Mrs. Green was happy to join the great demonstration that the Black community of Montgomery held in protest of this treatment. She was eager to join the movement against segregation in her city. There was one thing, she explained, that she had known all along: "I'm good for something, and they wasn't supposed to walk on me like you walk on a road."[7]

Mrs. Green was one of many spirited Montgomery women of modest means who were determined to end the racist indignities that they had endured for so long. Calling on one another for both support and leadership, Black women of Montgomery sporting pocketbooks, hats, and even high heels—the outside markers of their principled respectability—took on a city and a system that had historically disregarded them. Women from both the working and middle classes mobilized the crucial early support necessary to the success of the boycott. They took responsibility for recording and disseminating reliable information and regularly attended the church-based mass meetings that sustained the boycott for more than a year. The testimonies of their experiences before and during the boycott explain their reasons for joining this overtly political movement. Clearly, these women—

domestic workers, teachers, factory employees, and others—who had developed a political consciousness with respect to their oppression not only as Black people but also as women, could no longer accept their subordination or be "walk[ed] on . . . like you walk on a road."

Mobilizing the Women

Sometime in 1954 E. D. Nixon introduced Rosa Parks to Virginia and Clifford Durr, both natives of Alabama and renegade New Dealers who had relocated to Montgomery. Mrs. Durr had backed the Progressive Party candidate, Henry Wallace, for president in 1948, and her attorney husband had declined reappointment to the Federal Communications Commission by refusing to take Harry S. Truman's loyalty oath on the grounds that it was unconstitutional and insulting.[8] During the 1930s and 1940s the Durrs had been members of the Southern Conference for Human Welfare, an interracial group dedicated to increasing voter participation for Black people in the South. They fought the unfashionable fight against the poll tax through the Southern Conference for Human Welfare, took a stand against McCarthyism, defended suspected Communists, and staunchly advocated peace. They were two members of a rare breed of white southerner who were willing to forgo their social standing, or even their economic security, in order to uphold their convictions. Confident that he had an ally in Clifford Durr, E. D. Nixon brought him discrimination cases that other lawyers refused. The Black community also had a strong ally in Virginia Durr. Shortly before the 1954 *Brown v. Board of Education* decision, Senator William Jenner's Subcommittee on Internal Security—in its hunt for Communists—subpoenaed Mrs. Durr; Aubrey Williams, a radical friend who was the editor of the *Southern Farmer*; and Myles Horton a friend from the Highlander Folk School in Tennessee. Mrs. Durr refused to testify, preferring to "stand mute" before the "Kangaroo Court" that she held in such contempt. The public exposure that her behavior at the subcommittee hearings in New Orleans received blew her cover as a "proper" southern lady once and for all, freeing her to form her own associations with Black and white men and women whose political views aligned with her own.[9]

Mrs. Durr found allies among the members of the interracial Council on Human Relations, the United Church Women, and a group that she described as mainly composed of "teachers at Alabama State College [who were] later . . . prominent in Martin Luther King's struggle."[10] This group, which she referred to as the Women's Democratic Club, was most likely the Women's Political Council. Women from this club, including Mrs. A. W. West, had sent Mrs. Durr a telegram when she was in New Orleans: "We are with you and our prayers are with you and we are proud of you."[11] Mrs. Johnnie Carr, also a member of several of these groups, had become friendly with Mrs. Durr in 1954. In a continuing pattern of reciprocity and mutual political interest shared by two activist communities, Virginia Durr and Johnnie Carr maintained their friendship throughout the period of the boycott and beyond.[12]

Virginia Durr recommended her friend Rosa Parks for a ten-day Highlander Folk School workshop on the implementation of racial desegregation during the summer of 1955. Mrs. Durr recalled that she had to do a bit of maneuvering to get her there. Mrs. Parks was paid little for her job at Montgomery Fair, and she was stretched for time. She cared for her husband and mother, she worked with the youth of Montgomery on behalf of the National Association for the Advancement of Colored People (NAACP), and she worked with Nixon. Still, Mrs. Durr persisted:

> When Myles [Horton] called from Highlander, I immediately went over and asked Mrs. Parks if she would like to go. She said she would but she didn't have any money . . . so I said, "If I can get you some money, can you go?" She said yes. I went over and got the money from Aubrey Williams, who had more money than we did at that time. . . . Rosa Parks is one of the proudest people I've ever known in my life. . . . She was a very proud woman, so all of this had to be accomplished with a great deal of tact, which I am not noted for.[13]

Myles Horton was the son of a Tennessee sharecropper, who had studied with Reinhold Neibuhr at Union Theological Seminary.[14] Horton had founded Highlander, and under his direction it became an important resource for movement supporters, linking them to a national network of activists and material resources. Closely identified with radical political organizing in the 1930s, the school had acquired a reputation among its detractors as being a Communist institution. In any event, it offered important training to hundreds of movement people involved in labor organizing, voter registration, and civil disobedience. For instance, young members of the Student Nonviolent Coordinating Committee (SNCC)—Diane Nash, James Bevel, Marion Barry, and John Lewis—were among those who eventually made their way to the leadership workshops convened for youth organizers of the 1960s.[15]

While she was at Highlander, Mrs. Parks met Septima Clark (a gifted teacher from Charleston, South Carolina) and her colleague in citizenship education, Bernice Robinson (formerly a Charleston beautician). Mrs. Parks enjoyed the "peace and harmony" in the integrated workshops on how to desegregate schools. She recalled, "Everything was very organized.... [W]e shared the work and the play. One of my greatest pleasures there was enjoying the smell of bacon frying and coffee brewing and knowing that the white folks were doing the preparing instead of me."[16] The Highlander experience was one of many that preceded Mrs. Parks's decision to remain in her bus seat in December 1955. Certainly, her many experiences living in a white supremacist system—from her days with her grandparents in Pine Level, to her confrontations with the white bullies who targeted her and her younger brother in Montgomery, to her husband's activities on behalf of the Scottsboro defense, to her work for the NAACP—played a role in the stand she took on that fateful day. She recalled that on the evening of Thursday, December 1, 1955, when she refused to move on order from the same hostile driver who had put her off his bus in 1943, she thought about her defiant grandfather, armed and ready to protect himself.[17] "I was not tired physically," she explained. "I was not old.... I was forty-two. No, the only tired I was, was tired of giving in."[18]

The sequence of events that followed is now all but legendary. When Mrs. Parks was arrested, Bertha Butler, a friend and passenger on the same bus, told Mrs. Nixon what she had witnessed. Mrs. Nixon alerted her husband, E. D. Nixon, who called the jail. When the police refused to divulge to him the charges against Mrs. Parks, he sought legal counsel. Fred Gray, a young Black attorney, was unavailable at the time, so Nixon turned to Clifford Durr for help. After learning that Mrs. Parks was arrested for violating the segregation laws of Montgomery, Durr left for the jail in the company of both his wife and E. D. Nixon. Mrs. Parks, for her part, had since spoken to her mother and her husband, who was busy rounding up the money and a car to get her out. Meanwhile, Mrs. Parks's trial date had been set for Monday, December 5, 1955, and Nixon and the Durrs had managed to obtain her release. At the Parks home, Nixon proposed that Mrs. Parks allow hers to be the test case that the local NAACP had been looking forward to bringing against the segregated bus seating system in Montgomery. With the approval of both her mother and her husband, Rosa Parks agreed.[19]

By 4:00 A.M. on Friday, December 2, Mrs. Jo Ann Gibson Robinson of the WPC and two of her senior students at Alabama State had finally completed mimeographing thousands of leaflets to inform the Montgomery Black community of an impending bus boycott.[20] Having heard the news of Mrs. Parks's arrest the previous evening, late that same night Mrs. Robinson had conferred with Fred Gray, a friend and former student. She could no longer stand the waiting, the inaction, the indecision of the Black male leadership. Most of all, she was determined to make sure that Black Montgomery did not go about its "business as usual" and allow this important political moment to escape. The mood of many African Americans only increased her determination to "*do* something": "For that day and a half, black Americans rode the buses as before, as if nothing had happened. They were sullen and uncommunicative, but they rode the buses. There was a silent, tension-filled waiting. For blacks were not talking loudly in public places—they were quiet, sullen, waiting. Just waiting."[21]

Jo Ann Robinson was no stranger to what had been happening in Montgomery. Although as a professor at Alabama State College, she was protected by the privilege of her middle-class status from some of the harsher aspects of the U.S. version of apartheid, she was by no means immune to the indignities and dangers that Black women routinely faced. She too experienced the anger and frustration of living in a white supremacist state. On her way to the airport to visit family and friends in Cleveland, Ohio, just before Christmas 1949, a bus driver demanded that Mrs. Robinson vacate her seat in the fifth row of the bus. Stumbling off the bus that day, "tears blinded my vision," she remembered. "Waves of humiliation inundated me; and I thanked God that none of my students was on that bus to witness the tragic experience." Six years later, the memory remained fresh, and in a revelatory moment in the fall of 1955, she proposed that the WPC undertake a citywide boycott of the Montgomery buses. At that moment she had asked herself, "How long will this go on?" The answer seemed to come from all around her: "As long as black Americans will allow it!"[22]

The same night of Mrs. Parks's arrest, Mrs. Robinson received permission from a colleague at Alabama State to use the Business Department mimeograph equipment. She hammered out the first message:

> Another woman has been arrested and thrown in jail because she refused to get up out of her seat on the bus for a white person to sit down. . . . Negroes have rights, too, for if Negroes did not ride the buses, they could not operate. . . . [I]f we do not do something to stop these arrests, they will continue.

The next time it may be you, or your daughter, or mother. . . . We are, therefore, asking every Negro to stay off the buses Monday in protest of the arrest and trial. Don't ride the buses to work, to town, to school, or anywhere on Monday.[23]

Anxious to launch a boycott of the city buses, the WPC had been championing the civil and political rights of Black people in Montgomery since its inception in 1946. Mrs. Jo Ann Robinson, Mrs. Mary Fair Burks, Mrs. Irene West, Mrs. Euretta Adair, their lieutenants, and their membership were ready with a coordinated information distribution plan. According to Mrs. Burks, members of the WPC had appeared before the City Commission with their complaints about and proposed solutions to the bus abuses "at least six or seven times" before March 1955.[24] Indeed, after a WPC meeting with the city commissioners in March 1954, Mrs. Robinson had sent a letter on behalf of the WPC to Mayor W. A. Gayle, summarizing the main points of discussion with the commission regarding the "city-bus-fare-increase case." The WPC had suggested a new seating plan, whereby Black passengers would be seated from the back to the front and white passengers from the front to the back "until all the seats [were] taken." The WPC had also requested termination of the requirement that Black riders board the bus at the back after depositing their fare at the front and initiation of the requirement that drivers pick up passengers "at every corner in residential sections occupied by Negroes as they do in communities where whites reside." The WPC representatives offered examples of other cities—such as Atlanta, Macon, Savannah, and Mobile—that had implemented these conditions. They noted that the majority of riders on the buses were Black and that "if Negroes did not patronize them, they could not possibly operate." It was their belief that "forceful measures" were unnecessary to achieve fair treatment on the buses, but their requests fell on deaf ears.[25]

In the year that followed, the WPC had supported Claudette Colvin, a fifteen-year-old A-student at Booker T. Washington High School, who had been arrested for refusing to give up her seat to a white passenger. Mrs. Robinson characterized Miss Colvin as "quiet, well-mannered, neat, clean,"[26] and many believed that her ill treatment and arrest would make a compelling case against the bus company and perhaps a good reason for a boycott that would be orchestrated with the help of E. D. Nixon and others. It was determined, however, that as an unmarried pregnant teenager, Miss Colvin was too vulnerable a subject, one who might weaken the validity of the Black community's claims to respectability and demand for fair treatment. Much later, in her adulthood, Miss Colvin speculated that her family's working-class status prevented her from entering "the inner circle"[27] of the middle-class activists who organized the boycott. For his part, Nixon believed that the character of the subject of their test case must be spotless and capable of holding up under the pressure that was sure to come. Further, and most important, Miss Colvin's eventual conviction of assault and battery on a police officer, which yielded a probationary sentence, closed the door to the use of her case in a challenge against the city segregation laws.[28] Unwilling to let the matter of the buses die, however, the women of the WPC determined to keep the bus issue before both the public and the City Commission.

The years of segregated bus seating had tired and angered the Black residents of Montgomery. Black riders had stood over empty seats reserved for white passengers. They had watched drivers who hauled nearly empty buses pass them by as they waited on the street corners. They had witnessed the arrest of children for failing to follow the prescribed seating arrangements. They had watched drivers verbally and physically assault women riders and have them arrested by the police for minor infractions. They had witnessed as men were beaten, threatened, and thrown off buses for not having the correct change and then arrested for raising any kind of objection. As a means of both protest and self-protection, many Black men had abandoned their use of the buses.[29] Black people had voiced strong objections to their treatment; in 1953 the WPC received thirty bus-related complaints from the community at large.[30]

Mrs. Robinson reported that in 1952 a driver accused a rider named Mr. Brooks of having deposited his fare incorrectly. When the rider, who was noticeably intoxicated, denied that this was the case, the driver became incensed and called the police. Upon their arrival on the scene, the police shot and killed Mr. Brooks. Claiming that he had tried to resist arrest, the police were exonerated. In 1953 Mrs. Epsie Worthy received a transfer from the driver of the first of two buses that she rode to get home, and she offered it to the driver of the second bus. Refusing to accept the transfer, the second driver insisted that Mrs. Worthy pay the second fare. Mrs. Worthy held her ground, but when the driver would not relent, she decided to get off the bus rather than pay. Still unrelenting, however, the driver insisted that whether or not she remained on the bus, she would have to pay the second fare. As she descended from the bus, the driver overcame Mrs. Worthy and began to beat her. Vigorously defending herself, Mrs Worthy got in a few blows of her own but was then arrested and fined fifty-two dollars for disorderly conduct.[31] Frustrations increased as assaults on riders continued, and by December 1955—when Mrs. Rosa Parks was arrested—the WPC, E. D. Nixon, and the entire Black community of Montgomery were ready for a boycott.

Between Jo Ann Robinson's 8:00 A.M. and 2:00 P.M. classes on Friday, December 2, she and a number of supporters—including her two student helpers, who were members of the WPC—distributed the first batch of more than fifty-two thousand leaflets. She explained:

> I took out the WPC membership roster and called the former president, Dr. Mary Fair Burks, then the Pierces, the Glasses, Mrs. Mary Cross, Mrs. Elizabeth Arrington, Mrs. Josie Lawrence, Mrs. Geraldine Nesbitt, Mrs. H. Councill Trenholm, Mrs. Catherine N. Johnson, and a dozen or more others. I alerted all of them to the forthcoming distribution of the leaflets, and enlisted their aid in speeding and organizing the distribution network. Each would have one person waiting at a certain place to take a package of notices as soon as my car stopped and [we] could hand them a bundle of leaflets.[32]

Mrs. Irene West, a stalwart member of the WPC and a woman of great stature in the middle-class Black community explained some of the details of the WPC distribution plan:

> I was called and asked if I would help in initiating a one-day boycott and of course I was willing. I was sent a large stock of leaflets which I distributed among my workers, and they in turn put them on porches without ringing doorbells in order to keep the finger off of any [specific] persons.... [I]n the Women's Political Council we ... work in areas which are broken down into sub-areas and within these are persons who know the people a little better than I, and can reach some which I cannot, and these are called workers.[33]

Leaflets were distributed at schools, among both students and staff. Students carried them home to their parents, who redistributed them to neighbors. Leaflets were also handed out at small Black businesses, storefronts, beauty parlors, barbershops, bars, taverns, and factories. According to Mrs. Burks, the subsequent Saturday morning distribution of leaflets that announced both the boycott and the Monday night meeting at Holt Street

Baptist Church scheduled for December 5 was a slow process. She recalled, "Often we not only had to take time to explain the leaflet, but also first to read it to those unable to do so." On that Saturday morning, she admitted, she witnessed for the first time the living conditions of the "truly poor and disenfranchised." She remembered thinking "that not even a successful boycott would solve the problems of poverty and illiteracy that [she] saw that day."[34]

On Friday, members of the Black ministerial community of Montgomery were also called into action. E. D. Nixon called a number of ministers— including the Reverend Ralph Abernathy, of First Baptist Church; the Reverend H. H. Hubbard, of Bethel Baptist Church (who was also the president of the Baptist Ministerial Alliance); and the Reverend Martin Luther King, Jr., of Dexter Avenue Baptist Church—to inform them of Mrs. Parks's arrest and to gain their support for the idea of a boycott. Nixon helped arrange a meeting of the ministers to be held that evening at King's Dexter Avenue Church. Forced to miss the meeting to work his route as a Pullman porter, he left strict instructions that the ministers refrain from creating a permanent organization until he could be present. In the meantime, the WPC distribution plan had included a fortuitous drop-off at the Hilliard Chapel African Methodist Episcopal Zion Church, pastored by the Reverend E. N. French, who happened to be hosting a meeting of ministers. On Friday evening a full contingent of the Black leadership of Montgomery, including a sizable number of clergymen, met in the basement of Dexter Baptist to discuss boycott plans. Before Nixon left town on Friday, he had alerted Joe Azbell, a white columnist for the *Montgomery Advertiser*, about the imminent boycott. According to Mrs. Robinson, a domestic worker added to this publicity on Friday by carrying the story to her employer, who then helped it find its way to the bus company, the police, the City Commission, and more members of the press. However inadvertently, the weekend publicity, via newspaper, radio, and television, helped spread the word to those who otherwise would not have been reached.[35]

When, at last, Monday morning, December 5, 1955, dawned over the city, buses that serviced the Black communities of Montgomery followed their usual route accompanied by contingents of motorcycle police who claimed that their presence was intended to protect Black riders from "goon squads" that the authorities assumed would intimidate any Black people who attempted to ride. The boycott of the buses that day reached nearly total compliance—far beyond anyone's expectations—as workers and students walked, took ten-cent cab rides, or found alternative means of transportation. As Nixon elatedly reported, "Ended up at eight o'clock that morning, the buses ain't hauled nobody, hadn't hauled nobody, didn't haul nobody else for the next 381 days." By 7:00 P.M. on Monday, the mass meeting convened at Holt Street Baptist Church, with a jubilant crowd of between six thousand and seven thousand boycotters. Packed nearly to the rafters in the balcony, in the basement, in the aisles, in the surrounding churchyard, and up and down the street for several blocks, the people cheered Mrs. Parks and the leaders of their community. Unanimously, they agreed to continue the boycott until their modest demands were met: (1) courteous treatment of Black passengers by the bus operators, (2) first-come, first-served seating (Black people seating themselves from back to front and white people seating themselves from front to back), and (3) the hiring of Black bus drivers on predominantly Black routes.[36]

On the subject of the three-part objective of the boycott, Mrs. Robinson quietly disagreed. In the early stages of the action, it seemed, Black people sought not integration but better treatment on the buses. For the sake of unity, Mrs. Robinson cooperated, although she strongly believed that segregation must end:

> It may seem that my sentiments contradict Dr. King's press statements at the time that "blacks were not seeking integration." Certainly he was not demanding integration. However, the women of the WPC had started the boycott, and we did it for the specific purpose of finally integrating those buses. We were tired of second-class citizenship, tired of insults on buses by drivers who were cruel in order to make themselves appear big. The WPC wanted integration because of the abusive treatment of blacks on buses. Women have always gotten away with the truth. Men lie sometimes to get by. Integration was the ultimate end of our struggle. Can you envision 45,000 boycotters *not* wanting to integrate the buses? We just did not get up on the housetops to yell it and thus make our task a harder one. For the sake of a peaceful fight, we kept silent on integration. We were not obnoxious about it, but quietly demanded it. It was Dr. King who said, "Keep them in the dark."[37]

King's published statements surrounding the boycott notwithstanding, his memoir of the Montgomery movement noted, "We were sure . . . that the Rosa Parks case, which was now in the courts, provided the test that would ultimately bring about the defeat of bus segregation itself."[38] In subsequent discussions the leadership of the Montgomery Improvement Association (MIA)—the group organized to lead the boycott—acknowledged that the case might take years to move through the state and federal courts of appeal before it resulted in a favorable ruling and that even a favorable ruling might exonerate Mrs. Parks without outlawing segregated bus seating. Moreover, in view of the complete intransigence of the City Commission, its manipulation of bus company compliance with city and state law, the boycott leadership saw no possibility of a negotiated settlement with the city. Adding insult to injury, in the first two months of 1956, the threat of white violence erupted with the bombings of the homes of King and Nixon. The city enacted a new "get tough" policy against people who operated and participated in car pooling, and the Montgomery County solicitor helped the county grand jury charge King and eighty-eight others with violation of a thirty-five-year-old law prohibiting boycotts. The late January bombings in particular proved to the MIA, the NAACP, and others the necessity of waging a full-scale attack on the segregationist laws. On February 1, 1956, in Federal District Court in Montgomery, the attorney Fred Gray filed the MIA suit that would eventually upend the policy of segregated seating. On behalf of five women, including young Claudette Colvin, the suit charged the City Commission, the bus company, and two of its drivers with the unconstitutional act of enforcing "segregation on intra-state buses."[39]

In the remarkably short May 11, 1956, case known as *Browder v. Gayle*, a three-judge panel listened to the arguments prepared by Fred Gray, Charles Langford (another young, Black Montgomery attorney), and Robert Carter (assistant to Thurgood Marshall of the NAACP). One of the original plaintiffs, Jeanetta Reese, had dropped out of the suit, claiming that she wanted "nothing to do with that mess."[40] The remaining four women were asked to describe the treatment they had experienced on the buses. Mrs. Aurelia Browder explained, "I had stopped riding [the buses] because I wanted better treatment. I knew if I would cooperate with [those of] my color I would finally get it." Then she recounted her April 29, 1955, experience on the Day Street bus: "After I rode up by the Alabama Gas Company the bus driver had three of us get up and stand to let a white man and a white lady to sit down—myself and two other Negroes. I was sitting in a seat and another lady [was] beside me. And the seat just across from me there was just one colored person in there. And he made all three of us get up because he said we was in the white section of the bus."[41] Attorney Gray asked Mrs. Browder whether she would be willing to ride the buses again if she were allowed to sit wherever she pleased. Mrs. Browder responded without hesitatation that she would. After three hours of testimony, the judges adjourned to reach a decision. On June 5, the word came down that, in a majority opinion, the judges had found that the defendants had violated the equal protection and due process clauses of the Fourteenth Amendment.[42]

An injunction issued against the segregated buses as part of the decision of the court was suspended to allow the defense lawyers to mount an appeal to the Supreme Court. The MIA determined to continue the boycott until the Supreme Court decision was rendered. In the meantime, Mayor Gayle and his administration were busy seeking an injunction against the MIA car pool, which they claimed constituted an illegal jitney service that was operating without a license. On November 13, Judge Eugene B. Carter found in favor of the city, but the loss was trumped that same day by the Supreme Court decision in favor of the MIA. Until the Supreme Court desegregation order reached Montgomery on December 20, however, the Black community voted to continue the boycott even if the defeated car pool system meant that they had to walk.[43] Finally, early on the morning of Friday, December 21, 1956, a group of people—including the Reverend Martin Luther King, Jr.; the Reverend Ralph Abernathy; E. D. Nixon; the Reverend Glenn Smiley (of the Fellowship of Reconciliation); and Mrs. Inez J. Baskin—boarded the first integrated bus and completed their journey without major incident. Mrs. Baskin, a Black reporter who worked on the one Black page of the *Montgomery Advertiser*, was covering some of the events of the boycott. A now famous photograph that memorialized this most important victory includes Mrs. Baskin's image, which remained unidentified in Dr. King's memoir and a number of other sources, representing so many unidentified women whose participation was crucial to the success of the enterprise.[44]

Through the 381-day duration of the boycott—through every step of the long ordeal—in their organization, in their participation, and through their example, Black women were by no means invisible. In fact, they led the struggle in Montgomery to its successful conclusion. From the founding of the MIA in the first week of the boycott—an organization designed to coordinate efforts among the many volunteers, funnel funds to areas in need, poll the thousands of participants on key issues, and provide people with inspiration and support—to the victory bus ride on December 21, 1956, women participated in every aspect of the movement. Their participation

in the MIA often overlapped with their participation in such political organizations as the NAACP, the WPC, the Progressive Democratic Association, and the Citizens' Steering Committee. Jo Ann Robinson, Irene West,
Euretta Adair, Erna Dungee, and Rosa Parks were among those who served
as the first set of MIA Executive Board members. Mrs. Erna Dungee
served as the first financial secretary and, along with Euretta Adair and Ida
Caldwell, sat on the Finance Committee. She also served as secretary for
the WPC. Mrs. Euretta Adair also sat on the Transportation Committee of
the MIA, and Mrs. Rosa Parks and Mrs. Irene West served as members of
the Program Committee.[45] Mrs. Maude Ballou, Dr. King's personal secretary at the MIA, handled innumerable pieces of correspondence, requests,
and other MIA business with great efficiency and dispatch. Mrs. Martha
Johnson and Mrs. Hazel Gregory, also members of the WPC, managed
the MIA offices and performed secretarial and other duties. Jo Ann Robinson, who also sat on the boycott Negotiations Committee, took meticu-
lous notes at every meeting she attended, including every Monday night
mass meeting, which she used to produce the monthly MIA newsletter.
Mrs. Hazel Gregory and Mrs. Erna Dungee then reproduced the newsletter and mailed it to thousands of people in Montgomery, in other areas of
the state, all over the United States, and even in various foreign countries.
The newsletter provided the boycott effort with an important communications and fund-raising tool. Mrs. Erna Dungee described their efforts as
follows: "Oh, you just worked. . . . Sometimes, I'd go there in the morning
and I'd be there until midnight. And I'd leave and Mr. Nixon and some of
the others, they'd still be there. I don't know when they'd sleep. I'd never
seen that before or since."[46]

Women fund-raisers who operated on both the local and national levels were crucial to the boycott effort. For instance, through her office as
president of the Woman's Convention, Auxiliary to the National Baptist
Convention, seventy-seven-year-old Nannie Helen Burroughs—herself a
founding leader of the Woman's Convention and an ardent advocate of
Black women's leadership in the male-led Baptist church and beyond—
helped raise money for Dr. King and the MIA. In March 1956 she reported
to Dr. King that she had authorized her national treasurer, Mrs. H. M.
Gibbs of Tuscaloosa, Alabama, to send him two hundred dollars, adding,
"[We] wish we could do more."[47] Some of the Baptist Woman's Convention members were acquainted with Mrs. Alberta W. King, who was the
organist for Ebenezer Baptist Church in Atlanta and the wife of its widely

respected pastor, the Reverend Martin Luther King, Sr. Mrs. King also served as organist for the Woman's Convention.[48] In August 1956 Martin Luther King, Jr., was one of the featured speakers at the annual meeting of the Woman's Convention in Denver. In a letter of response to Mrs. Burroughs after the meeting, Dr. King thanked her for her continued support and "interest . . . in our struggle." He concluded, "I can assure you that your moral support and financial contributions have given me renewed courage and vigor to carry on."[49]

On the local level, few Montgomery activists were as enthusiastic about or effective at raising money as Mrs. Georgia Gilmore. Mrs. Gilmore, a single parent with seven children, worked as a cook in a downtown cafe on Court Street. Mrs. Hazel Gregory, an MIA secretary who knew Mrs. Gilmore well, recalled that Mrs. Gilmore's Court Street café employers fired her when they found out about her membership in the MIA.[50] Mrs. Gilmore was renowned on South Jackson Street for her barbecue and fish dinners, which students from nearby Alabama State College eagerly bought up. To contribute to the MIA coffers, Mrs. Gilmore organized the Club from Nowhere, through which supporters helped her raise money by selling cakes, pies, sandwiches, and other prepared foods. Her success helped to create a healthy competitive spirit among the MIA fund-raisers. Mrs. Inez Ricks headed another successful fund-raising group, known as the Friendly Club. Monday nights at the Black churches in Montgomery were lively events, as each club at the mass meetings proudly announced its total donations to the MIA. According to Mrs. Gilmore:

> The maids, the cooks, they were the ones that really and truly kept the bus running. And after the maids and the cooks stopped riding the bus, well, the bus didn't have any need to run.
>
> In order to make the mass meeting and the boycott be a success and keep the car pool running, we decided that the peoples on the south side would get a club and the peoples on the east side would get a club, and so we decided we wouldn't name the club anything, we'd just say it was the Club from Nowhere. I had a lot of white people who contributed. The Club from Nowhere was able to collect maybe a hundred and fifty or maybe two hundred dollars a week. I collected the money and I'd always reported it at the mass meetings, the same day that they would give it to us, so there never was any conflict.[51]

Those who were not raising money were providing rides. Many MIA and WPC women donated their own automobiles to the car pool effort;

others filled in as dispatchers and drivers, using borrowed, church, or MIA vehicles. Women who were already driving to work offered rides to their co-workers and to others who worked in the same vicinity. Especially during the morning and evening rush, drivers with an empty seat picked up any walker on their route. Mrs. Zecosy Williams, a member of the WPC who was employed as a domestic worker for the Stanhope Elmore family (in-laws to the Durrs), drove Beatrice Albert, the Elmores' cook, to and from work most days. Occasionally, Mrs. Elmore would save Mrs. Williams the cost of gas and the wear on her vehicle by lending her the family car to pick up people and take them home. "The Elmores never said anything. They quietly supported us," Mrs. Williams reported.[52] Mrs. Gregory recalled that, like Dr. King, she gave people rides on her way to and from work at the MIA office on South Union Street. Mrs. Beautie Mae Johnson volunteered as a driver from her church dispatch station at Bethel Baptist Church on a weekly basis.[53] MIA car pool drivers received a nominal sum to cover the cost of gasoline.[54]

Mrs. Johnnie Carr, a member of the WPC who had gone to school with Rosa Parks and was a fellow member of the NAACP, had bought her own car in 1941, when she went to work as an insurance agent for the Birmingham-based People's Burial Insurance Company. In addition to helping with the distribution of the WPC boycott notices, she provided rides to people from her Hall Street neighborhood near the Alabama State College campus. She remembered a day when it rained hard and she hurried downtown to give people a lift: "Some of them [white people] said that we'd be back on the buses the first day that it rained hard. I can just remember that so. And the first day it rained, I got in my car and drove down and saw a group of people down on Decatur Street and I stopped and said, 'As many of you as can, get in this car. . . .' Rain just dripping down off of 'em. . . . [P]eople were willing to do these things, to sacrifice."[55] These and other women drivers, especially those who were able to use their own cars, were crucial to the car pool effort. Because, early on, the city had put a stop to Black taxi drivers' attempt to charge the boycotters bus fare rates, alternative methods had been devised. During the week of November 1, 1956, seventeen of the forty-three volunteer car pool drivers (or nearly 40 percent) were women.[56]

The largest contingent of boycott participants was from among the Black working-class communities of Montgomery—they were the thousands of women who had pledged that first Monday night to stay off the buses until their demands were met, and they were the vital links to the success of the boycott. Without the participation of the domestic workers, footsoldiers in the nearly thirteen-month ordeal of the Montgomery movement, the efforts of the women who served as car pool drivers, fund-raisers, and organizers would all have been for naught. Of the approximately ten thousand "nonwhite" female members of the Montgomery workforce in 1950, roughly seventy-seven hundred worked in factories, in commercial service, and in domestic service. Domestic workers in private homes composed the vast majority, at more than five thousand women.[57]

Maids, Madams, and the Politics of Resistance

On the whole, women in domestic service and other working-class jobs depended on public transportation to get to and from work. Most could not afford their own cars—especially single heads of households like Ora Lee Bell. Others, like Mrs. Amy Harris, shared the family vehicle with their husbands, who used the car to get to their own jobs. Most working-class women used the buses not only to get back and forth to work but also to shop at the downtown department and grocery stores. Over the years, harsh treatment on the public buses had led some women to abandon this means of transportation. Mrs. Mary Harris, a domestic worker, testified in court that she had stopped riding the buses in 1954. She had not always been a regular rider, but she had finally stopped riding altogether "So many different complications came up on the buses [that] I decided to walk." As she explained:

> When the Cloverdale bus would come along it would be so crowded [that] naturally, I had to stand, and the driver told me to get another bus for I couldn't stand over white people. I said I had to be at work at seven-thirty. He said, "I just operate the bus[;] I don't care whether you ride the bus, or not." I said, "The next one runs around eight-fifteen and that is too late for me to get to work." He handed me a new transfer and told me I would have to wait for another bus. Another bus came along and it was the same thing. I waited down at the corner of Perry and Adams, and every bus [that] came along I had to wait for another bus. It was after eight-thirty [when] I got to work that morning.[58]

Given the frequency of such demeaning incidents, it is surprising that Black women were able to tolerate the system for so long. Clearly, the decision to boycott the buses en masse was long overdue. Mrs. Allean Wright, another domestic worker, expressed the feelings of many when she told an interviewer at the time, "Honey, I don't care if they don't ever run again!"[59]

The boycott provided a cathartic release from the longtime pressures of living under a system of white domination. When Mrs. Wright saw the WPC flyer announcing the boycott, she was more than just relieved: "I found a note on my porch and it said they had put Mrs. Parks in jail and next time it may be me and it said for us not to ride the buses. I felt good[;] I felt like shoutin''cause the time done come for them to stop treating us like dogs. I got them flat shoes back there, put my foot in the road and walked!"[60] The boycott freed her from the cycle of white power and Black deference. Mrs. Wright had no trouble telling her employer that she was participating in the boycott: "She asked me how did I get to work and I told her I walked and she ain't said nothing to me [about it] since[;] she get in that car and drive me home, though."[61] Mrs. Wright expressed a growing consciousness of the economic leverage at the disposal of the Black citizens of Montgomery: "Ol' Sellers [Police Commissioner Clyde Sellers] . . . might as well give up 'cause we ain't gonna be pushed around no more. Our eyes are open and they gonna stay open. Even the white folks in the stores are scared. They just as nice as they can be 'cause they think we'll boycott them, and they believe right, 'cause we sure will do it."[62]

Beatrice Charles also felt the demise of the lopsided power dynamic between white employers and Black servants. She had no compunction about speaking her mind to her employer, Mrs. Prentiss:

You see I work out in Cloverdale for Mrs. Prentiss, and she hates it [that I don't ride the bus], but it sure ain't nothing she can do about it. She said to me when I went to work that Wednesday, "Beatrice you ride the bus, don't you?" I said I sure didn't. She said, "Why Beatrice, they haven't done anything to you." I said, "[L]isten Mrs. Prentiss, you don't ride the bus, [so] you don't know how those ole nasty drivers treat us and further when you do something to my people you do it to me too." . . .

[She said,] "I'm going to tell you this, Beatrice, because I know you can keep your mouth shut. In the White Citizen Council meeting, they discussed starving the maids for a month. They asked us to lay our maid off for a month[;] then they'd be glad to ride the buses again. If they do it I still want you to come one day a week."

[I said,] "Well, Mrs. I just won't come at all and I sure won't starve. You see my husband is a railroad man, my son and my daughter have good jobs and my daddy keep plenty of food on his farm. So I'm not worried at all, 'cause I was eating before I started working for you." . . .

[She said,] "You know I heard that Rev. King is going to take all of your money and go buy a Cadillac with it. He's going from door to door asking for $2.00. Beatrice, don't you give him $2.00."

[I said,] "Whoever told you that, told you a lie, but if he did, it ain't no more for me to pay $2.00 than it is for you to pay $3.50 for that White Citizen thing."

[She said,] "And you know, Beatrice, ole Rev. King want people to go to church together and I just can't see it."

[I said,] "I didn't ask you to come to my church and I ain't particular about going to yours. . . . You don't want to go to church with us when down in the 5th ward until a couple of years ago, you couldn't go in or leave after dark 'cause all those white men and women were after those colored people." . . .

She stood there looking at me like a sick chicken [and] then hurried off, talking about she had to go to town. She didn't say anymore after that. I came right home and called Rev. Abernathy, my pastor, and told him about them talking about firing the maids.[63]

Mrs. Charles's ability to speak her mind to her employer represents an important turn in the racial dynamic of personal power relations.[64] Certainly, for Mrs. Charles the unmistakable first message of her response was the warning not to attempt the ruse of dividing Black people: "When you do something to my people you do it to me too." Second, Mrs. Charles let it be known that she had the same right to decide where and how to spend her money as Mrs. Prentiss did. Finally, Mrs. Charles stripped bare the hypocrisy of racial segregation to expose the deepest concerns about the loss of a system that kept Black bodies cheaply and readily accessible through the most exploitive sexual, social, and labor practices.[65]

The boycott changed Black people's lives in a number of ways. Mrs. Amelia Scott Green remembered the boycott era as a time when she helped others by participating in the voter registration effort and also received help from others in the form of literacy instruction at Hutchinson Street Missionary Baptist Church:

I can remember Willie Elmore, Mattie Presley—we'd walk together. Coach [Rufus] Lewis, he'd usually take us around to help get folks registered to vote. . . . There were five of us women and him, one man. He'd go all down Elmore County, [to those] little country towns. I learned how to read and write in Hutchinson Street [Church] basement. This church where [I'm] at now, it was on the ditch then. Reverend H. H. Johnson was there; he was the pastor. The church was bombed while I was going to school there. Coach Lewis used to take us five women, and sometimes it would be two o'clock in the morning before we get back home—me and Mattie Presley. I learned how to vote by going to Hutchinson Street.[66]

Mrs. Thelma Glass, a member of the WPC and a teacher at Alabama State, remembered feeling like a new person from the time of the boycott onward:

What happened to me as a result of my participation in this movement is what some . . . [have] describe[d] as the New Negro, or the new Black—a new person, a new spirit, [a] new feeling that did something for me—[made me] proud, fearless, [and taught me] self-control. I became more sympathetic to people's problems, government problems, and built up my faith, hope, and dreams. It was an exciting time to be involved with sixty thousand others in seeking justice for all. It was a pleasure to refute the stereotyped picture held by many in the world. . . that Black people are [a] happy-go-lucky, self-satisfied, complacent, lazy, good-for-nothing race.[67]

With predictions that Black people would never be able to sustain the boycott long enough to win, the victory was that much sweeter.

The example of the boycott victory proved meaningful to Ms. Gwen Bell later in life. When Gwen and her friends came home from elementary school, Gwen's mother, Ms. Ora Lee Bell, would ask them to run to whichever church was hosting the Monday or Thursday mass meetings to save some front-row seats for their parents. The children were happy to oblige, because it gave them a role to play in the boycott effort. By the time Gwen Bell attended college at Alabama State, she had become fully involved in the Black freedom movement: "As I got older over at Alabama State, I would attend a lot of the marches. I didn't march all the way from Selma to Montgomery [in 1965], but we met [the marchers] on the highway . . . on the Lowndes County line. We wouldn't go to Lowndes County, because we were afraid. . . . It was a dangerous place. So we met them on the creek, and we marched from there to St. Jude's and from St. Jude's to the [state] capitol."[68]

The bus boycott and the freedom movement beyond also became a family affair for Ethel Mae and Ezekiel Alexander and their children. During the boycott, Mrs. Alexander, who did day work for various families sta-

CHAPTER SEVEN

tioned at Maxwell Air Force Base, managed to find rides to and from work. Although she suspected that one of her employers was sympathetic to the cause, she took no chances. When one employer asked where she was going as she left work, Mrs. Alexander replied, "'I don't tell my husband everything I do!' I wasn't doing that to throw her off," she explained. "She knew I was going to the [mass] meeting, [but] that wasn't her business." [69] In the meantime, Mr. Alexander was among the men who were called on to help protect their own church (Bethel Baptist) and others, including Mt. Olive Baptist Church, which had been bombed. Although the movement emphasized nonviolent action, the church security team was armed and prepared for defense. As Mr. Alexander explained, "We got in there, and we stayed in there. If they had thrown the bomb, we [would] turn loose in that car. We was going to shoot in that car whoever it was if they throwed anything toward that church. We had a couple of windows cracked. They had no idea that somebody was there. We was. There were six of us." [70]

By the time the Freedom Riders came to Montgomery in the spring of 1961, the older Alexander sons were demonstrating in support of the beleaguered civil rights activists. As Mrs. Alexander rushed her family to First Baptist Church for the mass meeting, her third son William was already assisting the MIA organizers. She remembered clearly the tear gas and the vitriol lobbed by the white mob outside the church, holding those inside hostage until the U.S. marshalls and later the National Guard appeared. She recalled the ride home the next morning at daybreak, with the assistance of the National Guard. The children with her were sleepy, but no one was hurt. Despite the danger posed by white citizens who refused to give up segregation without a fight, Mrs. Alexander wanted her children to be involved in the struggle against white supremacy. "Yes, they were there," she said. "Sometimes they didn't want to go, but as my son say, 'You made us went!'" [71]

Mrs. Alexander's involvement in the freedom struggle was directed toward the younger generations. She housed young activists, the Freedom Riders, and people who helped with voter registration. She participated in the movement to open the door for young people to have economic equality and equal opportunities for achievement: "I know that I wasn't qualified like, say, to work the cash register. I was working for the younger people. We was concerned about them. That was my thought. I wanted them to have a better learning—a good learning—to be qualified for that job. I wanted

·{ 200 }·

them to have that job. Like I said, I was just ready: time to make a move and change things."[72]

Mrs. Alexander's brand of participation helped bring about an important change in the expression of race relations in Montgomery and across the South. Her role as one of the many "mothers of the movement" provided crucial support for those who would organize, mobilize, and help to lead direct actions.[73] Mrs. Alexander knew that a complete about-face in race relations in her city would require more than just a change in the bus seating policy; it must also include better education, more economic opportunity, and increased political power. In another part of the Black world—Johannesburg, South Africa—this same fundamental concept was being touted by the women who "joined politics."

"WE WILL NOT RIDE!" — "WE DON'T WANT PASSES!"

South African Women Rising in Political Movement, 1950–1960

Across the Atlantic, in Johannesburg, South Africa, the theme of personal dignity combined with ardent political activism is evident in the life of Mrs. Kate Mxakatho. Like Mrs. Amelia Scott Green in Alabama, Mrs. Mxakatho, who was a domestic worker in the white suburbs of Johannesburg, gladly participated in the 1950s movement to eradicate white supremacy. The story of her involvement reveals a spirited and purposeful woman whose criticism has remained sharp.

From her home in Soweto, a feisty eighty-six-year-old Kate Mxakatho clearly remembered 1944 as the year she stopped teaching elementary school in rural Transvaal to find work in Johannesburg. She had been educated through Standard Nine and had attained her Junior Certificate. In the city, however, her education qualified her for little more than domestic service—in which, she understood, Black people were never permitted to "enter by the front door." She arranged accommodations in Western Native Township among her paternal aunts and quickly found work in the wealthy suburb of Rosebank. "Then, " she recalled, "jobs were not that scarce. You meet a white woman, and she will say, 'Are you looking for work?' . . . And she would give you the address to . . . her house." During her married life, her income was crucial to the household. "I got married to a fool," she explained. Having a husband who was fond of spending money on other women caused Mrs. Mxakatho and her family a great deal of emotional and economic distress. As the mother of five children born between 1938 and 1957 and (after her divorce in 1959) as the head of a household that also included her elderly parents, however, Mrs. Mxakatho had no choice but to find a way to support herself and her family.[1]

Displaying the same resourcefulness as Mrs. Green, Kate Mxakatho left domestic work to take advantage of a vigorous wartime economy. She had good reason to want to leave her domestic job and move on: "The husband was a Mr. Heath from England. I remember them. His brother was the Prime Minister of England. I worked for them for two years and left them. The wife was a South African. She was too racist. I did not want to work anymore as a domestic servant. There were too many posts then. I started working at the NEH, [or] Non-European Hospital."[2] At the hospital, which served African people, Mrs. Mxakatho interpreted for patients who spoke little or no English.

During this time in her life—after having been forced to leave teaching and having determined that she was not cut out for serving racist "MaBoers"—Mrs. Mxakatho set out to "join politics." She was clear about why she wanted to participate in organized resistance as a member of the Women's League of the African National Congress (ANC): "It's the love I have for my people. And the suffering I saw because of pass laws." This was the beginning of a life devoted to the liberation of African people. Mrs. Mxakatho, who eventually became the secretary for the Transvaal ANC Women's League (ANCWL), never missed a campaign or any other opportunity to fight for freedom. A veteran activist, she was proud of her role: "Every little campaign I was in [including] marching to Pretoria on the 9th of August, 1956. . . . I know almost the whole of Transvaal organizing women from far and near."[3]

Mrs. Mxakatho threw herself wholeheartedly into her organizing work for the ANCWL. She proved both indefatigable and cunning in the face of the serious constraints—such as the Suppression of Communism Act—that the apartheid state placed on activists and organizers, especially those who were affiliated with interracial groups. She remembered how she and her colleagues in the ANC, the Federation of South African Women (FSAW), and the Congress of Democrats (COD) found ways to get their message out to women in rural areas: "You know what we used to do? Helen [Joseph], Marshall Goldberg[4]—it was either one of them going with two Black women in their car. If we say we're coming today, we don't come that day; we come two days earlier. When the police come there, we are long past [and off] to another area. When the informers have told them that on such and such a date they are addressing a meeting there, they will find only our dust!"[5]

Mrs. Mxakatho's face lit up as she recalled the march in which twenty thousand women from all over the country converged on Prime Minister Johannes Gerhardus Strijdom (known as the Lion of the North) at the Union Buildings in Pretoria:

> We expected more than twenty thousand. Only because of the laws of this country, only twenty thousand women went. Even getting there, we had to go in dribs and drops. When we got to Marabastad, an African policeman (he was a sergeant) said to us—I got out of the bus first, and he came to us and said, "Please, don't walk in big groups." I said, "Thank you." I went back to the bus and said, "That man says we mustn't walk in [big] groups." Two, three, four, two, three, four—[we walked] until we reached the Union Buildings. And we did it! And we told them straight off, "You have touched the women; you are going to die! *Watint a bafazi; watint imbokotho uzokufa!*" And [the prime minister] died within months—from the curse of Black women![6]

Mrs. Mxakatho had stood among those bold women on that day in Pretoria, and on subsequent days of defiance as well, to inform the prime minister and the apartheid state that African women would not take the pass and would not submit to unjust laws. For her determination to fight for the right, as she puts it, to "walk on the soil of my land," Mrs. Mxakatho was jailed and banned from her home; it grieved her greatly to be barred from attending the full complement of her mother's funeral ceremonies in the Cape Province in 1963. The 1956 Pretoria demonstration was one of many of her activist achievements designed to bring an end to a system that perpetuated virtual slavery. Mrs. Mxakatho lived to see the "MaBoers" defeated and the ANC victorious. Still, she observed, "There's a lot of work . . . to be done. . . . So we must go down again, underground, do spade work." Teaching the current generation of young women about the history and defiance of the ANCWL of her day, she has admonished them to "build up the branch!" insisting, "We want this branch to produce women who will work for the branch!"[7] Persisting in the continuation of the necessary "spade work" of the current movement by connecting those succeeding her to the legacy of their predecessors, Mrs. Mxakatho has pledged her mind and heart to the freedom of her people and to the organization that has demanded it.

Mrs. Green in Alabama and Mrs. Mxakatho in South Africa both rolled up their sleeves and committed themselves to a long and demanding struggle. In Mrs. Mxakatho's case, the struggle has lasted longer, encompassing a movement for national liberation. Both women started with the understanding that they were entitled to fair treatment. Each exploited the cracks in her respective system, left domestic work for more suitable employment, and took political action to free herself and others from untenable conditions.

This chapter is dedicated to the South African women who refused to be "slaves in our own country."[8] From their political practice, organizational strategies, ideologies, and motivations the meaning of their movements can be assessed. The 1957 Alexandra Bus Boycott and the 1955–1960 national campaign against passes for women form the focus of the discussion. Activist women from various geographical, educational, and socioeconomic backgrounds eloquently define a unique political consciousness, which—at a critical juncture in the history of their country—demanded nothing less than a total dismantling of South African apartheid power.

"I am a defier!"

By the early 1950s the Nationalist government in South Africa had set about implementing a spate of legislative initiatives to further constrict the political and economic space occupied by Black South Africans. The acts were designed to keep Black people out of white areas, severely limit their economic options, and eliminate any possibility that they might legally exercise their political voice. Black opposition to the set of six "unjust laws"—the pass laws, stock limitation, the Bantu Authorities Act, the Group Areas Act, the Voter Representation Act, and the Suppression of Communism Act—met with serious state counteractions. In December 1951 the ANC and the South African Indian Congress (SAIC) agreed to join forces in mass action, and in January 1952, the top leadership of the ANC first called for the Nationalists to repeal the acts. The request was denied. In late May—following successful counterdemonstrations held during the three hundredth anniversary celebrations in honor of the founding of Cape Town by the Dutchman Jan van Riebeeck—the ANC, the SAIC, and the largely Colored and trade unionist Franchise Action Committee (FRAC) announced that the Campaign for the Defiance of Unjust Laws would begin on June 26. One source touted the Defiance Campaign as "the most sustained and—in terms of numbers of participants—the most successful organised resistance the ANC was ever to initiate."[9]

Nelson Mandela, who was appointed national volunteer in chief by the ANC leadership, recalled that the idea for the Defiance Campaign came from Walter Sisulu and that Sisulu had no trouble convincing the National Executive Committee (NEC) of the ANC to undertake the project. Over the next five months, between late June and early November, small groups of people from across racial, class, and gender lines, totaling approximately eighty-five hundred people, volunteered to participate in minor acts of civil disobedience aimed at courting arrest. The activists broke curfew and pass laws; non-Africans entered African areas without permits; and Black people made use of "whites' only" facilities at post offices, train stations, and other public spaces. The venerable Nana Sita (a longtime Indian activist) and Chief Albert Luthuli (who was elected the national president of the ANC in December 1952) joined the effort, lending legitimacy to the campaign and proving to the ANC and SAIC memberships that their leaders would not ask the rank and file to do anything that they themselves were unwilling to do. In Mandela's view the well-publicized campaign succeeded in a variety of ways, not the least of which was the significant subsequent increase in national ANC membership—from twenty thousand to one hundred thousand.[10] Among the new recruits to the organization, many of whom were attracted by its latest brand of militancy, were women who were eager to replace tea making with more important political contributions.

In fact, earlier in 1952, African women had found their political voice with reference to the recently enacted Abolition of Passes and Co-ordination of Documents Act. The new act, which called for tighter influx control, would eventually require their submission to passes. Women also rallied against Section 10 of the Urban Areas Act, which allowed for the extension of "urban residence permits" to both women and men who lived in any urban area. In June 1952, for example, when the municipality of Odendaalsrus in the Orange Free State announced the extension of passes to women, demonstrations broke out that resulted in the death of one African man, the injury of one woman, and the arrest of seventy-one people. Of the forty-seven arrested activists who were prosecuted, forty-four were women.[11] It seemed, then, that for some women the Defiance Campaign was a timely successor to the earlier anti-pass actions.

In the Cape Province, where the campaign began and defiance was the greatest, large numbers of women participated. In one sample group in the Eastern Cape, of the 2,529 total defiers, 1,067 were women. In another sample group from the Transvaal, 173 of 488 were women.[12] The campaign evinced a strong spiritual element, especially in the Eastern Cape, where prayer meetings were held in conjunction with the defiance actions. Participating *manyano* women wearing colorful uniforms led demonstrators in hymn singing and praying.[13] Eastern Cape women were well represented according to the figures of Florence Matomela (regional president of the ANCWL) and Frances Baard (leading Port Elizabeth activist in both the Food and Canning Workers' Union [FCWU] and the ANCWL). Mrs. Matomela, who served six weeks in prison during the campaign, was tried along with many among the ANC leadership for violating the Suppression of Communism Act.[14] Mrs. Baard, who had joined both the ANC and the African section of the FCWU in 1948, did not serve time in jail, but she helped organize the defiers who did. In addition to being responsible for recruiting elderly people to look after the children and the homes of the activists who were arrested, she helped raise money to pay the rent and grocery bills for the families of the defiers in their absence. In her narrative, she recalled both the enthusiasm of the campaign and the hardships that many women defiers had to endure:

> During this campaign everybody wanted to break the laws and go to jail so that the jails would be too full of people who didn't like the *apartheid* laws.... During that time the husband would come to the house and tell his wife, "I am going to jail now."
> And then the wife says, "Well, I am going to jail too."
> And what about the children? Perhaps the wife has a small child, and then what can she do? Sometimes they took their babies with them to the jail. Sometimes they leave the child at home.... So I was told that I must not go and defy. I must stay at home and look after these children and houses that people have left. That was my job.[15]

One of the most important women from the Transvaal region to join the ANC and participate in the Defiance Campaign was Lilian Ngoyi, an active trade unionist in the Garment Workers' Union of Johannesburg. Inspired by the activities of the campaign, she was arrested for using the "whites only" facilities of the post office. Thereafter, she immersed herself in the work of the ANCWL, serving as president after the campaign had ended. She also served as president of the FSAW, which she helped to form in 1954. With the support of her family and other women in the movement, Mrs. Ngoyi became one of the preeminent leaders in the ANC and the first woman to serve on its NEC. Her fearless work on behalf of her people, of course, made her a target for harassment, imprisonment, and banning by the apartheid state. She was arrested in 1956 along with Nelson Mandela,

Robert Resha, Helen Joseph, Walter Sisulu, and others, and her 1961 acquittal was one of the last among the Treason Trialists.[16] A friend, co-worker, and admirer, Maggie Resha has described Lilian Ngoyi as the source of her inspiration:

> Many of those who worked closely with her were greatly inspired by her determination, and were ready to face any odds in pursuit of our goal. We certainly benefitted a great deal from her courage. . . .
>
> Lilian was one of those people who had a great deal of charisma; even those people who did not like her as a person were nowhere, because she was the queen bee with the masses. After she lost her first husband, Lilian got married again, but that second marriage did not work. It was at that time that she played a leading role in the trades union movement. At her house she was modest; she kept a lot of souvenirs which she had collected during her travels. As she went around, addressing meetings and rallies all over the country, she called on women to be in the forefront of the struggle, in order to secure a better future for our children. Women, she said, had a duty to protect their offspring, to preserve their dignity as mothers, who produced the future leaders and workers of the country. . . .
>
> It was during my frequent visits to Lilian's house that I thought I discovered the source behind Lilian's bravery: her mother. . . . Now, Lilian's mother was not the type to tell her to lay off [political activism]; rather, she encouraged her in her political work. She rejoiced with her when, through hard work, she climbed to senior positions both in the trade union and in the ANC, and during hard times, when the regime pointed its sharp knives at her, trying to stop her from campaigning against the injustices towards black people, her mother was there to comfort her. . . . [Lilian's] plow remains deep in the furrow of the field which was begun by ANC women pioneers like Charlotte Maxeke, Mrs. Mapikela, Mary Mqhweto, Ida Mtwana and many other (some unknown) names.[17]

Under Lilian Ngoyi's stewardship, the ANCWL broadened its definition of liberation to include a forthright articulation of women's concerns. In 1953, for instance, in an apparent first for the organization, the Transvaal ANCWL participated in celebrations on behalf of International Women's Day (which had previously been sponsored by the Communist Party of South Africa [CPSA]). In April 1953 in Port Elizabeth, Florence Matomela, Frances Baard, and Ray Alexander (the white general secretary of the FCWU, who worked tirelessly on behalf of fellow women) agreed to have the women from the various participating Defiance Campaign organizations meet to discuss their part in the struggle for national liberation. The three women distributed their personal invitations to co-workers and others by word of mouth, asking them to congregate that same April evening to discuss the basic issues of concern to Black South African women: the pass system and rising food and transportation costs. The thirty to forty women who gathered concluded that they needed a national strategy and a national framework in order to confront these issues. A proposal was submitted that a larger conference of women be convened to form an organization that would address these issues, and the responsibility for carrying out the proposal was placed in the hands of Ray Alexander.[18]

With the help of her considerable network of political friends from across the country, especially Hilda Watts, a friend and former comember of the Communist Party in Johannesburg, Ray Alexander worked diligently between April 1953 and April 1954 to organize the women's conference. Women and even some men affiliated with such organizations as the ANC, the former CPSA, the tiny all-white COD, the SAIC, the FCWU, and other trade unions were solicited in an effort to foment interest and assistance in formulating the agenda. Among the many who were included were Helen Joseph, a member of the COD and an advocate for Black workers in the Transvaal clothing industry; Lucy Mvubelo, a prominent trade unionist in the Garment Workers' Union; Dora Tamana and Ida Mtwana, ANCWL activists; Annie Silinga, a Cape Town ANC activist; Fatima Meer, a Durban SAIC activist; and Josie Mpama, a former member of the CPSA. This group of ground-floor organizers, who were responsible for the historic first conference of South African women, met at Trades Hall in Johannesburg on April 17, 1954.[19]

On the official invitation, dated March 16, 1954, the conference organizers set out the purpose of the gathering. Their goal—which, although modest by today's standards, was unprecedented in 1950s South Africa—was to bring together a group of "women of all races . . . to discuss women's disabilities, and to promote women's rights." The invitational letter pointed to the unfair system under which women who labored under the strictures of customary law (i.e., as minors), some few of whose husbands were allowed the limited right, were barred from the franchise. The letter clearly highlighted the "double battle" for women: "to achieve justice and happiness for our children, and to achieve equal status and rights in all fields with men." In some of its final paragraphs the letter addressed both women's pursuit of equality with men and their devotion to the struggle for national liberation. The letter contended, however, that the struggle for national liberation could not be waged without the full participation of women who shared equally in the overall effort:

> While our main struggle is with men against racialism and the colour bar, to make our national struggle more effective, we ask that men support us in our fight for equality.
>
> The battle for democracy and liberation can only be won when women, *mothers of the nation*—a half of the whole population—can take their rightful place as free and equal partners with men. Throughout history women have struggled side by side with men for justice.[20]

Concluding the letter by urging "any group of women, from factories or [rural?] areas" to attend or send delegates to the meeting, some sixty-three women from all over the country signed their names to the historic document.[21]

Using the phrase "mothers of the nation" as a potent symbolic device both to frame their argument and to galvanize their constituents, the conference organizers couched their bid for equality with men in maternalist and feminist terms. Although the national organizers took care to position their conference well within the ideological terrain of the national liberation movement, their intentions were unmistakable. They made every effort to ensure that their language did not alienate men as they sought to launch their new organization, but their unity empowered them to claim full equality and partnership with their male colleagues. In the early stages, they were unwilling to antagonize potential allies. Clearly, however, their goal was to frame a distinctly feminist argument within the more accepted notion of a historical struggle for justice. Still, during the initial phases, few men of note within the Congress Alliance of the Defiance Campaign took much interest in the activities of the new women's association.[22] As a function of organizing only women, gender held equal priority with racial difference in the political strategy, as the call to action was made to a wide variety of women from the racial categories imposed by apartheid. Indeed, the fact that the two primary organizers of the group were white women—Ray Alexander and Hilda Watts—raised no apparent objections.

Once the actual conference was under way, the women joined together with a great deal of enthusiasm for the effort they were about to undertake. The work of the first conference established a rudimentary framework for a national organization that included the election of an NEC. The delegates also created a Women's Charter and defined the broad goals of the organization. Interestingly, they did not, at this point, establish a formal name. Reflecting their decidedly leftist-to-radical viewpoint, the vast majority of the estimated 140 delegates present were drawn from the various political groups of the Congress Alliance network—the ANC, the SAIC, the COD, the South African Coloured People's Organization, and the more radical trade unions. Although the organizers had sought the participation of women who lived outside the cities, all of the delegates were women from urban areas, most of whom were working-class African women with families to support. Many of the delegates were already seasoned activists who were involved in resisting the use of passes and removal from their homes or in agitating for better wages or more affordable food, rent, and transportation. It was the responsibility of the organization to identify a number of campaigns in which to become involved. As the conference proclaimed, "This organisation is formed for the purpose of uniting all women in common action for the removal of all political, legal, economic and social disabilities."[23]

Although the inaugural conference did not accomplish all that the organizers had hoped, the delegates elected to the NEC a president (Ida Mtwana); four regional vice presidents, representing the four regions of South Africa (Gladys Smith, Lilian Ngoyi, Bertha Mkize, and Florence Matomela); a secretary (Ray Alexander); a treasurer (Hetty McLeod); and a host of general committee members (the Committee of Twenty included, among others, Dora Tamana, Annie Silinga, Albertina Sisulu, Fatima Meer, Hilda Watts, Helen Joseph, Frances Baard, and Elizabeth Mafeking).[24] Although Ray Alexander later commented to Hilda Watts that she would like future meetings to include only "serious discussion and no songs," the exuberance of the women often spilled over into long impromptu speeches and songfests.[25] African women transformed the physical space and political discussion into an occasion that included their own politically infused cultural forms. The organizers may have convened the group, but the rank and file would have a hand in its form, shape, and substance.

In her memoir Frances Baard testified to the feistiness of some of the women who spoke at the first conference:

> It was a very exciting conference. We felt very strong with all the women coming together. We felt very proud that we were all together. . . .
> We spoke at that conference about women and their problems and how we

can organize to change things. Some people gave speeches, Ida Mtwana and some others, and we all spoke our problems and ideas. I told the women at that conference about the passes in Port Elizabeth, and how the women didn't want them.

I remember Lilian [Ngoyi] stood up and she said that there would have been many more women there but their husbands didn't want them to go. The husbands say they want democracy, but then they won't let their wives go to meetings.

My friend Florence Matomela was there too from Port Elizabeth and she also spoke. It was getting late and there was a lot to do, so the chairwoman said, "Time is getting short; each speaker is only allowed three minutes."

When Florence was talking the chairwoman reminded her that she could only talk for three minutes, and Florence—she was a big woman—she stood there and she folded her arms and she said, "I am a defier," meaning that she had been a volunteer in the Defiance Campaign; "I am a defier, and I shall speak for as long as I like!"

And she did! And she said that the conference would bring tears to Dr. [Daniel François] Malan, because he did not want the women to be united. She said, "We want to go to war with [Prime Minister] Malan. We have no guns for our war, but we shall fight till he gives in." [26]

The conference itself was a critical expression of voice—of the power and importance of women's voices. In a context in which men predominated in the organizational hierarchy and were reluctant to allow space for women to address the direction and form of the freedom struggle, African women—the majority of the membership—in particular were proclaiming their ideas worthy of respect. For another woman to attempt to silence them would be sororial betrayal. White women, even those who were pledged to a spirit of cooperation and nonracialism, could not wholly understand the political import of what was being wrapped in the attributes of African performative culture. The metaphorical speechmaking and the traditional singing signaled the importance of the political moment.

Mrs. Baard revealed another inspired aspect of the design of the conference. To prevent the women conferees from having to perform the double duty of preparing the conference meals while they conducted important political business, Hilda Watts suggested that the conference meals be prepared and served by men: "While we were having our meetings at that conference, and talking about this and this, there were some men looking after the tea and food and everything so we didn't have to waste time with that.

I think it was the men from the Indian Youth Congress. They served us with tea and everything while we had our meeting!"[27] Unlike the husbands who kept their wives from attending the conference, the young men of the SAIC joined with the women in pursuit of a mutual cause.

In addition to electing the NEC of the future FSAW, the delegates adopted a Women's Charter as a strong manifesto on the conditions of women, particularly wives and mothers, followed by eight distinct goals of the organization. The charter declared upfront the women's solidarity with men in forming "A Single Society." It stated, "We women do not form a society separate from the men. There is only one society, and it is made up of both women and men. As women we share the problems and anxieties of our men, and join hands with them to remove social evils and obstacles to progress."[28] The charter then went on to describe the particularly debilitating nature of "Women's Lot" in a society divided by class and race—the special responsibility of having to "make small wages stretch a long way," of having to raise children alone when husbands were absent. The manifesto proclaimed the women's commitment to national liberation as well as to the removal of the social differences, which have kept "our sex in a position of inferiority and subordination." In a respectful nod to the customs and traditions of their African ancestors, who had been independent peoples, the charter acknowledged radical changes that had incorporated African and other women into the financial economy but had left them with few tools to protect themselves. Because women had not been extended "complete and unqualified equality in law and practice," women in the liberation movement would take it upon themselves to educate others about women's concerns. Last, the FSAW charter appealed to "all progressive men and women" to assist the organization in its "great and noble endeavour."[29]

In the last section of the charter, entitled "Our Aims," the women pledged "to strive for women to obtain" the following:

1. The right to vote and be elected to all State bodies, without restriction or discrimination.
2. The right to full opportunities for employment with equal pay and possibilities of promotion in all spheres of work.
3. Equal rights with men in relation to property, marriage and children, and for the removal of all laws and customs that deny women such equal rights.

4. For the development of every child through free compulsory education for all; for the protection of mother and child through maternity homes, welfare clinics, creches and nursery schools in countryside and towns; through proper homes for all, and through the provision of water, light, transport, sanitation, and other amenities of modern civilisation.

5. For the removal of all laws that restrict free movement, that prevent or hinder the right of free association and activity in democratic organisations, and the right to participate in the work of these organisations.

6. To build and strengthen women's sections in the National Liberatory movements, the organisation of women in trade unions, and through the peoples' varied organisation.

7. To cooperate with all other organisations that have similar aims in South Africa as well as throughout the world.

8. To strive for permanent peace throughout the world.[30]

The FSAW women possessed an outlook that was international in scope, advocating their connection to other women who were fighting common injustices. Advocating peace within a 1950s context of Cold War and nuclear weapons development linked them ideologically to women peace activists in the United States, Europe, Asia, and Latin America. To this end, Dora Tamana and Lilian Ngoyi spent eight months in Europe, the Soviet Union, and China in 1955, traveling, meeting groups of women, and attending the World Congress of Mothers in Switzerland. The Congress was sponsored by the Women's International Democratic Federation (which had funded their trip). Because the two South African women did not have permission to own a passport, they traveled outside their country illegally, for which Dora Tamana, a former member of the CPSA, was banned under the Suppression of Communism Act.[31]

Through the rest of 1954 and much of 1955, the organization concentrated on (as Ray Alexander described it) putting its diverse house in order. Unfortunately, this was not an easy task, with the problems of logistics, resources, and state repression that had to be overcome. The organization hammered out the particulars of its constitution, which included a lengthy argument about membership. Members of the NEC had to overcome such obstacles as distance, political inexperience, and bannings. Moreover, before the organization lost all the momentum from its first national gathering, it had to come up with a plan of action.

To begin with, the organization suffered a serious blow when two of the leading members of its NEC—its treasurer, Hetty McLeod, and its secretary, Ray Alexander—were banned from political activity. Bannings, arrests, police surveillance, the four-year-long Treason Trial, and additional state-sponsored harassment were pervasive from the founding of the FSAW to its demise in the early 1960s. Ray Alexander, a tough and intensely committed activist, refused to be stopped by her banning, but the proscriptions against her attendance at meetings, her correspondence, and mobilization of people to carry out assignments hindered her efforts. Her activities had to be clandestine, and her communications had to be anonymous. In addition, by 1955 her home base of Cape Town had become a seething receptacle of African resentment as the state began forced removals to turn over the Western Cape to white and Colored inhabitants. This policy put African working women, in particular, at risk, since they could not claim a right to legal residence by birth. The intimidation by the state also discouraged some women from becoming politically outspoken, hindering the growth of Cape Town membership in the FSAW and the ANCWL.[32]

Dora Tamana and Cecelia Rosier (a COD member) stepped in to fill the vacancies left by Ray Alexander and Hetty McLeod, but further disabilities plagued the NEC. With inadequate operating funds, the organization could not afford a full-time organizer. Services performed on behalf of the organization were paid for out of the pockets of the activists. Members who wanted to attend meetings faced the high cost and poor state of transportation; the logistics of arranging for child care; and, in some cases, lack of support from their husbands. The NEC suffered again in March 1955, when Ida Mtwana resigned from her post as president; the reasons for her resignation were unclear. Gladys Smith assumed the role of president and, when Dora Tamana was banned in October 1955, had to fill in as secretary as well.[33]

Still, particularly during 1955, several significant accomplishments gave emotional uplift and renewed determination to the initial commitment of the group. By the end of 1954, the volatile issue of membership qualification was laid to rest after thorough consideration of opposing viewpoints. Ray Alexander and others advocated a policy of individual membership to enable those who were not affiliated with another group to join. In addition,

Alexander pointed out, if individuals were banned from any of FSAW affiliates, they would avoid being automatically banned from the FSAW, which could retain the membership of a larger group. Opposing the individual-membership view were some of the leaders of the ANC and the ANCWL, the largest association of FASW members. One of the chief concerns of the ANC was that no organization should be in a position to compete for members or for precious resources with the larger and more seasoned body. An additional objective may have been to mute the degree to which the FSAW acted as an independent agent. In any case, within its draft constitution, the condition of membership was eventually established as "organisations or groups of females above the age of 18 years," with dues set at one pound, one shilling per year.[34]

In 1955 the FSAW conducted several campaigns, two of which stand out for their show of wide-scale enthusiastic support. Prior to the more successful campaigns, the Congress Alliance sponsored actions against removals in the Western Cape, Natal, and the Transvaal. The most notable of the actions against removals on the Rand was the one performed to prevent the demolition of Sophiatown, the freehold township located in central Johannesburg. Transvaal ANCWL and FSAW women took the opportunity to voice their indignation at the prospect of the loss of their homes and community. The initial round of removals came as a demoralizing defeat in 1955, and by the early 1960s Sophiatown had been completely decimated. The Bantu Education Act of 1953 also inspired resistance from FSAW affiliate groups, which helped to sponsor boycotts of schools that adopted this new, inferior form of education intended for Black children.[35] The alternative Cultural Clubs, suggestive of the Freedom Schools established in the rural U.S. South and in some areas of the urban U.S. North during the early days of the Black freedom movement, could not hope to provide the boycotting students with a viable alternative education over the long term.[36] In the meantime, the activities connected with the 1955 Alliance-sponsored Congress of the People and the first and wholly independent FSAW demonstration against the issuing of passes to women, which took place in Pretoria in October, may have seemed more promising.

According to Nelson Mandela and others, the idea for the Congress of the People originated with Z. K. Matthews, a noted professor from Fort Hare who taught social anthropology and African law. Upon returning from a year of teaching in the United States, he came up with the idea of a national convention composed of representatives of all of the people of

South Africa. Through a completely democratic process, they would create a Freedom Charter that incorporated principles by which all might live justly in a reconstituted nation.[37] The member organizations of the Congress Alliance took up the idea in an effort to become more engaged in the struggle. Organizers such as Bertha Mashaba (Gxowa) and Helen Joseph solicited ideas for the new statement of principles and mobilized people for the event, which was to take place from June 25–26, 1955, in the racially mixed area of Kliptown (adjacent to Soweto, outside Johannesburg). The Congress Alliance solicited the help of the FSAW in finding places for people to stay, and the women used this opportunity to reach additional women. Helen Joseph recalled:

> The Federation of South African Women had been asked to arrange overnight accommodation for the delegates to the coming Congress of the People. We had no idea how many people to expect, but we estimated it could run into 1,000 or more. We did not view this request as any sort of implied relegation of women to the domestic area. On the contrary, it gave us several weeks of intensive organising through small house meetings, mainly of women, at which we could discuss more important issues as well as beds.[38]

By nightfall of the first day of proceedings, the more than three thousand weary delegates were glad to bed down in their own homes or in the homes of those who had volunteered to house them.

In addition to helping to arrange accommodations for the delegates as the convention drew near, the FSAW urged local and regional groups of women to hold meetings to publicize the event and to solicit ideas for incorporation in the charter. At one such meeting of Transvaal women, held in the Johannesburg Trades Hall in May, Josie Mpama presided over some two hundred women who put together a list entitled "What Women Demand"—a more detailed reiteration of what the Women's Charter and Aims had already created. The demands covered fair employment conditions, the provision of child care, free and universal education, adequate housing and affordable rent, clean and safe living conditions, nutritious food supplies, food subsidies, land ownership, women's right to vote, equal rights for women, and peace among nations. The draft demands also included a section that called for improved conditions on the reserves and a section that called for the provision of birth control clinics.[39] Helen Joseph admitted that in the draft stage the population-control implications of these two items, which might have appealed to the apartheid state, were not considered fully. Once the women and the ANC activists identified the demands that could be used against them, the items were removed from the list.[40]

The participation of the FSAW, and of women in general, in the Congress of the People yielded positive results for the young organization and gave women increased visibility and partnership in the freedom struggle. Although the full list of women's demands was not incorporated into the final version of the Freedom Charter, Helen Joseph's proposal for "free medical treatment with special care for mothers and young children" was accepted.[41] Through the important role that the organization played in the Congress of the People, it gained recognition from the Congress Alliance. With the recognition of women as crucial players in the struggle, they became increasingly confident that their own demands would be heard and that their concerns would be taken seriously.

Like the Defiance Campaign, the Congress of the People helped to increase the politicization of women. Not yet a card-carrying member of either the ANCWL or the FSAW, Emma Mashinini was a young mother with children, who listened with great interest to the Congress of the People proceedings that took place in her community:

> I was in Kliptown when the Freedom Charter was drawn up there, and the square that became known as Freedom Charter Square was like a stone's throw from where I was living. . . .
>
> There were many papers that were going about, and the meeting was clearly advertised, but it was only when my friends approached me that I really took notice of it.
>
> I remember there were very many people there, and friends of mine who knew I was living in Kliptown wanted a place to sleep while they were there. This was before the African National Congress (ANC) was banned. All my friends were members, and I think the reason why I was not was because I had just got back from the rural area, and nothing meant anything to me apart from my children. It was when my friends came and spoke about this Congress that I took an interest.
>
> The ANC had a uniform then, and these women were wearing black skirts and green blouses. . . . So my friends were all in their colours, and I didn't have that, but every other thing which affected them and made that occasion so wonderful for them affected me as well. I was not a card-carrying member, but at that meeting I was a member in body, spirit and soul.

It was so good to be there, just to hear them speaking. Every race was there, everybody, intermingling. I would sit under the shade of a tree and listen to everything, and it was as though everything I heard was going to happen, in the next few days. . . . I take heart that it will all come true, that there will be houses for everyone, schooling, prosperity, everything we need.

There were speeches against the pass laws, and cheering, and clapping, and we sang "*Mayibuye Afrika!*"—"Africa come back!"—and "*Nkosi Sikelel' i Afrika*"—"God Bless Africa." It was a moving meeting, yet with all this—the shouting, the strong talk, the mixing of races—it was a peaceful meeting. . . . Maybe the police were there, enjoying the meeting as well. . . .

So I think that Congress was really an eye-opener for me. That, maybe, is when I started to be politicised. Although there is another thing, which I have always felt, which is that I have always resented being dominated.[42]

Emma Mashinini's vivid recollection illustrates the attraction of the high energy and purpose of the proceedings. Women who faced the double burden of the violence or lack of cooperation of their husbands and attacks against their persons, homes, families, and work by the state must have "take[n] heart" at the promises made during those days. When the Security Branch of the South African police interrupted the conference on the second afternoon, taking down the name of every delegate in attendance, the people—refusing to be harassed or intimidated—kept right on with their business. As one of the additional two thousand or more "unofficial" participants, Mrs. Mashinini was most impressed by the message implicit in the gathering. Mrs. Mashinini saw in the making a multiracial national liberation movement of South Africans whose representatives could articulate a much improved future taking place in their own lifetimes.[43]

On the heels of the enthusiasm generated by the Congress of the People, the FSAW and the ANCWL continued to gather momentum for further action. This time the target was the hated pass. In September 1955 the government announced that as of January 1956 women would be issued passes. Prime Minister Strijdom, who represented the interests of Transvaal Afrikaner workers and farmers, now led the Nationalists in an economic policy shift away from British mining interests. The new emphasis favored policies that supported the labor needs of commercial agriculture. The intent of the shift was to reduce the competition between poor white and Black workers in the towns and cities. Enacting a newer system of "influx control," the government intended to keep greater numbers of African women on the reserves and out of manufacturing jobs. African women's increased numbers in better-paying secondary industry jobs was helping to create a nationwide shortage of Black women in domestic service. The shortage prompted several municipalities either to attempt to recruit women domestic workers (which met with little success) or to regulate the service contracts between Black women and their employers. Either way, Black women would soon become subject to the same rigors of the pass laws as had their husbands and male children.[44]

Meanwhile, in June 1955, the all-white women's group known as the Black Sash (the Defend the Constitution League, which was known by the black sashes worn by its members to symbolize the imminent death of the South African constitution) had held a silent vigil in Pretoria protesting the final loss of the Colored vote. At a FSAW meeting in Johannesburg in August, Helen Joseph reported to the membership on her attendance at the Pretoria vigil. Without awaiting a directive from the leadership, a woman rose from the floor to make an astounding charge to the attendees. As Helen Joseph has reported, "Margaret Gazo, a veteran of the ANC Women's League, spoke from the floor. 'The white women did not invite us to join their protest,' she said, 'but we must go to the Union Buildings ourselves to protest against the laws which oppress us and we shall invite the white women to join us. We too shall sleep there, for we shall not leave the Union Buildings until our demands have been granted.'" The idea was greeted with immediate approval, which Helen Joseph knew would mean finding accommodations (including available "loos" [bathrooms]) for hundreds of women over an indefinite span of time. Before the meeting adjourned, however, the women had decided on a one-day protest at Pretoria to be held on October 27. Two months of frantic organizing ensued.[45]

Florence Siwedi, who was living in Mofolo (which would eventually become part of Soweto) at the time and who had become a member of the FSAW through her work in the ANCWL, explained why the idea of passes for women—indeed, for anyone—was so fiercely rejected:

When the first laws were introduced to women, then more women came together.... [W]e came together into one [organization] now, opposing these pass laws, and we told ourselves that we are not going to take these passes because they've been enslaving our husbands. Then especially we in the African National Congress, especially in the Federation of South African Women, we were so strong that we wouldn't take it because we saw them—our husbands and our male children—and we know they were caught on each and every corner. Even you can forget your pass, [and then] you are going to be arrested, be charged, be sent to jail without committing any crime. So we hated them.

And they had these qualifications of theirs that [if] you don't belong to a certain area, you are not allowed in a certain area. Say maybe a person is from Natal or from the Cape or just from Pretoria here, looking for a job in Johannesburg. Just because you don't qualify to be in Johannesburg, you are going to be arrested for that. Maybe now you're "special"; [for example,] it's toward an end [of the period during which your permit is valid]. . . . You get to your pass office to get it [renewed]. Maybe that day you are not attended to because people are such a lot. When you move away, you are going to be arrested for that. And you come out [of the permit area, for instance,] to look for [a] person, you don't get [your stamp], you go for another "special," [and then] you are going to be locked in. . . .

And when you go to those places where they [people accused of permit infractions] are arrested, you find they are sleeping on a cement [floor]. They usually used to put mats on a cement [floor], with those raffia blankets, usually those blankets . . . and sometimes they will sleep without blankets on the floor, and they will be molested—the women and the men. And they were not able to lay their cases that they were molested; they would not be allowed, as long as they are Blacks, you see? So that is why we were against the passes.[46]

Most people suffered the repercussions of one permit infraction or another. Because Mrs. Siwedi resisted carrying a pass for as long as she could get away with it, she did not have a pass to burn in protest with her comrades. "I did not go in and take a pass," she explained. "I was supposed to, [but I decided] I'm not going to take it; they can rather kill me!" In 1959, however, the police showed up at her door and demanded that she accompany them to the municipal office where she paid her rent. There she was forced to sit for her identification photo, and she was issued her pass. Later that same day, when her husband returned from work, she was arrested, "leaving the child whom I am breast-feeding to remain with the father, with the little children. . . . They've [thus] defeated the ANC woman, you see?" For two days the police kept her in jail, beating her and cuffing her about the head so severely that she was left with a hearing problem. To this day she shudders at the memory.[47]

The ANCWL and the FSAW had never before attempted an anti-pass campaign on the scale of the October 1955 protest that would bring them face-to-face with those who executed apartheid policy. For the first time,

Black women marched right up to the citadel of the Nationalist government to show Prime Minister Strijdom and the other cabinet ministers how much they hated the pass and how determined they were not to accept it. The women organizers, who again included the resourceful Bertha Mashaba (Gxowa) and Helen Joseph, concentrated largely on the cities and other African locations in the Transvaal. Apparently, there was some skepticism among the leadership of the ANC as to the ability of the FSAW to mount such a large demonstration of Black, white, and Indian women, especially in the face of the government effort to obstruct their actions. With public transport companies refusing to issue the women permits to arrange for public transportation, the organizers faced a major obstacle. Railroad companies declined to add extra coaches and refused to sell the women railway tickets to Pretoria. Police detained women who rode in private cars and harassed those who attempted to make their way to the Union Buildings. Finally, the cabinet ministers refused to meet with the women, and the municipal administration denied them permission to hold a meeting on public grounds or to hold a procession through the city streets. Nevertheless, the demonstration of October 27, 1955, was an unprecedented success that boosted confidence in the women's organizing ability for not only the participants but also many of the original skeptics. Some two thousand women had made their way to Pretoria that day.[48]

After mounting the terraced steps to the ministers' offices, the women approached the closed doors of the Union Buildings and deposited their signed protests. Instead of retreating to their homes, the group accomplished another first for Black women by assembling in the shade of the beautiful grounds of the executive offices. Lilian Ngoyi made a brief statement about the fulfillment of their task, and the group broke out in the song "*Nkosi Sikelele.*" No arrests or harassment of the demonstrators were attempted, and the women returned unmolested. At home the women received praise and a hearty welcome from those who did not attend. Helen Joseph recalled:

> In the townships, African men were waiting to welcome the women home. They gathered in crowds at the railway stations and the bus stops, even with their own local bands, in demonstration of their pride, in tribute to the courage of their women. That night I too went to a party. It was certainly not for me and I don't remember the occasion, but Nelson Mandela and Walter

Sisulu, the ANC leaders were there. From them I had an unforgettable welcome, and felt immensely rewarded for the weeks of organising.[49]

Even so, it was a slow process for the male leadership of the ANC to include women in their top-level decision-making body. In December 1955, however, members of ANCWL and the FSAW celebrated the ANC election of Lilian Ngoyi to the NEC.[50]

Beginning in January 1956, the mobile teams of government officials who issued passes to women began their work in the rural areas. There they met little resistance from women who were not as well politicized as their urban counterparts and who were easily intimidated by the threat of job loss. Once the mobile teams reached the towns, however, some of the women began to protest. Lacking a clear directive from the ANC parent body on the method or nature of an anti-pass response, the women of the FSAW and the ANCWL organized their own ardent meetings, conferences, protests, and demonstrations. As Lilian Ngoyi crisscrossed the country, traveling to towns and cities to address large groups of women and men who gathered to protest the passes, the women's mood became increasingly militant.[51]

In the town of Winburg, located in the Orange Free State—where African women had also protested the 1913 pass effort—the government had managed to issue just under fifteen hundred passes in the month of March without protest. In April, however—once the ANC had finally held its national conference on passes in Johannesburg and had determined to try to counter the developments in Winburg—Lilian Ngoyi and Robert Resha traveled to Winburg to speak with local members of the ANCWL and discovered that they were already preparing a vigorous public protest. Although the parent body had urged caution, at a meeting with their local leaders, the women collected their passes and prepared to dispose of them. At dawn the next day, April 9, the women gathered at the magistrate's office and defiantly burned their passes. The pass resisters were arrested for the offense, with some refusing to post bail.[52] As more towns and municipalities persisted in the attempt to issue passes to women, ANCWL and FSAW activists organized local women to lead mass protests. According to FSAW estimates, in thirty different locations in the Transvaal, including Johannesburg, Evaton, and Pretoria, some fifty thousand women participated in thirty-eight demonstrations against passes over the next several months. The women had succeeded in mobilizing nearly six times as many people as had the ANC-led Defiance Campaign. Like Florence Siwedi, these women had boycotted the mobile units and the pass offices, refusing to take the "dirty document of slavery" right up to its compulsory enactment in 1963.[53]

The largest single mobilization of any group of people involved in the freedom struggle of the 1950s was the second of the women's anti-pass demonstrations in Pretoria, which took place ten months after the first. On what has become known as Women's Day—Thursday, August 9, 1956—twenty thousand women gathered at the Union Buildings for a direct confrontation with Prime Minister Strijdom. Once again, they presented their petitions to closed doors, but their energy, their united show of defiance, and their overwhelming numbers proved their ability as leaders in not only the FSAW and the ANCWL but the national liberation movement as well.

For the Pretoria demonstration, Bertha Mashaba (Gxowa) and Helen Joseph once again served as the point persons in the mobilization of the national FSAW and ANCWL membership. Mrs. Gxowa recalled her experiences as a twenty-one-year-old woman traveling with Helen Joseph to promote the event:

I['d] never as a youth enjoyed not working, going to bioscopes [movie theaters] and . . . [other] social activities. My whole life was dedicated to the struggle. I was involved in all the campaigns—the Defiance Campaign, the introduction of the Bantu Education laws in '54, the writing of the Freedom Charter, the Women's March to Pretoria. I was the national organizer for the Women's March to Pretoria in 1956, for the Women's League. I went around the country organizing it.

We did this by going around to the provinces in a little car . . . Helen Joseph had. . . . We used to take special unpaid leave. For six weeks we went 'round the country with Helen, meeting women in various provinces, various areas, and at the same time we were organizing locally. We were organizing local protests to local authorities.

In all the provinces you have the ANC office, an ANC Women's League. We were going to these offices and other organizations. The ANC office there would know which women to call and [would] address the women—address our women, address churchwomen, address women from all walks of life. Sometimes we used to meet them in church; sometimes we used to invite them to general meetings, where we talked to them, and we found them receptive.[54]

Mrs. Gxowa remembered the spirited attitude of the women in Pretoria, with their colorful uniforms that indicated their organizational affiliation. The women were creative and resourceful in their efforts to arrive at their destination. Organizing women was not an easy task, Mrs. Gxowa recalled, but the hard work was rewarding:

> They [put on] a colorful march. We said churchwomen must wear their church uniforms, nurses must wear their nurses' uniforms, [and] ANC women must wear theirs. That was our identity. The *manyano* women came in their *manyano* uniforms. Whoever wanted to come in the uniform of their organization, society, whatever, they came. Traditionally, some of them would come in their own uniforms.
>
> [Some came] by road. Others came by train. The women from the Eastern Cape came by train. They booked their own coach and paid [for it]. Women from Natal came by trains and buses. In fact, we had booked a group of buses, which, at the end, the last minute, the government pulled out. We had to use trains, private cars . . . our own money, own food. [They have little money], yes, but they are determined to come. And the organization had no money. When we actually started this campaign, we had only ten pounds. We were using our own money for transport, for petrol. We were prepared to pay if we wanted to get there.
>
> No one helped us with petrol money. . . . It was not very easy to convince women to come out, to come out of where they were or they are, to come out and fight. It was difficult to organize women to a campaign, but once they are organized, you can never stop them. Once they're organized, you'll never stop them![55]

According to Mrs. Gxowa, the husbands sometimes hindered their wives' attendance: "It was difficult because some of the husbands refused [to allow] them to join with the others. . . if they had little children [, for example]. . . . There were a number of reasons . . . but their conscience always told them that if they are oppressed . . . [that is,] once the women have made up their minds that they will do it, the women will . . . organize and fight, and you will never stop them."[56]

For many of the women activists who had small children, this circumstance did not prevent them from making their way to Pretoria. A neighbor cared for Mrs. Siwedi's youngest child. Others simply took their children with them. While Mrs. Maggie Resha was organizing women for the campaign, she encountered two young mothers who determined that they would transport their children to the demonstration using the traditional method—carrying them on their backs. The two women remembered how their own mothers had carried them on their backs to and from the fields, balancing baskets of grain on their heads in the process. Moreover, they reasoned, "When we are arrested for pass offenses, we will either have to go to jail and take our babies with us, or be separated from them!"[57]

Organizing for the Women's March to Pretoria gave Maggie Resha new insights into her own connection with the legacy of women's resistance in South Africa. Earlier, as the ANCWL Sophiatown branch was forming, Mrs. Resha had become aware that her landlady (Mrs. Edith Senaoane) and her landlady's sister (Matilda Kopo) had been members of the ANC since the 1913 pass resistance. Mrs. Mary Mqhweto, another elder woman in the community who was also a relative of Mrs. Senaoane's, had also taken part in the 1913 campaign. These women advised Mrs. Resha and the other women activists that in the new generation as in their own "unity begets bravery and strength":

> When I went to see my landlady in 1956, for the signing of the petition to Pretoria, because I knew she would not be able to go—she was no longer young, and she suffered from arthritis—and when she saw my anxiety, she told me that she would call Mary Mqhweto so that she could give us tips about how the 1913 women's resistance had been successful. . . . Auntie Mary told us that it would be a shame if women of our day, who were enlightened and educated, could not defeat the regime, whereas her generation had been successful, although they had not gone to school. She still hated the pass![58]

These reminders from the still-defiant elder women renewed the courage of Maggie Resha and others.

Still, Strijdom and his ministers remained obstinate. Helen Joseph recalled that the women rejected his endeavor to meet with a delegation of African women but not with a multiracial group. Government and police interference proceeded as they had before. Public transportation in several areas was once again unavailable to the women marchers, all public gatherings of more than three people were banned, and the Security Branch police made sure that their presence was known. Up to the last moment, the leaders of the march were unsure whether their efforts would prove successful. Lacking complete confidence in the women's organizing abilities, the ANC leadership had summoned the resistance leaders to a meeting to inquire about a contingency plan in case of police hostility. Lilian Ngoyi responded that if the leadership was arrested, they were sure that others would rise to the occasion and that the members of the rank and file would manage to participate in their own guidance. Mrs. Ngoyi purposely did not reveal that in the face of police intimidation, their plan of civil disobedience was to kneel and pray. In any case, they had no concerns about the women's ability to remain calm.[59]

By Wednesday evening, with Lilian Ngoyi and Helen Joseph already in Pretoria to help ease the women's arrival, contingents of women coming from long distances had begun to reach the city in joyous anticipation. In the public hall of the township, where the women had been accommodated, they began to sing, continuing through most of the night. The next day, as the city was deluged with thousands more protesters, the momentous outpouring of women who came to register their rejection of the pass proved the organizers' success. A delegation was chosen from among the leadership to deliver the thousands of petitions to Strijdom, who, in the words of Frances Baard, "was just too scared to see us."[60] The women stood in silence in the amphitheater, "the holiest of places for the Boer,"[61] waiting for their leaders to return. The office workers at the Union Buildings hung out their windows and stood on the balconies to observe the unprecedented scene. When the leaders returned, Lilian Ngoyi asked the women to offer thirty minutes of uninterrupted silence in protest. As the silence ended, the women taunted the prime minister with a song composed for him:

> *Heyi Strijdom! [W]atint a bafazi[,] watint' imbokotho uzokufa!*
> Strijdom beware! Now that you have touched the women,
> you have struck a rock, and you will die![62]

Maggie Resha was powerfully moved by what her community of women accomplished that day:

> Before the day was wound up with *"Nkosi Sikelel' i Africa,"* Lilian's voice echoed from the walls of the Union Buildings as she cried out: "A . . . frika!" The atmosphere seemed electrified by the power of her voice, and the crowd responded: *"Mayibuye!"* (May it [r]eturn!). By this time, many of the women, myself included, were weeping quietly. Yes, the women had done it! Women from the ghettoes of the [African] locations, from the farms, from the villages, young and old, had dared to invade the very citadel of oppression in order to express their indignation and detestation for apartheid laws.[63]

Singing as they left in twos and threes, the women made their way back to the bus and train terminals. Some went straight home; others stopped in Johannesburg for the two-day (second ever) FSAW national conference. It was reported that as women prepared to board the buses leaving Pretoria, some of the men who were just getting off work paid tribute to them by allowing them to board first.[64]

For two days immediately following the August 9 demonstration, 450 women from all over the country attended the second national FSAW conference, again held at the Johannesburg Trades Hall. The delegates adopted a constitution, Lilian Ngoyi was elected president, Helen Joseph was elected secretary, and the regional vice presidents were also elected. As part of a full schedule of speakers, Helen Joseph gave a report on the overall work of the organization, Bertha Mashaba (Gxowa) reported on the anti-pass struggle, Robert Resha addressed the issue of the Bantu Education Act, and Frances Baard spoke about the "Houses, Security, and Comfort" clause of the Freedom Charter. In December a regional conference was convened in the Transvaal, where the focus of the coming year was placed on two important issues—the pass laws and the Group Areas Act (which stimulated the forced removal of, especially, members of Colored and Indian communities).[65]

On December 5 (only three days after the regional conference), in a sweeping move directed against the increasingly militant and mass-based freedom movement, 156 of the leading activists of the Congress Alliance were rounded up at dawn and arrested on charges of treason. Lilian Ngoyi, Helen Joseph, Bertha Mashaba (Gxowa), Frances Baard, Annie Silinga, Florence Matomela, and Ida Mtwana were among the women of the ANCWL and the FSAW who were included in the original number of "Treason Trialists." Helen Joseph and Lilian Ngoyi, the only women who had to endure the entire four-year trial, were not acquitted of the charges until March 1961.[66] With leaders of the cause tied up in court proceedings on a daily basis, the trial greatly debilitated the overall strategy of the movement. Nevertheless, large numbers of women and some men, at times moving in protest ahead of their leaders, managed to sustain the liberatory struggle at least through 1959.

"*Azikhwelwa!*": The Alexandra Bus Boycott

Among the many resistances on the Rand during the 1950s was the Alexandra bus boycott of 1957. A popular movement with roots that stemmed from the 1940s, the boycott illuminated household and family economic concerns that women had been articulating with renewed fervor since the time of the Defiance Campaign. Although both men and women participated fully in the campaign, the boycott shared important elements with the women's campaigns in South Africa and in Montgomery, Alabama.

Mary Mkosi—a well-respected member of the ANCWL in Alexandra, a participant in the bus boycotts, and a supporter of the freedom movement—recalled her experiences growing up in Alexandra during the 1940s and 1950s, when gangsters reigned. She remembered the violence of the Stonebreakers, the Spoilers, and the Msomi gangs: "We just ran away when we saw them! Or we would wear trousers and a cap like a boy." Her parents were hard-working people, who struggled to provide a home for their five children. Her mother earned a living taking in laundry from white families and washing linens at a downtown Johannesburg hotel. Her father was a chef at one of the downtown cafes near Park Station. After Ms. Mkosi finished secondary school, she and one of her brothers helped her mother and her aunt wash and iron thirty-four bundles of laundry per week. When the boycott took place, she was working two jobs. In addition to taking in laundry during the day, she earned five shillings a night working at a nursing home in Alexandra. She eagerly participated in the boycott:

> [When the Public Utility Transport Company (PUTCO) raised the price], we were walking. If you were riding the bus, they were burning the buses! Just here were the bus sheds . . . where the organizers from ANC would come . . . or at Number 3 Square. I would go to Number 3 Square—aahwu!—the singing and what[not]: "*Azikhwelwa!*" [and] "*Amandla!*" every time! We used to light candles there at Number 3 Square. [If the police bothered us,] we took stones and hit them. . . . It was important for us to do because we were suffering. We had to struggle.[67]

Everybody in her family worked, and every shilling they could bring in was important. The economic dimensions of the boycott were an acute reality.

In January 1957, as the Montgomery, Alabama, bus boycott was winding down in victory, the Alexandra boycott was just beginning. Patterned after the earlier bus boycotts of the 1940s, the later boycotts took place under conditions quite similar to those of the boycotts that had preceded them. When PUTCO announced that its fare increase would take effect on January 7, 1957, the riders' refusal to pay the one-cent increase precipitated a successful three-month boycott. The complaints in Alexandra resembled those of the Montgomery boycotters: Bus routes and schedules in Alexandra were not convenient to riders; because the number of buses on the routes was inadequate, the buses were overcrowded; and the bus staff was rude to the riders. Women riders faced the dangers of waiting for buses at unsheltered and unlit terminals or walking the long distances to their homes in the dark of night from the one terminal where the drivers chose to deposit them. Washerwomen, who carried laundry bundles and had to fight for space on the overcrowded buses, were especially active in picketing the bus stops. Moreover, for many families, the fares charged by the partially subsidized bus company were second in cost only to rent.[68]

A matter of days before the scheduled fare increase, representatives from at least seven community organizations met to form the Alexandra Peoples' Transport Committee (APTC). They organized a mass meeting for January 6, during which some two thousand people voted to boycott the buses until the old fares were restored. Walking the nine miles each way between Alexandra and Johannesburg, some fifteen thousand people managed to widen the movement to encompass the townships of Sophiatown and Pretoria, keeping some sixty thousand people all told off the PUTCO buses. For Mrs. Naomi Setshedi, a militant activist who campaigned against passes for women and bus fare increases, the miles were of little consequence: "We didn't even feel the distance from home to work going on foot. [The white people who gave us lifts] felt pity for us, [and] they somehow supported us in the struggle because we were working for them."[69]

White people from the COD and from the Liberal Party supported the boycott effort by organizing a relay system of rides, and the members of the Liberal Party were especially helpful as liaisons between the APTC, the business community, and the Johannesburg City Council. Within the business sector, however, opinion was divided. Support by the Chamber of Commerce came in the form of the suggestion that employers add a one-shilling-per-week transportation allowance to workers' wages. The Transvaal Chamber of Industries, however, aligned itself with the outright state rejection of the boycott, refusing to support the wage increase. In any case, the APTC rejected the idea on the grounds that not every Black person had an employer and many employers whose hiring took place as individuals (for example, heads of families who employed domestic workers) would be reluctant to raise wages to include the transportation allowance.[70]

The fractured APTC managed to draft a set of proposals of its own. In the meantime, in its impatience, PUTCO threatened to withdraw the buses from service permanently if the boycott did not end by March 1. The Johannesburg City Council proposed that an employers' fund subsidize a one-cent return on a canceled bus ticket. APTC opinion of the proposal was split, but at a mass meeting organized by Alexandra women (among them, Rachel Motshele) to vote on the proposal, it was resoundingly defeated. Rachel Motshele's husband, Michael, one of the boycott leaders, was among the contingent that rejected the offer. The people jubilantly pressed on, walking, singing, and shouting, *"Azikwelwa!"* (We will not ride!), *"Asinimali!"* (We have no money!), and *"Mayibuye!"* (May Africa come back to us!). Meanwhile, between 1950 and 1954, the difference between the average income earned and the income needed to subsist had risen from four pounds, seventeen shillings, ten cents to seven pounds, eleven shillings, five cents.[71]

With the buses removed, the APTC threatened to have workers stay at home on Monday, March 18, if the Johannesburg City Council did not provide transportation for the boycotters. Instead, however, on March 18 a more disposed faction of the APTC, the ANC, PUTCO, the Johannesburg City Council, the Chamber of Commerce, and members of the Liberal Party generated a fresh round of proposals, featuring a coupon plan whereby the Chamber of Commerce would, for all practical purposes, make up the difference between the four-cent coupons and the five-cent fare. A series of public meetings in Alexandra indicated that the plan would be accepted if it were to include Pretoria. In a meeting on March 31, however, the Alexandra residents rejected the proposal on the grounds that it included neither a guarantee that the four-cent fare would continue once the subsidy ran out nor any provision for compensation for police arrests and destruction of property. As Mrs. Setshedi explained:

> No one is forced to join the strikes; your conditions compel you to support anyone that promises to change your bad living conditions. We started with the bus boycotts[;] when the bus fare rose from 3 penny to 4 penny we agreed reluctantly to the increase, but when they increased it to 5 penny we joined our hands and refused to travel on buses. We walked to and from work sometimes getting lifts from sympathetic whites. . . . We stayed at home during the *Azikhwelwa* (Don't ride the bus) strikes and those that had walked to work were returned in the evening by their madams in cars.[72]

Nevertheless, the buses began to roll again the following day, April 1, and people began to ride them, with many using the coupons. The people of Alexandra wished to continue the boycott, if not to widen its scope, and more radical factions criticized the ANC for failing to comply with the people's wishes.[73]

Mrs. Alina Serote, a nurse working in Johannesburg, however, was among those who were not completely aligned with the boycotters:

> I used to travel to work by the PUTCO buses. But sometimes I would walk with them. I wasn't politically interested. I didn't know the meaning—all I saw was hardships. If they won, at least they worked together ... but it was a political weapon in a sense—it mobilized the mentality of people working together—but at the time I didn't think so.
>
> One paper [a political cartoon] I read [showed] a big eye on Ghana, and then it showed the toes in South Africa moving: "A big giant in South Africa wakes up." This is politics during the boycott. I got to understand that it was politically motivated, but I hadn't seen it that way.[74]

The boycott began to awaken Mrs. Serote's political consciousness. She wanted to see the residents of Alexandra improve their lives—particularly women and children, who seemed hardest hit by conditions in the townships. By 1976 politics were an unavoidable fact of life in her household: Both her son, Wally Serote—poet of the people—and her grandchildren had escaped into exile.

Mrs. Martha Dlamini, a resident of Alexandra since the late 1940s and an ANCWL veteran, supported the boycott and every campaign before and since. A friend and colleague of activists Florence Mophosho and Rachel Motshele, she attended many political meetings at Number 3 Square. "I was long in the struggle," she stated. "We were untouchable! ANC used to live!" During the bus boycott, Mrs. Dlamini cleaned rooms at a hotel in nearby Berea, and she walked when the people voted not to pay the one-cent increase: "We walked from here to Johannesburg, to and from, raining or not raining, and they decreased the fare. Today we just pay; we don't question. There were whites who were sympathetic to Blacks, and we shouldn't hate whites, because some were on our side. I used my feet! Here are my feet! We were still young in those days, very young. I thought we would be successful because we were united as members of [the] ANC." Today Mrs. Dlamini lives a modest life with members of her extended family, who continue to deal with the economic consequences of long years under white rule. Still, she takes pride in the spirited activism of her youth: "We were not educated, but we liberated this country—especially the mamas!"[75]

In the end, although it did not generate a wider campaign to eliminate white supremacy, the Alexandra boycott provided important lessons for the coming struggle for liberation. First was the lesson that unity was a potent force and that factionalization undermined the object of that unity. Second, was the lesson of the high cost of underestimating the intransigence of the Nationalist government. Third, was the lesson that the consciousness, strength, and militancy of the rank and file could surge beyond those of the leadership. Effective mass protest required a strategy to prevent the depletion of monetary resources, the disaffection of the constituency, and the potential for annihilation by opposing state forces. For its part, the boycott contributed to the larger context of Black militancy of the decade, supported by those who were convinced that change must come.

"We don't want passes!"

True to Lilian Ngoyi's 1956 call "to organize all the various organizations of African women and individuals against this inhuman and wicked decision of the Government," a variety of Black women—housewives, domestic workers, nurses, farmers—in the townships and rural areas resisted the pass through 1959. In a speech to her ANCWL constituents Mrs. Ngoyi announced, "Only direct mass action will deter the Government and stop it from proceeding with its cruel laws."[76] In nonviolent mass protest, women demonstrated against forced removals and against municipal beer halls; confronted the police and withstood their baton charges against the protesting masses; and endured arrest, even sometimes refusing to pay bail or fines. In March 1958 Maggie Resha, Helen Joseph, and busloads of women confronted police and hospital officials at Baragwanath Hospital in Soweto in vigorous protest of the requirement that nurses obtain passes in order to register with an identity number. The action forestalled the pass policy for nurses for several years. Between two thousand and three thousand women from the East and West Rand converged on the Johannesburg City Council to register their objections to the pass and to the squalid conditions of the African locations. In Durban between June 1958 and June 1959, African women—many of them beer brewers—raged against forced removals and against those who produced, sold, and consumed beer in municipal beer halls in Cato Manor. As some two thousand women clashed with the police over a period of several weeks, city property was destroyed, beer halls were burned, and three people were shot. Groups of rural women all over Natal—who were adversely affected by new laws and regulations that re-

quired their participation in the objectionable cattle dipping[77] or who faced
the loss of their farmlands even in the reserves—demonstrated against the
Bantu Authority and were imprisoned for their efforts. Others marched
against women's passes and demanded a minimum wage of one pound per
day. The women's revolt in Natal yielded some twenty thousand protesters,
about a thousand of whom filled the jails.[78]

Maggie Resha recalled a spontaneous anti-pass demonstration from
Sophiatown to central Johannesburg in 1958. Early one late October morning, two women appeared at Mrs. Resha's house in Sophiatown to inform
her, as chairwoman of the branch ANCWL, that protest marchers were
gathering at Freedom Square to make their way downtown to Market
Street. Rushing out to find her ANCWL branch secretary, Kate Molale,
Mrs. Resha tried to persuade the women to put the march on hold until
they could solicit advice from the executive officers. Refusing to delay the
protest, however, the women walked or (in the case of those who were elderly or who carried babies) took the bus, undeterred by the presence of the
Security Branch police. As they marched through the white neighborhoods,
domestic workers spontaneously joined in. "It was one of those times," Mrs.
Resha said, "when the masses march ahead of the leaders instead of vice
versa." At a police roadblock, the women were ordered to disperse, but
Mrs. Resha—speaking in a combination of Xhosa and Sesotho—urged the
women to move forward. Later arrested for her participation, Mrs. Resha
was informed that the group of women who had arrived earlier by bus had
been taken into police custody at the pass office on Market Street. She
learned too that a large contingent of Alexandra women, led by the forceful Florence Mophosho, was also arrested for demonstrating that day. The
1,200 Alexandra and Sophiatown women, including 170 with babies, served
two of the four weeks of their sentence in the notorious Johannesburg Fort
before the ANC paid the remainder of their fines.[79] Showing that they
would control their own destiny, the rank-and-file women redefined the
concept of leadership by taking command of their resistance.

Ernestina Mekgwe, a domestic worker who lived in Alexandra, recalled
her own indirect participation in one of the Alexandra women's 1950s anti-
pass campaigns. She raised money for and took food to the protesters who
were arrested and taken to Station Number 4:

After [collecting money for those arrested,] I went home. I went back to work.
I left that place. When I went to the kitchen to work, the son to the white

man came in. The son to the white man asked me, "What is that badge for, Dorothy?"[80] I told him, "This is your language[;] read it." He read it. "Away with passes." He told his parents. His parents came. They asked me, "What's away with the passes?"

I told [them], we don't want passes in our land. They gave us passes, both men and women. Passes are for men. Even if it's a pass, it must be a relevant pass because the pass is able to identify the person. You must not be arrested for it. They forced blacks to carry it. It must be like the one carried by whites. [Black people] must [be able to] move around and no police should be asking for it in the streets.

They said to me, "You are now safe[;] you got away[;] if you can be arrested you will be in trouble." I can rather be in trouble. I don't want a pass in my own country. What can I say if I am arrested? I was born without such troubles but now I have troubles. I am going to try to get rid of these troubles with my people. I am trying to fight for my own country.[81]

Mrs. Mekgwe did not hesitate to state her position to her employers—she had no use for the policy of passes for women. She would not be forced to carry a document of humiliation *in her own country*. Her white employers, newer arrivals to South Africa, were not required to carry such passes, and Mrs. Mekgwe was committed to the struggle to equalize the privileges and rights that she and all those who were born in South Africa should be entitled to enjoy.

Mrs. Naomi Setshedi, of Bafokeng heritage, a street hawker in and resident of Alexandra, took part in the local meetings designed to advise women about pass resistance and participated in the Pretoria demonstration in 1956. Arrested for her participation, she understood that state success in issuing passes to some would divide the women's resistance and eventually doom their efforts as a whole:

Yes, women were furious, [and] no one could stop them from doing what they thought was right. I started to realize that women are militant sometimes. If they could have been sent to war during that time, they would have carried their arms without hesitation. Police vans came in large numbers to the scene, and women packed themselves therein. They instructed the police to arrest them because they were not willing to apply for passes.

Xhosas and Shangaan women remained behind, selling vegetables on the streets. One Tswana woman went to them and said, "Hey you are busy here making profits because you don't care for what happens since your land has been long taken away from you by whites. Your chiefs have sold your land

to the whites, [and] now you have come here to work for your children and
you don't care to join in our struggle. You are satisfied when you rent a house,
[whereas] we [Tswanas] rent houses with the hope that we would go back to
our villages and settle there eventually. Do you think we should fight for your
rights while you are here making profits? Let's go[;] join the struggle all of
you, Pedi, Shangaan, and Xhosa."[82]

Mrs. Setshedi identified herself as a proper BaTswana woman, who could
still claim productive lands in the reserves of Bophuthatswana. She blamed
the failure of other women to grasp the importance of collective struggle on
their less-independent status. When the women excused their behavior by
invoking their family responsibilities, Mrs. Setshedi had a ready response:

> Towards sunset these Shangaan women told us that they had to go back to
> their homes because they had left their houses locked and their husbands
> expected them home to cook the evening meal. We told them that we also
> had husbands who expected us home but because we had responsibilities be-
> yond our homes, which we were presently attending to, we couldn't go home,
> so how could they go home. They should not expect themselves to go about
> their hawking business while we did not work but took part in demonstrations
> which if proved successful would benefit them as well as us. In other words, we
> could not struggle for them.[83]

Mrs. Setshedi wasted no time wrestling with conflicting loyalties. In fact,
the women's resistance linked home and national liberation; women fought
for greater control over and protection of the comfort and security of their
families. Therefore, even if it put a kink in gender relations, business as
usual was not an option.

As the decade progressed, the women would have to adapt their forms
of resistance against an increasingly repressive regime that turned openly to
violence against both women and men. Activists were banned, leaders were
jailed and killed, workers' strikes were outlawed, and (as witnessed in 1976),
tear gas and guns were used against even small schoolchildren. In spite of
international protest that made South Africa a pariah in the world community, apartheid power would not go gently into the good night. This bitter
state tenacity forced the national liberation struggle to change its tactics
or face annihilation. In 1960, when sixty-nine unarmed people were killed
at Sharpeville—most of them shot in the back as they ran from police—
the ANC and Pan-Africanist Congress (PAC) leadership took the strug-

gle underground. The ANC concentrated its efforts on the creation of a military wing: *Umkonto we Sizwe*, or "Spear of the Nation."[84] PAC formed its own militarized organization, known as Poqo.[85] As the ANC and the PAC—both of which had been banned—operated from exile during the long span of continued conflict, other organizations that were less political in appearance but still dedicated to human dignity and freedom took their place. Through the ebb and flow of liberatory movement, women on the ground acted as committed agents of change, both within their own country and in exile.[86]

Spurred by the children's uprisings of 1976, Black consciousness, and heavy state repression, the mass-based protests of the 1980s took a form that differed greatly from that of the protests of the 1950s. The character of the liberation movement had become more youth centered, trade unionist, and masculinist. In the 1950s, in contrast, the women had given impetus and leadership to the enormous outpouring of political activity and had succeeded in bringing their demands to bear on a movement and a government finally forced to take them seriously.

The women had revived their auxiliary branch of the ANC and had brought it into full membership within the parent body. They had significantly increased their numbers within the organization and had developed their own leaders and strategizers. In addition, the ANCWL had been among the founding bodies—indeed the most significant in terms of numbers and leadership—of the FSAW. Through this vital national network of South African women freedom fighters, they had broadened their view of the meaning of liberation, insisting that all of South Africa belonged equally to the women and men who lived there. They had opened the discussion of liberation to include their relationships with men at home and within the freedom struggle, and they had entered into political friendships with a racially and ethnically diverse base of women. With the ANC reluctant to give women the go-ahead to take to the streets en masse to burn and protest passes, the women had forged ahead. They had faced arrests, beatings, heavy fines, angry husbands, and the logistics of arranging for the care of small children—all in the name of pass resistance. Throughout the 1950s, assisted by their radical white and Indian counterparts, Black South African women—old and young; middle class, working class, and impoverished; some more politicized than others—had led their country's struggle for freedom.

At the same time, Black women in Alabama—operating perhaps in a narrower context—played an equally important role in the freedom movement. Since the 1940s, and especially during the early 1950s, Montgomery women helped to open and to continue the discussion of the inequalities of racial segregation. Agitating for the vote and joining men in political organizations designed to change the power structure in state and local governments, they kept their eyes on the prize in the personal and political struggle against white supremacy. Struggling to hold the attention of their male counterparts, Black women in Montgomery formed their own political organization, the Women's Political Council. Bus segregation in the South, demeaning to both Black men and Black women, inflicted special indignities on Black women. They were extended no courtesy as working mothers who carried packages and children and they faced gruff manhandling, insults, and routine abuse. The members of the Women's Political Council—who shared these abuses, regardless of class status—came together, in part, to address these issues. For their part, the women were prepared to lead the boycott campaign. Organized and prepared for action, they stepped out with faith in their plan to see the death of white supremacy in their city and across the South. Their Montgomery protest precipitated a wider movement for racial justice and social change in the South and in the nation. By staying off the buses, by keeping out of the downtown stores, and by vigorously defending their positions to the white people who wielded power over them, Black women in Alabama put the system of white supremacy on notice—old power relationships and the status quo were about to come to an end.

The importance of the actions of the South African and U.S. women to their respective movements is beyond dispute. The energy, determination, and defiance characteristic of the 1950s women's demonstrations spurred both their movements and their societies toward irrevocable change.

CONCLUSION

Perhaps initially, it is easier to point to the differences than to the similarities between 1950s Black women's resistance in Montgomery, Alabama, and Johannesburg, South Africa. To begin with, the close-up histories of Black people in the two locations differ. Black South Africans were, at the outset, a free people in the land of their birth, but they were forced to surrender their sovereignty to Dutch and British imperial powers and their land to Boer farmers. Black Alabamians in the United States, in contrast, began by being treated as commodities in a multifaceted colonial project of economic exchange in which Europeans, followed by white Americans, kept them enslaved. In addition, geographically and economically, Montgomery was established as the capital seat of a cotton agriculture–rich region sustained by a large reservoir of Black labor. Johannesburg, for its part, admitted a wider ethnic mix of people subject to special labor migrancy regulations. In fact, in search of a route to meaningful Black citizenship, African Americans used any and all means, including migration, mass protest, and court action, to attain adequate freedom. Black South Africans, in contrast, saw their scant constitutional rights steadily dwindle until, by the mid-twentieth century, legal redress was no longer an option. By 1960, as mass Black protest heated up across the southern United States and beyond, mass protest in South Africa was forced underground.[1]

With the analysis couched in different terms, however, the points of similarity become clearer. As two sites of the African diaspora, for instance, Montgomery and Johannesburg were both created and developed as racially segregated cities that inflicted severe social, political, physical, and economic hardships on their Black inhabitants. Under systems of white domination and Jim Crow, African diasporan women and men responded to these conditions in ways that ultimately included similar forms of protest. Throughout the 1950s and 1960s, the Third World was ablaze with popular anticolonial movements that help contextualize the connections between the political actions of the women in Montgomery and Johannesburg. In the important decade of the 1950s, in both locations, Black women's protests involved a broad understanding of the meaning of democracy that led their movements to a new form of militancy.

History: A Legacy of Struggle, Memory, and Place

Black women in Alabama and in the Transvaal share a fundamental connection to the land in which they were born (see chapters 1 and 2). African American women in the U.S. South learned early on that their sex was no protection against the dehumanization of being treated as the property of another and being forced to labor on land that was not their own. The scars of slavery cut deep, yet the resilience, tenacity, and agency with which Black women cared for their families and homes, pursued freedom, and in many cases expressed their understanding of faith helped them persevere in the face of these challenges. The children of these enslaved women, grandmothers and great-grandmothers of the 1950s women activists, assimilated these strengths from their mothers and passed them on to coming generations. Lessons learned at the feet of these great-grandparents or indirectly from stories passed down through generations forged in the women activists an important understanding of the long history of struggle—individual and collective—that their people waged against white supremacy.

African women, for their part, recalled a time when their people were masters of their own domain, when the land belonged to them, and when the results of their labor directly benefited their families and communities. African people on the Highveld remained free well into the last third of the nineteenth century, their land and labor still not wholly subject to the political economy of the land-hungry white "baases." Resistance to the encroaching Boers was fierce among the BaSotho-BaTswana peoples; the legacy of Moshoeshoe's tireless campaign against the white people left an important point of reference for those who held onto their land and their independence until all options seemed exhausted. Their history provided future generations of South African women with crucial lessons of struggle, models of resistance, and reminders of the objective—freedom in their own country.

Resistance in Urban Contexts

As Montgomery and Johannesburg developed into two distinct centers of urban commerce and politics connected to developing world economies by trade, Black women and men had to find ways to cope with the segregated structures within. Like Kimberley before it, early Johannesburg developed a complicated pass system for Black male migrant workers who traveled between their rural homes and the mines. During enslavement and Reconstruction, African Americans were also subject to a pass system that limited their whereabouts and their occupations to confined spaces and job categories. As Johannesburg surpassed Montgomery as an urban outgrowth of heavy manufacturing and secondary industries, the pass system became institutionalized as a much more onerous network of rules and regulations that impacted every facet of life for Black men, women, and children. Both cities delineated the physical spaces in which Black people were allowed to travel, conduct business, enjoy leisure time, and live; however, only in Johannesburg were Black people subject to the practice of having their homes and neighborhoods removed. It was the assault on Black households, on Black women's livelihoods, on Black children's safety and education that brought Black women in South Africa into a particular kind of vocal opposition with the state. In Montgomery it was primarily the "moving theaters" of contested space—the segregated buses[2]—but also the parks and ultimately any place demarcated as "White Only" or "Colored," that helped galvanize many women into action. On the buses, their persons were not respected or safe, but although working women formed the majority of the ridership, the articulation of their objections did not come in overtly gendered terms. U.S. and South African women responded with forms of resistance that were both similar (bus boycotts) and different (women's passes).

Specifically, in the late nineteenth and early twentieth centuries, Black women established important models of successful political resistance in Atlanta and Bloemfontein, not far from Montgomery and Johannesburg, respectively. Relegated to some of the lowest-paying jobs in their cities, Atlanta washerwomen struck for higher wages and control of their own industry and Bloemfontein domestic workers refused to carry passes. Within increasingly urban settings, women who were generally regarded as powerless demonstrated two early momentous examples of political thought and action. On the heels of the entrenchment of Jim Crow, Black people in Montgomery similarly set an early precedent with their first boycott of city trolley cars.

Black women who migrated from their rural share-cropping or independent farms and villages to the growing urban centers brought with them crucial forms of cultural expression and systems for accessing networks of friends and relatives that helped them to form groups essential to the

urban-based struggles they would face (see chapters 3 and 4). These circles of women, based on the circles first established in the country among
those who migrated, were responsible for teaching women necessary survival skills and maintaining a connection that would prove invaluable in the
years to come. Through these groups, women could partake in the wealth
of knowledge, wisdom, and faith accumulated over time and shared in the
fields, kitchens, and churches enriched by their presence. Baptist women's
circles, beer-brewing groups, *manyano* organizations, and *stokvel* meetings
taught urban women how to organize and helped politicize them around
shared issues. Many of these women became "bridge leaders,"[3] linking their
constituents on the ground to the male leadership of the national, parent,
or larger groups.

Many who migrated to the cities made the transition with the mental
paraphernalia of old tools that would prove useful in new contexts. For future women activists who were born into the urban context, access to such
resources as schools and churches was less limited than it had been for their
rural ancestors. The city offered a more diverse cultural life that presented
new economic, social, and political opportunities.

In the city the daughters of sharecroppers and independent farmers
joined those born and raised in the urban locations in coming face-to-face
with the intimate particularities of white domination in an urban setting.
Black people could not, for example, try on shoes in a downtown department store; even owning a pair of shoes was often considered a luxury. In
the city, it was assumed that young Black women looking for work sought
employment as domestic workers; thus, white women felt free to seek them
out on town or city streets. The nature of the relationship between mistress
and servant mirrored that between Black and white people in the wider
society. Because of the racialized subordination of their workers' position,
white women employers assumed they were entitled to speak for their employees, to call them by other than their proper names, to intimidate them,
to overwork them, to pay them in food or in reduced wages, and to exploit their labor and their good will as they saw fit. For their part, Black
women domestic workers resisted this subordination by speaking out to
their employers about intolerable conditions or by seeking new employment (see chapters 7 and 8). Buttressed by the periods of political resistance
in the 1950s, Black women domestic workers turned the tables on these
dominant-subordinate roles and put their employers on notice that they
would no longer tolerate the racial status quo.

Radical Antecedents and Cross-Class Relationships

In addition to enacting the more personal forms of resistance to white domination, Black women activists of the 1950s participated in a wider movement for social change rooted in the political activism of the 1930s and 1940s. The Communist Party in both South Africa and the United States, labor organizers, New Dealers, Liberal Party members, the early African National Congress (ANC), members of the National Association for the Advancement of Colored People (NAACP), Garveyites, and the more middle-class Black clergymen and educators espousing a theory of racial uplift contributed greatly to the pool of resources and expertise shared by the 1950s activists. In both locations the Communist Party inspired many workers to participate in the first round of mass actions against racial and economic injustice. The Communist Party critique of the political and racial status quo was significant to Black people, rural and urban, many of whom had yet to hear a more compelling articulation of their condition. Throughout the World War II era, expanded work opportunities, increased exposure to democratic rhetoric, and a rise in anticolonial activities in the Third World made the promise of improved conditions appear more immediate to African Americans and Black South Africans alike. For Black women and men in both locations and throughout the African diaspora generally, direct participation in the war created an important political opening that returning war veterans were quick to exploit. Within the labor movement too there existed tools (augmented in many ways by members of the Communist Party) that easily lent themselves to other contexts: worker education and politicization, coalitional relationships, the practice of negotiation, strike organizing, and mobilization techniques (see chapter 5). Labor organizing catapulted some working-class activists into the forefront of their wider freedom movements.

At least in the twentieth century, the NAACP and the ANC—working from a more middle-class sensibility, which emphasized the merits of seeking legal redress on behalf of a literate and pious Black community—first took the lead in the establishment of a Black protest tradition. Members of these organizations excelled at forming bridges to members of the sympathetic white liberal leadership, who could be called on to extend their influence in pushing for necessary, if more gradual, change. Within these organizational frameworks and others—such as those of the Black Baptist, Methodist, and African Methodist Episcopal churches and later the

Women's Political Council—women made space for the articulation of their own particular viewpoints.

Middle- and working-class women filled the ranks of the Baptist women's circles and Methodist *manyanos*. Indeed, the class lines of these and other organizations were often blurred: factory workers, teachers, nurses, and domestic employees formed the ANC Women's League (ANCWL) membership. A member of the Women's Political Council, which was originally founded as a professional women's organization, might be employed as a teacher for most of the year but earn money as a domestic or factory worker as well. Teachers and domestic workers formed a large majority of the membership of the Baptist Woman's Convention and the National Association of Colored Women's Clubs, who shared a dedication to both the defiance of the conventional wisdom held about them (stereotypical Mammies or women with loose personal morals) and the improvement of the conditions under which Black people lived. Adhering to what some have labeled the politics of respectability, Black women fearlessly and visibly entered the realm of overt political activity to protect their own interests and those of their communities (see chapter 6).

Daughters, mothers, urban householders, and workers understood and responded to the issues at hand. They were skilled, capable, autonomous, independent, active agents of change who bore no resemblance to the Eurocentric passive ideal. In South Africa, far more than in the United States at this time, the work of such forceful women took on a decidedly feminist outlook.

An Early Feminist Critique Informs Black Women's Activism

The economic and political interests of Black women, for which the state and the women's employers had such little regard, lay at the center of much of their protests. Although these interests were contained within wider movements for social justice, Black women identified and ardently fought against practices and policies that especially affected them as women. Assaults by white bus drivers and by the police when the women did not carry a pass left them both physically abused and disrespected. Their children and households suffered, by extension, from the meager wages, the physical and emotional abuse, and the arrests that the women endured. Black women rebelled against not only these assaults but also the many limitations on their personal freedom, the meager compensation for their productive and reproductive labor, the high price and poor quality of their children's education, and the vulnerability of their children to violence.

Plainly articulating the reasons for their resistance, the women's political organizations, in particular, laid claim to a feminist critique. Black women worked effectively within heterogeneous groups of men and women activists, but in the women's organizations they found the space to discuss issues of special interest to them. The goal was freedom from domination—by the state, by their husbands, by their male counterparts in political leadership. The message was "[Don't] walk on me like you walk on a road."[4] In South Africa, when the multiracial group of activists from the Federation of South African Women (FSAW) and the ANCWL proclaimed their dedication to the cause of liberation, their concept of liberation (much more fully realized than that of their U.S. counterparts) included an argument against male domination. The resistance that South African women—who faced state-sponsored attacks against their persons, households, and children—mounted especially, but not exclusively, in defense of women's issues constitutes decisive feminist practice. Their actions greatly enhanced the tenor and mass appeal of their overall movement, and by the mid-1950s the vanguard approach of the women of the WPC and the FSAW-ANCWL had yielded even more vigorous and advanced freedom movements.

Finally, although the process was gradual in most cases, the development of the political activism of these women—which had fully flowered by the mid-1950s—had a great deal to do with their own particular makeup, ethnicity, history, class status, color, and personal courage. The legacy of enslavement ran deep for the Alabama women, whereas African women learned of their lineages as long, proud, and free. Black women in both societies were taught by their mothers and other female family members and friends what it meant to be women—to be the caretakers of the household, the children, and the men and to engage in economic activities that benefited them, their families, and their communities. They learned of a different sort of domesticity that confined them neither to the household nor to passivity. They learned how to stand on their own, free from dependence on men. Work experiences outside their homes highlighted the economic disadvantages under which they labored. Thus, the upbringing and early experiences of the Black rural daughters and urban workers greatly influenced their subsequent activism.

By 1960 the movements for Black liberation in the United States and South Africa had taken different trajectories toward uncertain outcomes.

Still, the politically aware women activists saw their sometimes difficult and dangerous participation as wholly worth their continued efforts. In their own children and in the children of others, they helped to nurture the next generation of freedom fighters. Their political practice transformed the idea of motherhood from the 1950s Cold War ideal of Hollywood June Cleavers to social justice activists, militant pacifists, and "mothers of the[ir] nation[s]."[5]

. . .

The oral histories of these women activists, generously offered for the benefit of younger generations, connect listeners (especially young Black women) to a deep reservoir of strength and determination. This connection is fortified by images that portray, for instance, streams of women walking in small groups along the streets of Montgomery wearing coats and hats, carrying pocketbooks, and sporting high-heeled shoes or a tired but resolute woman in worn-down shoes balancing a large box of turnip greens on her head in the tradition of her African foremothers. All the women captured in the photographs herein and in the memories of those who were present—women standing at pickup stations, piling out of church station wagons, filling up front pews at the weekly mass meetings—are dignified, purposeful, and glad to be actively involved in the effort to obliterate Jim Crow.

Images from the other side of the Atlantic portray, for example, the women (some of whom are carrying their babies on their backs) who stormed the Union Buildings at Pretoria to inform Prime Minister Johannes Gerhardus Strijdom that they would not accept the pass. They are pictured in hats, traditional dresses, and ANC colors, and they are shown giving the thumbs up sign to indicate their tremendous enthusiasm, confidence, and mutual support. Victory would come soon, they believed, because Strijdom had "touched the women, [and] struck a rock."[6] The final dismantling of apartheid would not come for three more long and arduous decades, but the faces of the women who marched to Pretoria that August day revealed confidence that victory would be theirs.

These "defiers" challenge all who listen to follow suit. "Stand tall," they seem to say. "Be tenacious, give no quarter to injustice, and do not fail to give full voice to the stories of connection, of purpose, and of hope!"

Notes

INTRODUCTION

1. Mrs. Idessa Redden, interview by the author, Montgomery, Alabama, April 13, 1997.

2. Mrs. Bertha Mashaba Gxowa, interview by the author, Shell House, Johannesburg, South Africa, July 22, 1997.

3. See Jo Ann Gibson Robinson, *The Montgomery Bus Boycott and the Women Who Started It* (Knoxville: University of Tennessee Press, 1987), 19–43.

4. Tom Lodge, *Black Politics in South Africa since 1945* (New York: Longman, 1983), especially chap. 7; Ruth First, "The Bus Boycott," *Africa South*, July 1957, 55–58.

5. For a good understanding of "Black women's standpoint" or "special angle of vision" and the process of turning thought into action within the context of resistance, see Patricia Hill Collins, *Black Feminist Thought: Knowledge, Consciousness, and the Politics of Empowerment* (New York: Routledge, 1991), especially chaps. 1 and 2.

6. On new patterns of contemporary Black women's activism at the grassroots level in the United States and South Africa, see Temma Kaplan, *Crazy for Democracy: Women in Grassroots Movements* (New York: Routledge, 1997).

7. Because of the very political nature of its social construction in the United States (and similarly in South Africa), race has functioned as a "metalanguage" in the lives of Black women, strongly influencing their choices of when, where, how, and with whom common cause might be made in the interests of liberation and equality. In one sense, according to Higginbotham, this has meant that at important historical moments Black women have had to acknowledge and act on their understanding of the negative implications of race as more immediate than gender. See Evelyn Brooks Higginbotham, "African-American Women's History and the Metalanguage of Race," *Signs* 17, no. 21 (Winter 1992): 251–74. See also Audre Lorde, "Age, Race, Class, and Sex: Women Redefining Difference," in *Sister Outsider* (Freedom, Calif.: Crossing Press, 1984), 114–23; Deborah K. King, "Multiple Jeopardy, Multiple Consciousness: The Context of Black Feminist Ideology," *Signs* 14, no. 1 (August 1988): 42–72; and E. Frances White, "Africa on My Mind: Gender, Counter Discourse and African-American Nationalism," *Journal of Women's History* 2, no. 1 (Spring 1990): 73–97.

8. According to the feminist scholar Joy James, "Historical women or 'protofeminists' who preshadowed contemporary black feminism [she uses Ida B. Wells and Ella Baker as examples] provided models and strategies for resistance that rejected strict black female adherence to middle-class norms." Joy James, *Shadowboxing: Representations of Black Feminist Politics* (New York: Palgrave, 2002), 41.

9. For detailed accounts of Jamaican women in slavery, see Lucille Mathurin Mair, *A

Historical Study of Women in Jamaica, 1655–1844 (Kingston: University of the West Indies, 2007) and "Women Field Workers in Jamaica during Slavery," in *Women in Africa and the African Diaspora*, 2nd ed., ed. Roslyn Terborg-Penn and Andrea Benton Rushing (Washington, D.C.: Howard University Press, 1996). On Claudia Jones, see her daughter's memoir, Buzz Johnson, *I Think of My Mother: Notes on the Life and Times of Claudia Jones* (London: Karia Press, 1985), and Carol Boyce Davies, "Claudia Jones Anti-Imperialist/Black Feminist Politics,"in *Decolonizing the Academy: African Diasporan Studies*, ed. Carole Boyce Davies, with Meredith Gadsby, Charles Peterson, and Henrietta Williams (Trenton, N.J.: Africa World Press, 2003). See also Adelaide M. Cromwell, *An African Victorian Feminist: The Life and Times of Adelaide Smith Casely Hayford, 1868–1960* (Washington, D.C.: Howard University Press, 1992); Amy Jacques Garvey's columns in *The Negro World*, the journal of the Universal Negro Improvement Association; and Amy Jacques Garvey, *Garvey and Garveyism* (New York: Collier Books, 1970).

10. Differing in status and means from such charismatic male leaders as Martin Luther King, Jr., and Nelson Mandela, who exhorted their listeners with prophetic visions of the future, the women activists—or organic intellectuals—resist the notion that only the educated class of Black men can define and bring change to the contours of Black life. In Gramscian terms, such women demonstrate their "active participation in practical life, as constructor[s], organiser[s], 'permanent persuader[s]' not just simple orator[s]." See Antonio Gramsci, *Selections from the Prison Notebooks*, ed. Quintin Hoare and Geoffrey Nowell Smith (New York: International Publishers, 1971), 10.

In her excellent study of local Black women of the southern freedom movement, Belinda Robnett situates the women's activism between the more formal political organizations and the communities from which they came. Robnett calls such women "bridge leaders" and sees their participation in terms of their roles as both consummate organizers and mobilizers of masses of Black people to act and, in the process, become transformed by their complete immersion in a powerful and emotional set of interactions. As Robnett asserts, "The day-to-day interactions between bridge leaders and potential adherents and constituents provide the basis for the emotional intimacy so necessary for persuading the masses to take risks. Additionally, bridge leaders provide a leadership . . . as the trusted leader who constructs a kind of local charismatic authority." The consistent, dedicated work of Mrs. Redden and Mrs. Gxowa fits Robnett's framework of bridge leadership and underscores their many talents beyond the "women-as-organizers" model. See Belinda Robnett, *How Long? How Long? African-American Women in the Struggle for Civil Rights* (New York: Oxford University Press, 1997), 193.

11. For a discussion of oral subjects as historians, see Susan Geiger's adaptation of Marjorie Mbilinyi's term "life historian" in Susan Geiger, "What's So Feminist about Women's Oral History?" *Journal of Women's History* 2, no. 1 (Spring 1990): 171. See also Rhonda Y. Williams, "'I'm a Keeper of Information': Voice and History-Telling," *Oral History Review* 28, no. 1 (Winter 2001): 41–63.

12. See Gwendolyn Etter-Lewis, "Black Women's Life Stories: Reclaiming Self in Narrative Texts," in *Women's Words: The Feminist Practice of Oral History*, ed. Sherna Berger Gluck and Daphne Patai (New York: Routledge, 1991), 43–58.

CHAPTER ONE

1. Miss Gwendolyn Bell, interview by the author, Montgomery, Alabama, May 19, 1998.
2. Emma Mashinini, *Strikes Have Followed Me All My Life* (New York: Routledge, 1991), 3; Emma Mashinini, interview by the author, Pretoria, South Africa, July 21, 1997.
3. Mashinini, *Strikes Have Followed Me*, 4–6.
4. William Warren Rogers, Robert David Ward, Leah Rawls Atkins, and Wayne Flint, *Alabama: The History of a Deep South State* (Tuscaloosa: University of Alabama Press, 1994), 9, 639 n. 12; D. R. Morris, *The Washing of the Spears* (1964; reprint, New York: Simon and Schuster, 1986); Shula Marks, *Reluctant Rebellion* (New York: Oxford University Press, 1970); J. B. Peires, *The House of Phalo: A History of the Xhosa People in the Days of Their Independence* (Johannesburg: Ravan Press, 1981); Robert Ross, *Cape of Torments: Slavery and Resistance in South Africa* (London: Routledge and Kegan Paul, 1983); Elizabeth Eldredge, *A South African Kingdom: The Pursuit of Security in Nineteenth-Century Lesotho* (New York: Cambridge University Press, 1993).
5. U.S. Bureau of the Census, *Fourth Census of the United States, 1820*, vol. 1 (Washington, D.C.: Department of the Interior, 1821), 29.
6. James Benson Sellers, *Slavery in Alabama* (University, Ala: University of Alabama Press, 1950), 3–4; Rogers et al., *Alabama*, 94.
7. Sellers, *Slavery in Alabama*, 5.
8. Ibid., 144; Rogers et al., *Alabama*, 105.
9. See the definition of *laborlords* in Gavin Wright, *Old South, New South* (New York: Basic Books, 1986), 18.
10. U.S. Bureau of the Census, *Seventh Census of the United States, 1850*, vol. 1 (Washington, D.C.: Department of the Interior, 1851), 421.
11. Steven F. Miller, "Plantation Labor Organization and Slave Life on the Cotton Frontier: The Alabama-Mississippi Black Belt, 1815–1840," in *Cultivation and Culture: Labor and the Shaping of Slave Life in the Americas*, ed. Ira Berlin and Philip D. Morgan (Charlottesville: University of Virginia Press, 1993), 159–60.
12. Quoted in Sellers, *Slavery in Alabama*, 163.
13. Deborah Gray White, *Ar'n't I a Woman? Female Slaves in the Plantation South* (New York: W. W. Norton, 1985), 101.
14. Kenneth M. Stampp, *The Peculiar Institution: Slavery in the Ante-bellum South* (New York: Vintage Books, 1956), 245.
15. Quoted in Benjamin A. Botkin, ed., *Lay My Burden Down: A Folk History of Slavery* (Chicago: University of Chicago Press, 1945), 161–62.
16. See White, *Ar'n't I a Woman?* See also Melton A. McLaurin, *Celia, a Slave* (Athens:

University Georgia Press, 1991); Adrienne D. Davis, "Slavery and the Roots of Sexual Harassment," in *Directions in Sexual Harassment Law*, ed. Catharine MacKinnon and Reva Siegel (New Haven, Conn.: Yale University Press, 2003); Jean Fagan Yellin, ed., *Incidents in the Life of a Slave Girl: Written by Herself* (Cambridge, Mass.: Harvard University Press, 1987); and Margaret Washington, ed, *The Narrative of Sojourner Truth* (New York: Vintage Books, 1993).

17. See, for instance, John Blassingame, *The Slave Community: Plantation Life in the Ante-bellum South* (New York: Oxford University Press, 1972), especially chap. 3; Angela Y. Davis, *Women, Race and Class* (New York: Random House, 1981), chap. 1; Jacqueline Jones, *Labor of Love, Labor of Sorrow: Black Women, Work, and the Family, from Slavery to the Present* (New York: Vintage Books, 1985), chap. 1; Eugene Genovese, *Roll, Jordan, Roll: The World the Slaves Made* (New York: Vintage Books, 1972), especially Book Three, Part Two, "Wives and Mothers"; and Herbert G. Gutman, *The Black Family in Slavery and Freedom, 1750–1925* (New York: Vintage Books, 1976).

18. Quoted in George P. Rawick, ed., *The American Slave: A Composite Autobiography*, supplement, series 1, vol. 1, *Alabama Narratives* (Westport, Conn.: Greenwood Press, 1977), 15.

19. Quoted in Botkin, *Lay My Burden Down*, 89.

20. Quoted in Rawick, *American Slave*, 1:117–18. It is likely that the term *orsanberg*, or, more correctly, *osnaburg*—a coarse, heavy cotton used for grain sacks, draperies, upholstery, and clothing for slaves—is derived from Osnaburg, or Osnabrück, an industrial city in Germany. The term *brogan* is the diminutive form of the Irish-Gaelic word *brog*, or *brogue*, which means "shoe."

21. Quoted in Botkin, *Lay My Burden Down*, 89–90.

22. Quoted in Rawick, *American Slave*, 6:157.

23. Rawick, 1:56.

24. Quoted in Rawick, *American Slave*, 6:157.

25. Wilma King, *Stolen Childhood: Slave Youth in Nineteenth-Century America* (Bloomington: Indiana University Press, 1995), 30.

26. White, *Ar'n't I a Woman?* 94–95.

27. Quoted in Rawick, *American Slave*, 1:18. On plowing and hoeing, see White, *Ar'n't I a Woman?*

28. Quoted in Rawick, *American Slave*, 1:99–100. Elsewhere in the Alabama narratives, Callie Williams defined a cut as three hundred yards of spun cotton. According to Williams, four cuts was "a hard day's work." Quoted in ibid., 6:426.

29. Quoted in ibid., 1:100.

30. King, *Stolen Childhood*, 92.

31. Angela Davis, *Women, Race and Class* (New York: Random House, 1981), 23–24.

32. Quoted in Botkin, *Lay My Burden Down*, 189.

33. See Stephanie M. H. Camp, "'I Could Not Stay There': Enslaved Women, Truancy and the Geography of Everyday Forms of Resistance in the Antebellum Plantation South," *Slavery and Abolition* 23, no. 3 (December 2002): 1–20.

34. See Frederick Douglass, *Narrative of the Life of Frederick Douglass, an American Slave, Written by Himself* (New York: Signet, 1968), 22.

35. Quoted in Rawick, *American Slave*, 1:99.

36. Quoted in ibid., 1:25–26.

37. Quoted in ibid., 6:47.

38. On the connections between African and African American traditions in slavery and their link to an African American identity, see, for instance, Albert J. Raboteau, *Slave Religion: The "Invisible Institution" in the Antebellum South* (New York: Oxford University Press, 1978); Lawrence W. Levine, *Black Culture and Black Consciousness: Afro-American Folk Thought from Slavery to Freedom* (New York: Oxford University Press, 1977); and Sterling Stuckey, *Slave Culture: Nationalist Theory and the Foundations of Black America* (New York: Oxford University Press, 1987).

39. The lyrics to "Steal Away to Jesus" are quoted in Henry Louis Gates and Nellie Y. McKay, eds., *The Norton Anthology of African American Literature* (New York: W. W. Norton, 1997), 13.

40. U.S. Bureau of the Census, *Ninth Census of the United States, 1870*, vol. 1, *Population by Counties—1790–1870* (Washington, D.C.: Department of the Interior, 1872), 11, table 2.

41. Ibid., 11–12.

42. Quoted in Rawick, *American Slave*, 6:163.

43. Eric Foner, *Reconstruction: America's Unfinished Revolution, 1863–1877* (New York: Harper and Row, 1989), 110.

44. Quoted in "Testimony of Witnesses before the Joint Congressional Committee," in *Black Women in White America: A Documentry History*, ed. Gerda Lerner (New York: Vintage Books, 1972), 185–86.

45. Walter L. Fleming, *Civil War and Reconstruction in Alabama* (New York: Columbia University Press, 1905), 564.

46. See Elsa Barkley Brown, "To Catch the Vision of Freedom: Reconstructing Southern Black Women's Political History, 1865–1880," in *African American Women and the Vote, 1837–1965*, ed. Ann D. Gordon, Bettye Collier-Thomas, John H. Bracey et al. (Amherst: University of Massachusetts Press, 1997), 83.

47. Foner, *Reconstruction*, 112, 352, 538 n. 48; W. E. B. Du Bois, *Black Reconstruction in America, 1860–1880* (1935; reprint, New York: Atheneum, 1973), 490–91.

48. Charles Sumner and Thadeus Stevens were the two leading Radical proponents of land redistribution in the South. See Foner, *Reconstruction*, 308–9.

49. See Eric Foner, *Nothing but Freedom: Emancipation and Its Legacy* (Baton Rouge: Louisiana State University Press, 1983), especially chap. 2.

50. Ibid., 60.

51. Jones, *Labor of Love*, 58.

52. Leon Litwack, *Been in the Storm So Long: The Aftermath of Slavery* (New York: Vintage Books, 1979), 475.

53. Jones, *Labor of Love*, 96.

54. Litwack, *Been in the Storm So Long*, especially, chap. 9.

55. Bureau of the Census, *Ninth Census, 1870*, vol. 1, 401; idem, *Twelfth Census of the United States, 1890*, vol. 2, *Population, Part II* (Washington, D.C.: Department of the Interior, 1891), cxi.

56. Sociologist Jacklyn Cock found that the image many Black domestic workers held of themselves in the late 1970s under apartheid was as slaves. See Jacklyn Cock, *Maids and Madams: Domestic Workers under Apartheid* (London: The Women's Press, 1989) 104. In addition, Mrs. Kate Mxakatho, a former domestic worker and African National Congress Women's League member, argued that the pass was actually "that dirty document of slavery." Mrs. Kate Mxakatho, interview by the author, Johannesburg, South Africa, July 29, 1997.

57. G. W. Stow (a nineteenth-century geologist), quoted in Monica Wilson and Leonard Thompson, eds., *A History of South Africa to 1870* (Boulder, Colo.: Westview Press, 1983), 134. This is a revised edition of Monica Hunter Wilson and Leonard Thompson, eds., *The Oxford History of South Africa* (London: Oxford University Press, 1969).

58. Wilson and Thompson, *History of South Africa*, 134.

59. Ibid., 132.

60. Ibid., 133–34. See also Isaac Schapera and John L. Comaroff, *The Tswana* (1953; rev ed., London: Kegan Paul and the International African Institute, 1991), 8–9.

61. Wilson and Thompson, *History of South Africa*, 142–43.

62. Ibid., 153–54. See also Eileen Jensen Krige, "The Place of the North-Eastern Transvaal Sotho in the South Bantu Complex," *Africa* 11, no. 3 (July 1938): 265–93.

63. Krige, "Place of the North-Eastern Transvaal Sotho," 145.

64. Schapera and Comaroff, *Tswana*, 21.

65. Researching BaTswana life in the Bechuanaland Protectorate during the 1930s and 1940s, the anthropologist Isaac Schapera found that the primary division of labor between men and women and the types of labor performed had remained relatively unchanged since pre-European times. He noted, however, the changes that had come about since contact with the Europeans. See ibid., 13–27.

66. I take my definition of the Sotho-Tswana household from Elizabeth Eldredge, "Women in Production: The Economic Role of Women in Nineteenth-Century Lesotho," *Signs* 16, no. 4 (Summer 1991): 710.

67. Schapera and Comaroff, *Tswana*, 21; Eldredge, "Women in Production," 713–14.

68. Schapera and Comaroff, *Tswana*, 21; Wilson and Thompson, *History of South Africa*, 148.

69. Eldredge, "Women in Production," 712.

70. See Margaret Kinsmen, "'Beasts of Burden': The Subordination of Southern Tswana Women, ca. 1800–1840," *Journal of Southern African Studies* 10, no. 1 (October 1983): 39–54.

71. Iris Berger, "'Beasts of Burden' Revisited: Interpretations of Women and Gender in Southern African Societies," in *Paths toward the Past: African Historical Essays in Honor of Jan Vansina*, ed. Robert W. Harms, Joseph C. Miller, David S. New-

bury et al. (Atlanta: African Studies Association Press, 1994), 130. Iris Berger wisely chooses to employ the work of several anthropologists, who were far better equipped to interpret the cultures under study than were the missionaries and colonial administrators and even some much later (class-oriented) historians.

72. Ibid.

73. Monica Hunter, "The Effects of Contact with Europeans on the Status of Pondo Women," *Africa* 6, no. 3 (July 1933): 260.

74. Ibid.

75. Eldredge, "Women in Production," 707–31.

76. Hunter, "The Effects of Contact with Europeans," 265–66.

77. Schapera and Comaroff, *Tswana*, 45–46.

78. Krige, "Place of the North-Eastern Transvaal Sotho," 266, 272. The information included in this paragraph is from ibid., 265–93.

79. John Campbell, *Travels in South Africa*, 3rd ed. (London: Black, Parry, 1815).

80. Quoted in ibid., 208–9.

81. Between 1801 and 1850, among the Tswana of what would become the Orange Free State and the Transsvaal, Western "civilization" in the form of missionaries, traders, hunters, and explorers, along with the Boer farmers who trekked east from the Cape Colony after 1836, established permanent stations among the BaTlhaping (1816), BaRolong (1822), BaHurutshe (1836), BaKgatla (1843), and BaKwena (1846). The intrepid David Livingstone reached Lake Ngami in 1849 and opened up the northern route to ivory and other important trade goods. See Schapera and Comaroff, *Tswana*, 9.

82. Ibid., 199–200.

83. For a fuller treatment of the *Difaqane* and its consequences, see Wilson and Thompson, *History of South Africa*, vol. 1, especially chap. 9.

84. See Sol Plaatje, *Mhudi* (1930; reprint, Portsmouth, N.H.: Heinemann, 1978), a beautiful novel set during this period, told from the point of view of a resourceful woman.

85. Robert Moffat, *Missionary Labours and Scenes in Southern Africa* (1842; reprint, New York: Johnson Reprint, 1969), 340.

86. J. C. MacGregor, quoted in Eldredge, *South African Kingdom*, 138.

87. Quoted in Wilson and Thompson, *History of South Africa*, 398.

88. Ibid., 398.

89. Eldredge, *South African Kingdom*, 139.

90. Mrs. Maggie Resha, interview by the author, Ramohlakoana, District of Matatiele, South Africa, July 10–11, 2001. See also Maggie Resha, '*Mangoana O Tsoara Thipa Ka Bohaleng: My Life in the Struggle* (Johannesburg: Congress of South African Writers, 1991).

91. See Leonard Thompson, *Survival in Two Worlds: Moshoeshoe of Lesotho, 1786–1870* (Oxford: Clarendon Press, 1975), and Eldredge, *South African Kingdom*.

92. Wilson and Thompson, *History of South Africa*, 445.

93. Ibid., 445–46.

94. Quoted in ibid., 401.

95. See Eldredge, *South African Kingdom*, 136.

CHAPTER TWO

1. Mrs. Thelma Glass, interview by the author, Montgomery, Alabama, April 24, 1997.

2. Mrs. Joyce Piliso Seroke, interview by the author, Soweto, South Africa, August 16, 1997.

3. Seroke, interview.

4. Graduates of Wilberforce University in Ohio, an African Methodist Episcopal Church–sponsored school, founded Wilberforce Institute between 1905 and 1906. The institute offered teacher training and industrial education courses to young, Black South Africans. The Maxekes, both graduates of Wilberforce University, taught at the institute in its early days. See James T. Campbell, *Songs of Zion: The African Methodist Episcopal Church in the United States and South Africa* (New York: Oxford University Press, 1995), 178, 283.

5. Deborah Gaitskell and Elaine Unterhalter, "Mothers of the Nation: A Comparative Analysis of Nation, Race and Motherhood in Afrikaner Nationalism and the African National Congress" in *Woman–Nation–State*, ed. Nira Yuval-Davis and Floya Anthias (New York: St. Martin's Press, 1989), 58–78.

6. See Aldon D. Morris, *The Origins of the Civil Rights Movement: Black Communities Organizing for Change* (New York: Free Press, 1984).

7. U.S. Bureau of the Census, *Tenth Census of the United States, 1880*, vol. 1, *Population* (Washington, D.C.: Department of the Interior, 1881), 380–81.

8. Leon Litwack, *Been in the Storm So Long: The Aftermath of Slavery* (New York: Vintage Books, 1979), 432.

9. Wayne Flint, *Montgomery: An Illustrated History* (Woodland Hills, Calif.: Windsor Publications, 1980), 48.

10. Ibid., 48; Howard Rabinowitz, *Race Relations in the Urban South, 1865–1890* (New York: Oxford University Press, 1978), 41–42, 265.

11. Alfred Lewis Bratcher, *Eighty-three Years: The Moving Story of Church Growth Including Significant Sermons and Addresses* (Montgomery: Paragon Press, 1950), 7; Taylor Branch, *Parting the Waters: America in the King Years* (New York: Simon and Schuster, 1988), 4.

12. Bratcher, *Eighty-three Years*, 7–8.

13. Ibid., 13–14.

14. Evelyn Brooks Higginbotham, "Religion, Politics, and Gender: The Leadership of Nannie Helen Burroughs," in *This Far by Faith: Readings in African-American Women's Religious Biography*, ed. Judith Weisenfeld and Richard Newman (New York: Routledge, 1996), 142.

15. Bratcher, *Eighty-three Years*, 15.

16. Ibid., 14–15.

17. Flint, *Montgomery*, 50.

18. Branch, *Parting the Waters*, 3–4.

19. Norman W. Walton, "A Brief History of Alabama State University," Montgomery, 1970, Alabama State University Archives, Levi Watkins Library, Alabama State University.

20. Joseph Darnel Caver, "Marion to Montgomery: A Twenty Year History of Alabama State University, 1867–1887" (master's thesis, Alabama State University, 1982), 31; Robert G. Sherer, *Subordination or Liberation? The Development and Conflicting Theories of Black Education in Nineteenth Century Alabama* (University, Ala.: University of Alabama Press, 1977), 25, 160 n. 16.

21. William Burns Paterson to Booker T. Washington, January 5, 1887, In *Booker T. Washington Papers*, ed. Louis R. Harlan and Raymond W. Smoch, vol. 2 (Urbana: University of Illinois Press, 1982), 319–20.

22. Caver, "Marion to Montgomery," 88. In several letters between Booker T. Washington and his Montgomery associates—including his physician, Cornelius Nathaniel Dorsette, one of the few Black physicians in Alabama—Washington made clear his opposition to having the school move to the capital: "My object is to prevent the Marion school from being located here." Quoted in a letter from Booker T. Washington to Warren Logan, Harlan and Smoch, *Booker T. Washington Papers*, 2:331; see also 2:321, 2:376.

23. Walton, "Brief History of Alabama State University," 6; Rabinowitz, *Race Relations*, 102.

24. Caver, "Marion to Montgomery," 109–12; Levi Watkins, *Alabama State University: A History of the First One Hundred and Fourteen Years, 1867–1981* (Montgomery: Alabama State University, 1994), 35.

25. Quoted in Charles William Dabney, *Universal Education in the South*, vol. 2 (Chapel Hill: University of North Carolina Press, 1936), 439. Charles Dabney reports that from the outset Alabama State Normal School employed a racially integrated teaching faculty, which included Paterson's wife, whom he does not name, a graduate of Oberlin College. Additionally, Black women faculty members were in the majority: seventeen out of a total of twenty-eight in the 1904–1905 school year. See also William Burns Paterson's letter to Booker T. Washington, September 3, 1897, in Harlan and Smoch, *Booker T. Washington Papers*, 4:325.

26. Quoted in Booker T. Washington, "The Atlanta Exposition Address," in *Up From Slavery* (New York: Dell, 1965), 156. And see, for instance, Gavin Wright, *Old South, New South* (New York: Basic Books, 1986), and C. Vann Woodward, *Origins of the New South, 1877–1913* (Baton Rouge: Louisiana State University Press, 1971), especially chap. 8.

27. For insightful comparisons with other educational approaches—including that of W. E. B. Du Bois—from Washington's personal and political perspective, see the excellent biography of Washington by Louis R. Harlan, *Booker T. Washington: The Wizard of Tuskegee, 1901–1915* (New York: Oxford University Press, 1983), especially chaps. 7 and 8.

28. In 1931 Alabama State awarded (to students who completed a four-year teacher training program) its first bachelor of science degrees; by 1969 the school had achieved university status. Watkins, *Alabama State University*, 59; Walton, "Brief History of Alabama State University," 9.

29. Rabinowitz, *Race Relations*, 66.

30. Ibid., 62, 67–68.

31. Ibid., 77.

32. Quoted in ibid., 72.

33. Several historians, including Howard Rabinowitz, have examined the case of the 1881 Atlanta washerwomen's strike. I take as my main source the discussion by Tera Hunter, who perceives a great deal of agency among the women and provides the full context for and a positive interpretation of the outcome of the strike. Tera W. Hunter, *To 'Joy My Freedom: Southern Black Women's Lives and Labors after the Civil War* (Cambridge, Mass.: Harvard University Press, 1997), chap. 4.

34. Quoted in ibid., 93 (italics mine).

35. Quoted in ibid. (italics mine).

36. Ibid., 95.

37. See Dorothy Sterling, ed., *We Are Your Sisters: Black Women in the Nineteenth Century* (New York: W. W. Norton, 1984), 355–57. See also Dorothy Sterling's rendition of the "Washing Society" of Atlanta in ibid., 357–58.

38. August Meier and Elliott Rudwick, "The Boycott Movement against Jim Crow Streetcars in the South, 1900–1906," *Journal of American History* 55 (March 1969): 756–75.

39. A new incarnation of the Ten Times One Club shows up again during the 1955–1956 Montgomery bus boycott, as does the family name Dungee. Erna Dungee (Allen) was the original financial secretary for the Montgomery Improvement Association and secretary for the Women's Political Council. At the 1899 NACW convention in Chicago, Margaret Murray Washington nominated a Mrs. Dungee of the first Ten Times One Club to the post of statewide organizer for Alabama. *Records of the National Association of Colored Women's Clubs, 1895–1992*, ed. Lillian Serece Williams and Randolph Boehm (Bethesda, Maryland: University Publications of America, 1993), microfilm reel 1, part 1, Minutes of National Conventions, Publicity, and President's Office Correspondence, Oberlin College Library, p. 29.

40. Ibid., 58–59, 118–19.

41. Ibid., 49 (italics mine).

42. Ibid., 25 (italics mine).

43. Meier and Rudwick, "Boycott Movement," 775.

44. Flint, *Montgomery*, 76–77.

45. Quoted in William Warren Rogers, Robert David Ward, Leah Rawls Atkins et al., *Alabama: The History of a Deep South State* (Tuscaloosa: University of Alabama Press, 1994), 351–52.

46. Mrs. Booker T. Washington, "The Tuskegee Woman's Club," *Southern Workman* 49, no. 8 (August 1920): 365–69.

47. William H. Worger, *South Africa's City of Diamonds: Mine Workers and Monopoly Capitalism in Kimberley, 1867–1895* (New Haven, Conn.: Yale University Press, 1987), 9.

48. Ibid., 15–20.

49. Peter Richardson and Jean Jacques Van-Helten, "Labour in the South African Gold Mining Industry, 1886–1914," in *Industrialisation and Social Change in South Africa: African Class Formation, Culture, and Consciousness, 1870–1930*, ed. Shula Marks and Richard Rathbone (New York: Longman, 1982), 79.

50. Monica Hunter Wilson and Leonard Thompson, eds, *The Oxford History of South Africa*, vol. 2, *1870–1966* (London: Oxford University Press, 1971), 14.

51. Richardson and Van-Helten, "Labour in the South African Gold Mining Industry," 83.

52. Worger, *South Africa's City of Diamonds*, 68–69.

53. Ibid., 70 n. 14.

54. Ibid., 82–85.

55. Ibid., 86–87.

56. See Elizabeth A. Eldredge, *A South African Kingdom: The Pursuit of Security in Nineteenth-Century Lesotho* (New York: Cambridge University Press, 1993), 139–46.

57. Worger, *South Africa's City of Diamonds*, 110–11.

58. Building from the example set by the Cape in regulating the movements and labor of the "native foreigner," the administration at Kimberley required that the African migrant, upon his entry into the town, register and receive a one-day pass until employment was procured. At that point, a second pass was issued certifying employment; this pass was to be carried on his person at all times and produced on demand. A third pass was required of the migrant worker returning home, who first required certification by his employer as having satisfactorily completed his term of work. By the mid-twentieth century, the pass laws had been multiply augmented to include a wide variety of restrictions on the movements of African men. Quoted in ibid., 114; see additional stipulations on 114–16.

59. Rob Turrell, "Kimberley: Labour and Compounds, 1871–1888," in Marks and Rathbone, *Industrialisation and Social Change in South Africa*, 65. In Alabama, the leasing of convict labor actually began in the 1840s, but it was particularly successful in the 1880s and 1890s, both in rewarding political greed and providing the nascent Alabama mining industry with a pool of the cheapest Black labor; the industry could also use these workers (whom they housed) as strikebreakers. Rogers et al., *Alabama*, 284.

60. Worger, *South Africa's City of Diamonds*, 139–44.

61. Turrell, "Kimberley," 61.

62. Cherryl Walker, "Gender and the Development of the Migrant Labour System circa 1850–1930: An Overview," in *Women and Gender in Southern Africa to 1945*, ed. Cherryl Walker (Cape Town, South Africa: David Philip, 1990), 173.

63. Elizabeth Eldredge, "Women in Production: The Economic Role of Women in Nineteenth-Century Lesotho," *Signs* 16, no. 4 (Summer 1991): 723–24.

64. Walker, "Gender and the Development of the Migrant Labour System," 189.
65. Ibid., 188–89.
66. P. L. Bonner, "'Desirable or Undesirable BaSotho Women?' Liquor, Prostitution and the Migration of BaSotho Women to the Rand, 1920–1945," in Walker, *Women and Gender in Southern Africa*, 228.
67. Walker, "Gender and the Development of the Migrant Labour System," 190.
68. Interestingly, Deborah Gaitskell finds that the number of African women in Johannesburg more than tripled between 1896 and 1911, increasing from 1,234 to 4,357. Deborah Gaitskell, "Female Mission Initiatives: Black and White Women in Three Witwatersrand Churches, 1903–1939" (Ph.D. diss., University of London, 1981), 106–7. See also Charles van Onselen, "The Witches of Suburbia: Domestic Service on the Witwatersrand, 1890–1914," in *Studies in the Social and Economic History of the Witwatersrand, 1886–1914*, vol. 2, *New Ninevah* (New York: Longman, 1982), 16.
69. Quoted in van Onselen, "The Witches of Suburbia," 16.
70. Ibid., 16–17.
71. Gaitskell locates the beginning of the shift from male to female domestic workers in the late 1920s and the 1930s, when secondary industry added to the mining industry made further demands on the labor of Black men. Gaitskell, "Female Mission Initiatives," 118–19.
72. Both quoted in Sean Moroney, "Mine Married Quarters: The Differential Stabilisation of the Witwatersrand Workforce, 1900–1920," in Marks and Rathbone, *Industrialisation and Social Change in South Africa*, 261.
73. Ibid., 261; Andre Proctor, "Class Struggle, Segregation and the City: A History of Sophiatown 1905–1940," in *Labour, Townships, and Protest: Studies in the Social History of the Witwatersrand*, ed. Belinda Bozzoli (Johannesberg: Ravan Press, 1979), 58; Gaitskell, "Female Mission Initiatives," 113–14.
74. Moroney, "Mine Married Quarters," 261, 263.
75. See Julia C. Wells, "Why Women Rebel: A Comparative Study of South African Women's Resistance in Bloemfontein (1913) and Johannesburg (1958)," *Journal of Southern African Studies* 10, no. 1 (October 1983): 55–70. See also Cherryl Walker, *Women and Resistance in South Africa*, rev. ed. (New York: Monthly Review Press, 1991), 27–32.
76. See Maggie Resha's testimony in chapter 8.
77. Emerging first at the Cape Colony in the seventeenth century, these Afrikaans-speaking mixed race descendants of European, Asian, and African peoples, though minimally advantaged over other groups, sometimes made common cause with African people. For a comparative view of U.S. and South African "colored" peoples see George M. Fredrickson, *White Supremacy: A Comparative Study in American and South African History* (New York: Oxford University Press, 1981), especially chap. 3.
78. The Black journalist and early South African Natives National Congress (SANNC) leader Sol Plaatje recounted the conviction of a white location super-

intendent for the rape of a Colored woman who had been arrested because she did not have a residential pass. See Sol T. Plaatje, *Native Life in South Africa* (1916; reprint, Randburg, South Africa: Ravan Press, 1982), 115–16.

79. See Julia C. Wells, "The History of Black Women's Struggle against Pass Laws in South Africa, 1900–1960" (Ph.D. diss., Columbia University, 1982), chaps. 2–4. The 1913 women's resistance is also chronicled in Plaatje, *Native Life in South Africa*, chap. 7.

80. The SANNC, which convened in Bloemfontein in January 1912, was formed partly in response to formal recognition of the Boer-dominated Union of South Africa. During the 1920s, the organization dropped the words *South* and *Native* from its name, became known as the African National Congress (ANC), and continued its mission of African unity and full citizenship rights. See Andre Odendaal, *Black Protest Politics in South Africa to 1912* (Totowa, N.J.: Barnes and Noble Books, 1984), 270–71, 289.

81. Headed by Dr. Abdullah Abdurahman (the first Black medical doctor in South Africa and the first Black member of the Cape Town City Council), the APO was founded at Cape Town in 1902 to protect and extend the political rights of Colored men throughout South Africa, especially the right to vote. See ibid., 97–98.

82. Wells, "History of Black Women's Struggle against Pass Laws," 141.

83. Wells, "Why Women Rebel," 56–57; idem, "History of Black Women's Struggle against Pass Laws," 120–50.

84. Walker, *Women and Resistance in South Africa*, 30–31; quoted in Wells, "History of Black Women's Struggle against Pass Laws," 123.

85. GG 1542 50/396 Katie Louw, Circular letter of the OFS Native and Colored Women's Association, February, 18, 1914, National Archives of South Africa, Pretoria Transvaal Archives Depot.

86. Bonner, "Desirable or Undesirable BaSotho Women?" 242; Wells, "History of Black Women's Struggle against Pass Laws," 158.

87. Wells, "Why Women Rebel," 60–62.

88. Walker, *Women and Resistance in South Africa*, 35–40.

89. See ibid., 36–40, and the portrait of Maxeke in Campbell, *Songs of Zion*, 282–94. See also Alfred Xuma, *Charlotte Manye (Mrs. Maxeke) or What an Educated African Girl Can Do*, ed. Dovie King Clarke, Women's Parent Mite Missionary Society of the African Methodist Episcopal Church, 1930, Hallie Quinn Brown Black Collection, Hallie Quinn Brown Library, Wilberforce University.

90. See Judy Kimble and Elaine Unterhalter, "'We opened the road for you, now you must go forward': ANC Women's Struggles, 1912–1982," *Feminist Review* no. 12 (October 1982): 11–35.

91. Washington was the third wife of Booker T. Washington and held the title Lady Principal of Tuskegee Institute. See Hallie Quinn Brown, *Homespun Heroines and Other Women of Distinction* (1926; reprint, New York: Oxford University Press, 1988), 224–30; Cynthia Neverdon Morton, *Afro-American Women of the South and*

the Advancement of the Race, 1895–1925 (Knoxville: University of Tennessee Press, 1989), 122–38; and Dorothy C. Salem, *To Better Our World: Black Women in Organized Reform* (New York: Carlson, 1990).

CHAPTER THREE

1. Mrs. Amy Collins Harris, telephone interview by the author, July 20, 1999.
2. Mrs. Amy Collins Harris, interview by the author, July 20, 1999.
3. Harris, interview, July 20, 1999.
4. Ibid., July 20, 1999.
5. Ibid., July 20, 1999.
6. Ibid., July 20, 1999, and Montgomery, Alabama, March 21, 1998.
7. Ibid., July 20, 1999.
8. Maggie Resha, *'Mangoana O Tsoara Thipa Ka Bohaleng: My Life in the Struggle* (London: SA Writers, 1991), 2–3.
9. As Ntsiuoa remained an only child, this presented a dilemma with regard to male succession. Her family decided that "instead of her getting married, . . . a husband should be married for her," which meant that the sons from the proxy-marriage took her place as the next heirs. Thus Ntsiuoa herself was eliminated from the direct line of succession. See Resha, *'Mangoana O Tsoara Thipa Ka Bohaleng*, 3.
10. Ibid., 3.
11. Kadalie, who was from Nyasaland (Malawi), formed the ICU in Cape Town in 1919 and went on to organize an impressive, although ultimately unsuccessful, strike of African and Colored dock workers there. Influenced in part by the Pan-Africanist philosophy of Marcus Garvey and by the class-based ideology of the Communist Party, Kadalie sought to organize the masses of Black workers in the countryside, as well as in the cities. He moved his organizational base to Johannesburg (where Tsekiso Tsiu apparently came in contact with the organization) and increased ICU membership to well over 150,000. Significantly, in addition to organizing industrial workers, the ICU also organized and represented women who brewed beer in competition with the municipally subsidized beer halls. See George M. Fredrickson, *Black Liberation: A Comparative History of Black Ideologies in the United States and South Africa* (New York: Oxford University Press, 1995), 168–71. See also William Beinart and Colin Bundy, "The Union, the Nation and the Talking Crow: The Ideology and Tactics of the Independent ICU in East London," in *Hidden Struggles in Rural South Africa: Politics and Popular Movements in the Transkei and Eastern Cape, 1890–1930*, ed. William Beinart and Colin Bundy (London: James Currey, 1987), 302–8.
12. Resha, *'Mangoana O Tsoara Thipa Ka Bohaleng*, 4–5.
13. Quoted in ibid., 5.
14. Ibid., 13.
15. U.S. Bureau of the Census, *Fourteenth Census of the United States, 1920*, vol. 2, *Population: General Report and Analytical Tables* (Washington, D.C.: Department of the Interior, 1921), 44.

16. Ibid., 98.

17. U.S. Bureau of the Census, *Fifteenth Census of the United States, 1930*, vol. 3, pt. 1, *Population: Alabama-Missouri* (Washington, D.C.: Department of the Interior, 1931), 83, 88.

18. Ibid., 83.

19. Ibid.

20. U.S. Bureau of the Census, *Negro Population in the United States, 1790–1915* (New York: Arno Press and the *New York Times*, 1968), 415.

21. Bureau of the Census, *Fourteenth Census, 1920*, vol. 3, *Population: Composition and Characteristics of the Population by States*, 56; idem, *Fifteenth Census, 1930*, 3 (pt. 1), 88.

22. William Warren Rogers, Robert David Ward, Leah Rawls Atkins et al., *Alabama: The History of a Deep South State* (Tuscaloosa: University of Alabama Press, 1994), 414. The Russell Sage Foundation Report, which was commissioned by Governor Charles Henderson in 1918, concluded that the failure of the Alabama state legislature to fund necessary health and educational programs fully and equitably had adversely affected Black and white children alike. In 1920, for instance, more than 130,000 children aged ten to seventeen—both Black and white, in equal numbers—worked the mines, mills, and fields of the state. Rogers et al., *Alabama*, 413–15.

23. Bureau of the Census, *Fourteenth Census, 1920*, 2:1065; ibid., vol. 4, *Population: Occupations*, 875–76.

24. Bureau of the Census, *Fifteenth Census, 1930*, 3 (pt. 1), 87.

25. For a detailed sociological study of Black farming families in Macon County at the onset of the Depression, see Charles S. Johnson, *Shadow of the Plantation* (Chicago: University of Chicago Press, 1934).

26. Mrs. Ethel Mae Smith Alexander, interview by the author, Montgomery, Alabama, April 23, 1997.

27. Bureau of the Census, *Fifteenth Census, 1930*, 3 (pt. 1), 120.

28. Johnson, *Shadow of the Plantation*, 124–25.

29. Quoted in ibid., 121.

30. Alexander, interview.

31. Quoted in Thordis Simonsen, ed., *You May Plow Here: The Narrative of Sara Brooks* (New York: W. W. Norton, 1986), 102–3.

32. Ibid., 103.

33. Ibid., 103–4.

34. Alexander, interview.

35. Quoted in Simonsen, *You May Plow Here*, 88, 89.

36. Ms. Rose Zell Lawrence, interview by the author, Montgomery, Alabama, April 26, 1997.

37. Mrs. Lillie Means Lewis, interview by the author, Montgomery, Alabama, April 18, 1997.

38. Alexander, interview.

39. Quoted in Simonsen, *You May Plow Here*, 33.

40. Quoted in Horace Mann Bond, *Negro Education in Alabama: A Study in Cotton and Steel* (Washington, D.C.: The Associated Publishers, Inc., 1939), 265, 267. See also James D. Anderson, *The Education of Blacks in the South, 1860–1935* (Chapel Hill: University of North Carolina Press, 1988), 137–47.

41. Anderson, *Education of Blacks in the South*, 79–83. James Anderson sees a distinct ideological split among the various factions that competed for hegemony in educational policy—especially among planters, industrialists, and northern philanthropists, all of whom harbored their own notions of white supremacy—which ultimately came to rely on the Hampton-Tuskegee model of industrial education for young Black people.

42. Lawrence, interview.

43. Mrs. Amy Collins Harris, interview by the author, Montgomery, Alabama, March 21, 1998.

44. Ibid., July 20, 1999.

45. Alexander, interview.

46. Harris, interview, March 21, 1998.

47. Quoted in C. Eric Lincoln and Lawrence H. Mamiya, *The Black Church in the African American Experience* (Durham, N.C.: Duke University Press, 1990), 96.

48. Simonsen, *You May Plow Here*, 31; Lewis, interview.

49. Harris, interview, July 20, 1999.

50. See Elizabeth Clark-Lewis, *Living In, Living Out: African American Domestics in Washington D.C., 1910–1940* (Washington, D.C.: Smithsonian Institution Press, 1994), 18–19.

51. Mrs. Beautie Mae Johnson, interview by the author, Montgomery, Alabama, April 16, 1997.

52. Ibid.

53. Quoted in ibid.

54. Ibid.

55. Rosa Parks with Jim Haskins, *Rosa Parks: My Story* (New York: Dial Books, 1992), 15.

56. Ibid., 16. For a convincing explanation of Sylvester Edwards's brand of resistance to white domination, see James C. Scott, *Weapons of the Weak: Everyday Forms of Peasant Resistance* (New Haven, Conn.: Yale University Press, 1985), especially 289–303. See also the work of the psychologist John Dollard, who uses the notion of white southerners' expectation of deference as a means of subordinating Black people in his *Caste and Class in a Southern Town*, 3rd ed. (1937; reprint, Garden City, N.Y.: Doubleday Anchor Books, 1949), 174–78. Additionally, the evolution of the system known as Jim Crow, which encompasses the laws and practices of a racially segregated society in the United States, is well documented in C. Vann Woodward, *The Strange Career of Jim Crow*, 3rd ed. (1955; reprint, New York: Oxford University Press, 1974).

57. Parks with Haskins, *Rosa Parks*, 30.

58. William J. Snell, "Fiery Crosses in the Roaring Twenties: Activities of the Revised Klan in Alabama, 1915–1930," *Alabama Review* 23, no. 4 (October 1970): 256–59.
59. Parks with Haskins, *Rosa Parks*, 32.
60. Lewis, interview.
61. Sol T. Plaatje, *Native Life in South Africa: Before and since the European War and the Boer Rebellion* (Athens: Ohio University Press, 1991), 21.
62. See Monica Hunter Wilson and Leonard Thompson, eds., *The Oxford History of South Africa*, vol. 2, *1870–1966* (London: Oxford University Press, 1971), 127–31.
63. For a full account of the law, see Plaatje, *Native Life in South Africa*, chap. 3. See also William Beinart, *Twentieth-Century South Africa* (New York: Oxford University Press, 1994), 261, and Leonard Thompson, *A History of South Africa* (New Haven, Conn.: Yale University Press, 1995), 163.
64. Plaatje, *Native Life*, 86–87.
65. Quoted in ibid., 100. Plaatje reported that some Boer wives—fearing both the loss of their domestic workers and a loss in income—resisted imposition of the law, insisting that their African clients remain undisturbed on their land. See ibid., chap. 6.
66. The following account is from Ted Matsetela, "The Life Story of Nkgono Mma-Pooe: Aspects of Sharecropping and Proletarianisation in the Northern Orange Free State, 1890–1930," in *Industrialisation and Social Change in South Africa: African Class Formation, Culture, and Consciousness, 1870–1930*, ed. Shula Marks and Richard Rathbone (New York: Longman, 1982), 213–37.
67. Quoted in ibid., 218.
68. Ted Matsetela defines *trekgoed* as "material goods used for hauling," such as chains and yokes. Ibid., 235 n. 26.
69. Quoted in ibid., 221.
70. Quoted in ibid., 224.
71. Quoted in ibid., 224.
72. Matsetela defines *bywoner* as a landless white farmer, tenant, or sharecropper. Ibid., 236 n. 33.
73. Quoted in ibid., 226.
74. Colin Bundy, *The Rise and Fall of the South African Peasantry* (Berkeley: University of California Press, 1979), 46.
75. The *akkoord* was a yearly contract or agreement entered into in winter, once the harvest was completed; it contained all of the terms under which the sharecropper, tenant, or laborer would work. See Matsetela, "The Life Story of Nkgono Mma-Pooe," 235 n. 28.
76. Quoted in ibid., 231–32.
77. Mrs. Ernestina Mekgwe, interview by Mmantho Nkotsoe, September 11, 1981, English trans. #01, box Ab, Collection AG 2738, p. 2, Institute for Advanced Social Research, William Cullen Library, University of the Witwatersrand.
78. Belinda Bozzoli with the assistance of Mmantho Nkotsoe, *Women of Phokeng:*

Consciousness, Life Strategy, and Migrancy in South Africa, 1900–1983 (Portsmouth, N.H.: Heinemann, 1991), 28.

79. Mekgwe, interview, September 11, 1981, p. 2.

80. Mrs. Ernestina Mekgwe, interview by Dennis Mashabela, February 2, 1983, #32, pp. 5, 13, Institute for Advanced Social Research, William Cullen Library, University of the Witwatersrand.

81. Bozzoli with Nkotsoe, *Women of Phokeng*, 45.

82. Ellen Kuzwayo, *Call Me Woman* (1985; reprint, Randburg, South Africa: Ravan Press, 1996), 68.

83. Ibid., 68–69.

84. Ibid., 69–70.

85. Naboth Mokgatle, *The Autobiography of an Unknown South African* (Berkeley: University of California Press, 1971), 20–21.

86. Ibid., 21–22.

87. See, for instance, the discussion of women's resistance to municipal beer halls in Tom Lodge, *Black Politics in South Africa since 1945* (New York: Longman, 1983), 148.

88. Kuzwayo, *Call Me Woman*, 62.

89. Resha, '*Mangoana O Tsoara Thipa Ka Bohaleng*, 5.

90. Isaac Schapera and John L. Comaroff, *The Tswana*, rev. ed. (1953; reprint, London: Kegan Paul International and the International African Institute, 1991), 32.

91. Ibid., 32–33.

92. Kuzwayo, *Call Me Woman*, 70–71.

93. Ibid., 71.

94. See, for instance, Darlene Clark Hine's explanation of a "cult of secrecy, a culture of dissemblance" designed to combat the negative sexual images about Black women, wherein especially middle-class women could protect their own "private, empowering definitions of self." Given the emphasis on female propriety, it seems unlikely that this dissemblance nurtured within Black women a willingness to discuss issues of sex frankly and openly among themselves or with their daughters in settings other than homes for unwed mothers sponsored by the National Association of Colored Women Clubs (NACW). Darlene Clark Hine, "Rape and the Inner Lives of Black Women in the Middle West: Preliminary Thoughts on the Culture of Dissembance," in *Unequal Sisters: A Multicultural Reader in U.S. Women's History*, ed. Ellen Carol DuBois and Vicki L. Ruiz (New York: Routledge, 1990), 292–97.

95. Mekgwe, interview, September 11, 1981, p. 7; Mekgwe, interview, February 2, 1983, p. 16. Ernest Penzhorn, Sr., was the first German Lutheran missionary to the Bafokeng who became fluent in SeSotho, preached his sermons in that language, and taught the Bafokeng to read the Bible in SeSotho. He and his son brought their version of orderly and godly European village life to the Bafokeng during the late nineteenth and early twentieth centuries. See Mokgatle, *Autobiography of an Unknown South African*, 60–65.

96. Kuzwayo, *Call Me Woman*, 60–61.

97. Mokgatle, *Autobiography of an Unknown South African*, 66–68. See also James T. Campbell, *Songs of Zion: The African Methodist Episcopal Church in the United States and South Africa* (New York: Oxford University Press, 1995), 160.
98. Mokgatle, *Autobiography of an Unknown South African*, chap. 12.
99. Quoted in S. M. Molema, *The Bantu Past and Present: An Ethnographical and Historical Study of the Native Races of South Africa* (Cape Town, South Africa: C. Struik, 1963), 221.
100. Ibid., 232.
101. Ibid. See also Manning Marable, "John L. Dube and the Politics of Segregated Education in South Africa," in *Independence without Freedom: The Political Economy of Colonial Education in Southern Africa*, ed. Agrippah T. Mugomba and Mougo Nyaggah (Santa Barbara, Calif.: ABC-CLIO, 1980), 113–28.
102. Molema, *Bantu Past and Present*, 233. See also David Chanaiwa, "African Humanism in Southern Africa: The Utopian, Traditionalist, and Colonialist Worlds of Mission-Educated Elites," in Mugomba and Nyaggah, *Independence without Freedom*, 11.
103. Wilson and Thompson, *Oxford History of South Africa*, 2:76.
104. Kuzwayo, *Call Me Woman*, 61.
105. Ibid., 95.
106. Ibid., 95–96.
107. See the educational tables in Molema, *Bantu Past and Present*, 228–29.
108. Ibid., 231.
109. Pam Christie and Colin Collins, "Bantu Education: Apartheid Ideology and Labour Reproduction," in *Apartheid and Education: The Education of Black South Africans*, ed. Peter Kallaway (Johannesburg: Ravan Press, 1984), 165–66.
110. Resha,'*Mangoana O Tsoara Thipa Ka Bohaleng*, 8–9.
111. Ibid., 14–15. There are twenty shillings in a pound.
112. Ibid., 15–16.
113. Ibid., 21.
114. Ibid., 24–25.

CHAPTER FOUR

1. Founded by Alice L. White and H. Margaret Beard, its co-principals, the Montgomery Industrial School for Girls was supported by the American Missionary Association until it closed in 1928. Centennial Celebration Committee, *100 Years: A Century of Negro Progress in Montgomery City and County, 1863–1963*, p. 46, Alabama Department of Archives and History, Montgomery, Alabama.
2. Rosa Parks with Jim Haskins, *Rosa Parks: My Story* (New York: Dial Books, 1992), 33–54.
3. Rosa Parks, interview by Marcia M. Greenlee, Detroit, Michigan, August 22–23, 1978, in *Black Women Oral History Project*, ed. Ruth Edmonds Hill and Patricia Miller King (Cambridge, Mass.: Radcliffe College, 1984), 248.
4. Parks with Haskins, *Rosa Parks*, 48–49.

5. One of the strongest critics of Booker T. Washington's Tuskegee idea, W. E. B. Du Bois, trenchantly argued *against* the educator's campaign for the hearts and minds (and hands) of Black youth and *for* an education that would encourage a worldly curiosity and thorough preparation to confront all forms of injustice. See W. E. B. Du Bois, *The Souls of Black Folk* (New York: Fawcett, 1961), especially chaps. 3 and 6.
6. Parks with Haskins, *Rosa Parks*, 49.
7. Ibid., 22.
8. Horace Mann Bond, *Negro Education in Alabama: A Study in Cotton and Steel* (New York: Atheneum, 1969), 257.
9. According to Mrs. Parks, the city of Montgomery did not provide a public high school for Black students until 1938, and the school was not allocated its own building until 1947. Parks with Haskins, *Rosa Parks*, 53–54.
10. Kate Mxakatho, interview by the author, Soweto, South Africa, July 29, 1997.
11. Ibid.
12. Ibid.
13. Earl Lewis, "Expectations, Economic Opportunities, and Life in the Industrial Age: Black Migration to Norfolk, Virginia, 1910–1945," in *The Great Migration in Historical Perspective: New Dimensions of Race, Class, and Gender*, ed. Joe William Trotter, Jr. (Bloomington: Indiana University Press, 1991), 24–25.
14. Mrs. Ethel Mae Smith Alexander, interview by the author, Montgomery, Alabama, April 23, 1997.
15. See Charles S. Johnson, *Shadow of the Plantation* (Chicago: University of Chicago Press, 1934), 90–100.
16. Alexander, interview.
17. Ibid.
18. Mrs. Amy Collins Harris, interview by the author, Montgomery, Alabama, March 21, 1998.
19. Ibid.
20. A. Harris, interview.
21. Ibid.; Mr. George Harris, interview by the author, Montgomery, Alabama, March 21, 1998.
22. For a discussion of the differences between the migratory patterns of Black women and Black men, see Darlene Clark Hine, "Black Migration to the Urban Midwest: The Gender Dimension, 1915–1945," in Trotter, *Great Migration in Historical Perspective*, 127–46. On the migration of Black women, see Jacqueline Jones, *Labor of Love, Labor of Sorrow: Black Women, Work and the Family, from Slavery to the Present* (New York: Vintage Books, 1986), chap. 5.
23. U.S. Bureau of the Census, *Sixteenth Census of the United States, 1940*, vol. 2, pt. 1, *Population: Characteristics* (Washington, D.C.: Department of the Interior, 1941), 323; ibid., vol. 3, pt. 2, *The Labor Force*, 29.
24. Bond, *Negro Education in Alabama*, 259.

25. Mrs. Irene Williams, interview by the author, Montgomery, Alabama, April 17, 1997.

26. Ibid.

27. Mrs. Amelia Scott Green, interview by the author, Montgomery, Alabama, April 13, 1997.

28. Mrs. Idessa Redden, interview by the author, Montgomery, Alabama, April 13, 1997.

29. Frank Gregory, a former cutter at Reliance, recalled that teachers from the surrounding areas of Montgomery and Lowndes Counties found work at the shirt factory in order to augment their annual salaries. Mr. Frank Gregory, interview by the author, Montgomery, Alabama, April 16, 1997.

30. For a full account of the instrumental participation of women in the Baptist Convention movement, see Evelyn Brooks Higginbotham, *Righteous Discontent: The Women's Movement in the Black Baptist Church, 1880–1920* (Cambridge, Mass.: Harvard University Press, 1993).

31. Ms. Gwen Bell, interview by the author, Montgomery, Alabama, May 19, 1998.

32. Ibid.

33. Mrs. Rachel Maredi Motshele, interview by the author, Alexandra, South Africa, August 18, 1997.

34. The Bantu Education Act did not come into effect until 1953; however, the ideological shift, as Mrs. Motshele describes it, had begun as early as 1949. Ibid.

35. Ibid.

36. Frances Baard (as told to Barbie Schreiner), *My Spirit Is Not Banned* (Harare, Zimbabwe: Zimbabwe Publishing House, 1986), 15.

37. Ibid., 15–16.

38. Ibid., 16–20.

39. Ray E. Phillips, *The Bantu in the City: A Study of Cultural Adjustment on the Witwatersrand* (Alice, South Africa: Lovedale Press, n.d.), 33.

40. Mrs. Naomi Setshedi, interview by Mmantho Nkotsoe, January 31, 1983, box Ab30, Collection AG 2738, #30, p. 27, Institute for Advanced Social Research, William Cullen Library, University of the Witwatersrand.

41. Mrs. Naomi Setshedi, interview by Mmantho Nkotsoe, March 12, 1982, box Ab18, #18, Collection AG 2738, p. 5, Institute for Advanced Social Research, William Cullen Library, University of the Witwatersrand.

42. Belinda Bozzoli, ed, *Labour, Townships, and Protest: Studies in the Social History of the Witwatersrand* (Johannesburg: Ravan Press, 1979), 99; André Proctor, "Class Struggle, Segregation and the City: A History of Sophiatown, 1905–1940," in ibid., 73.

43. Ibid., 100–101.

44. Ellen Hellmann, *Rooiyard: A Sociological Survey of an Urban Native Slum Yard* (Cape Town, South Africa: Oxford University Press, 1948), 38.

45. Ibid., 39–42.

46. Phillips, *Bantu in the City*, 34.
47. Bozzoli, *Labour, Townships, and Protest*, 144; Hellmann, *Rooiyard*, 41–49.
48. Proctor, "Class Struggle, Segregation and the City," 82–83.
49. Ida Molefe, interview by Dennis Mashabela, March 24, 1983, box Ab43, Collection AG 2738, #43, p. 11, Institute for Advanced Social Research, William Cullen Library, University of the Witwatersrand.
50. For a fascinating account of the evolution of Black urban culture in Johannesburg, see David Coplan, *In Township Tonight! South Africa's Black City Music and Theatre* (Johannesburg: Ravan Press, 1985).
51. Ibid., 150.
52. Ibid., 163; Hugh Masekela, Sunday Afternoon Jazz Program, KAYA FM, 95.9, August, 1997.
53. This is a popular term that refers to the large police vans.
54. Taken from the Xhosa word *ukumanya*, meaning "to join" or "to unite," *manyano* is the noun formed from the shortened verb form. Among other peoples, such as the Zulu and Southern Sotho, other forms of the word are used: *Inhlangano yomanyano* for the Zulu and *Bamanyano* for the Southern Sotho. Mia Brandel-Syrier, *Black Woman in Search of God* (London: Lutterworth Press, 1962), 15.
55. Deborah Gaitskell, "Female Mission Initiatives: Black and White Women in Three Witwatersrand Churches, 1903–1939" (Ph.D. diss., University of London, 1981), 142–51.
56. Ibid., 151–58, 197.
57. See Elizabeth Clark-Lewis, "From 'Servant' to 'Dayworkers': A Study of Selected Household Service Workers in Washington, D.C., 1900–1926" (Ph.D. diss., University of Maryland, 1983), 123–28.
58. Hellmann, *Rooiyard*, 43–45. See also David Coplan, "The Emergence of an African Working-Class Culture," in *Industrialisation and Social Change in South Africa: African Class Formation, Culture, and Consciousness, 1870–1930*, ed. Shula Marks and Richard Rathbone (New York: Longman, 1982), 367, and Bozzoli, *Labour, Townships, and Protest*, 141–42. On July 27, 1997, I participated in a Johannesburg *stokvel* meeting that included several prominent women activists in the anti-apartheid national liberation campaigns. They had formed their group in Soweto as young wives and mothers in need of mutual support, and thirty years later the group was still active.
59. Quoted in Bozzoli, *Labour, Townships, and Protest*, 141, 142.

CHAPTER FIVE

1. Frank Gregory, interview by the author, Montgomery, Alabama, April 16, 1997. Frank Gregory was one of the original organizers of the all-Black union local at the factory; his wife, Hazel Gregory, was managing secretary of the Montgomery Improvement Association during the 1955–1956 bus boycott.
2. Gregory, interview.

3. Mrs. Beautie Mae Johnson, interview by the author, Montgomery, Alabama, April 16, 1997.
4. Ibid.
5. Ibid.
6. Helen Joseph, *Side by Side: The Autobiography of Helen Joseph* (New York: William Morrow, 1986), 10.
7. See also Helen Joseph, *Tomorrow's Sun: A Smuggled Journal from South Africa* (New York: John Day, 1967), which was written closer to the period she describes and which includes additional details.
8. Mrs. Bertha Mashaba Gxowa, interview by the author, Johannesburg, South Africa, January 27, 1998.
9. Mrs. Bertha Mashaba Gxowa, interview by the author, Johannesburg, South Africa, July 22, 1997.
10. John Mashaba worked closely with Gana Makabeni, who served as a Communist Party organizer among African workers in the Johannesburg and Germiston areas. In early 1928 some ten thousand furniture, clothing, bakery, laundry, and garage workers formed the South African Federation of Non-European Trade Unions, which was heavily influenced by the ideology and led by members of the Communist Party. Federation demands for the workers stressed the modest goals of a forty-eight-hour work week and "equal pay for equal work." See H. J. Simons and R. E. Simons, *Class and Colour in South Africa, 1850–1950* (Baltimore: Penguin Books, 1969), 376–77, 388 (quote on 377).
11. Gxowa, interviews, July 22, 1997, and January 27, 1998. Quote from January 27, 1998 interview.
12. Gxowa interview, July 22, 1997.
13. Belinda Robnett, *How Long? How Long? African-American Women and the Struggle for Civil Rights* (New York: Oxford University Press, 1997), 193. See also Aldon Morris, *The Origins of the Civil Rights Movement: Black Communities Organizing for Change* (New York: Free Press, 1984).
14. Emma Mashinini, *Strikes Have Followed Me All My Life: A South African Autobiography* (New York: Routledge, 1991), 14.
15. Officially formed in 1910 by a group of white progressives with the African American scholar-activist W. E. B. Du Bois, the NAACP incorporated a liberal, reformist ideology based on political and social equality for Black people. Much of the work of the organization was promulgated through the courts, which had pointedly neglected most of the concerns of Black workers. For a favorable comparison with the ANC, see George M. Fredrickson, *Black Liberation: A Comparative History of Black Ideologies in the United States and South Africa* (New York: Oxford University Press, 1995), 266.
16. For two outstanding works on the Scottsboro case, see Dan T. Carter, *Scottsboro: A Tragedy of the American South* (Baton Rouge: Louisiana State University Press, 1969), and James Goodman, *Stories of Scottsboro* (New York: Vintage Books, 1994).

17. Quoted in Haywood Patterson and Earl Conrad, *Scottsboro Boy* (New York: Doubleday, 1950), 246.
18. Robin D. G. Kelley, *Hammer and Hoe: Alabama Communists during the Great Depression* (Chapel Hill: University of North Carolina Press, 1990), 90. For a compelling discussion of the Black, mass-based ILD, which fearlessly entered the fray in the Scottsboro case despite the virulent polemics of white supremicists who vowed never to allow any Black man or Communist "free possession of White women," see ibid., 79 and chap. 4. At the same time, Robin D. G. Kelley does not overlook the failure of the ILD, the NAACP, and other organizations to advocate on behalf of Murdis Dixon, a Black twelve-year-old girl who was raped by her white employer in 1934. On this case, see also Nell Irvin Painter, *The Narrative of Hosea Hudson: The Life and Times of a Black Radical* (New York: W. W. Norton, 1979), 104–6.
19. Angelo Herndon, who was born in 1913 in Wyoming, Ohio, was the son of working-class parents who had migrated from Birmingham, Alabama. He and his brother later found work, as their father had, in the Kentucky and Birmingham coal mines, and by 1930 Angelo Herndon had become an ardent activist in the Communist Party. When Herndon was arrested in Georgia on the charge of inciting to insurrection in 1932, the ILD assisted in his successful defense. See Angelo Herndon, *You Cannot Kill the Working Class* (New York: International Labor Defense and the League of Struggle for Negro Rights, [1937?]), and Charles Martin, *The Angelo Herndon Case and Southern Justice* (Baton Rouge: Louisiana State University Press, 1976).
20. Quoted in Rosa Parks with Jim Haskins, *Rosa Parks: My Story* (New York: Dial Books, 1992), 59.
21. Kelley, *Hammer and Hoe*, 95, 161.
22. Parks with Haskins, *Rosa Parks*, 64, 66, 67.
23. Ibid., 69, 70.
24. For a fine account of the efforts to organize workers in Alabama, see Philip Taft, *Organizing Dixie: Alabama Workers in the Industrial Era* (Westport, Conn.: Greenwood Press, 1981), especially chaps. 7 and 8.
25. Painter, *Narrative of Hosea Hudson*, 16. Further excavating the radical landscape in Alabama during the same period, Kelley reports findings consistent with those of Nell Painter. See Kelley, *Hammer and Hoe*.
26. Quoted in Theodore Rosengarten, *All God's Dangers: The Life of Nate Shaw* (New York: Avon Books, 1974), 333; see also 311–33.
27. Quoted in Kelley, *Hammer and Hoe*, 51; see also 40–42, 49–54. See also Philip S. Foner, *Organized Labor and the Black Worker, 1619–1973* (New York: Praeger, 1974), 192–93.
28. Kelley, *Hammer and Hoe*, 67, 121–22.
29. Harvard Sitkoff, *A New Deal for Blacks—The Emergence of Civil Rights as a National Issue: The Depression Decade* (New York: Oxford University Press, 1978), 255. Sitkoff is very convincing in his description of the critical internal rift within the NAACP that pitted Walter White (who was consumed by his campaign against lynching)

and the board on one side against W. E. B. Du Bois (assisted by the able thinking of Ralph Bunche and Abram Harris of Howard University) and some of the
younger members of the NAACP on the other. See ibid., especially 246–58.

30. On the turn of the Communist Party from "self-determination in the Black Belt"
to popular-front coalition building, see Kelley, *Hammer and Hoe*, chaps. 6–10. For
ideological and strategic links between the Communist Party of the United States
and the Communist Party of South Africa, see George Fredrickson, *Black Liberation: A Comparative History of Black Ideologies in the United States and South Africa*
(New York: Oxford University Press, 1995), chap. 5.

31. Quoted in Studs Terkel, *Hard Times* (New York: Avon Press, 1970), 145.

32. Quoted in ibid., 144; On the differences between the ideologies and practices of
the Ladies Auxiliary of the BSCP and the National Congress of Negro Women,
see Deborah Gray White, *Too Heavy a Load: Black Women in Defense of Themselves,
1894–1994* (New York: W. W. Norton, 1999), 160–75.

33. Quoted in Terkel, *Hard Times*, 146–47.

34. Gregory was the first vice president of Local 490. Gregory, interview; Taft, *Organizing Dixie*, 125.

35. Mrs. Amy Collins Harris, interview by the author, Montgomery, Alabama, March
21, 1998.

36. Ibid.

37. Ibid.

38. See Morris, *Origins of the Civil Rights Movement*, 141–43.

39. Septima Pointsette Clark (1898–1987) was born and educated in Charleston, South
Carolina, where she became a teacher. She began her career in 1916 teaching children and adults on Johns Island, South Carolina. Having dedicated her life to the
liberation of Black people—demanding greater respect for Black women and working tirelessly on behalf of Black citizenship education—Clark was a revered figure
in the freedom movement. See Cynthia Stokes Brown, ed., *Ready from Within: Septima Clark and the Civil Rights Movement, a First Person Narrative* (Trenton, N.J.:
Africa World Press, 1990), and Grace Jordan McFadden, "Septima P. Clark and the
Struggle for Human Rights," in *Women in the Civil Rights Movement: Trailblazers and Torchbearers, 1941–1961*, ed. Vicki L. Crawford, Jacqueline Anne Rouse, and
Barbara Woods (Bloomington: Indiana University Press, 1993), 85–97.

40. Morris, *Origins of the Civil Rights Movement*, 144–57; Brown, *Ready from Within*,
41–62; Donna Langston, "The Women of Highlander," in Crawford et al., *Women
in the Civil Rights Movement*, 145–67; Aimee Horton, *The Highlander Folk School:
A History of Its Major Programs, 1932–1961* (Brooklyn, N.Y.: Carlson Publishing,
1989).

41. "South Holds First Education Parley," *The Advance* 34, no. 17 (September 1,
1948): 9.

42. Zilphia Horton (the wife of Myles Horton), who directed Highlander's music and
drama programs in collaboration with Pete Seeger, adapted the song "We Shall
Overcome" for use in the labor movement in the 1940s from a Black church song

called "I'll Overcome Someday." The potency of the song as a galvanizing force and symbol of unity in the Civil Rights Movement is legendary. See Langston, "Women of Highlander," 148–49, and Guy and Candie Carawan, *We Shall Overcome! Songs of the Southern Freedom Movement* (New York: Oak Publications, 1963), 11.

43. E. S. (Solly) Sachs, *Rebels Daughters* (Manchester, England: MacGibbon and Kee, 1957), 104.

44. Bernard Makhosezwe Magubane, *The Political Economy of Race and Class in South Africa* (New York: Monthly Review Press, 1979), 83.

45. William Beinart, *Twentieth-Century South Africa* (New York: Oxford University Press, 1994), 121, 265. In Kenya the population of Nairobi reached 220,000, and in Nigeria the population of Lagos reached 267,000 during the 1950s. See Philip Curtin, Steven Feierman, Leonard Thompson et al., *African History: From Earliest Times to Independence*, 2nd ed. (New York: Longman, 1995), 508–9.

46. See Sachs, *Rebels Daughters*, 36–39.

47. Between 1944 and 1945, African women received only 20.6 percent of white men's wages; by 1957 that figure had dropped to 14 percent. See Iris Berger, *Threads of Solidarity: Women in South African Industry, 1900–1980* (Bloomington: Indiana University Press, 1992), 167–68, 170.

48. Beinart, *Twentieth-Century South Africa*, 124. See also Dan O'Meara, "The 1946 African Mine Workers' Strike and the Political Economy of South Africa," *Journal of Commonwealth and Comparative Politics* 12, no. 2 (1975): 147–73.

49. Indentured Indians were also excluded from the employee classification. See Simons and Simons, *Class and Colour in South Africa*, 320. See also Monica Horrell, *South African Trade Unionism: A Study of a Divided Working Class* (Johannesburg: South African Institute of Race Relations, 1961), 8–10. In certain instances in the Cape and the OFS, where pass laws did not as yet apply to Africans and where some Indians were not indentured, however, these men and women were legal members of registered unions in Cape Town, Port Elizabeth, and Johannesburg, making their unions multiracial from the start. Horrell, *South African Trade Unionism*, 61.

50. Edward Roux, *Time Longer Than Rope: A History of the Black Man's Struggle for Freedom in South Africa* (1948; reprint, Madison: University of Wisconsin Press, 1964), 400.

51. Ibid., 207–11; Horrell, *South African Trade Unionism*, 67–68.

52. Horrell, *South African Trade Unionism*, 69–70; Roux, *Time Longer Than Rope*, 332–33; Ken Luckhardt and Brenda Wall, *Organize or Starve! The History of the South African Congress of Trade Unions* (New York: International Publishers, 1980), 60–61.

53. Sachs, *Rebels Daughters*, 114–16.

54. Quoted in Berger, *Threads of Solidarity*, 175.

55. Berger, *Threads of Solidarity*, 173–77; Sachs, *Rebels Daughters*, 118–27.

56. Mashinini, *Strikes Have Followed Me All My Life*, 13–14.

57. Ibid., 14–18.

58. Mashinini, *Strikes Have Followed Me All My Life*, 16.

59. Ibid., 16–17.

60. Ibid., 17. On July 26, 1997, I participated in a *stokvel* meeting of past and present Soweto residents, including Mrs. Emma Mashinini. All of the women present had in some clear way participated in the movement for the liberation of South Africa. In the new South Africa, one of the women is a former Truth and Reconciliation Commission member, and another formerly headed the South African Council of Churches.

61. In 1942 Smuts philosophized about the nature of trusteeship in "African Native policy," musing, "Isolation has gone and I am afraid segregation has fallen on evil days too." Simons and Simons, *Class and Colour in South Africa*, 540–41 n. 36.

62. Roux, *Time Longer Than Rope*, 315–17.

63. Quoted in ibid., 308.

64. In 1960 South Africa officially made the transition from pounds to rands (at the time, one pound equaled two rands). Monica Hunter Wilson and Leonard Thompson, eds., *The Oxford History of South Africa*, vol. 2, *1870–1966* (London: Oxford University Press, 1971), 36 n. 2.

65. Michael Motshele, interview by the author, Alexandra, South Africa, August 7, 1997. See also Rachel Motshele, interview by the author, Alexandra, South Africa, August 7, 1997.

66. Mrs. Florence Nomathamsangqa Siwedi, interview by the author, Soweto, South Africa, August 6, 1997.

67. Ibid.

68. For migrant women's perspectives on the violence that they encountered in Alexandra and Sophiatown, see Belinda Bozzoli, with Mmantho Nkotsoe, *Women of Phokeng: Consciousness, Life Strategy, and Migrancy in South Africa, 1900–1983* (Portsmouth, N.H.: Heinemann, 1991), especially chap. 7. For various aspects of the political economy of the township during this period, see "Challenge to Democracy: Rand's Problem Township," *Libertas*, August 1942, 16–29; David Duncan, "Liberals and Local Administration in South Africa: Alfred Hoernle and the Alexandra Health Committee, 1933–1943," *International Journal of African Historical Studies* 23, no. 3 (1990): 475–93; A. W. Stadler, "A Long Way to Walk: Bus Boycotts in Alexandra, 1940–1945," in *Working Papers in Southern African Studies*, vol. 2, ed. Philip Bonner (Johannesburg: Ravan, 1981), 228–57; and Mike Sarakinsky, *Alexandra: From "Freehold" to "Model" Township* (Johannesburg: Development Studies Group, University of the Witwatersrand, 1984).

69. In August 1944 a study of the transportation issue on the Rand commissioned by the state the previous year reported that transportation charges for African workers were already "beyond [their] capacity to pay." Quoted in Sarakinsky, *Alexandra*, 16, and Stadler, "A Long Way to Walk," 229. In 1951 the South African Institute of Race Relations sponsored a study of the average incomes of African families relative to their expenditures. The study found that for a family of five in 1944 the aver-

age income of nine pounds, eighteen shillings, one cent was insufficient to cover the average expenditure of twelve pounds, eighteen shillings, six cents. See Cherryl Walker, *Women and Resistance in South Africa*, 2nd ed. (New York: Monthly Review Press, 1991), 71.

70. Stadler, "A Long Way to Walk," 237.

71. Ibid., 240–41.

72. Quoted in ibid., 244.

73. Hilda Watts, "They Marched to Victory!" *Fighting Talk*, November 1954, 9.

74. Ibid.

75. Quoted in Stadler, "A Long Way to Walk," 246, 247.

76. James "Sofasonke" ("We Shall All Die Together") Mpanza was the most well-known of the squatters' movement leaders. His strong leadership appealed to many women and won the squatters favorable concessions from the Johannesburg City Council. See A. W. Stadler, "Birds in the Cornfields: Squatter Movements in Johannesburg, 1944–47," in *Labour, Townships and Protest: Studies in the Social History of the Witwatersrand*, Belinda Bozzoli, ed. (Johannesburg: Ravan Press, 1979), 19–47. See also Walker, *Women and Resistance in South Africa*, 75–85, and Simons and Simons, *Class and Colour in South Africa*, 547–48.

77. Walker, *Women and Resistance in South Africa*, 76–79.

78. See P. Olisanwuche Esedebe, *Pan-Africanism: The Idea and Movement, 1776–1991*, 2nd ed. (Washington, D.C.: Howard University Press, 1994), 138–41.

79. Simons and Simons, *Class and Colour in South Africa*, 548.

CHAPTER SIX

1. Mrs. Irene Williams, interview by the author, Montgomery, Alabama, April 17, 1997.

2. Mrs. Cora McHaney, interview by the author, Montgomery, Alabama, April 17, 1997. Mrs. McHaney is most likely referring to the case known as *Browder v. Gayle*, held in the Federal District Court in Montgomery in May 1956, challenging the constitutionality of segregated seating on intra-state buses (see chapter 7).

3. Ibid.

4. Williams, interview.

5. Mrs. Maggie Resha, interview by the author, Ramohlakoana (Eastern Cape), South Africa, July 10–11, 2001.

6. Maggie Resha, *'Mangoana O Tsoara Thipa Ka Bohaleng: My Life in the Struggle* (Johannesburg: Congress of South African Writers, 1991), 28.

7. Ibid., 39.

8. Ibid., 41.

9. Emphasis added.

10. See Richard Kluger, *Simple Justice: The History of Brown v. Board of Education and Black America's Struggle for Equality* (New York: Vintage Books, 1975), 202–13.

11. Quoted in Studs Terkel, *Hard Times* (New York: Avon Books, 1970), 145–46.

12. Mrs. Carr had joined in the late 1930s or early 1940s to help a member of her church

(Hall Street Baptist) who was participating in the branch membership drive. Mrs. Johnnie Carr, interview by the author, Montgomery, Alabama, May 25, 1995.

13. Mrs. Parks succeeded Mrs. Johnnie Carr as secretary of the NAACP branch in Montgomery. Rosa Parks with Jim Haskins, *Rosa Parks: My Story* (New York: Dial Books, 1992), 80–81.

14. Quoted in Steven M. Millner, "The Montgomery Bus Boycott: A Case Study in the Emergence and Career of a Social Movement," in *The Walking City: The Montgomery Bus Boycott, 1955–1956*, ed. David J. Garrow (Brooklyn, N.Y.: Carlson Publishing, 1989), 560.

15. Parks with Haskins, *Rosa Parks*, 76.

16. Ibid., 83–86.

17. Ibid., 77, 78, 79.

18. Patricia Sullivan, "Southern Reformers, the New Deal, and the Movement's Foundation," in *New Directions in Civil Rights Studies*, ed. Armstead Robinson and Patricia Sullivan (Charlottesville: University of Virginia Press, 1991), 86.

19. Quoted in ibid., 87. See also William Warren Rogers, Robert David Ward, Leah Rawls Atkins et al., *Alabama, the History of a Deep South State* (Tuscaloosa: University of Alabama Press, 1994), 539.

20. Quoted in Sullivan, "Southern Reformers," 90; See also the references to Baker's work with the NAACP in Patricia Sullivan, *Days of Hope: Race and Democracy in the New Deal Era* (Chapel Hill: University of North Carolina Press, 1996), 139, 142–43, 195.

21. Sullivan, "Southern Reformers," 96.

22. Big Mule is a political term that refers to rich planters and industrial bosses.

23. Rogers et al., *Alabama*, 530.

24. Quoted in Charles G. Dobbins, "Alabama Governors and Editors, 1930–1955: A Memoir," *Alabama Review* 29 (April 1976): 154.

25. Quoted in Taylor Branch, *Parting the Waters: America in the King Years, 1954–1963* (New York: Simon and Schuster, 1988), 22.

26. See the vivid portrait of the Reverend Vernon Johns in ibid., 6–26.

27. Mary Fair Burks, "Trailblazers: Women in the Montgomery Bus Boycott," in *Women in the Civil Rights Movement: Trailblazers and Torchbearers, 1941–1965*, ed. Vicki Crawford, Jacqueline Anne Rouse, and Barbara Woods (Bloomington: Indiana University Press, 1993), 71–83.

28. J. Mills Thornton III, "Challenge and Response in the Montgomery Bus Boycott of 1955–1956," in Garrow, *Walking City*, 330.

29. Burks, "Trailblazers," 78.

30. Several sources list Mrs. Burks's founding of the WPC in 1946. See Burks, "Trailblazers," 75; Jo Ann Gibson Robinson, *The Montgomery Bus Boycott and the Women Who Started It*, ed. David J. Garrow (Knoxville: University of Tennessee Press, 1987), 22; and David J. Garrow, "The Origins of the Montgomery Bus Boycott," in Garrow, *Walking City*, 608. The Reverend Vernon Johns became the pastor at Dexter in 1948. It is possible that Mrs. Burks confused her organization of the WPC with

another action that was precipitated by Johns's pulpit address, or his address may have inspired Mrs. Burks to reinvigorate a flagging group.

31. Quoted in Burks, "Trailblazers," 78.

32. Quoted in ibid., 79, The 1896 Supreme Court decision in *Plessy v. Ferguson* upheld the constitutionality of the "separate but equal" accommodations doctrine in public life, including in schools, in hospitals, in hotels, and with respect to seating arrangements on public conveyances. For an excellent discussion of the *Plessy v. Ferguson* case and decision see Richard Kluger, *Simple Justice* (New York: Vintage Books, 1977), 72–83.

33. Quoted in Burks, "Trailblazers," 79.

34. On an earlier version of southern Black women's overt political activism, see Glenda Elizabeth Gilmore, *Gender and Jim Crow: Women and the Politics of White Supremacy in North Carolina, 1896–1920* (Chapel Hill: University of North Carolina Press, 1996). Gilmore highlights the importance of middle-class Black women's educational and civic work—intersected by race and gender—in Black politics and interracial relations before the advent of the vote for women.

35. Burks, "Trailblazers," 78–79.

36. Mrs. Thelma Glass, interview by the author, Montgomery, Alabama, April 24, 1997.

37. Ibid. See also Stephanie J. Shaw, *What a Woman Ought to Be and to Do: Black Professional Women Workers during the Jim Crow Era* (Chicago: University of Chicago Press, 1996), especially chap. 6. Shaw argues that Black professional women were socialized to engage in unpaid work that might more fittingly be termed community development.

38. Quoted in Burks, "Trailblazers," 80.

39. As a response to the liberalizing effect of *Smith v. Allwright*, Democratic leaders in Alabama proposed the Boswell amendment to their state constitution in May 1945, which would require that any applicant be able to understand any portion of the U.S. Constitution. In November 1946 the general electorate ratified the plan. In the spirit of the new law, the Jefferson County Board of Registrars, for example, designed new and more ingenious questions with which to discourage any potential Black voters, such as "What is meant by the veto power of the UN?" "How are members of the Cabinet elected?" and "What is meant by the pocket veto?" The NAACP in Birmingham and the Voters and Veterans Association in Mobile combined their efforts in the federal district court to overturn the amendment, but their victory was "Pyrrhic": The justices declined to overturn the use of literacy tests, and Alabama boards simply "invented new measures to thwart enrollment." Steven F. Lawson, *Black Ballots: Voting Rights in the South, 1944–1969* (New York: Columbia University Press, 1976), 90–97; quotes on 93, 97.

40. Burks, "Trailblazers," 80.

41. Ibid., 80. According to Mrs. Thelma Glass, the League of Women Voters' segregated branches in the South were an impetus for the formation of the WPC. Glass, interview.

42. Quoted in Sullivan, *Days of Hope*, 207; see also ibid., 172–73, 215–16.

43. On the derivation of the SNYC and its links to the Communist Party, see Robin D. G. Kelley, *Hammer and Hoe: Alabama Communists during the Great Depression* (Chapel Hill: University of North Carolina Press, 1990), 200–219.

44. Mrs. Beautie Mae Johnson, interview by the author, Montgomery, Alabama, April 16, 1997; Mrs. Amy Collins Harris, taped interview by the author, Montgomery, Alabama, July 20, 1999; Mrs. Idessa Redden, interview by the author, Montgomery, Alabama, April 13, 1997.

45. Harris, interview.

46. Redden, interview.

47. Ibid.

48. Tom Lodge, *Black Politics in South Africa since 1945* (New York: Longman, 1983), 18; Dan O'Meara, "The African Mine Workers' Strike and the Political Economy of South Africa," *Journal of Commonwealth and Comparative Politics* 12, no. 2 (1975): 146–73.

49. In addition, miners were compelled to provide their own boots, blankets, and cigarettes, which were offered at inflated prices. H. J. Simons and R. E. Simons, *Class and Colour in South Africa, 1850–1950* (Baltimore: Penguin Books, 1969), 569.

50. O'Meara, "African Mine Workers' Strike," 146–47; T. Dunbar Moodie, "The Moral Economy of the Black Miners' Strike of 1946," *Journal of Southern African Studies* 13, no. 1 (October 1986): 1–35.

51. Moodie, "Moral Economy of the Black Miners' Strike of 1946," 15–27; O'Meara, "African Mine Workers' Strike," 155–60; Simons and Simons, *Class and Colour in South Africa*, 569–73.

52. Quoted in Moodie, "Moral Economy of the Black Miners' Strike of 1946," 27.

53. Ibid., 28–29; Simons and Simons, *Class and Colour in South Africa*, 575–78.

54. Simons and Simons, *Class and Colour in South Africa*, 388.

55. Ibid., 406.

56. Ibid., 392.

57. On the derivation of this program and the similarities between the U.S. South and South African Communist Party interpretations of the Communist International directive see Kelley, *Hammer and Hoe*, 13; George Fredrickson, *Black Liberation: A Comparative History of Black Ideologies in the United States and South Africa* (New York: Oxford University Press, 1995), 192–202; and Mark Solomon, *The Cry Was Unity: Communists and African Americans, 1917–1936* (Jackson: University Press of Mississippi, 1998), 68–89.

58. Simons and Simons, *Class and Colour in South Africa*, 388–400.

59. Quoted in ibid., 492–93; see also 402–3, 414–15. On Kotane, see also Thomas Karis and Gwendolen M. Carter, eds., *From Protest to Challenge: A Documentary History of African Politics in South Africa, 1882–1964*, vol. 4, *Political Profiles*, ed. Gail M. Gerhardt and Thomas Karis (Stanford, Calif.: Hoover Institution Press, 1977), 50–52.

60. In fact, according to one historian, Xuma had begun to change his perspective on the general direction that African protest should take. He became less disposed

toward working with white liberals and more disposed toward working with people who accepted Black equality. His politics, which became increasingly "proto-Africanist," advocated an ideology of "African self-reliance and solidarity" that many future Youth Leaguers would represent. Stephen D. Gish, *Alfred B. Xuma: African, American, South African* (New York: New York University Press, 2000), 107–9; quotes on 108.

61. See Lodge, *Black Politics in South Africa*, 29. For a favorable comparison between the roles of Communists in the United States and in South African freedom movements during the World War II era, see George M. Fredrickson, *Black Liberation*, 214–24.

62. Anthony Sampson, *Mandela* (New York: Knopf, 1999), 62–63.

63. Karis and Carter, *From Protest to Challenge*, vol. 2, *Hope and Challenge*, 98–99.

64. Ibid., 4:55–57, 2:100.

65. Ibid., 2:101–2.

66. "Trumpet Call to Youth," Congress Youth League flyer, n.d., quoted in ibid., 2:308–9.

67. See Ellen Kuzwayo, *Call Me Woman* (1985; reprint, Randburg, South Africa: Ravan Press, 1996), 139.

68. Mrs. Florence Nomathamsangqa Siwedi, interview by the author, Soweto, South Africa, August 6, 1997. At the time of Florence Siwedi's membership in the CYL (after her service in the war), Oliver Tambo had already been expelled from Fort Hare (having earned his bachelor's degree, he was working toward a second degree). As a founding member of the CYL and a popular secondary school teacher in Johannesburg at the time, however, Tambo certainly appeared as a guest at the Bantu Men's Social Centre with fellow past and present student Youth Leaguers. See Karis and Carter, *From Protest to Challenge*, 4:151–53.

69. "Congress Youth League Manifesto," issued by the Provisional Committee of the Congress Youth League, March 1944, quoted in Karis and Carter, *From Protest to Challenge*, 2:306.

70. "Basic Policy of Congress Youth League," manifesto issued by the National Executive Committee of the ANC Youth League, 1948, Item 5, "Two Streams of African Nationalism," quoted in Karis and Carter, *From Protest to Challenge*, 2:328.

71. "Two Streams of African Nationalism," quoted in ibid., 2:328.

72. Quoted in Lodge, *Black Politics in South Africa*, 22.

73. "Programme of Action," Statement of Policy adopted at the ANC Annual Conference, December 17, 1949, quoted in Karis and Carter, *From Protest to Challenge*, 2:337.

74. Ibid., 107.

75. During this era Hallie Quinn Brown, Nannie Helen Burroughs, Anna Julia Cooper, Alexander Crummell, W. E. B. Du Bois, Mary Church Terrell, Booker T. Washington, and Margaret Murray Washington were some of the best-known proponents of racial uplift ideology, which included self-help, racial solidarity, a

Christian moral ethic, educational improvement, and ministering to those who were less fortunate. Brown and Du Bois either taught at or were affiliated with Wilberforce University while Charlotte Manye was a student there. See August Meier, *Negro Thought in America, 1880–1915: Radical Ideologies in the Age of Booker T. Washington* (Ann Arbor: University of Michigan Press, 1963); Wilson J. Moses, *The Golden Age of Black Nationalism* (Hamden, Conn.: Archon Books, 1978); Paula Giddings, *When and Where I Enter: The Impact of Black Women on Race and Sex in America* (New York: William Morrow, 1984); Hallie Q. Brown, *Homespun Heroines and Other Women of Distinction* (New York: Oxford University Press, 1988); and Kevin Gaines, *Uplifting the Race: Black Leadership, Politics, and Culture in the Twentieth Century* (Chapel Hill: University of North Carolina Press, 1996).

76. According to her younger sister, Kate Manye Makanya, who was born in 1873, Charlotte was six years old in 1878. See Margaret McCord, *The Calling of Katie Makanya, a Memoir of South Africa* (Cape Town, South Africa: David Philip, 1995), 4–5, 10.

77. See L. L. Berry, *A Century of Missions of the African Methodist Episcopal Church, 1840–1940* (New York: African Methodist Episcopal Church, 1942), 186. See also A. B. Xuma, *Charlotte Manye (Mrs. Maxeke): "What an Educated African Girl Can Do"* (Women's Parent Mite Missionary Society, 1930), Hallie Quinn Brown Black Collection, Hallie Quinn Brown Library, Central State University.

78. Berry, *Century of Missions*, 186. On W. E. B. Du Bois and Reverdy Ransom, see David Levering Lewis, *W. E. B. Du Bois: Biography of a Race, 1868–1919* (New York: Henry Holt, 1993), especially chap. 12.

79. C. M. Manye, "Our Work in South Africa," July 5, 1900, Women's Mite Missionary Session, and "Synopsis of Address by C. Manye, Our African Daughter," Ohio Conference Branch Fifth Annual Convention, Women's Mite Missionary Society, July 18, 19, 20, and 21, 1901, Archives and Special Collections, Rembert E. Stokes Learning Resources Center, Wilberforce University.

80. Xuma, *Charlotte Manye (Mrs. Maxeke)*, 13–17; Berry, *Century of Missions*, 186–87.

81. Quoted in James Campbell, *Songs of Zion: The African Methodist Episcopal Church in the United States and South Africa* (New York: Oxford University Press, 1995), 287. See Campbell's thoughtful description of her life, 252–94.

82. Quoted in ibid., 287–88.

83. Quoted in Campbell, *Songs of Zion*, 288.

84. Charlotte Maxeke, "Social Conditions among Bantu Women and Girls," Address by Charlotte Maxeke at the Conference of European and Bantu Christian Student Associations at Fort Hare, June 27–July 3, 1930, quoted in Karis and Carter, *From Protest to Challenge*, vol. 1, *Protest and Hope, 1882–1934*, ed. Sheridan Johns (Stanford, Calif.: Hoover Institution Press, 1972), 344–46.

85. Quoted in ibid., 346.

86. See Anna Julia Cooper, *A Voice from the South* (New York: Oxford University Press, 1988), especially chaps. 3 and 4.

87. See Xuma, *Charlotte Manye (Mrs. Maxeke)*; Cherryl Walker, *Women and Resistance in South Africa*, 2nd ed. (New York: Monthly Review Press, 1991), 38–39; and Campbell, *Songs of Zion*, 288–94.

88. Quoted in Walker, *Women and Resistance in South Africa*, 89.

89. Quoted in Nat Nakasa, "Mummy Goes Home—but Her Job's Done," *Drum*, March 1963, 41.

90. Quoted in ibid., 39.

91. Walker, *Women and Resistance in South Africa*, 91. See also "Annual Report of the Johannesburg Zenzele Club," n.d., "Witbank Zenzele Club Report," n.d., and untitled report from Evaton, n.d., A. B. Xuma Papers, box O, microfilm reel 5, Dodd Research Center, University of Connecticut.

92. Quoted in Emily Herring Wilson and Susan Mullaly, *Hope and Dignity: Older Black Women of the South* (Philadelphia: Temple University Press, 1983), 144–45.

93. Ibid., 143, 145–47.

94. "American Negro Revue: The Making of a People," *Umteteli wa Bantu*, June 5, 1943, and Review of "American Negro Review," *Forward*, June 18, 1943, box U, Xuma Papers, Dodd Research Center, University of Connecticut. See also Gish, *Alfred B. Xuma*, 117, and Walker, *Women and Resistance in South Africa*, 91.

95. Catherine Higgs, "Helping Ourselves: Black Women and Grassroots Activism in Segregated South Africa, 1922–1952," in *Stepping Forward: Black Women in Africa and the Americas*, ed. Catherine Higgs, Barbara A. Moss, and Earline Rae Ferguson (Athens: Ohio University Press, 2002), 60–62.

96. For profiles of both Jabavu and his father, John Tengo Jabavu, see Karis and Carter, *From Protest to Challenge*, 4:39–43. Neither father nor son was a proponent of the ANC; their politics, which were far less confrontational, advocated interracial cooperation with white South Africans. Both men were, however, ardent believers in the Cape franchise for Africans.

97. For an excellent portrait of the Yergans, which addresses Max Yergan's turn from radical leftist to reactionary politics, see David H. Anthony III, *Max Yergan: Race Man, Internationalist, Cold Warrior* (New York: New York University Press, 2006). See also Mrs. Booker T. Washington, "The Tuskegee Woman's Club," *Southern Workman* 49, no. 8 (August 1920): 366–67, and Higgs, "Helping Ourselves," 61–62, 67.

98. Quoted in Nakasa, "Mummy Goes Home," 39. For an insightful analysis of Mrs. Xuma's work, see Iris Berger, "An African American 'Mother of the Nation': Madie Hall Xuma in South Africa, 1940–1963," *Journal of Southern African Studies*, 27, no. 3 (September 2001): 547–66.

99. Quoted in Nakasa, "Mummy Goes Home," 39.

100. "Witbank Zenzele Club Report," n.d., Xuma Papers, box O, microfilm reel 5, Dodd Research Center, University of Connecticut.

101. See Kuzwayo, *Call Me Woman*, 160–79; Ms. Joyce Piliso Seroke, interview by the author, Soweto, South Africa, August 16, 1997.

102. Walker, *Women and Resistance in South Africa*, 92.

103. Mrs. Kate Mxakatho, interview by the author, Soweto, South Africa, July 29, 1997. Seme was president from 1930 to 1936; see Francis Meli, *South Africa Belongs to Us: A History of the ANC* (Bloomington: Indiana University Press, 1989), 209. Recall that Mandela and Resha came into the ANC by way of the Youth League, which was formed under the presidency of A. B. Xuma in 1943.

104. Mxakatho, interview.

105. Quoted in Resha, *'Mangoana O Tsoara Thipa Ka Bohaleng*, 31.

106. Ibid., 38–39.

107. Ibid., 39.

108. Although she participated in the Youth League, Ida Mtwana was from an earlier generation of activists. Born in 1903, she became a dressmaker and joined the Industrial and Commercial Workers Union in 1927. In addition to leading the Transvaal Women's League, she was elected to the Transvaal ANC Executive Committee in 1953. Karis and Carter, *From Protest to Challenge*, 4:91.

109. Resha, *'Mangoana O Tsoara Thipa Ka Bohaleng*, 40.

110. Quoted in ibid., 40.

111. William Beinart, *Twentieth-Century South Africa* (Oxford: Oxford University Press, 1994), 137.

112. Roux, *Time Longer Than Rope*, 380–81.

113. Simons and Simons, *Class and Colour in South Africa*, 605.

CHAPTER SEVEN

1. Mrs. Amelia Scott Green, interview by the author, Montgomery, Alabama, April 13, 1997.

2. Ibid.

3. Ibid.

4. Ibid.

5. Ibid.

6. Ibid.

7. Ibid.

8. Virginia Durr, *Outside the Magic Circle: The Autobiography of Virginia Foster Durr* (Tuscaloosa: University of Alabama Press, 1985), 201, 217.

9. Quoted in ibid., 259; see also 254–73.

10. Ibid., 272.

11. Quoted in ibid., 272.

12. Before the boycott, Mrs. Durr was fortunate to have Coretta Scott King, an Antioch College alumna, conduct an admissions interview with her daughter, Tilla. Ibid., 271–75. See also Mrs. Johnnie Carr, interview by the author, Montgomery, Alabama, May 25, 1995.

13. Virginia Durr, *Outside the Magic Circle*, 178.

14. In his doctoral dissertation at Boston University, Martin Luther King, Jr., addressed the work of Niebuhr, especially his philosophy of "pragmatic realism," or morally based coercion within a framework of nonviolent resistance. See George

Fredrickson, *Black Liberation: A Comparative History of Black Ideologies in the United States and South Africa* (New York: Oxford University Press, 1995), 226.

15. Aldon Morris, *The Origins of the Civil Rights Movement: Black Communities Organizing for Change* (New York: Free Press, 1984), 139–57.

16. Rosa Parks with Jim Haskins, *Rosa Parks: My Story* (New York: Dial Books, 1992), 105.

17. Recall that Mrs. Parks's first rebellion against the City Bus Lines Company occurred when she failed to board the bus at the crowded rear door after having deposited her money at the front, insisting that it made no sense for her to reboard. The enraged bus driver, James Blake, responded by pulling her to the front of the bus by her sleeve, and he demanded she get off his bus. Rosa Parks with Jim Haskins, *Rosa Parks*, 78–79; 113–16.

18. Ibid., 116.

19. Ibid., 116–24. See also the E. D. Nixon interview in Henry Hampton and Steve Fayer with Sarah Flynn, *Voices of Freedom: An Oral History of the Civil Rights Movement from the 1950s through the 1980s* (New York: Bantam Books, 1991), 20–21.

20. Jo Ann Gibson Robinson, *The Montgomery Bus Boycott and the Women Who Started It: The Memoir of Jo Ann Gibson Robinson*, ed. David J. Garrow (Knoxville: University of Tennessee Press, 1987), 45.

21. Ibid., 44.

22. Ibid., 16, 26–27.

23. Quoted in Ibid., 45–46.

24. Mary Fair Burks, "Trailblazers: Women in the Montgomery Bus Boycott," in *Women in the Civil Rights Movement: Trailblazers and Torchbearers, 1941–1965*, ed. Vicki Crawford, Jacqueline Anne Rouse, and Barbara Woods (Bloomington: Indiana University Press, 1993), 82.

25. Jo Ann Robinson, letter to Mayor W. A. Gayle, Montgomery County District Attorney's files, Montgomery County Courthouse, Montgomery, Alabama, quoted in *Daybreak of Freedom: The Montgomery Bus Boycott*, ed. Stewart Burns (Chapel Hill: University of North Carolina Press, 1997), 58.

26. Robinson, *Montgomery Bus Boycott*, 37.

27. Richard Willing, "History's Forgotten Soldiers: Civil Rights' Untold Story," *USA Today*, November 28, 1995, 4.

28. Robinson, *Montgomery Bus Boycott*, 37–42; Howell Raines, *My Soul Is Rested: Movement Days in the Deep South Remembered* (New York: Bantam, 1978), 29–30; Willing, "History's Forgotten Soldiers"; J. Mills Thornton III, "Challenge and Response in the Montgomery Bus Boycott of 1955–1956," in *The Walking City: The Montgomery Bus Boycott, 1955–1956*, ed. David J. Garrow (Brooklyn, N.Y.: Carlson Publishing, 1989), 339–40.

29. Robinson, *Montgomery Bus Boycott*, 37.

30. Ibid., 22.

31. Ibid., 21–22. Rosa Parks remembered a slightly different version of the Brooks in-

cident. Hilliard Brooks was a military veteran who, in August 1950, was shot and killed by the police, accused of being drunk and disorderly. See Parks with Haskins, *Rosa Parks*, 149–50.

32. Quoted in Robinson, *Montgomery Bus Boycott*, 50; see also 46.

33. Mrs. Irene West, interview, Preston Valien Papers, Amistad Collection, Tulane University; Preston Valien, "The Montgomery Protest as a Social Movement," in Garrow, *Walking City*, 96.

34. Burks, "Trailblazers," 82–83. See also Robinson, *Montgomery Bus Boycott*, 46–47.

35. Raines, *My Soul Is Rested*, 36–37; Martin Luther King, Jr., *Stride Toward Freedom: The Montgomery Story* (New York: HarperCollins Publishers, 1958), 44–48; Robinson, *Montgomery Bus Boycott*, 53–56.

36. Quoted in Raines, *My Soul Is Rested*, 37–38. See also King, *Stride Toward Freedom*, 63, and Robinson, *Montgomery Bus Boycott*, 80.

37. Robinson, *Montgomery Bus Boycott*, 78.

38. King, *Stride Toward Freedom*, 109.

39. Quoted in Thomas J. Gilliam, "The Montgomery Bus Boycott of 1955–1956," in Garrow, *Walking City*, 262. See also Fred. D. Gray, *Bus Ride to Justice* (Montgomery, Ala.: Black Belt Press, 1995).

40. Quoted in Taylor Branch, *Parting the Waters: America in the King Years, 1954–63* (New York: Simon and Schuster, 1988), 167; and in Gilliam, "The Montgomery Bus Boycott of 1955–1956," 263. Mrs. Jo Ann Robinson reported that Mrs. Reese "could not stand the pressure" of being involved in the suit against the mayor, the Board of Commissioners of the city of Montgomery, the City Lines bus company, and the two bus drivers, James Blake and Robert Cleere. See Robinson, *The Montgomery Bus Boycott*, 142 and 137.

41. Civil Action #1147-N: *Browder v. Gayle*, in the U.S. District Court of the Middle District of Alabama, Northern Division, Montgomery, Alabama, 1956, box 69, folder 1, pp. 3–4, National Archives–Atlanta Branch.

42. Ibid., 4. See also Gilliam, "Montgomery Bus Boycott of 1955–1956," 263, 270–71.

43. Gilliam, "Montgomery Bus Boycott of 1955–1956," 271–78. See also Robinson, *Montgomery Bus Boycott*, chaps. 7 and 8.

44. Mrs. Inez J. Baskin, interview by the author, Montgomery, Alabama, April 21, 1997. See also King, *Stride Toward Freedom*, 168–74, and Clayborne Carson, ed., *The Papers of Martin Luther King, Jr.*, vol. 3, *Birth of a New Age, December 1955–December 1956* (Berkeley: University of California Press, 1997), photograph 23.

45. King, *Stride Toward Freedom*, 225–26.

46. Quoted in Steven M. Millner, "The Montgomery Bus Boycott: A Case Study in the Emergence and Career of a Social Movement," in Garrow, *Walking City*, 524. See also Robinson, *Montgomery Bus Boycott*, 66, 74–75, and Mrs. Hazel Gregory, interview by the author, Montgomery, Alabama, May 24, 1995.

47. Nannie Helen Burroughs, letter to Martin Luther King, Jr., March 17, 1956, box 67, VIII 34 W (MIA Correspondence), Martin Luther King, Jr., Papers, Special Collections, Mugar Library, Boston University.

48. In ibid., Mrs. Alberta W. King is listed on the Woman's Convention stationery as the organist for the Auxiliary. See also Branch, *Parting the Waters*, 32–33.
49. Martin Luther King, letter to Nannie Helen Burroughs, September 18, 1956, in Carson, *Papers of Martin Luther King, Jr.*, 3:370–71.
50. Gregory, interview.
51. Ibid.; Robinson, *Montgomery Bus Boycott*, 71–72; quoted in Hampton and Fayer, *Voices of Freedom*, 29–30.
52. Mrs. Zecosy Williams, interview by the author, Montgomery, Alabama, May 23, 1995.
53. Mrs. Beautie Mae Johnson, interview by the author, Montgomery, Alabama, April 16, 1997.
54. Gregory, interview; Transportation Payroll, box 6, F 38 (MIA Correspondence), Martin Luther King, Jr., Papers, Special Collections, Mugar Library, Boston University.
55. Quoted in Millner, "The Montgomery Bus Boycott," 529. See also Carr, interview.
56. King, *Stride Toward Freedom*, 75–76; Robinson, *Montgomery Bus Boycott*, 91; MIA Transportation Payroll, box 6, F 38 (MIA Correspondence), Martin Luther King, Jr., Papers, Special Collections, Mugar Library, Boston University.
57. U.S. Bureau of the Census, *Seventeenth Census of the United States, 1950*, vol. 2, pt. 2, *Characteristics of the Population* (Washington, D.C.: Department of the Interior, 1951), 2–100.
58. *M. L. King, Jr. v. State of Alabama*, Montgomery County, Alabama, District Attorney of Montgomery County file #2279, "Bus Boycott," 3/19–22/56, p. 455, Alabama Department of Archives and History, Montgomery, Alabama.
59. Mrs. Allean Wright, interview by Willie Mae Lee, January 24, 1956, Preston Valien Papers, Amistad Collection, Tulane University.
60. Ibid. The dialect speech originally recorded by Mrs. Wright's interviewer, Willie Mae Lee, has been dropped.
61. Ibid.
62. Ibid.
63. Mrs. Beatrice Charles, interview by Willie Mae Lee, January 20, 1956, Preston Valien Papers, Amistad Collection, Tulane University.
64. On the several facets of the racialized power dynamic between white women employers and their Black domestic servants, see Judith Rollins, *Between Women: Domestics and Their Employers* (Philadelphia: Temple University Press, 1985).
65. The personal observations of Mrs. Charles and other working-class Black women, based on their own lived experiences, represent an important dimension of and value placed on the production of knowledge. For an important explication of this and other ways of knowing on the part of Black women, see Patricia Hill Collins, *Black Feminist Thought: Knowledge, Consciousness, and the Politics of Empowerment* (New York: Routledge, 1991), 208–19.
66. Green, interview. The Reverend H. H. Johnson, who was among the first MIA Executive Board members, also sat on the MIA Finance Committee. Early in Janu-

ary 1957—after the peaceful victory of the boycott and while King and Abernathy were away in Atlanta preparing to convene a group of Black leaders—Hutchinson Street, First Baptist, Bell Street, and Mt. Olive Baptist Churches were bombed, along with the homes of the Reverend Ralph Abernathy and the Reverend Robert Graetz. The Reverend Mr. Graetz was the activist white pastor of the all-Black Trinity Lutheran Church. See King, *Stride Toward Freedom*, 175–76.

67. Mrs. Thelma Glass, interview by the author, Montgomery, Alabama, April 24, 1997.

68. Ms. Gwen Bell, interview by the author, Montgomery, Alabama, May 19, 1998.

69. Mrs. Ethel Mae Alexander, interview by the author, Montgomery, Alabama, April 23, 1997.

70. Mr. Ezekiel Alexander, interview by the author, Montgomery, Alabama, April 23, 1997.

71. Mrs. Ethel Mae Alexander, interview. The tense and extremely dangerous integrated bus ride through Alabama was originated by the Congress of Racial Equality (CORE) but was implemented by SNCC and CORE with support from Dr. King and the MIA and with the protection of the U.S. marshalls. The violence and the terror suffered by the riders and by other Black activists in Montgomery during the siege of First Baptist Church is vividly described in the following works: Harvard Sitkoff, *The Struggle for Black Equality, 1954–1992*, rev. ed. (New York: Hill and Wang, 1993), 93–98; David J. Garrow, *Bearing the Cross: Martin Luther King, Jr., and the Southern Christian Leadership Conference* (New York: Vintage Books, 1988), 156–58; and Branch, *Parting the Waters*, 454–65.

72. Mrs. Ethel Mae Alexander, interview.

73. On "mothering the movement," see Françoise N. Hamlin, "Vera Mae Pigee (1925—): Mothering the Movement," in *Mississippi Women: Their Histories, Their Lives*, ed. Martha H. Swain, Elizabeth Anne Payne, and Marjorie Julian Spruill (Athens: University of Georgia Press, 2003), 281–98.

CHAPTER EIGHT

1. Mrs. Kate Mxakatho, interview by the author, Soweto, South Africa, July 29, 1997.

2. Ibid.

3. Ibid.

4. This might have been Dennis Goldberg, a member of the COD, a white allied organization, who helped organize the 1955 Congress of the People, or Norman Levy, another member of the COD, who helped Helen Joseph and Bertha Mashaba (Gxowa) organize the 1956 women's protest at Pretoria. See Thomas Karis and Gwendolen M. Carter, eds., *From Protest to Challenge: A Documentary History of African Politics in South Africa, 1882–1964*, vol. 4, *Political Profiles*, ed. Gail M. Gerhardt and Thomas Karis (Stanford, Calif.: Hoover Institution Press, 1977), 32, and Helen Joseph, *Side by Side: The Autobiography of Helen Joseph* (New York: William Morrow, 1986), 17.

5. Mxakatho, interview.

6. Ibid. Prime Minister Strijdom died in office in 1958.

7. Ibid.

8. Quoted in Jacklyn Cock, *Maids and Madams: Domestic Workers under Apartheid* (London: The Women's Press, 1989), 104.

9. Tom Lodge, *Black Politics in South Africa since 1945* (New York: Longman, 1983), 43.

10. Nelson Mandela, *Long Walk to Freedom: The Autobiography of Nelson Mandela* (London: Abacus, 1994), 141–52.

11. Cherryl Walker, *Women and Resistance in South Africa* (New York: Monthly Review Press, 1991), 130–31.

12. Ibid., 131.

13. Lodge, *Black Politics in South Africa*, 44.

14. Walker, *Women and Resistance in South Africa*, 131–32; Karis and Carter, *From Protest to Challenge*, 4:78.

15. Frances Baard, *My Spirit Is Not Banned* (Harare, Zimbabwe: Zimbabwe Publishing House, 1986), 40, 41, 42.

16. Karis and Carter, *From Protest to Challenge*, 4:113–14; Ezekiel Mphahlele, "Guts and Granite," *Drum*, March 1956, 63–65.

17. Maggie Resha, *'Mangoana O Tsoara Thipa Ka Bohaleng: My Life in the Struggle* (Johannesburg: Congress of South African Writers, 1991), 46, 47–48, 49, 50.

18. Walker, *Women and Resistance in South Africa*, 132–36.

19. Ibid., 138–39.

20. Letter announcing Conference to Promote Women's Rights, box Ac 1.1, Federation of South African Women Papers, Cullen Library, University of the Witwatersrand (emphasis added).

21. Among the signers were Josie Palmer (Mpama), Ida Mtwana, Hilda Watts, Lucy Mvubelo, Helen Joseph, Hetty du Preez, Betty du Toit, M. Cachalia, M. Sita, Dora Tamana, and Ray Alexander. In a second version of the letter, Albertina Sisulu, Winnie Mandela, and Mrs. Nokwe, wives of the Transvaal ANC leadership, added their names to the list. Ibid.

22. Walter Sisulu and Duma Nokwe were two of the early male supporters of the women's organization. Nokwe, a leftist ANC Youth League leader, spoke for Sisulu at the FSAW organizing conference. Report of the Organizing Conference, April 17, 1954, box Ac 1.5.1 Federation of South African Women Papers, Cullen Library, University of the Witwatersrand; Walker, *Women and Resistance in South Africa*, 143, 153.

23. Quoted in Walker, *Women and Resistance in South Africa*, 153. See also ibid., 160–63.

24. Federation of South African Women Minutes, box Ac 1.5.2, Federation of South African Women Papers, Cullen Library, University of the Witwatersrand.

25. Quoted in Walker, *Women and Resistance in South Africa*, 154.

26. Baard, *My Spirit Is Not Banned*, 44–45.

27. Ibid., 45. According to Cherryl Walker, two of the radical journals that reported on the proceedings of the conference, *Advance* and *Fighting Talk*, noted the unusual

role reversal in the food preparation and service. Walker, *Women and Resistance in South Africa*, 154.

28. Women's Charter, box AD1137/Ac 1.5.4, Federation of South African Women Papers, Cullen Library, University of the Witwatersrand.

29. Ibid., 1, 2, 4, 4–5.

30. Ibid., 5.

31. Helen Joseph tells the inspiring story of the women's determination to leave the country to attend the Lausanne conference. See Joseph, *Side by Side*, 6–7. The socialist-inspired Women's International Democratic Federation was formed in Paris in 1945 to enable international groups of women to advocate for peace collectively. Hilda Watts attended the 1947 conference in Prague, where she spoke about the adverse conditions for women and children in South Africa. In 1953 the Women's International Democratic Federation announced its Declaration of the Rights of Women, important aspects of which were strongly aligned with FSAW principles. See Walker, *Women and Resistance in South Africa*, 100–101.

32. Walker, *Women and Resistance in South Africa*, 166–68.

33. Ibid., 168–70.

34. Draft Constitution, box A.a.1, Federation of South African Women Papers, Cullen Library, University of the Witwatersrand, 1. See also Walker, *Women and Resistance in South Africa*, 170–71.

35. The Bantu Education Act was criticized as an insidious attempt at the retribalization of Africans by instructing children in their own languages and witholding the instruction of English and Afrikaans until the secondary grades. Under Hendrik Frensch Verwoerd's Ministry of Native Affairs, the more tightly controlled administration of African education became the full responsibility of the state, complete with state-prescribed syllabi. As the numbers of Black children increased, gross underfunding of their education persisted. See William Beinart, *Twentieth-Century South Africa* (Oxford: Oxford University Press, 1994), 153–54. On the intention of Bantu education, Verwoerd was known to have remarked, "If the native in South Africa today in any kind of school in existence is being taught to expect that he will live his adult life under a policy of equal rights, he is making a big mistake." Quoted in Leonard Thompson, ed., *A History of South Africa*, rev. ed. (New Haven, Conn.: Yale University Press, 1995), 196.

36. Walker, *Women and Resistance in South Africa*, 176–78. For a more detailed analysis of the campaigns, see the discussion of the Sophiatown removals and the school boycotts in Tom Lodge, *Black Politics in South Africa*, chaps. 4 and 5. Don Mattera's memoir of his early coming of age and political awakening in Sophiatown provides a more personal view of the effects of the removals. See Don Mattera, *Sophiatown: Coming of Age in South Africa* (Boston: Beacon Press, 1987).

37. Mandela, *Long Walk to Freedom*, 52, 199.

38. Joseph, *Side by Side*, 43–44.

39. Walker, *Women and Resistance in South Africa*, appendix C.

40. Joseph, *Side by Side*, 44–45; Walker, *Women and Resistance in South Africa*, 182–83.
41. Quoted in Walker, *Women and Resistance in South Africa*, 184.
42. Emma Mashinini, *Strikes Have Followed Me All My Life* (New York: Routledge, 1991), 12, 23–24. Mrs. Mashinini has admitted that her frequent flights to her mother-in-law's house in the rural Transvaal were made in order to escape the beatings of her husband, Roger, which may help explain her preoccupation with her children and lack of much political awareness until 1955.
43. Several participants noted the aggressive police presence, among them Helen Joseph (who also estimated the number of additional participants), Nelson Mandela, Maggie Resha, and Frances Baard. See Joseph, *Side by Side*, 47–48; Mandela, *Long Walk to Freedom*, 202–3; Resha, '*Mangoana O Tsoara Thipa Ka Bohaleng*, 92–93; and Baard, *My Spirit Is Not Banned*, 56. Interestingly, the Africanist faction within the ANC, an increasingly nationalist group that paid strict attention to the principles embedded in the 1949 Programme of Action, did not agree with the multiracial sentiment of the charter. This faction believed that the ANC had deviated from its original Programme of Action philosophy, which stressed African "freedom from white domination and the attainment of political independence." Quoted in Benjamin Pogrund, *How Can Man Die Better: The Life of Robert Sobukwe* (Johannesburg: Jonathan Ball Publishers, 1990), 46; see also 46–47, 61–62.
44. See Julia Wells, "Why Women Rebel: A Comparative Study of South African Women's Resistance in Bloemfontein (1913) and Johannesburg (1958)," *Journal of Southern African Studies* 10, no. 1 (October 1983): 61–62.
45. Joseph, *Side by Side*, 10.
46. Mrs. Florence Siwedi, interview by the author, Soweto, South Africa, August 8, 1997.
47. Ibid.
48. Walker, *Women and Resistance in South Africa*, 184–88; Joseph, *Side by Side*, 10–13.
49. Joseph, *Side by Side*, 13.
50. Walker, *Women and Resistance in South Africa*, 187.
51. Ibid., 190–92; Lodge, *Black Politics in South Africa*, 143.
52. Ibid.; Joseph, *Side by Side*, 15; Walker, *Women and Resistance in South Africa*, 192–93. See also Julia Wells, "The History of Black Women's Struggle against Pass Laws in South Africa, 1900–1960" (Ph.D. diss., Columbia University, 1982), 308–9.
53. Quoted in Mrs. Kate Mxakatho, interview by author, July 29, 1997; Lodge, *Black Politics in South Africa*, 143; Walker, *Women and Resistance in South Africa*, 193.
54. Mrs. Bertha Mashaba Gxowa, interview by the author, July 22, 1997, Shell House, Johannesburg, South Africa.
55. Ibid.
56. Ibid.
57. Quoted in Resha, '*Mangoana O Tsoara Thipa Ka Bohaleng*, 114. See also Siwedi, interview.
58. Resha, '*Mangoana O Tsoara Thipa Ka Bohaleng*, 111–12.

59. Joseph, *Side by Side*, 19.
60. Baard, *My Spirit Is Not Banned*, 59–60.
61. Quoted in Resha, '*Mangoana O Tsoara Thipa Ka Bohaleng*, 117.
62. Quoted in ibid., 117; Baard, *My Spirit Is Not Banned*, 60; and in Kate Mxagatho, interview by author, July 29, 1997.
63. Resha, '*Mangoana O Tsoara Thipa Ka Bohaleng*, 117.
64. Joseph, *Side by Side*, 19.
65. Agenda for National Conference to Be Held August 11 and 12, 1956, at the Trades Hall, Johannesburg, box Ac 2.2, Federation of South African Women Papers, Cullen Library, University of the Witwatersrand; Report on the Work of the Federation of South African Women, April 1957, box Ab 2, Federation of South African Women Papers, Cullen Library, University of the Witwatersrand.
66. Walker, *Women and Resistance in South Africa*, 199–200.
67. Ms. Mary Mkosi, interview by the author, July 30, 1997, Alexsan Community Center, Alexandra, South Africa.
68. Lodge, *Black Politics in South Africa*, 155–59.
69. Mrs. Naomi Setshedi, interview by Mmantho Nkotsoe, March 1, 1983, box Ab30, Collection AG2738, p. 9, Institute for Advanced Social Research, William Cullen Library, University of the Witwatersrand. See also Lodge, *Black Politics in South Africa*, 158–61.
70. Ibid., 161–62.
71. Ibid., 162–63; Rachel Motshele, interview by the author, August 18, 1997, Alexandra, South Africa; Michael Motshele, interview by the author, August 18, 1997, Alexandra, South Africa; Ruth First, "The Bus Boycott," *Africa South*, July 1957, 55–58.
72. Mrs. Naomi Setshedi, interview by Mmantho Nkotsoe, January 31, 1983, box Ab 30, Collection AG2738, pp. 37–38, Institute for Advanced Social Research, William Cullen Library, University of the Witwatersrand.
73. Lodge, *Black Politics in South Africa*, 165–67.
74. Mrs. Alina Serote, interview by the author, August 2, 2006, Alexandra, South Africa.
75. Mrs. Martha Dlamini, interview by the author, August 11, 2006, Alexandra, South Africa.
76. Lilian Ngoyi, Presidential Address, Annual Conference of the African National Congress Women's League (Transvaal), Jabavu, Johannesburg, November 11, 1956, Federation of South African Women Papers, Cullen Library, University of the Witwatersrand.
77. The practice of cattle dipping to combat disease-carrying ticks began in the late nineteenth century as part of a state-sponsored program to extend further control over rural Africans and their cattle. Cattle represented an African family's economic well being and were a means to bride-wealth, important in the process of joining couples (and families) in marriage. See William Beinart, *Twentieth-Century South Africa* (New York: Oxford University Press, 1994), 96, 130. Tom Lodge reports that

in the late 1950s many believed that dipping made cattle more susceptible to other diseases, and that women became the unwilling custodians of the dipping tanks, a "tiring" and "irrational" duty. See Lodge, *Black Politics in South Africa*, 149.

78. Resha,'*Mangoana O Tsoara Thipa Ka Bohaleng*, 118–21; Lodge, *Black Politics in South Africa*, 145–50.

79. Quoted in Resha,'*Mangoana O Tsoara Thipa Ka Bohaleng*, 124. See ibid., 124–32; see also Lodge, *Black Politics in South Africa*, 146.

80. In her study of the relations between Black South African domestic workers and their employers in the late 1970s, Jacklyn Cock finds that employers rarely knew the actual names of their workers. Rather, employers used names such as "Cookie" or "Sissie," or, in this case, "Dorothy." See Cock, *Maids and Madams*, 117.

81. Ernestina Mekgwe, interview by Mmantho Nkotsoe, March 2, 1982, box Ab17, Collection AG2738, p. 2, Institute for Advanced Social Research, William Cullen Library, University of the Witwatersrand.

82. Setshedi, interview, March 1, 1982, p. 15.

83. Setshedi, interview, January 31, 1983, p. 40.

84. See Nelson Mandela, *Long Walk to Freedom*, 279–82. For the ANC decision to turn to controlled violence, see Nelson Mandela, *No Easy Walk to Freedom* (Portsmouth, N.H.: Heinemann, 1990), chaps. 13 and 15. For an important view of PAC ideology—including the ideas of its leader, Robert Sobukwe—which spawned the 1960 pass resistance that led to the Sharpeville massacre, see Gail M. Gerhart, *Black Power in South Africa: The Evolution of an Ideology* (Berkeley: University of California Press, 1978), chaps. 6 and 7.

85. For the story of one Poqo adherent see Mxolisi "Bra Ace" Mgxashe, *Are You With Us? The Story of a PAC Activist* (Cape Town, South Africa: Tafelberg, 2006).

86. For a view of the experience of one *Umkonto we Sizwe* woman in exile, see the portrait of Thenjiwe Mtintso in June Goodwin, *Cry Amandla! South African Women and the Question of Power* (New York: Africana Publishing, 1984).

CONCLUSION

1. On the South African retreat from mass political mobilization and the attempts at mounting an armed struggle, see Joe Slovo, *The Unfinished Autobiography* (Randburg, South Africa: Ravan Press, 1995). A founding member of the Congress of Democrats and the South African Communist Party, Joe Slovo also served as the commandant of the military wing of the African National Congress (ANC), the *Umkonto we Sizwe*.

2. Robin D. G. Kelley writes persuasively about acts of resistance that Black people in Birmingham performed on segregated buses, or "moving theaters," that were quite unlike the rebellion of Mrs. Parks. See Robin D. G. Kelley, *Race Rebels: Culture, Politics, and the Black Working Class* (New York: Free Press, 1994), chap. 3.

3. Belinda Robnett, *How Long? How Long? African-American Women in the Struggle for Civil Rights* (New York: Oxford University Press, 1997), 193.

4. Mrs. Amelia Scott Green, interview by the author, Montgomery, Alabama, April 13, 1997.

5. For the origin of the phrase "mother of the nation," see Letter announcing Conference to Promote Women's Rights, box Ac 1.1, Federation of South African Women Papers, Cullen Library, University of the Witwatersrand. On the post–World War II transformation of the idea of motherhood in the United States, see Joanne Meyerowitz, ed. *Not June Cleaver: Women and Gender in Post-war America, 1945–1960* (Philadelphia: Temple University Press, 1994), especially chap. 12.

6. Quoted in Maggie Resha, '*Mangoana O Tsoara Thipa Ka Bohaleng: My Life in the Struggle* (Johannesburg: Congress of South African Writers, 1991), 117.

Index

The abbreviation "illus." refers to the gallery following page 98.

PAM BROOKS is associate professor of African American studies at Oberlin College, where she has taught since 2000. Born in Boston, Ms. Brooks spent many years as a high school teacher in the Boston area after completing a BA degree in history from New York University and before earning her PhD in global history from Northeastern University. She is the parent of a daughter who she likes to say accompanied her in her graduate education and who continues to inspire her in her work. Currently, Ms. Brooks is engaged in working with her father on a memoir of his life in the Black Freedom movement.